COLOMBIA: A BRUTAL HISTORY

Published books by Geoff Simons include:

Geoff Simons

COLOMBIA

A BRUTAL HISTORY

SAQI

British Library Cataloguing-in-Publication Data
A catalogue for this book is available from the
British Library

ISBN 0 86356 758 4
EAN 9-780863-567582

This edition first published 2004

SAQI
26 Westbourne Grove
London W2 5RH
www.saqibooks.com

Contents

Introduction

The Colombia story is one of colonialism, liberation, class struggle and civil war – a long and bloody chronology given extra dimensions by the grim imperatives of the international drugs trade and United States intervention. The result is a complex of contending groups and alliances, a 'labyrinth'[1] of military forces, political interests and people's struggle. The Colombian people, half of them existing in abject poverty, live their lives in one of the most violent societies on earth. They continue to combat a residual feudalism, industrial exploitation, state terrorism and the mounting encroachments by a regional superpower intent on poisoning their land with toxic chemicals and biological agents, bolstering the forces of social repression and rolling back their hard-won political gains.

The circumstances of the struggle against oppression and for social justice should not be confused with the exigencies of the 'war on drugs'. The political struggle of the Colombian people for social justice has existed for the entire history of the country, with US intervention escalating over the decades in firm opposition to this aspiration. Washington had an ideological and commercial interest in Colombia long before the explosion of the drugs trade in the 1960s and 1970s. The US-hyped 'war on drugs' developed as a useful pretext for the escalating American campaign against the Colombian people's struggle for social justice

Alexander Lopez, leader of the Cali Municipal Workers Union, Sintraemcali, which continues to resist the privatisation of Colombian public services, has been targeted by rightwing death squads. In recent years he survived several assassination attempts but other trade unionists have been less fortunate: over the last decade more than 3000 trade unionists have been murdered by paramilitaries committed to the protection of corporate interests. Lopez has described the plight of the Colombian people:

> In Colombia today, we have a class struggle – a neoliberal economic model has been imposed by the IMF and the World Bank. It is being implemented by the Colombian government, which is probably the most corrupt in the world ... 20 out of 40 million of the people live below the poverty line. The UN has recognised that the right to life in Colombia does not exist. Seven children are disappearing [by death squads] every day. In the last six years, 1.5 million people have been displaced ... and 35,000 have died ... since 1990 .[2]

Hector Fajardo, general-secretary of the United Labour Confederation (CUT), and others have typically worn bullet proof vests on their way to work and operated from offices with enough armour-plating to withstand a bomb blast. Fajardo, a teacher, received his first death threat in 1984. Six years later, he said: 'Today, the killings are carried out by paramilitaries [rightwing death squads] and the state security forces. I would not dare say that this is state policy, but they still kill and threaten us. My life no longer depends on good health but on the will of another person who can attack you at any moment. Each day when you leave the house, your wife wonders if you will return.' During the course of a strike in October 1998, nine trade unionists were shot dead and the killings have continued.[3] Trade unionists, teachers, journalists, human rights workers, community leaders, indigenous peoples – all are targeted if they are perceived as political opposition, as an obstacle to the business interest. This is the context in which a national population is repressed, in which the Colombian military collaborates with death squads, in which the decades-long civil war continues, and in which the United States pours arms, training and military personnel into the maelstrom.

Through the 1990s, Colombia became the leading recipient of US military aid in Latin America, and boasted the worst human-rights record in the region – 'in accord with a well-established correlation' (Chomsky). Each year, the Colombian military and their death-squad allies drive 300,000 from their homes, contributing to the world's largest displaced population, after Sudan and Angola. Such matters did not discourage President Bill Clinton from proclaiming Colombia a leading democracy, or from stimulating a new escalation in the supply of arms to the Colombian military, known to collaborate with the death-squad factions. The purpose, in accord with the American Way, is to protect the business interest in a country where the top three per cent of the landed *élite* own over 70 per cent of arable land, 57 per cent of the poorest farmers subsist on under three per cent, and 18 per cent of the people live in absolute misery, unable to meet basic nutritional needs. In one estimate, by the Colombian Institute of Family Welfare, 4.5 million children under 14, half Colombia's children, are hungry.

The US attitude to the Colombian drug trade is ambivalent and hypocritical. It is plain that the traffic in cocaine and heroin has provided all the advantages of a 'moral' excuse for a massive intervention in Colombian affairs; and while Washington has agitated over the years for the extradition of Colombian drug barons to stand trial in the United States a range of US companies have derived benefits from a business that is predictably denounced in American rhetoric. It is north American (and other) companies that supply the chemicals for processing cocaine and heroin, and north American (and other) banks that benefit immensely from the vast financial flows generated by the drugs trade. It was useful to the drug traffickers that certain limitations on the international dealings of Colombian banks have not always applied to exchange houses. Thus a Colombian bank may have required a specific licence to deal in foreign exchange, and was allowed only to exchange dollars for pesos domestically, at the official rate. But exchange houses often required no licences, were able to pay more than the banks, were able to offer a greater degree of anonymity, and were able to deal more easily with the United States. It was possible in these circumstances to exploit exchange houses as a financing facility for the drugs trade, allowing the development of a secure procedure for the depositing of vast drug funds in Miami banks.[4]

At the same time drug money was being fed via circuitous routes into a wide range of other US banks. For example the authorities managed to seize money deposited in an account at the Marine Midland Bank of New York, but were quick to admit that the $7.7 million account represented 'only about 10 per cent of the money these particular [Colombian] traffickers had

laundered in this way over a two-year period.'[5] Similarly, the Bank of Credit
and Commerce International (BCCI) – with links to former US president
Jimmy Carter, the then Panama dictator Manuela Noriega, the then
Peruvian president Alan Garcia, and Colombian drug traffickers – derived
substantial financial benefits from handling drug money before the bank
was exposed as perpetrating 'the largest bank fraud in world financial
history.'[6] At one time links were established between BCCI and the then
Colombian leader, President Andres Pastrana: BCCI took over Banco
Mercantil, the board of which included Pastrana and at least one man with
very close links to Rodriguez Orejuelas of the Cali cocaine cartel.[7] The drug
trade continues to thrive and there has never been a full exposé of the extent
to which its vast profits help to guarantee the business successes of US
corporate enterprise.

It is well known that the Central Intelligence Agency (CIA) has
supported the international drug trade as a source of covert revenues,[8] and
that many Third-World dictators have derived funds from drug trafficking.
Thus Guillermo Endara, installed in Panama after the overthrow of Manuel
Noriega by US forces, was known to be linked with drug traffickers and
money launderers; and the Chilean dictator Augusto Pinochet, a favourite
of Washington after the US-inspired *coup d'état* against the democratically-
elected Salvador Allende, is now known to have collaborated with
Colombian drug dealers.[9] The United States may be taking some initiatives
against the international drugs trade, but the free-enterprise trafficking in
drugs has provided a useful pretext for an escalating US intervention in
Colombia, covert funds for the CIA, substantial revenues for US industrial
and financial companies, income for US-friendly Third-World dictators,
and – some observers have alleged – a source of revenue for the Bush family
and Vice-President Richard Cheney.[10] And even when the US took practical
steps against the drug barons, American narcotics agents were sometimes
fooled into aiding some cartels at the expense of others.[11] Such details
should be remembered when US officials tour the world inviting Europe,
Japan, and Middle-East and Latin American states to underwrite
Washington's plans for a wider 'war on drugs' in Colombia.

The international corporations are active in Colombia – variously
despoiling the land, conspiring with death-squad paramilitaries and
funding private armies. Some 6000 U'wa Indians threatened to commit mass
suicide in protest at plans by a US oil giant to explore their ancestral lands
for oil. The tribesmen made it plain that the issue was not negotiable,
arguing that the extraction of oil would destroy their culture and ruin their
physical environment.[12]

It was all part of a global pattern – massive oil companies riding roughshod over local interests in the desperate quest for profits; for example, companies moving into the Caspian Sea to develop huge oil and natural-gas reserves, and becoming embroiled in disputes about brutal security forces, inadequate judiciaries and the abuse of vulnerable ethnic minorities. And while companies fund security forces that are linked to the death squads the United States organises systematic chemical warfare – 'an attack against human life, the community and the environment' – to destroy local crops and local communities. Tons of glyphosate, a chemical poison, are being sprayed on coca and poppy plantations in Colombia, and on banana, maize and rubber, on fish stocks and livestock, on schools and churches, and on people:

> This week, four governors from southern Colombia came to Washington to ask policymakers to stop the fumigation, which they say has harmed humans, livestock and destroyed legal crops that are essential to the farmers' subsistence ... It is remarkable that the United States, which sprayed Vietnam with Agent Orange, could proceed with a widespread, intensive fumigation program in another country without knowing the long-term effects on humans, vegetation, livestock, birds and fish. It is cruel and inhumane for us to try to solve our drug problem – which is one of demand – by attacking the livelihoods and environment of peasant farmers ... But that's exactly what we're doing.[13]

There was evidence also that spraying of toxic chemicals was having catastrophic effects on countries beyond Colombia.[14]

Then it seemed that perhaps the widespread use of chemical warfare against the helpless peasant enemy might be insufficient to do the job. In September 2000 it emerged that Britain, keen to bolster US initiatives, was working to develop a lethal fungus that could be sprayed over Colombia. Despite the concerns of environmentalists this fungus, *fusarium oxysporum*, had already been field-tested in the three central Asian states: Uzbekistan, Tajikistan and Kazakhstan. Critics were emphasising that this form of biological warfare would kill food crops, ruin the environment and seriously endanger human life.[15]

Other documents, from the US State Department, revealed that the United States wanted to involve other countries in the spraying of *fusarium* on Colombia 'in order to avoid a perception that this is solely a US government initiative.'[16] Washington evidently saw no ethical or legal objection to the use of chemical and biological warfare against Colombian peasants – despite the prohibition of such practices in international law – but perceived nonetheless that the matter needed to be finessed for public consumption.

Through 2001 and particularly after 11 September there were ample signs that the US intervention in Colombia were set to escalate, leading to an effective 'Vietnamisation' of the region. The ambitious military components of Plan Colombia, launched under the Clinton administration, were rolling into effect: the momentum of the scheme was evident before George W. Bush entered the White House but the new administration, run by an unprecedented coterie of rightwing ideologues, quickly made plain its attitude to international affairs – by invading Iraq, by threatening North Korea, by unilaterally abrogating international treaties, by pressing ahead with the ridiculous 'Son of Star Wars', by opposing the International Criminal Court, by abusing the United Nations and in countless other ways. It was obvious, even before the US-led wars on Afghanistan (2002-...) and Iraq (2003-...), that Colombia – in the US 'backyard' – would soon be given particular increased attention.

The essentially military Plan Colombia, cloaking a war on the Colombian people with the so-called 'war on drugs', was set to escalate. President Bush would not talk with rebel factions – in Colombia or anywhere else. In what laughably passes for the Bush philosophy one never sups with any species of devil, however long the spoon. The Colombian turmoil would continue, freshly fuelled by a brazenly arrogant White House and with no side in the conflict powerful enough to impose a decisive peace. US policy on Colombia would be managed by the State Department, the CIA and the Pentagon. The president could be relied on to read aloud to the public when required.

This book offers a profile chronology, a history of Colombian political affairs, with focus on recent times and with particular attention to human rights and US involvement. Again it is possible to identify the common themes of international politics, too often ignored by the literature and in public discourse:

– the battles over land and other natural resources;
– the desperate struggles against wealth and other forms of privilege;
– the remarkable brutalities of commercial and military élites;

- the universal instinct of power to exploit and oppress;
- the measureless costs of foreign intervention;
- and the incredible resilience and fortitude of ordinary people.

The case of Colombia is part of a global story. In February 2003 the Colombian activist Berenice Celeyta quoted the words of a peasant in Valle del Cauca, said soon after he had seen a dozen of his friends and comrades killed by the rightwing death squads: 'We all mobilise or we all die.' Celeyta commented, voicing the growing awareness of millions around the world:

> The US and the great world powers ... are not moved by the knowledge that children die from hunger all over the world, or by the impact on the environment ... Their multinational corporations in league with the Pentagon have decided on the policies of domination and subjecting the peoples of the world, a policy they call national security. In Colombia ... they have decided in cold blood on the extermination of entire communities.
>
> In Iraq the war is directly related to economic interests. Oil is the objective, the methods to achieve it: missiles, bombs, the extermination of thousands of men, women, and children. The conflict in Colombia, as in Iraq, has structural reasons based on the imposition of the economic policies of the International Monetary Fund, the World Bank, the World Trade Organisation and other multilateral organisations.
>
> There are people responsible for this war [against the Colombian people], with names and clear interests. It is our duty to remove their masks and the blanket of impunity that covers them.

The war with Iraq is not yet over. The war with Colombia continues, as does the war in Afghanistan. They will not be the last that the United States fuels in defence of the corporate interest.

PANAMA

VENEZUELA

• Medellin

• Bogota

• Cali   COLOMBIA

• San Vicente

BRAZIL

PERU

0 100 200 km

100   200 m

ONE

The Historical Roots

The Pre-Colonial Era

Colombia, a spectacular country and the fourth largest in Latin America, has snow-capped peaks and tropical regions, deep gorges and vast planes. Three Andean ranges cross the country from southwest to northeast: the Western Cordillera with five peaks over 4000 metres (13,000 ft), the central Cordillera, with six peaks over 4900 metres (16,000 ft) and the Eastern Cordillera, reaching heights in excess of a 5000 metres (17,000 ft) and branching off into Venezuela. Two major rivers, the Cauca and the Magdalena, run through the valleys on either side of the Central Cordillera and at times surge through chasms in the towering rock. The mountain ranges divide Colombia into the three major regions of the highland core, the coastal lowlands and the eastern plains. It seems that this was not a geography that encouraged the emergence of high civilisation in the centuries before the European conquest.

The people boasted no civilisation comparable to what had emerged elsewhere in the Americas. In the region now called Colombia there were no cultural developments akin to those of the Incas, the Mayas or the Aztecs. Some of the people existed in large families grouped into larger units that served to define local monarchies; smaller communities were ruled by local chieftains of minor importance. Carved stone figures have been found in San Augustin, and primitive pottery and jewellery were discovered in the region that now comprises Tolima and Caldas. The people had found emeralds and gold, which pleased the Spanish conquistadors, and the modern Banco de la Republica in Bogota collected specimens of gold work that were nonetheless generally judged to be inferior to Mayan or Incaic artefacts.

Significant political systems existed among the Tairona tribes, between the coast and the Sierra Nevada de Santa Marta; among the Cenu, to the southwest; and among the Chibcha of the Muisca people in the high valleys of the Eastern Cordillera. These polities, individually occupying 10,000 to 25,000 square kilometres, were larger than the Inca community before its phase of imperial expansion but none could rival the development of the Inca empire at the height of its power.

It was the Chibcha, like their neighbours definable ethnic groups, that were to feature as principal regional victims of the Spanish conquest. The Chibcha mined and worked the emeralds they had discovered, just as the Tairona shaped and embellished the shells they collected from their Caribbean beaches. The tribes produced cotton textiles, artefacts in gold, and in a gold-copper alloy (*tumbaga*). It would all prove enough to impress the Spanish, while at the same time the natives would be brutally coerced to 'take the Cross'. The Muisca, for example, were weavers, potters and metalworkers, but as typical pagans they worshipped the sun and the moon. This was quite enough for the Spanish invaders to regard the Muisca and all the other tribes as benighted heathens fit only for slavery, despite all their skills and political arrangements. The resistance of the local people to Spanish ambition was insignificant.

Colonial Colombia

The first Spanish settlement was established in 1509, as a precursor to the conquest of the territory. The methods employed by the Europeans were well-tried: local populations were conquered, pressed into servitude and tortured and killed if they resisted. Vasco Nunez de Balboa, for example, behaved as a typical conquistador when he used fighting dogs to hunt down the local people. At the same time his displays of terror were said to be carefully judged. He would intimidate local chiefs and only if they remained recalcitrant treat them with ferocity. Alonso Zuazo, a Spanish inspector general of the Indies, wrote in 1518 that 'the Indians willingly gave him much gold and also their sisters and daughters to take with him to be married or used as he wished', and noted that by the means employed by Vasco Nunez 'peace was spread and the revenue' to Spain 'greatly increased'.[1] Balboa also developed his reputation as an explorer, commanding a series of expeditions in what is now Colombia and elsewhere. It is recorded that on occasions he lost his patience and from time to time 'the dogs were loosed'.[2]

It took some time for the Spanish to settle what is now Colombia, not least because of the prodigious difficulties of the terrain – mangrove swamps on the coast and inaccessible mountain highlands in the interior. In 1500 Alonso de Lugo, who had sailed with Columbus, sailed along the Venezuelan coast to reach the Goajira Peninsula. In 1525 Santa Marta was founded; in 1533 Cartagena; and in 1535 a fresh expedition set out from Spain to expand Spanish control of the region. Gonzalo Jimenez de Quesada, an Andalusian lawyer and explorer, then led five hundred Spaniards and several hundred Indians to explore the interior of what is now Colombia. For a year this expedition, facing appalling difficulties, reached the Magdalena river and made its way along the swampy and uncharted banks. The jungle-covered and disease-infested journey took a dreadful toll. A mere 165 survivors eventually reached the tributary river Opon and finally the northern end of Bogota.

Quesada then embarked upon an orgy of torture and killing as yet another characteristic phase in the Spanish hunt for gold, after which he resolved to establish a permanent colony. On 6 August 1538 he founded 'the New City of Granada', soon renamed 'Santa Fé de Bogota'. Two further Spanish expeditions, both unaware of each other and of Quesada and his survivors, then managed to reach the location. Sebastian de Belalcazar, one of Pizzaro's generals, had conquered Quito and travelled north to found Cali in 1536 and Popayan in 1537. And Nicholas Federman, journeying from what is now Venezuela, had taken three years to cross the Llanos Orientales and over the Eastern Cordillera. The leaders of the various expeditions, intense rivals with competing ambitions, almost resorted to conflict amongst themselves, and in subsequent years plotted various intrigues, lawsuits and political machinations in the struggle for power. With

Quesada's brother and other lieutenants left in uneasy charge of the new colony, Quesada himself returned to Spain and in 1550 went back to Colombia with the title of Marshal. For twenty years he embarked upon no adventures but then began a disastrous three-year exploration of the Orinoco in search of 'El Dorado'. In 1579 he helped to crush an Indian rebellion in Mariquita and died soon afterwards.

The Spanish had ravaged the land in typical conquistador style, stealing all that they coveted and mutilating and killing anyone who resisted. In 1536 the conquistadors had reported back to Charles V on the Paramount Chibcha chief, the 'Bogota' (hence the speedy renaming of 'the New City of Granada'): 'This Bogota is the principal lord of this land, with many other nobles and chiefs subject to him. He is a personage of great wealth, because the natives say he has a house of gold and many rich emerald mines ... He has conquered and tyrannised over much of the land.'[3] Perhaps the natives lied, to impress the Spanish interlopers; perhaps there was no house of gold. The conquistadors relied on torture and terror to find out. Native tombs had revealed quantities of gold and the Spanish were happy to assume that there was always more to be found. The Chibcha and the other tribes had been ruthlessly intimidated and suppressed in what was a major phase of the Spanish conquest.

On 17 July 1549 Charles V signed a royal decree which created the *Audiencia de Santa Fé* and assigned the region a judicial, legislative, and administrative focus. In 1550 a Supreme Court (*Real Audiencia*), comprising three judges with full political and administrative authority, was established in Bogota to expand the political status of the colony. In 1564 Spain appointed the first President of what was called 'the New Kingdom of Granada' (more often 'New Granada', today Colombia). The new system of rule continued until 1718 when the first Viceroy, Andres Venero de Leiva, was installed with expanded powers. This government by Viceroys continued, except for a break between 1723 and 1739, until the end of colonial rule early in the 19th century.

The principal purpose of Spanish colonialism, like all colonialisms, was a campaign of economic exploitation – in this case designed to enrich a European monarchy. In New Granada this exploitation took various forms. For example, an early lure was the promise of gold. After 1550 New Granada was producing two thirds of all the gold shipments from New Granada, New Spain and Peru, with one estimate suggesting that gold worth 48.46 million silver pesos was shipped from these regions to Spain between 1521 and 1610. But even this substantial product was exceeded in financial terms by the 400 million silver peso worth of silver itself, produced in Spanish America to 1610. It was at some point in the 1540s that the value of silver mined exceeded that of the gold acquired through various means. Gold drew Spain to America but silver emerged as the more lucrative product.

New Granada saw also the development of native servitude, effective slavery, in the *encomienda* and *repartimiento* systems of forced labour. Before 1600 the *encomienda* defined the relationship between the Spanish settlers and the native population. Here Indians were forced to work for their *encomenderos*, leaving no other option if the native adults wanted to survive. *Repartimiento* (state-run draft Labour) was set up in New Granada at the end of the 16th century, but then only in a relatively small highland region dominated by Bogota. The involvement of the state brought a measure of official control, allowing a marginal improvement in native working conditions, but the *encomenderos* in New Granada were able to maintain what was basically a system of slavery.

After 1700 the scale of gold production in the region was rapidly increasing. According to records of both royalties collected and gold coins struck, mining output increased up to six fold between the early and late decades of the century. Thus where annual gold output at 1715-19 was around 440,000 silver pesos, by the 1790s the yearly output was worth around 1,890,000 silver pesos. By then, black slaves had been brought in to do much of the mining work.

New Granada was also deriving income from other products: notably, after the 1750s, from the royal monopolies on tobacco and brandy (*aguardiente*). But New Granada was spending most of its income on defence, and with this as a rising burden Spain was deriving little financial benefit from its colony. In 1781 the *comuneros*, protesting at the growing range of economic pressures, demonstrated the mounting disaffection with the colonial administration. In March 1781 a reforming visitor general, Guitierrez de Pineres, did nothing to improve the situation when he attempted to enforce *alcabala* measures that involved a loss of profit to local growers and higher prices for local consumers. In early May 1781 a force of *comuneros* managed to overwhelm soldiers sent to crush the protests. When perhaps 20,000 *comuneros* assembled to threaten Santa Fé (Bogota) the authorities decided that negotiation would be prudent and in due course acceded to most of the *comuneros'* demands. This movement, like many eruptions in New Granada, has been interpreted as a preliminary bid to oust the colonial power. Other commentators have argued that the rebels would have been satisfied with reasonable reforms within the system of Spanish administration.

In reality there was a swelling national opposition to Spanish colonialism. The odious use of Indian and black slavery, however mediated by different administrative models, had been discredited in both ethical and economic terms; and local growers and consumers were becoming equally disenchanted with what was being increasingly perceived as a system of foreign exploitation. By the start of the 19th century various nationalist movements committed to the ending of Spanish rule were gaining in strength. A number of these were to fall under the sway of Simon Bolivar (1783-1830), destined to become known as 'The Liberator'. In 1805 Bolivar declared on one of the hills of Rome: 'I swear before the God of my fathers, by my fathers themselves, by my honour and by my country, that my arm shall not rest nor my mind be at peace until I have broken the chains that bind me by the will and power of Spain.'[4]

The Bolivar Liberation

It was in 1810 that Simon Bolivar, born in Caracas to a wealthy landowning family, emerged as the leader of the revolutionary forces struggling to bring an end to Spanish rule. On 4 July 1811 he contributed to the Declaration of Independence in Venezuela and was soon fighting against counter-revolutionary forces in Valencia, 100 kilometres west of Caracas. On 12 August 1812 Bolivar left Venezuela for New Granada after the first Venezuelan republic had been crushed by Spanish forces. On 15 December, in New Granada, he issued his 'Cartagena manifesto', explaining the failure of the first republic in Venezuela and urging a fresh attempt to expel the Spanish from that country.

After defeating a large Royalist force near Cucuta, Bolivar re-entered Caracas on 6 August 1813 and was proclaimed the 'Liberator of Venezuela'. The second republic survived for 13 months, until he was forced to withdraw again to Cartagena. Spain then dispatched General Pablo Morillo and a large force to crush the remaining resistance in Venezuela and to attack the revolutionary forces in New Granada. On 9 May 1815 Bolivar left New Granada, soon to be retaken by Spanish forces, and sought refuge in Jamaica. In September he issued his 'Jamaica letter', summarising the current state of affairs in Spanish America and urging a fresh struggle for independence. In May 1816 Morillo, called the 'the Pacifier,' arrived in

Bogota and began a reign of terror. Bolivar, after a period in Haiti and several unsuccessful attempts to regain territory in Venezuela, established a hold in December east of Caracas and began his third and ultimately successful campaign to expel the Spanish from the north of South America.

The installation of the Congress of Angostura in February 1819 provided a legal basis for an insurgent government in Venezuela, after which Bolivar began a campaign in May to achieve the final liberation of New Granada. In July he defeated the Royalists at the Battle of the Swamps of Vargas, and on 7 August he thoroughly routed the Royalists at Boyaca, 110 kilometers northeast of Bogota. Francisco de Paula Santander, who for years had led a separate revolutionary struggle, was appointed Vice-President of New Granada, now called 'Gran Colombia'. He worked to organise the new country while Bolivar went on to complete the liberation of Venezuela, Ecuador and Peru. On 17 December 1819, at Bolivar's urging, the Congress of Angostura proclaimed the Republic of Colombia, comprising what was New Granada and Venezuela. The new republic was divided into three Departments of Venezuela, Quito and Cundinamarca, with Bolivar as President of the whole and Santander as vice-president of Cundinamarca. In 1821 the first Congress of Gran Colombia established Bogota as the capital.

On 17 September 1821 the constituent Congress of Cucuta, having been drafting a liberal constitution since May, appointed Bolivar as the first President of Colombia, whereupon he marched south from Bogota to complete the liberation of the new republic. Later in the year, Bolivar won the Second Battle of Carabobo to finally expel the Spanish from Venezuela, and the following year Antonio José de Sucre, one of Bolivar's ablest generals, won the Battle of Pichincha in Quito (Ecuador) to end Spanish rule in the region. On 13 July 1822 Bolivar incorporated Quito into Colombia. Panama was incorporated in the same year, and after independent victories in 1824 by Bolivar and Sucre fighting in Peru the Spanish armies were scattered without further combat. On 10 February 1824 a Peruvian congress made Bolivar dictator, and on 30 April 1826 he was re-elected President of Colombia. On 25 May 1826 Bolivar completed his constitution for Bolivia (a centralist document providing for a life-long president) which Colombia, against his wishes, declined to adopt.

Bolivar's instincts were for a strong centralist authority, an unambiguous dictatorship. But this approach grated on many of his revolutionary allies. The Centralists, headed by Bolivar, were opposed by the Federalists, of which Santander was a leading protagonist, urging the creation of a separate Colombia under a democratic government on loose federal lines. It seemed increasingly obvious that Bolivar's union of Gran Colombia, combining four liberated states (Venezuela, Colombia, Panama and Ecuador), was too cumbersome to admit of one central authority and that some form of dissolution would prove inevitable. But in 1826 Bolivar was urging an even greater union. At the first Pan-American Congress in Panama he strongly advocated a union of American Republics.

In 1827 the divisions between Centralists and Federalists came to a head at the Convention of Ocana, and the Federalists walked out. Bolivar quickly assumed dictatorial powers to quell the disturbances that followed and in 1828 an assassination attempt was made against him in Bogota. Then a territorial dispute with Peru erupted, generating further political instabilities. Now many people were inclined to see Bolivar as less the 'Liberator' and more the 'Tyrant.' Late in 1829 Venezuela seceded from the federation, and in May 1830 Ecuador followed suit. Bolivar had resigned from the presidency because of serious ill-health, and soon afterwards Marshall Sucre was assassinated. On 19 November 1830 Bolivar wrote to Juan José Flores, president of Ecuador and once one of Bolivar's generals in the independence wars. He had derived 'only a few short conclusions':

> first, America is ungovernable for us; second, he who serves a revolution ploughs the sea; third, the only thing that can be done in America is to emigrate; fourth, this country will fall without fail into the hands of an unbridled multitude, to pass later to petty, almost imperceptible, tyrants of all colors and races; fifth, devoured as we are by all crimes and destroyed by ferocity, the Europeans will not deign to conquer us; sixth, if it were possible for a part of the world to return to the primeval chaos, the latter would be the final stage of America.[5]

Six weeks later Simon Bolivar, ill and morose, died near Santa Marta on the coast of Colombia.

In 1831 the Provinces of Boyaca, Cauca, Cundinamarca, Magdalena and Panama formed themselves into 'the Republic of New Granada', defining their boundaries as those of the old Viceroyalty ruled by Spain. The secession of Panama from Colombia, stimulated in part by long-standing ambitions in the United States, was yet to come. In 1832 a centralised Constitution was adopted and Santander was elected President, whereupon he returned from his exile in New York for alleged complicity in the assassination plot against Bolivar. Santander, known as 'the Man of Laws', organised Colombia, provided a legal framework, introduced a workable system of finance, founded schools and reduced the influence of the Church in education (he further estranged the clergy by encouraging the study of advanced thinkers in various fields). The Centralists, the Church and the religious laity were now identified as the 'Conservatives', their opponents as the 'Liberals'. A Conservative, Tomas Cipriano de Mosquera, became President in 1845, to be supplanted by a Liberal in 1849. Bolivar and his revolutionary allies had secured the independence of much of South America from the Spanish monarchy, but the years of turmoil, civil war and foreign intervention were set to continue.

The Bidlack Treaty (1846)

The United States was well aware of the developments in South America. The US government, at this time under the presidency (1845-49) of James Knox Polk, was not about to abandon the thrust of the Monroe Doctrine, enunciated by President James Monroe on 2 December 1823 to buttress US hegemony in the Americas. The aim had been to exclude the European powers from expansion in the South American states (and to discourage Russian ambitions over Alaska). President Polk was happy to reiterate the principles of the Doctrine and to take whatever other steps were necessary to safeguard US interests in the region. One persistent concern was the possibility of a canal being built to link the Atlantic and the Pacific, a notion that had been considered since the time of the Spanish conquest of much of South America. Perhaps a canal would come to be built through Panama or Nicaragua (and various other routes were considered). In any event, Washington would work to guarantee US access to the region. Britain too was aware of the possibilities and was developing a presence at Belize (British Honduras) on the Mosquito Coast.

On 12 December 1846 at Bogota, capital of Colombia, the US chargé d'affaires Benjamin Alden Bidlack (in one account acting entirely on his own initiative[6]), signed a treaty with the Colombian government of President Tomas Cipriano de Mosquera. Colombia (again New Granada) guaranteed to the United States the exclusive right of transit across the Isthmus of Panama; and in exchange the United States guaranteed the 'perfect neutrality' of the Isthmus and New Granada's rights of sovereignty in that region. There was anxiety in Washington about the implications of 'entangling' alliances, whereupon New Granada despatched special envoy Pedro Alcantara Herran to lobby for the treaty. After more than a year of deliberation the US Senate acted to ratify the agreement, and seven months later congressman Bidlack, formerly a small-town lawyer and newspaper editor, died.

Washington may have pretended relative indifference to the Bidlack Treaty (also called the New Granada Treaty) but it certainly granted remarkable rights to the United States. Most of the Articles convey equal rights to New Granada and the United States, which in itself is significant in view of New Granada's sovereign status in its own territory. But the meat of the treaty is conveyed in Article 35, by far the longest section. A few extracts convey the scale of US presumption:

> ... The citizens, vessels and merchandise of the United States shall enjoy in the ports of New Granada ... all the exemptions, privileges and immunities, concerning commerce and navigation, which are now, or may hereafter be enjoyed by Granadian citizens, their vessels and merchandise; and that this equality of favours shall be made to extend to the passengers, correspondence and merchandise of the United States in their transit across the said territory ...

Transit across the Isthmus of Panama 'upon any modes of communication that now exist *or that may be, hereafter, constructed*, shall be open and free to the Government and citizens of the United States ... no other tolls or charges shall be levied or collected upon the citizens of the United States or their said merchandise thus passing over any road *or canal that may be made by the Government of New Granada ...*' (my italics). Any US produce, passing from one sea to the other, 'shall not be liable to any import duties whatever ... nor shall the citizens of the United States be liable to any duties, tolls, or charges of any kind to which native citizens are not subjected for thus passing the said Isthmus ...'

In short, the Bidlack treaty enshrined a US hegemonic presence in the territory of the Isthmus of Panama, at the time a part of sovereign Colombia; and the right also to use any future canal that may be built across the Isthmus, without the need to pay duties to the Colombian government. The Bidlack Treaty laid the ground for the subsequent US-aided secession of Panama from Colombia, for the conversion of Panama into a US protectorate, and for the exclusive US control of the Panama Canal Zone. Such matters were to bear directly on the development of Colombia as a sovereign state in the 20th century and beyond.

The Canal Enterprise

The United States was not the only country with an interest in building a canal to link the Pacific and the Atlantic. The French too were examining the possibilities and in 1875, at an international congress of the Paris-based Société de Géographie, Ferdinand de Lesseps, builder of the Suez Canal, made his first public declaration of interest in the creation of a canal across the Isthmus of Panama. The best route for such a waterway would have to be determined and the decision taken on whether the canal would be built at sea level or constructed with a series of locks. And various political events were weighing heavily in the debate. England had gained control of the Suez Canal, and the Interoceanic Canal Commission supported in the United States by President Ulysses Simpson Grant had decided that a canal through Nicaragua would be the best option. The Société announced that it would sponsor an international congress to evaluate the technological aspects of building a Central American canal.

A French intermediary was then dispatched to Bogota to secure permission to conduct explorations within Colombian territory, and six months later, in early November 1876 a seventeen-man expedition sailed in the steamer *Lafayette* to assess the options for a canal route. The expedition was ordered to limit its activities to Darien, east of the transisthmian railroad completed by a US company in 1855 – a limitation that severely constrained the Société's original concept. The expedition was not a great success. Two men died in the jungle, one during the voyage home. A second French expedition fared little better – in marked contrast to an American exploration three years before during which more than a hundred men had worked to chart an ocean-to-ocean route, exploring the Chagres watershed and preparing maps and statistical tables. The US Government Printing Office in Washington subsequently produced a composite document of several hundred pages summarising the expedition findings and rejecting the option of the Panama route.

In the event, despite the seeming success of the American Nicaragua Expedition, Colombia granted the Société Civile the exclusive privilege, valid for ninety-nine years, to build a canal across the Isthmus of Panama. The terms of the agreement required the grantees to deposit 750,000 francs in a London bank to demonstrate good faith, the carrying out of appropriate surveys, the creation of a canal company, and a specification of Colombia's gross revenues from the canal over a 25-year period. Colombia conceded to the company 500,000 hectares (1,235,500 acres) of public lands, in addition to strips of land 200 metres wide on each side of the waterway. After ninety-nine years Colombia would assume ownership of the canal.[7]

The French duly created the required company (Compagnie Universelle du Canal Interocéanique) but, having opted for a Panama route, subsequently ran into a host of logistical and financial problems. It quickly emerged that the American ownership of the Panama Railroad was as big an obstacle as any that the canal company faced. The railroad was the sole means of transportation across the isthmus, and the Americans had no enthusiasm for the success of the French project. One French observer suggested that the Americans were under orders from New York 'to do everything to create the greatest possible difficulty for us'.[8] The answer, not unfavourable to the Americans, was for the canal company to buy the railroad. The eventual deal, concluded in June 1881, was remarkable. The relatively small piece of track cost the company $20 million, and on a per-share basis 'the stock actually wound up costing $292 at a time when the true par value was less than $100.'[9] At the same time the railroad company remained incorporated under the laws of the state of New York, with its franchise from the Colombian government still intact. Despite the fact that the canal company had purchased 68,500 of the existing 70,000 shares there was no guarantee that Yankee obstructionism would be brought to an end. Moreover, the Bidlack Treaty (1846), protecting US hegemony in the region, remained in effect. American gunboats were stationed off Colon and Panama City.

The nominal purchase of the railroad company did nothing to solve the French problems. Work on the canal had begun in 1881, but malaria, yellow fever and the difficult terrain were combining to convince the engineers that the project was not feasible. The financial problems increased, the canal company went bankrupt, and in 1887 the French-inspired scheme collapsed in chaos. Despite protracted salvage attempts, including demands for yet more prodigious injections of public money, the company could not be saved. On 15 December 1888 the French Chamber of Deputies turned down the company's final proposals by a vote of 256 to 181, whereupon the Tribunal Civil of the Department of the Seine appointed three receivers to administer the company's affairs. On 4 February 1889 a liquidator was appointed. The decade-long project had cost of 1435 million francs ($287 million) and perhaps the lives of 22,000 workers.

The United States, having contemplated the possibility of a canal for more than half a century, was well prepared to turn the French failure to American advantage. One requirement was to renegotiate the Clayton-

Bulwer Treaty (1850), drawn up between US Secretary of State John Clayton and British envoy Sir Henry Lytton Bulwer, which stipulated joint US and British control over an isthmian canal. Hence in 1898 President William McKinley directed Secretary of State John Hay to negotiate a new canal treaty with Britain, currently facing problems with the Boers in South Africa. In the circumstances British ambassador Sir Julian Pauncefote, reflecting London's disenchantment with South America as a 'sphere of influence', accepted the American proposals. On 5 February 1900 the first draft of the Hay-Pauncefote Treaty was signed in Hay's office (a second draft followed objections from the US Senate). Britain finally agreed an amended version of the treaty, the first important agreement of Theodore Roosevelt's presidency (1901-09), ending any lingering British ambitions over the canal. It only remained for the United States to exploit the unhappy French involvement and to sell fresh American proposals to the Colombian government.

There was still much American opinion in favour of building a canal through Nicaragua – until a general inventory of French property in the Panama region was made available. There were 30,000 acres of land, the Panama Railroad, more than 2000 buildings, a central headquarters in Panama City and hospitals at Panama City and Colon. In addition the French had provided tugs, launches, dredgers, excavators, pumps, cranes, locomotives, railroad cars, surveying instruments and large quantities of medical supplies. Already some 36,689,965 cubic yards had been excavated. There would be obvious advantage in acquiring the French assets and in exploiting the work already completed. On 28 January 1902 Senator John Colt Spooner, acting with White House approval, introduced an amendment to a canal-authorising Bill proposed by congressman William Peters Hepburn. The President would be authorised to acquire the French company's Panama property and concessions (at a cost not to exceed $40 million), to gain from Colombia perpetual control of a canal Zone, and to build a Panama Canal. The Nicaragua option was kept alive, but by now Roosevelt was committed to the vision of a successful Panama canal.

After prolonged negotiations the United States acquired the French interests and then began talks with Colombia to build the canal. The US-Colombian talks yielded the Hay-Herran Treaty (1903), enshrining all the American demands. But the Colombian senate withheld ratification in order to secure better terms, an intolerable ploy for the impatient Roosevelt. The United States set about organising the secession of Panama from Colombia, and the creation of a Panama Canal Zone over which Washington would enjoy an unambiguous military control.

The Secession of Panama

On 23 March 1911 Theodore Roosevelt uttered the subsequently much-quoted observation: 'I took the Isthmus, started the Canal and left Congress not to debate the Canal but to debate me.' There is no doubt that the United States intervened in Colombia at the beginning of the 20th century to encourage the secession of Panama and the resulting creation of a new state that would fall totally under US sway. Washington's 1903 intervention in Colombia was not its first. In 1856 a slice of watermelon was reportedly stolen from a US soldier, leading to rioting in which more than a dozen US citizens were killed. Months later, as an evident reprisal, 160 marines landed 'to protect the railroad'. The habit of intervention, not just in Colombia but throughout the region and elsewhere had become an important element in American foreign policy.

The United States, sensitive to Colombian procrastination over the Hay-Herran Treaty, had resolved to support the Panamanian secessionist movement, a faction that had made 33 attempts to secure independence since 1830. Washington had not created secessionism but had become determined to exploit its ambitions. The earlier attempts had all failed, despite two brief victories (in 1841 and 1855), but in 1903 the rebels could rely on the support of the US navy. Roosevelt knew where he stood: 'I do not think that the Bogota lot of jack rabbits should be allowed permanently to bar one of the future highways of civilisation.' It was helpful to the United States that the Colombian government had been seriously weakened by a devastating civil war, the so-called War of a Thousand Days (1899-1902).

President Roosevelt had discussed with Philippe Bunau-Varilla, a one-time director general of the canal excavation and shareholder in the French company, whether a revolution would be possible to secure Panamanian independence. At the time it had seemed unclear how the United States government would react to any such eventuality. In fact, Bunau-Varilla, himself keen to encourage a revolt against Colombian rule, judged that American gunboats might play the key role, and with this in mind set about preparing a proclamation of independence, a military plan, the draft of a constitution, and other elements designed to serve the rebellion. Bunau-Varilla and other plotters scheduled the uprising for 4 November 1903. It seemed that the United States was highly sympathetic to the revolution from the outset, though some doubts were raised when the USS *Nashville* made no effort to prevent Colombian troops from disembarking to counter the rebellion.

It was in fact an array of American warships that secured the creation of the new republic. Within a week, various vessels had arrived to discourage any Colombian attempt to thwart the rebel objectives: the *Dixie* was soon followed by the *Atlanta, Maine, Mayflower, Prairie, Boston, Marblehead, Concord* and *Wyoming*, variously deployed in such crucial places as Colon and Panama City. Roosevelt ('Speak softly and carry a big stick; you will go far') was wielding substantial naval forces for the first time – and the independence of secessionist Panama was assured.[10] Without the US naval presence Colombia could have landed several thousand troops on both sides of the isthmus to crush a Panamanian force that even a year later was described as 'not much larger than the army on an opera stage'. A Colombian force of two thousand men did attempt an overland march through the Darien region but, ravaged by fever, they abandoned the attempt to reach Panama.

Roosevelt was proud of his part in helping to secure the creation of a new and US-friendly republic: 'I did not consult Hay, or [Secretary of War] Root, or anyone else as to what I did, because a council of war does not fight; and I intended to do the job once for all.' He had already declared that the American flag would 'bring civilisation into the waste places of the earth' – 'We have no choice as to whether or not we shall play a great part in the world. That has been determined for us by fate.' There would now be no nonsense about Colombia delaying a treaty that was in Washington's interest. Already weakened by the civil war, Colombia had now lost control over what had seemed its most important geographic asset, the isthmus between two great oceans. There were riots in Bogota and elsewhere. The US role in the Panamanian secession had gravely harmed Washington's relations with much of Latin America. Thus in 1812 James T. Du Bois, an American minister at Bogota, commented:

> By refusing to allow Colombia to uphold her sovereign rights over a territory where she had held dominion for eighty years, the friendship of nearly a century disappeared, the indignation of every Colombian, and millions of other Latin Americans, was aroused and is still most intensely active.

It now seemed obvious that the 'confidence and trust in the justice and fairness of the United States ... has completely vanished, and the maleficent influence of this condition is permeating public opinion' throughout the region.

There was not much public disquiet in the United States, and President Theodore Roosevelt was happy to boast about the success of his Colombia policy. It was time for a new treaty that would deal with Panama and the matter of a canal. It was now plain that a new agreement to safeguard American interests would no longer face procrastination and uncertainty. The United States was strong enough to indulge its growing taste for *unequal* treaties.

The Hay–Bunau-Varilla Treaty (1903)

Only days after the Panamanian secession US Secretary of State John Hay was signing a new treaty with a leading architect of the rebellion, Philippe Bunau-Varilla. The latter, seen by one commentator as the 'midwife at the birth of Panama', was reliably pro-American. He had formerly operated out of Room 1162 at the Waldorf Astoria which, resorting to an analogous metaphor, he later dubbed 'the cradle of the Panama Republic'. In view of the subsequent US control of Panama and the canal it seemed appropriate that the Panamanian secession should be plotted in a hotel room in New York. Bunau-Varilla had promised the rebel leaders (Manuel Amador, Tomas Arias, Federico Boyd and José Agustin Arango) at least $100,000 – which may have induced them to name him 'envoy extraordinary and ambassador plenipotentiary' in Washington.

The treaty that Bunau-Varilla signed in haste (on 18 November 1903) with the United States was judged by John Hay to be 'very satisfactory, vastly advantageous to the US and we must confess … not so advantageous to Panama'. It begins by citing the US congressional Act (28 June 1902) authorising the President to acquire control of 'the necessary territory of the Republic of Colombia, and the sovereignty of such territory being actually vested in the Republic of Panama' with a view to constructing a ship canal across the Isthmus of Panama. Article II of the treaty 'grants to the United States in perpetuity the use, occupation and control of a zone of land … for the construction, maintenance, operation, sanitation and protection of said Canal … extending to the distance of five miles on each side of the center line of the route of the Canal …'. Panama would also grant the United States 'in perpetuity the use, occupation and control of any other lands and waters' (including islands in the Bay of Panama, named Perico, Naos, Culebra and Flamenco) that may be necessary to the project.

Subsequent Articles of the treaty emphasised the substantial transfer of sovereignty over what had been Colombian territory only days before to the United States:

> The Republic of Panama grants to the United States all the rights, power and authority within the zone mentioned ... and within the limits of all auxiliary lands and waters mentioned ... which the United States would possess and exercise if it were the sovereign of the territory ... to the entire exclusion of the exercise by the Republic of Panama of any such sovereign rights, power or authority. (Article III)
>
> ... the Republic of Panama grants in perpetuity to the United States the right to use the rivers, streams, lakes and other bodies of water ... for navigation, the supply of water or water-power as may be necessary for the project. (Article IV)
>
> The Republic of Panama grants to the United States in perpetuity a monopoly for the construction, maintenance and operation of any system of communication by means of canal or railroad across its territory between the Caribbean Sea and the Pacific Ocean. (Article V)

Under the presumed authority of the treaty (Panama ratification on 2 December 1903; US Senate ratification 23 February 1904; US presidential ratification 25 February), the United States removed all Panamanian judges from the Canal Zone and forced Panama to abolish its army. At the same time, Panama was made to adopt the US dollar (dubbed the *balboa*) as its currency and to abandon any pretence of an independent monetary or territorial independence. In the years to come, the United States would frequently use its assumption of Colombian/Panamanian sovereignty to quell unrest, to protect US business interests, to guarantee favourable election results and to generally expand and consolidate US hegemony in the region. The 1903 treaty was a bone of contention between Panama and the United States for much of the 20th century.

Towards Modern Colombia

Over a period of almost four centuries, Colombia had moved from the time of the Spanish conquest and colonialism, through the phase of the Bolivar liberation with all its attendant tensions and instabilities, to further episodes of unrest, civil war and foreign intervention. Colombia had been stripped of geographically important territory and dragged like all its neighbours into the sphere of unambiguous US hegemony. Foreign business interests, protected by unassailable foreign military power, continued the systematic exploitation of the Colombian people and other Colombian assets. None of this provided a basis for a stable and progressive development of the Republic of Colombia through the 20th century.

TWO

The Struggle for Stability (1903 to 1980s)

Political Tensions

The political turmoil of the 19th century, shaped in part by rivalry between the Conservative and Liberal factions, produced a series of armed conflicts that terminated in the bloody 'War of a Thousand Days' (1899-1902). President Rafael Nunez had sought to impose central control on the country during his term of office (1885-94), but after his death, the Conservatives and Liberals intensified their struggle. At the beginning of the 20th century the Liberals were in disarray, the Colombian economy was paralysed, the government was near to bankruptcy, and Colombia had lost the vital geographical asset of Panama to US protectorate status.

The horrendous losses of the civil war, followed by the US-aided secession of Panama, seemingly jolted the Conservative victors into serious efforts to end the instabilities that had characterised Colombian politics for decades. One commentator described the ensuing period as 'happily, not spectacular and only conspicuous for those qualities which need no record'.[1] From one perspective this was a time of national recuperation and modest material progress, though there were many simmering tensions, with border disputes, escalating factional rivalries, and the continued foreign exploitation of workers and peasants. The apparent stability was no more than an illusion: the scene was set for mounting turmoil through the subsequent decades.

General Rafael Reyes became president in 1904 and, ruling like a dictator, imposed authoritarian control. A National Constituent Assembly comprising members of both the main parties replaced the partisan Congress, and legislation providing for minority representation in government became effective in 1910. In the same year the Assembly adopted constitutional reforms that included an annual Assembly meeting, popular election of the President (voters having to satisfy literacy, property and income qualifications – so excluding much of the population), and an Assembly-elected 'Designado' to replace the post of Vice-President. Such measures did little to solve the basic problems of Colombia – the wholly disproportionate influence of the Church, the virtually feudal social patterns, and the gross economic exploitation of workers and peasants, not least by foreign interests. American investments in Colombia increased from $600,000 in 1919 to $617,400,000 in 1929.

To the persistent domestic problems were added various territorial border disputes. A long-standing border disagreement with Venezuela had been submitted to the Spanish king who adjudicated in 1891, but it was not until 1922 that the Federal Court of Switzerland ruled in favour of Colombia and delineated the border. Still the matter was not settled. In 1928, a treaty finally resolved the issue.

In 1911, as part of another border dispute, Peruvian troops attacked Colombian forces across the Putumayo River, a provisional boundary, and only a hastily contrived agreement served to prevent war between the two countries. The dispute continued to simmer through the 1920s and after, leading Cordell Hull, the US Secretary of State in 1933, to observe later that then a possible war between Columbia and Peru was 'in the skirmish stage'.[2] Hull, judging that Washington's 'high-handed, unilateral actions ... in dealing with countries to the south must stop',[3] decided to give full support to the League of Nations in efforts to end the dispute. In September 1932, a band of Peruvian troops had occupied Leticia, a small wedge of border territory ceded by Peru to Colombia in a recent treaty, and valued by Colombia because it provided an outlet to the Amazon.

On 13 March 1933 the League Council ruled unanimously that the Peruvian troops must quit Leticia, whereupon Peru appeared to be defiant, so inviting whatever sanctions the League may choose to impose. Then Colombian ships in the Putumayo River came under fire from Peruvian forts and under attack from Peruvian bombers. Then it was reported that four Peruvian warships were sailing into the Atlantic with the aim of steaming up the Amazon to strengthen the Peruvian forces. There seemed little chance that a full-scale war between Colombia and Peru could be averted, until a dramatic event entirely altered the situation. On 30 April 1933 an assassin shot and killed President Cerro of Peru. The new president quickly accepted the League Council report on the dispute, and on 25 May delegates from Colombia and Peru signed their acceptance of the League demands.

The following month, League representatives visited Leticia and received the surrender of the Peruvian commander. For the first time, a flag of the League of Nations, a white rectangle bearing the words in dark blue letters, 'League of Nations Commission, Leticia', flew proudly over an American territory. The League commission – whose membership included Americans, Brazilians and Spaniards – was in Leticia for a year, administering the territory while Peru and Colombia worked to settle their differences. The ending of the dispute, occasioned by unusual US forbearance and an assassin's bullet, was one of the League's few successes in its unhappy history.[4]

At the same time, Colombia, subservient to US economic interests, was happy to develop its growing influence in South America. Thus in 1936 the government proposed the creation of an 'Association of American Nations', a suggestion that was repeated at the Lima conference two years later. When the European war broke out in 1939 Colombia was quick to advocate inter-American solidarity and unity of action, with President Eduardo Santos initiating telegraphic consultation with the presidents of the other South American republics. In September, at the Meeting of American Foreign Ministers in Panama, Colombia affirmed her neutrality, and was subsequently represented in Washington on the Inter-American Financial and Economic Advisory Committee. Here the Colombian government was keen to support a plan for regional economic conferences, wholly in accord with Washington's international business policies.

In July 1940 Colombia attended the second meeting of foreign ministers, this time held in Havana, Cuba, then under the US-friendly dictator Fulgencio Batista. Colombia tended to resent Washington's growing aid to its European allies, though Batista was keen to emphasise that the United States 'can count on us as a factor in their plans for the defence of the Caribbean' (as part of the US war effort, American military personnel, stationed in Cuba, were allowed to travel and photograph anywhere on the island). In April 1941 Luis Lopez de Mesa, the Colombian foreign minister, worked to settle frontier differences with Venezuela in order to cultivate South American unity against the threat of being dragged into the Second World War. Under US pressure, Colombia eliminated German control of SCADTA, the national airline, and in December 1941 severed its diplomatic relations with Germany, Italy and Japan. In November 1943, despite all its earlier overt commitment to neutrality and yielding to US wishes, Colombia itself declared war. Washington rewarded Colombia by providing lend-lease aid amounting to $8,257,000 from 1941 to 1947, so consolidating yet further the US grip on the Colombian economy.

Colombia's posture during World War II, the provision of US lend-lease and the growing American business control over the Colombian economy did nothing to stabilise Colombia's internal politics. By 1948, the domestic tensions, caused in large part by the gross economic exploitation of the bulk of the population, had erupted in bloody civil conflict that was to yield a ruthless dictatorship and more than 250,000 deaths. Over much of the next two decades, the catastrophe of *La Violencia* (1948-53, 1958-65) indicated yet again that the Colombian economic system was rooted in harsh injustices and consequent instabilities sure to cause many more casualties in the years to come. The dictatorship of Gustavo Rojas Pinilla (1953-57) failed to halt the strife.

In 1957, Rojas Pinilla was overthrown by the military, and the Conservatives and Liberals decided to form a National Front government. The presidency of Alberto Lleras Camargo (1958-62), supporting the sort of economic and social plans called for in the US Alliance for Progress, attracted substantial loans from Washington and the US-dominated multilateral agencies. The United States was now keen to reckon Colombia a 'showcase' for democratic reformism, though there had been little reform in such crucial areas as workers' rights, social welfare and land redistribution. By the mid-1960s, US congressional critics, such as Senator J. William Fulbright, were denouncing Colombia for its lack of social and political progress, despite massive American investment and financial aid from various sources.

In 1978, after the period of the National Front, Turbay Ayala was elected as a Liberal president. Again, in an attempt to quell the growing disruption, the government imposed tough security laws but failed to stem the swelling people's revolt against repression and exploitation. By now, there was a strong guerrilla movement, allegedly supported by Cuba, committed to the violent overthrow of the US-friendly regime. In 1982, the Liberals won a majority in the National Assembly but a rift in the party allowed Belisario Betancur, a Conservative, to become president. Three years later, in November 1985, guerrillas seized the national courts building in Bogota, and about 100 people were killed in the government onslaught to recapture it. In 1986 a Liberal, Virgilio Barco Vargas, was elected president and was soon declaring war on the drug traffickers.

Colombia was now racked by a people's war of liberation, set against a growing drug trade (Colombian cartels controlling about 80 per cent of the cocaine smuggled into the United States) and mounting US involvement to combat both the drug cartels and the Marxist guerrillas. The country was sinking ever deeper into turmoil and violence, with all that this implied for government repression, the growth of paramilitary death squads, and massive abuses of human rights.

The Role of Violence

The use of violence to pursue political goals has a long history in Colombia, as in most countries. The Spanish conquest was inevitably a bloody affair and Spain itself could only be evicted from the land by war, after which civil strife took other forms. The historian Gonzalo Sanchez described Colombia as a 'country of permanent war' in the 19th century. After the fourteen years of the Independence wars, there were eight national civil wars, fourteen local civil wars, many small revolts, two wars with Ecuador and three *coups d'état*. The episodes of violence, never decisive, brought phases of uneasy peace, soon to be followed by fresh conflict. Many factors combined to fuel the wars – political ambition, the solidarity of exploited workers, legitimate peasant grievances, and family feud. Thus a Swiss professor, E. Rothlisberger, wrote of the 1885 revolution: 'The majority do not fight in one party or another out of conviction but because they must avenge some atrocity.' More commonly, the burdens imposed on the mass of the population by a privileged ruling élite stimulated a violent response as the only political recourse. A Jesuit, Francisco de Roux, commented: 'It is a simplification to say that the Colombian people were an aggressive people from the beginning. Rather what you find is a country where the political customs of the ruling class have led the people into war from the very first days of the republic.'[5] With the 'War of a Thousand Days', ushering in the 20th century, 'a gust of death had passed over the entire country', according to the political witness Jorge Holguin. It was a prelude to the mounting civil strife that would follow.

The peasants, the bulk of the population, had gained nothing from the economic developments of the early 20th century. Granted no labour rights, they lived in poverty and servitude that had changed little since the colonial era. Since they were unable to pay the levied taxes the peasants were forced to perform whatever tasks were specified by landowners and local authorities. They were, for example, obliged to act as human pack horses, trudging miles of highway with goods upon their shoulders. The resulting protests were invariably crushed. Thus the peasant leader Quintin Lame organised a series of revolts beginning in 1914 in the Cauca, Huila and Tolima, but nothing was achieved. Between 1928 and 1937, some 20,000 peasants took part in uprisings in eighteen areas of the country, with 11,000 dispossessed men and women demonstrating in Cundinamarca alone. In 1931 the then Liberal government was at last forced to grant the peasants the right to form trade unions. But peasant militancy was neutralised for a time in various ways. The leaderships were often subverted into conventional – and largely ineffective – political channels; some coffee workers were gradually transformed into conservative freeholders; and private armed squads were used increasingly to terrorise potential demonstrators into acquiescence. Such developments, of brief effect, had done nothing to remove the underlying tensions.

Between August 1946 and the end of 1947 the workers staged around 600 organised demonstrations, strikes and other forms of protest. In May 1947 some 1500 workers were arrested at the start of a general strike, and violence broke out in Boyaca, Santander and other places. An estimated 14,000 people were killed in the ensuing repression. On 7 February 1948 Jorge Eliecer Gaitan, the Liberal leader, led a silent protest of 100,000 people through the streets of Bogota and urged a peaceful resolution of the conflict: 'All we ask, Mr President, is guarantees for human life, which is the least that a nation can ask.' On 9 April Gaitan was assassinated. The scene was set for one of the most violent phases in Colombian history.

The immediate response to the assassination was a spontaneous people's uprising (the *Bogotazo*) that shook the capital. Men and women poured through the streets of the city in a rampage of fury and destruction. Soon the massive rebellion had spread to the provinces where for some time the Conservatives had been deploying death squads to crush any hint of opposition. In one account the repressive regime had sent armed thugs into the countryside to sever testicles, slash the bellies of pregnant women, and throw babies in the air to catch on bayonets – all under the injunction 'don't leave even the seed'.[6] The orgy of cruelty against the people knew no limits:

> New ways of killing came into vogue: the *corte corbata*, for example, left the tongue hanging from the neck. Rape, arson and plunder went on and on; people were quartered or burned alive, skinned or slowly cut into pieces; troops razed villages and plantations and rivers ran red with blood ... the repressive forces expelled and pursued innumerable families, who fled to seek refuge in the mountains ...[7]

Efforts were made to organise a people's resistance to the government-inspired slaughter. Rafael Rangel created a 'revolutionary council' in Barrancabermeja that lasted for two weeks, and bands of armed men and women were formed by Eliseo Velasquez in the Llanos and by Hermogenes Vargas in the south of Tolima. During 1948 the government action resulted in more than 43,000 deaths, the union movement was crushed, and thousands of workers were dismissed throughout the country. In May 1949 three Conservatives and three military officers (including General Gustavo Rojas Pinilla) were brought into the cabinet to replace the six Liberals, and in November 1949 – to the delight of rightwing mobs in the streets – three Liberal members of the Chamber of Representatives were shot dead, one in the Chamber itself. A law passed to bring in elections met Liberal opposition because of its lack of safeguards, whereupon the president closed Congress, prohibited public meetings and imposed press censorship. In 1949 Laureano Gomez, facing no opposition, was elected president and then set about intensifying the terrorist campaign against the people.

Some 200,000 people were killed between 1948 and 1965 as the country plunged into a barbaric chaos. Peasant armies, death squads (the *chulavitas*, *pajaros* and others), the loyal military forces – all contended for power as the violence intensified and the casualties mounted. The peasants, some organised in self-defence units by the Communist Party, were forced to take military initiatives to avoid extermination. At the same time the Liberal faction was split. Some Liberal leaders (Pedro Antonio Marin, Jacobo Prias Alape, Ciro Trujillo, etc) came to fight as guerrillas alongside the Communists; while others began collaborating with the army against the people. Many rich landowners fled, as did Liberals when they received the dreaded death threat (*boleteo*). Some peasants gained access to abandoned land, but many more were evicted from their homes, dispossessed or murdered. An estimated one million migrated, 150,000 of them to

Venezuela. The sustained slaughter was highly congenial to capitalism, now able to enjoy a remarkable period of capital accumulation. In 1949, during which 18,500 people died, the president of the National Association of Industrialists (ANDI) was happy to comment: 'The Colombian situation is the best we have ever known'; just as a government report observed in 1951, when 10,300 people were murdered, that 'social peace reigns'. The urban popular movement had been destroyed, wage levels had plunged, and industrial production had dramatically increased. General Pinilla, now president, urged an amnesty in order to disarm the guerrillas while he organised a further campaign of violence against the people. Any regions thought to harbour Communists, declared illegal, were indiscriminately attacked by the army and by aerial bombardment. The Communists responded by evacuating whole areas to safer zones, by working to create 'independent republics' within Colombia, and by developing systems of administration that were independent of the repressive state. The historian Alfredo Molano wrote of the Communist guerrillas: 'The same organisation which saved them from being killed by the *chulavitas* in 1950, which enabled them to confront the army in 1955, which defended their lives during the marches, allowed them in the 1960s and 1970s to limit the advance of the *latifundio*.'[8]

The creation of the National Front, nominally uniting the Conservatives and Liberals, officially ended *La Violencia* – though it was set to continue in a different form through its second phase (1958-65) when 18,000 more people would be killed. In 1952 Colombia had been one of the first five South American states to sign a mutual-defence assistance agreement with the United States, and the US influence had increased through the entire period of the violence. The United States was training Colombian officers, staging inter-American military conferences, and providing financial aid ($60 million between 1961 and 1967) for both counter-insurgency and 'economic development', as well as specific allocations ($100 million worth) of military equipment.

In 1964 the Colombian army, led by US-trained officers and using US-supplied equipment, launched *Plan Lazo* against what was taken to be a dissident peasant grouping. Some 16,000 troops, advised by US personnel, surrounded the narrow valley of Marquetalia where fewer than fifty peasants were working, while the US-equipped Colombian air force began bombing the area. Virtually all the peasants escaped and, with men and women from the other 'republics', came to develop a network of mobile guerrilla groups. In September 1964 they came together at the *Bloque Sur* (bloc of the south) conference. In 1966 a second conference officially founded the Revolutionary Armed Forces of Colombia (*Fuerzas Armadas Revolucionarias de Colombia*, FARC) which, by the start of the 21st century, had developed into the largest guerrilla organisation in the Western hemisphere. In 1966, at the end of the second phase of *La Violencia*, a new period of warfare was about to begin.

In its early days FARC was essentially a defensive organisation, too weak to launch military initiatives of its own. One early setback was when Ciro Trujillo was defeated in Qindio with many casualties and the loss of 70 per cent of the organisation's arms. FARC suffered constant harassment from the Colombian army and the large cattle ranchers keen to acquire land that the guerrilla colonisers were forced to abandon. Nonetheless, the FARC gradually expanded its influence, becoming increasingly able to offer protection to peasants, to take over fresh territory, and to provide basic services in the regions under its control. Other guerrilla organisations were experiencing mixed fortunes in the struggle against government forces that were being provided with ever increasing US support. Thus the National Liberation Army (*Ejercito de Liberacion Nacional*, ELN) first appeared on 7 January 1965 when 27 men and one woman held the town of Simacota for two hours; and the People's Liberation Army (EPL) fragmented under heavy army pressure, before regrouping in the 1980s. The government responded to all such groups by launching military campaigns, by intensifying the degree of social repression, and by inviting continued US support.

The administration of President Guillermo Leon Valencia (1962-66) increasingly left the army to combat the people's forces in any way it wished. These were depicted as essentially 'public order' matters to be dealt with in circumstances where the country was facing a 'state of siege' (today called a 'state of internal commotion'). The US organisation Human Rights Watch has pointed out that 37 out of the last 47 years (that is, the second half of the 20th century) have seen Colombia either under states of siege or states of internal commotion.

It is significant that during a state of siege the Colombian government executive implements decrees that abrogate rights by transferring judicial and other powers to the military, with little or no civilian involvement. For example, Decree 1290, implemented in 1965, sent suspect civilians to military courts martial where hearings were in secret and important judicial and political rights were suspended. In the same vein, Decree 3398, implemented in 1968 to create armed civil patrols, was later converted into permanent legislation by Law 48 which has been frequently cited as the legal foundation for all the paramilitary groups that roam the country to spread terror among the people.[9] At the same time the Colombian military distributes combat manuals designed to increase army effectiveness against the rebel forces. One instructs field commanders to disguise some soldiers in civilian clothes so that they can move among the people to identify those individuals who are not enthusiastic about the army presence. If a civilian's reaction to troops 'is indifferent or negative' the individual can be targeted as a suspected subversive. Selected individuals can then be sent death threats (*boleteos*) to 'frighten them and make them believe that they have been compromised and must abandon the area'.[10]

By the 1970s, despite all the efforts of the Colombian government advised by the United States, the FARC influence was rapidly expanding. In some areas the guerrilla organisation was adjudicating legal disputes, overseeing public works and carrying out police functions. Again the government intensified the repression to combat what US advisors were calling 'known communist proponents' – which came to mean suspected guerrilla supporters, government critics, trade unionists, community organisers, opposition politicians, civic leaders, students, human rights activists, health-care workers and others. General Luis Carlos Camacho Leyva, Colombian Defence Minister from 1978 to 1982, declared that any form of social protest was simply 'the unarmed branch of subversion'. Thus any appeal for better wages, adequate health care or clean water could invite a death threat deriving from an official source supported by the United States.

The long civil war continued. The two principal phases of *La Violencia* were now over but the armed struggle continued to take its terrible toll of casualties year by year. The war might have been brought to an end had it not been for the involvement of the United States. In Colombia, as in many other states, Washington fuelled civil turmoil to further its broader Cold-War agenda. In the Caribbean, South America and elsewhere the United States was determined to protect corporate interests. In the region of Colombia many people were unsympathetic to the tenets and presumptions of the American Way. One of these people was Fidel Castro.

Castro in Bogota

In April 1948 a Pan-American Conference was arranged with the intention of converting the old Pan-American Union of American States into a more tightly structured body, the Organisation of American States (OAS). The United States was represented by General George C. Marshall, with all the other South American states represented by their foreign ministers. Students from Cuba, Argentina and other countries, highly sympathetic to the people's plight in Colombia, were planning to stage a protest to coincide with the conference. The Argentinian president, Juan Domingo Peron, hostile to US and British imperialism in Latin America, had paid many of the students' fares. (In one account Diego Molinari, the chairman of the Argentinian Senate Foreign Relations Committee, visited Havana in February 1948 to pay the expenses of the Cuban delegation.[11]). Among those invited to Bogota were Alfredo Guevara, the Communist leader in the University of Havana, and Fidel Castro, representing the university's law faculty. One aim of the Cuban students was to inaugurate a new inter-American student organisation that would be a powerful political instrument in the region.

On 29 March 1948 Fidel Castro and Rafael del Pino, a Cuban-American (like Castro, a member of the *Union Insurrecional Revolucionaria*, UIR), arrived in Bogota and immediately began discussions with other students leaders. On 3 April the Pan-American meeting began, whereupon the students dropped thousands of leaflets, attacking US colonialism, from the balconies of the Teatro Colono where prominent members of the Colombian élite were meeting. Castro and del Pino were interrogated, ordered to report to the police two days later (which they refused to do) and were then arrested and told to cease their political agitation. Events were now moving towards a more violent confrontation.

On 9 April the Liberal populist Jorge Eliecer Gaitan was killed during a peaceful demonstration (as already noted). The assassin, Juan Roa Sierra, was soon branded a lone madman (for example, in the report by Sir Norman Smith, Scotland Yard chief) – which did nothing to defuse the political tensions. Today some observers claim that the CIA was involved in the assassination.[12]

Within hours massive demonstrations were taking place, rioting and destruction were spreading, and Bogota was out of control. Over several days of chaos around 3000 people were killed. General Marshall and others blamed the Communists, while William Pawley, the veteran anti-Communist US ambassador to the United Nations (and with business interests in Cuba), later commented: 'We had information that there was a Cuban there, a very young man who appeared to us not to be the real threat.' Then Pawley recalled hearing a voice on the radio just after Gaitan's assassination: 'This is Fidel Castro from Cuba. This is a Communist revolution. The President has been killed, all the military establishments in Colombia are now in our hands, the Navy has capitulated to us and this Revolution has been a success.'[13]

Other commentators suggested that Castro and del Pino had been sent in to organise the riots; and that Castro himself had killed thirty-two people during the period. A guest at the Hotel Claridge allegedly heard Castro and del Fino boasting about their successes, while Castro is believed to have shown Colombian detectives a pass book identifying him as 'Grade I agent of the Third Front of the USSR in South America'.[14] Sir Norman Smith reported that the two Cubans had arrived at their hotel on 9 April 'bringing a large quantity of arms and staying there for many hours, talking on the phone, in English, with various people'.[15]

Castro did become involved in the Bogota riots, but his precise role and degree of involvement remain uncertain. He was due to meet Gaitan about the time of his murder, but supposedly only to arrange the booking of a theatre for a meeting.

On 13 April Fidel Castro and Rafael del Pino were given sanctuary in the Cuban embassy, after which they travelled back to Havana in a cargo plane. Castro said later that the Colombian people had failed to gain power 'because they were betrayed by false leaders', but he was in no doubt about the power of a popular uprising and the need to channel the people's anger. Perhaps one of the significant fruits of the 1948 *bogotazo* was to fuel the passion behind the Cuban revolution.

The Mounting US Pressure

The United States massively expanded its hegemony over the South American states through the 19th century, 'stole' Panama from Colombia at the beginning of the 20th, and deepened its penetration of the Colombian economy through the rest of century. Through the period of the Cold War an escalating military presence was added to substantial injections of capital to enlarge and consolidate US control over the Colombian state.

Between 1913 and 1929 US investment in Colombia expanded from around $2 million to $4 million. The US-dominated United Fruit Company, with an odious reputation throughout Latin America, began investing in banana production on the Caribbean coast near Santa Marta; and after 1925 Tropical Oil, an affiliate of Standard Oil, began exporting oil near the port of Barrancabermeja on the Magdalena river. Such corporate enterprise had international ambitions. The United Fruit Company, for example, was to develop a vast network of plantations throughout the region – in Cuba, Jamaica, the Dominican Republic, Panama, Honduras, Nicaragua, Guatemala and Colombia. This was all part of an agricultural revolution that was set to have drastic consequences for peasant populations throughout the region.

The US-dominated World Bank also worked to shape the economic and political development of Colombia and other regional states. A Bank mission in 1949 laid the basis for growing influence in Colombia through the 1950s and beyond. It was not long before Colombia became the World Bank's fourth largest borrower – with all that implied for the country's loss of financial independence. Thus Colombia emerged as well prepared to observe the demands of international finance, and to become in due course a World Bank 'favourite child'.[16] In 1985 the richest 10 per cent of urban Colombian families received about 40 per cent of the total national income, while 50 per cent of families received less than 20 per cent; the poorest 20 per cent gained less than five per cent of the national income. It is significant that development loans were offered only within the context of real support for US business. Thus one World Bank loan was conditional upon the Colombian government specifying that railroad rails to be purchased be of a size manufactured only by US companies. [17]

The Colombian government of Laureano Gomez, keen to attract further US support, decided in 1951 to send a battalion of troops to fight in support of the Americans in the Korean War. This was a significant gesture of subservience to Washington. Colombia was the only Latin American country to send troops, and eventually the policy was rewarded. The Colombian army attracted increased amounts of US training and *matériel*, and Colombian officers who had fought in the war later rose to high ranks in the army. It was all useful background experience for the Colombian army's long war against the Colombian people. And where the Colombian government had been happy to yield to US military wishes, it was equally keen to accept the implications of US food aid. Thus when in 1954 the adoption of US Public Law 480 (PL 480) institutionalised food aid as yet another arm of American imperialism, with little of the aid reaching needy recipients, Colombia was one of the first countries to accept PL 480 products and the consequent destruction of the local farming economies (as a prelude to penetration by US agribusiness interests).[18] US policy in this regard was transparent, even when not overtly stated. Hence in 1957 Senator Hubert Humphrey told Congress:

I have heard ... that people may become dependent on us for food ...
that was good news, because before people can do anything they have
got to eat. And if you are looking for a way to get people to lean on
you and to be dependent on you, in terms of their cooperation with
you, it seems to me that food dependence would be terrific.[19]

In such a fashion, Colombian agriculture, as well as other Colombian
economic assets and the Colombian armed forces, were progressively
brought under American control. In 1952 Colombia was one of the first five
South American countries to sign a mutual-defence assistance agreement
with the United States, and in the same year became the site of the first US-
funded Latin American counter-insurgency training institute. By 1960 the
Colombian army, under General Alberto Ruiz Novoa, was in effect
controlled from the United States. Ruiz Novoa had fought in support of the
Americans in Korea and a growing number of Colombian officers were
being trained by US army personnel. Between 1961 and 1967 there was a
dramatic increase in US military aid to the Colombian armed forces.

By 1962 General Ruiz had brought in US Special Forces to train
Colombian officers in counterinsurgency methods, with Colombian officers
also being assigned for training at US bases.[20] In 1962 a US Army Special
Warfare team visited Colombia to help in the development of the *Plan Lazo*
counterinsurgency strategy, with US advisors proposing, amongst other
things, that the United States 'select [Colombian] civilian and military
personnel for clandestine training ...' and that Colombian personnel be
used 'to perform counter-agent and counter-propaganda functions and as
necessary execute paramilitary, sabotage and/or terrorist activities against
known communist proponents'.[21] This policy 'should be backed by the
United States'.[22]

In 1961 Bogota, acting in accord with US wishes, broke off diplomatic
relations with Cuba and continued to enjoy American military support.
Two years later, in a further attempt to bolster the US–Colombian
connection, President John Kennedy visited Bogota and received a rapturous
welcome – which appeared to be misplaced. Thus Alberto Lleras Camargo
of Colombia commented: 'Do you know why these people are cheering you?
It's because they think you're on their side against the oligarchs.'[23] Kennedy
had been promoting his Alliance for Progress, which the Colombian
military perceived as a recipe for upheaval. The radicals by contrast judged
the Alliance to be no more than a further weapon of US imperialism.

The panoply of US investors continued to benefit from their access to the open Colombian economy. In 1968 the Colombian government asked the Greek economist Constantine Vistas to investigate the benefits being derived by the mass of foreign investor companies, whereupon he exposed the common practice of 'transfer pricing': to avoid showing profits in countries where taxes or inflation were high, or to transfer money for other reasons, the companies could manipulate the costs in various ways. It was found that Colombia, massively exploited, was then losing substantial revenues: $20 million in lost foreign exchange and $10 million in tax revenues in the pharmaceutical industry alone.[24] The Colombian government then arranged for a renegotiation of royalty payments, saving the country $8 million and reducing by 90 per cent the provisions that forced subsidiaries to buy only from parent companies. The government had managed to claw back some of the revenue being extracted from Colombia by foreign companies, but the foreign investors remain broadly content. Not a single US company withdrew from Colombia as a result of the reforms.[25] The United States continued to dominate Colombia in the usual ways. The Colombian army was under *de facto* US control, the few critics of US policy (for example, General José Joachin Matallana) in influential posts were either forced to retire or otherwise marginalised, and the CIA was active in funding anti-Communist propaganda – for example, via Radio Sutatenza, a Church radio literacy program for some one million peasant listeners.[26]

The US pressure on Colombia has increased over the decades (see Chapter 9), using the drug wars and the need to safeguard US security as principal pretexts. Peasants have been expelled from the land in their hundreds of thousands with the government always ready to increase the levels of repression to protect the large landowners and the US agribusiness interest. Deliberate American pressure over the years, including the 'Food for Peace' program, has undermined the production of crops for domestic use. It is inevitable that small Colombian farmers have found it impossible to compete with cheap US agricultural exports which the United States encourages Latin America to consume while producing cash crops for the benefit of US consumers: 'flowers, vegetables for yuppie markets – or coca leaves, the optimal choice on grounds of capitalist rationality'.[27] In the case of Colombia, the consequences are obvious.

A report produced by Evan Valliantos, in the US Government Office of Technology Assessment, indicates the significance of the Colombian experience in the context of economic exploitation and US policy: 'Colombia's twentieth century history is above all stained in the blood of the peasant poor.' The US Agency for International Development (USAID), the Ford Foundation and other approved organisations have insisted that the rural poor in Latin America and elsewhere would be aided by 'the largely discredited trickle-down technology and knowledge transfer process', by investing in the military and business communities, and by relying on the mechanisms of 'competition, private property, and ... the free market'. One poor Colombian farmer described the system as one in which 'the big fish eats the little one', and it is not only the rural poor who have been punished in so merciless a fashion. Valliantos described the small Colombian city of Yumbo, rapidly becoming unfit for human habitation' because of uncontrolled pollution, decay, and 'corrosive slums' in which 'the town's spent humanity has all but given up'.[28]

It is easy to see the rationale behind the mounting US pressure. The current system of economic exploitation and political repression benefits the US corporate interest – which in turn means that army, police, paramilitaries, CIA, the media, large landowners and the Colombian and US governments must persevere with their broad and sometimes untidy alliance to maintain the status quo. It is just as easy to see why the Colombian people have struggled over the decades against the unholy capitalist conspiracy. 'The essential dynamics of the Colombian scene have been discernible for most of two centuries. Today the struggle continues.

The People's Struggle

The Colombian people have continually battled against exploitative élites backed by a powerful foreign neighbour. The seemingly endless struggle has taken many forms but with violent protest increasingly perceived as the only possible route to radical change. The workers were granted the right to strike in 1919, but with employers allowed the right to hire contract workers to replace the strikers. A socialist party was founded in the same year, set to win 23 per cent of the vote in Medellin in the 1921 legislative elections. In 1926 the Revolutionary Socialist Party (PSR) was founded in the wake of the oil workers' first strike. Here and elsewhere the state used the courts and the army to suppress the developing people's movement. When in 1928 the army fired on a peaceful demonstration of Cienaga banana workers, and pursued those who fled, an estimated 1000 workers were killed. The demonstrations continued.

In the 1920s the peasants also attempted to rebel over land rights, tenancy agreements and other matters. The large landowners, invariably supported by government and army, responded with intimidation, beatings and eviction. In 1931 the peasants were granted the right to unionise, while the government worked to transform the growing peasants' movement into a manageable mainstream faction. At the same time the Communist Party, a focus of radical agitation, called for 'revolutionary land seizures' and 'expropriation of landowners without compensation'. But it proved impossible for the radicals to unite the workers and peasants in a truly national movement, while the landowners were striving to enlist the peasants to fight their party battles.

The situation continued virtually unchanged into the fraught period of the Cold War. In the 1960s there were spontaneous peasant revolts against the impact of commercial agriculture and the expansion of the cattle ranches, but the peasants were confronted with the growth of paramilitary factions and successive regimes committed to the suppression of all forms of organised resistance. In 1967 a National Association of Peasants (ANUC) was set up by the Lleras Restrepo government in an attempt to contain the growing dissident factions within manageable mainstream politics. ANUC struggled to address specific peasant problems but was largely impotent when confronted by the large landowners enjoying predictable government support. In these circumstances the peasant movement sired various competing organisations, some even coming into conflict with the FARC, despite their nominally similar aims and ambitions.[29]

The labour movement has similarly been historically weak, suffering from deep fragmentation and the impact of successive repressive governments. The trade unions have proved unable to press for the company observance of current labour legislation, much less to urge the adoption of new laws to protect worker rights. Thus when the Colombian Ministry of Labour inspected 12,452 firms between 1982 and 1985, it was found that only 8.4 per cent were meeting the requirements of labour legislation, while 91.6 per cent were violating an average of 3.85 regulations.[30] At the same time it seemed unlikely that the mainstream political parties would do much to further union aspirations, with the consequence that through the 1980s union leaders struggled to achieve a breakaway from the influence of the mainstream parties. In October 1981 50 trade unionists were arrested days before the start of a national civic strike, with more arrests taking place later. The universities were shut down, trade unions were made illegal for a year, and teachers involved in the protest were dismissed. Now there were steps to unite the independent and Communist-led unions, while the civic movement began to expand. Between January 1982 and March 1984 there were some 78 local and regional civic strikes, involving 152 municipalities and around five million people from many different occupations.[31]

The FARC was also expanding its influence: by 1980 it had nine contested fronts, by 1984 some 27. In May 1982, acknowledging that a revolutionary situation now existed in Colombia, it added the letters EP (*Ejercito del Pueblo*, People's Army) to its name, and resolved to adopt more offensive military tactics. The FARC wanted peace but also something in return. When an agreement was negotiated with the government at the end of 1984, critics of the movement charged that only a few vague promises had been won. After an attack on its leaders, another guerrilla organisation, M-19, declared the truce with the government over – which in turn led in May 1985 led to a grouping of various guerrilla organisations, a National Guerrilla Coordination (*Coordinadora Nacional Guerrillera*) committed to continued armed struggle. At this time only the FARC continued to observe the negotiated truce. Then Colombia plunged headlong into a fresh civil war.

The paramilitary groups became more active, killing guerrilla leaders and also delinquents and homosexuals. During 1985 there were 800 murders in Cali alone. The army regained control of the slum districts of Cali, but on 6 November 1985 M-19 captured the Palace of Justice in Bogota. Hundreds of troops surrounded the building, reportedly occupied by 40 guerrillas. Soon the fire from tanks and rocket grenades had begun a blaze that raged out of control until the building was destroyed. The battle cost the lives of all the guerrillas, at least 17 soldiers, and Alfonso Reyes, president of the court.

The war continued, sucking all social sectors into the maelstrom. Many of Colombia's political and social institutions were ambivalent, desperately wanting stability but nervous about the scale of repression being perpetrated by the paramilitaries and the army. The Church had supported the Conservatives through the period of *La Violencia*, with priests and bishops even supporting the mass slaughter of the peasants[32]; but then the priests began taking up arms in firm alliance with the guerrillas (for example, the priest Camilo Torres died in his first encounter with the Colombian army, on 17 February 1966, in the Andes). In 1968 the bishops of Latin America met in Medellin to produce a revolutionary statement of human rights. It served to shatter the centuries-old bond of the Church, the military, and the rich élites of the region. Pope Paul told a huge crowd in Bogota: 'We wish to personify the Christ of a poor and hungry people'. And to the rich he declared: 'Your ears and your hearts must be sensitive to the voices crying out for bread, concern, justice, and a more active participation in the direction of society.' The Latin-American Episcopal Conference (CELAM) had prepared detailed documents for Medellin, carrying statistical surveys, theological appeals and sociological arguments, 'but the bishops had already seen the proof in the poverty outside their palace windows'.[33]

Colombia continued to suffer the US pressure and the continued capitalist exploitation. American companies dumped toxic DDT on the Colombian countryside, the US Information Agency issued propaganda comic books in which American supermen battled the Communist monster (causing university students to riot), and Washington continued to pump money, *matériel* and personnel into the Colombian conflict to fuel the bloody chaos. Many elements continued to shape the turbulence in modern Colombia: not least, coffee, water, oil and drugs. All provided their unique *raison d'être* for the expanding US involvement in the affairs of the country, but the issue of drugs was particularly congenial to American ambitions. Who could object to a war against the drug barons?

THREE

Ravaged by the Drug Trade (1980s to Late-1992)

War by Various Means

The civil conflict in Colombia continued through the 1980s and beyond, fuelled by the emergence of new paramilitary groups, the growing involvement of the drug traffickers, the guerrilla campaign, and the escalating US intervention. On all sides, funds were available to support the mounting carnage, and as successive government administrations came under revolutionary threat the United States felt compelled to support the procession of business-friendly regimes.

The Colombian army remained committed to the elimination of what it regarded as subversives, and looked to the Government to provide the appropriate legal justification. For example, the administration of President Julio Cesar Turbay Ayala (1978-82) imposed Decree 1923, the 'Security Statute', defining new crimes such as 'disturbing public order', implementing new levels of press censorship, and even giving the police judicial powers. Some Colombian observers denounced the Security Statute as a virtual 'occupation' of civilian life by the military, allowing the armed forces, according to historian Francisco Leal Buitrago, to expand their autonomy in matters of public order 'to unprecedented levels'. It was plain that the military intended to eliminate the 'subversive' organisations from top to bottom. Thus General Fernando Landazabal, who served as Defence Minister under President Belisario Betancur (1982-86), declared: 'As important as finding the subversives is finding their political leaders ... There is nothing more harmful for the development of counter-revolutionary operations than to dedicate all efforts to combat and the repression of the enemy's armed forces, leaving untouched the movement's political leaders, free to continue their activities.'

On 3 December 1981 a helicopter dropped leaflets over the city of Cali announcing the creation of a new organisation, Death to Kidnappers (*Muerte a Secuestradores*, MAS). The group was set up by 223 drug traffickers in retaliation for the M-19 kidnapping of Martha Nieves Ochoa, whose brothers were members of the Medellin cartel. Some Colombians outside the drug trade were prepared to welcome his development. For example, in the Middle Magdalena region people with land or business interests were facing increasing demands for guerrilla-imposed 'war taxes', food and other supplies. Perhaps an organisation such as MAS would offer an effective means of fighting back.

In 1982 the MAS approach was adopted by the Barbula Battalion in Puerto Boyaca, Santander, and by Captain Oscar de Jesus Echandia, the town's military mayor who convened a meeting of interested people – including not only local Liberal and Conservative Party leaders, businessmen and ranchers but also representatives from the US oil industry. It seemed likely that American oil money would be made available to fund a paramilitary onslaught on any people suspected of subversive's sympathies. The aim was to 'cleanse' the region of subversives, an ambitious plan that went far beyond simply protecting local businesses and landowners from guerrilla attack. A first step was to collect guns, food, clothing and money to equip the new paramilitary force for the anticipated confrontation with subversive elements. Businessmen, ranchers, political leaders and the military combined to provide the necessary support for the new MAS group. This meant that MAS, the name used by drug traffickers, would be encouraged by businessmen and the army to hunt down and kill suspected subversives. It was a recipe for intimidation, summary executions and a new wave of terror against the civilian population.

There were no legal constraints on the work of the MAS activists. Early victims included a Puerto Boyaca council member, political activists and a doctor, all of them members of the Liberal Party and all killed. Soon joint operations were being carried out by the army and MAS members, and local peasants were reporting many incidents of extrajudicial executions and other nominally illegal acts. After 240 murders had been attributed to MAS, President Betancur ordered an investigation by the Procuraduria, the government agency responsible for considering reports of abuses by government employees. It was found that 59 of 163 individuals with links to MAS were active police and military officers, including the commanders of the Barbula and Bombona Battalions. Procurador Carlos Jimenez Gomez, responsible for the investigation, described them as 'officials who go overboard when faced with the temptation to multiply their ability to act ... with this plan of hired killers, they can do officiously what they cannot do officially'. Jimenez pressed for further action but was ignored.

The Defence Minister, General Fernando Landazabal, ordered members of the armed forces to pay towards the legal defence of the accused men, while influential officers were prepared to describe the MAS paramilitaries as civilians rightly defending themselves against guerrillas. Finally the Disciplinary Tribunal, in charge of resolving disputes between military tribunals and civilian courts, ruled that the case properly belonged within military jurisdiction, whereupon all the charges were dismissed. None of the MAS officers was ever charged, and some were rewarded. For example, Colonel Ramon Emilio Gil Bermudez, whose name appeared in the Jimenez list, having already been trained in the United States, returned to Washington D.C. as the military attaché to the Colombian embassy. While being investigated for multiple murders in Colombia, Gil was offered additional military training in the United States. In 1994, after serving as commander of the Colombian armed forces, he retired with honours.

The MAS campaign continued, now involving a public entity to carry out civic improvement and to aid sympathetic peasants: the Association of Peasants and Ranchers of the Middle Magdalena (*Asociacion Campesina de Agricultores y Ganaderos del Magdalena Medio*, ACDEGAM). The new body issued propaganda against what it called 'communism', including any attempt to protect worker and peasant rights, and urged the legalisation of the so-called 'self-defence groups', unambiguously involved in covert attacks on suspect peasants, overt terror, death threats and assassinations. In 1984 FARC had signed a ceasefire with the government and was negotiating the creation of a new political Party, the Patriotic Union (*Union*

Patriotica, UP), but the killings by MAS and other paramilitary groups continued, including the murders of guerrillas who were involved in negotiations with the government. Other victims of the paramilitaries, working with the open support of the army, were UP members, human-rights leaders and community activists, most with no involvement with the guerrillas or other military groups.

By 1985 ACDEGAM was working actively with the drug traffickers to develop its various campaigns. Drug money was now available to increase the supply of weapons to the MAS paramilitaries, and to improve the group's intelligence gathering and other activities. During the period 1987-88 Britain and Israel were providing instructors to work in ACDEGAM training centres, in this way giving support to drug-linked paramilitaries whose declared purpose included the goal of attacking 'Patriotic Union members and government representatives or political parties that oppose drug trafficking'.[1] The witness Diego Viafara Salinas, at one time a MAS doctor, reported the close collaboration in MAS between army commanders, paramilitary leaders and drug traffickers (including Pablo Escobar, Gonzalo Rodriguez Gacha, Victor Carranza and others). Through the 1980s MAS became active in eight of the 32 regions of Colombia, enjoying the support of local political and military leaders. The weapons used by the MAS paramilitaries included R-15 rifles, AKMs, Galils, FALs and G-3 rifles, all nominally prohibited for civilian use, but supplied through drug-funded private sales, by the military, and by Military Industry (*Industria Militar*, INDUMIL), this latter the only organisation officially authorised to produce, store and distribute firearms in Colombia.

In 1988 a human-rights group, the Centre for Investigation and Popular Education (*Centro de Investigacion y Educacion Popular*, CINEP) recorded 108 massacres (a massacre defined as the killing of four or more people for political reasons). In one case, the massacre on the La Honduras and La Negra farms, the Colombian army had arrested people, tortured them, taken their photographs, and then handed the information over to the paramilitary killers. Major Luis Becerra Bohorquez, before the massacre, put up the killers at a Medellin hotel and reportedly paid the bill with his Diner's Club card.[2] On 18 January 1989 the paramilitaries killed two judges and ten investigators near La Rochela, Santander, working to collect information on killings in the area. Lieutenant Luis Andrade Ortiz, commander of the Rafael Reyes Battalion, was later linked to the massacre of the investigators and sentenced to a five-year prison term. Then a higher court overturned the decision and in 1990 Andrade mysteriously escaped from a military prison. In 1994 a civil court ruled that the Colombian security forces had organised the massacre.

In April 1989 President Virgilio Barco (1986-90) declared that the paramilitaries were 'terrorist organisations', and that the majority of their victims were not guerrillas: 'They are men, women, and even children, who have not taken up arms against institutions. They are peaceful Colombians.' Two military officers, Major Diego Velandia (commander of the Barbula Battalion) and Lieutenant-Colonel Luis A. Bohorquez (commander of the Puerto Boyaca base) were discharged, some training centres were dismantled, and a special police unit was created to hunt down the paramilitaries. In addition, President Barco issued Decree 815 to claim the sole power to establish 'self-defence' groups, with the Defence and Government (now Interior) Ministries required to give approval. In May, the Colombian Supreme Court abolished the Law 48 provisions that allowed the army to give restricted weapons to civilians; and in June government Decree 1194 established criminal penalties for civilians and members of the military who recruited, trained, financed, led or belonged to 'the armed groups, misnamed paramilitary groups, that have been formed into death squads, bands of hired assassins, self-defence groups, or groups that carry out their own justice'.

It remained to be seen how effective these government measures would be. The ACDEGAM organisation responded by creating the National Restoration Movement (*Movimiento de Restoracion Nacional*, MORENA), which was then investigated by a group under the authority of the president. The result was the issuing of arrest warrants for MORENA leaders on charges of murder, terrorism and the possession of illegal weapons. But none of this was able to abolish the power of the many paramilitary groups. Army officers continued to work with the paramilitaries, with some of the paramilitary leaders now claiming that they had fought successfully against the guerrillas until the drug traffickers had induced them to work on behalf of 'perverse interests'. In the Middle Magdalena military leaders were still supporting the MAS paramilitaries, even to the point of patrolling with them and helping to distribute pro-paramilitary propaganda. One former paramilitary leader, Luis Antonio Meneses Baez, testified in November 1989 that even after the Barco decrees army intelligence officers were continuing to meet with paramilitary leaders in Caqueta to discuss ideology and operations planning.

By 1990 it was plain that the Barco measures had achieved little. There were more paramilitaries than ever, most of them with access to revenue from the drug trade. In the 1970s there were some 1053 political killings recorded by human-rights groups; in the 1980s 12,859. Rafael Pardo, appointed Colombia's first civilian defence minister in 1981, later commented that by 1989 the paramilitary groups engaged in organised violence 'posed the greatest threat to the country's institutional stability'.[3] This was due in large measure to the massive revenues being derived from the traffic in drugs.

Development of a Drug Trade

All societies have toyed with drugs in one form or another throughout history, a cultural theme that has impacted on social attitudes, religions and national economies. In Colombia a rudimentary drug industry saw rapid expansion with the marijuana boom of the 1970s – partly by courtesy of the United States. The sons and daughters of the wealthy Colombian élite, returning home from American schools and universities, imported substantial elements of the prevailing hippy culture in which marijuana was a principal element. Thus in June 1971 tens of thousands of hippies, many from the United States, arrived in Medellin for a massive open-air rock concert. Marijuana had long been regarded as a low-life vice, used essentially by beggars, thieves and visitors to brothels. But now, what had been no more than a disreputable weed had become fashionable in the artistic, student and intellectual communities. The smoking of marijuana had become a potent symbol of social and political dissent, *de rigueur* for a young generation of men and women prepared to contemplate rebellion.

Days before the festival, there were riots in Medellin's biggest university and on the streets. Mayor Alvaro Villegas hoped that the concert, by 'bridging the generation gap', would defuse the violence, and so to a degree it proved, but there were casualties. Witnesses swore to an event which Medellin officials denied: that several young people, caught on a collapsing bridge, were swept away by a swollen river. The festival continued, encouraging experimentation with hallucinogenic mushrooms but not at this stage with cocaine. One girl remembered 'You couldn't breathe without getting stoned', but the authorities chose to ignore the extent of drug consumption. The scene was now set for a rapid and pivotal expansion of the drug trade.

As the marijuana market developed, there was a massive increase in the prison use of drugs – pot, barbiturates, tranquillizers and others. Already

Medellin's prisons were bursting as they struggled to accommodate the flood of peasants driven from the land and into urban crime. In the growing culture of brutality and exploitation prisoners were being killed and guards were being caught up in drug smuggling. The authorities tried to ignore the violence and the growing market in drugs but already a vast new criminal culture was emerging. Politicians, police and jailors were being bribed by drug money, with lawyers paid to defend the illicit dealers in pharmaceutical products. All this was laying the basis for the future traffic in cocaine.

In Mexico and Jamaica the marijuana plantations were being destroyed following the tough anti-drugs policies of President Richard Nixon in the United States – which served to boost the Colombian trade. In Uraba, northern Antioquia, marijuana was grown for shipment by boat and land transfers to California and the Florida Keys, a trade that relied heavily on the mercenary complicity of police and customs officials. Then pot cultivation shifted to La Guajira where it thrived between 1974 and 1978, but by then there were signs that the marketing of marijuana would be replaced by the cocaine trade, a more lucrative and more hazardous expression of free enterprise.

In 1978 the Colombian president, Julio Cesar Turbay Ayala, heading a repressive Liberal administration (1978-82), bowed to US pressure to stamp out marijuana production. Despite his suspected links to drug traffickers, he sent 10,000 troops into La Guajira to destroy the marijuana plantations and to terrorise the peasant producers. The army acted with extreme brutality, to the point that the local authorities in the region protested at its behaviour, while soldiers and army officers were themselves being corrupted by the lucrative attractions of the drug trade. The Minister of Defence terminated the disastrous military campaign and charged the local police with the task of suppressing the La Guajiri marijuana production. At the same time, while the United States was pressing for the eradication of the Colombian trade, there was a rapid expansion in pot production in various US states. In 1980 about 40 per cent of the US market was supplied by US producers, with Jamaica supplying the rest. Colombia, deprived of an important economic resource, was forced to look to alternative production. The subsequent massive trade in cocaine was the result.

The inhabitants of Peru, Bolivia, Ecuador and Colombia chewed leaves of the South American coca plant, *Erythroxylum coca*, a thousand years ago. The Incas regarded coca as sacred, a divine food planted by the sun god with the help of the moon. By the 20th century, cocaine, the principal alkaloid of the plant, was starting to emerge as the drug of choice for bohemians, though it was soon being denounced by Western politicians and Western media. Thus, an article in the *New York Times* declared in 1915: 'Most of the attacks on white women in the South [of the United States] ... are the direct result of a black brain driven crazy by coca.' During the Great Depression the US introduced stiffer laws to combat both marijuana and cocaine. In 1970 cocaine was classified as a 'category two' drug, permitted only for medical applications; the following year, customs officials in the United States impounded 197kg of cocaine, compared with 29kg in 1968 and 3kg in 1961. The trade was rapidly increasing and circumstances were combining to make Colombia a centre for cocaine production and distribution.

Until the 1973 *coup d'état* in Chile by General Augusto Pinochet, that country had dominated the supply of cocaine to the United States. Pinochet, grateful for US assistance in his successful attempt to destroy Chilean democracy, acceded to American pressure to combat the drug trade. He arrested leading traffickers, jailing dozens and deporting 20 to the United States. Some of the remaining coca chemists sought refuge in Colombia where they helped to provide the expertise for a burgeoning cocaine industry. By mid-1974 Colombians were successfully growing and cultivating the coca leaves. The US-aided *coup* in Chile had succeeded in bringing the cocaine threat nearer to home. In 1974 US Customs seized 320 kg of cocaine, and a survey by the US National Institute on Drug Abuse revealed that 5 million North Americans had used cocaine (22 million by 1982).[4] In 1978 about 15 tonnes of cocaine was exported to the United States; in 1988 270 tonnes, with another 40 tonnes arriving in Europe.[5] In 1987 the Colombian Health Ministry estimated that more than 400,000 Colombians were regular smokers of *basuco* (a mixture of cocaine paste, marijuana and/or tobacco).[6]

Through the 1980s Colombia, processing and marketing cocaine for its neighbours, planted 16,000-25,000 hectares of coca, a relatively small growing capacity (in Bolivia perhaps 50,000 hectares were planted; in Peru more than 100,000 hectares were being cultivated by 1990). In the late 1980s two drug barons, Jorge Luis Ochoa and Pablo Escobar, then among the 20 richest men in the world, had reportedly offered to pay off Colombia's foreign debt. The profitability of the cocaine trade, occasioned by its illegality, is remarkable: $1 million worth of crop can be converted into $5000 million profit; a kilogram of cocaine paste worth about $800 can be transformed into a product worth $50,000. Drug trafficking, 'the only successful transnational in Latin America' (according to former Peruvian

President Alan Garcia), represented 3 per cent of the national wealth of the Colombian economy, unable as it was to absorb more drug money.

By the 1980s the drug traffickers were buying land and setting up cattle ranches throughout Colombia. Thus in the Magdalena Medio some 130,000 hectares of fertile land were purchased, compared with the 12,605 hectares in the region bought by the Colombian Institute of Agrarian Reform (*Instituto Colombiano de Reforma Agraria*, INCORA) under the National Rehabilitation Plan in the period between 1983 and 1988. In addition, the traffickers were creating a complex network of companies with growing influence in the financial sector, sports clubs, mass communication media, the arts, and the cooperative sector. Penetration of the export sector gave the traffickers an even greater influence in the Colombian economy, just as drug money increasingly fuelled corruption in the justice, police and political structures of the country.

The drug traffickers declared at a meeting in Cali: 'We have to finance the campaigns of the politicians and keep them on our side. We can participate in business without causing a scandal, in family businesses so that they get used to dealing with us. In the end they receive innumerable benefits.'[7] During the 1980s the revenues derived from the drug trade had increasing importance for the national economy but was perhaps even more significant in its corruption of the political process. Army officers, lawyers, politicians, businessmen – all were corrupted by the prodigious fortunes to be made from drugs. Most judges, highly susceptible to bribery and intimidation, would automatically release any member of the drugs mafia who had been arrested. It has been suggested that by 1990 about 80 per cent of the Medellin police were on the mafia payroll.[8] Two ministers of defence were involved in drug scandals: General Miguel Vega Uribe and General Luis Camacho Leiva the latter's brother caught with cocaine aboard a government plane. In 1983 a general ordered an élite army corps to use air force planes to transport an entire cocaine laboratory from Colombia to the safety of the Brazilian jungle. The general was later promoted.[9]

From the 1970s prominent politicians in Colombian were increasingly linked with the drug trade. Thus in 1978 the American *60 Minutes* television programme showed that two cabinet ministers in the administration of President Alfonso Lopez Michelsen (1974-78) and a presidential candidate, Julio Cesar Turbay Ayala, later to form an administration (1978-82), were involved in drug trafficking. Since then many leading politicians have been associated with the Medellin-based drug cartel, with drug barons standing for Congress in 1982, and Pablo Escobar of the Medellin cartel elected to serve as a *suplente* (substitute) to another congressman.[10] In 1984 Rodrigo Lara, Minister of Justice, and Colonel Jaime Ramirez Gomez, head of the police narcotics unit, tracked down the source of ethyl ether, an essential chemical for processing coca, to Tranquilandia where they destroyed the largest cocaine-processing laboratory in the world. Seven weeks later Lara was murdered. Then a Bogota judge who implicated leading cartel members in the assassination was also killed. In November 1985 Colonel Ramirez was murdered. The mafia had bugged Lara's telephone and sent him copies of his own conversations – to indicate the extent to which the government security system had been compromised.

The government then pushed for an extradition treaty with the United States, opposed by the traffickers as a threat to their self-image and security. In response the mafia hired 50 top lawyers to urge the Supreme Court of Justice to annul the treaty. To persuade the Court judges responsible for the decision, the mafia sent them all the following message:

> We are writing to you to demand favourable positions for our cause. We do not accept resignations, we do not accept sabbaticals, we do not accept fictitious illnesses ... any position taken against us we shall take as an acceptance of our declaration of war. From prison, we will order your execution and with blood and lead we will eliminate the dearest members of your family.[11]

In November 1985 four magistrates connected with the case were murdered; one who survived the attack was killed in July 1986. Ten judges were assassinated by the end of the same year, as well as Guillermo Cano, editor of *El Espectador*, after publishing a report on the Colombian mafia. While the extradition treaty was in force, 18 people were arrested and taken to the United States for trial, but only one mafia boss, Carlos Lehder, was ever extradited. Then, under the campaign of mafia terror, the Supreme Court suspended the treaty.

The traffickers continued to seek security and tacit acceptance by the social and political establishment. In 1982 they created the National Latin Movement (*Movimiento Latino Nacional*), a political party to aid the war against the left, in an attempt to demonstrate their 'respectable' credentials; and they continued to invest in Colombian business and real estate (through the 1980s the mafia bought one million hectares of land in Cordoba, the Magdalena Medio, Uraba, Meta, Caqueta, Sucre and elsewhere). In addition, the mafia spent prodigious sums into converting MAS and other paramilitary groups into private armies that could help to defend the drug trade.

The assassinations continued through the 1980s. By the end of the decade the mafia was demonstrating that it could strike at leading politicians, prominent judicial figures, workers' leaders, presidential candidates and others. Thus on 4 July 1989 Antonio Roldan Betancur, Governor of Antioquia, was killed; on 29 July, Maria Diaz Perez, an active anti-mafia judge; on 7 July, Henry Cuenca Vega, President of the National Federation of Cement Workers; on 9 August, Daniel Espitia, national treasurer of the National Association of Peasant Users (*Asociacion Nacional de Usuarios Campesinos*, ANUC); on 16 August, Carlos Ernesto Valencia, an anti-mafia magistrate; and on 18 August, Colonel Franklin Quintero, Commander of the Antioquia police, and also Luis Carlos Galan, likely to be a presidential candidate committed to rolling back the influence of the drug cartels over the political establishment. At the same time the Colombian press had dared to publicise a list of nine congressmen linked to the traffickers, and another list of 20 journalists on the mafia payroll. The mafia were also bribing candidates for public office, in addition to congressmen, and army and police officers. In September 1989 Alfonso Gomez Mendez, Attorney-General, said that the drug barons 'have informers in the police and the army who warn them in advance when there are operations to arrest them'.[12] The banks, other financial institutions, motor manufacturers and the construction industry were all accepting cocaine dollars. By means of terror and investment the drug barons were tightening their grip on the Colombian economy.

In the wake of the Galan murder the government announced that it would resume the extradition treaty with the United States, whereupon the mafia announced that ten judges would be killed for every one of their members extradited. Then the government launched a serious crackdown on the traffickers: 11,000 cocaine linked individuals were arrested; laboratories were destroyed; 2000 properties were raided; 900 vehicles and aircraft seized; and more than 1200 weapons were captured in the first weeks of the campaign.[13] The United States provided financial and military help, though much of this was judged unsuitable for the task in hand. The extradition treaty was accomplishing little. One high-ranking mafia figure, Evaristo Porras Ardila, was extradited but other arrested individuals were being released. The death threats against public employees continued, resulting in Barco running through eight ministers of justice in September 1989. Some appointees lasted a few hours before resigning; the 32-year-old

Monica de Greiff received constant death threats and managed to stay in post for a mere two months.

The United States continued to expand its presence in the country, with the US State Department declaring that it would be sending up to 100 military advisors to supplement the ones already in Colombia. Many observers suspected that the aim of Washington was to combat the leftist guerrillas rather than the cocaine traffickers. At the same time it seemed convenient to the American propagandists to link the two. Thus in 1989 General Charles Brown told the Senate Foreign Relations Committee: 'The greatest increase in arms will be destined for Colombia, where the drugs barons and insurgent groups often work together, threatening the survival of the legal system and the democratic government'. Some reports said that by that end of 1990 Colombia would have received about $167 million in US military aid.

In reality, the Colombian government was doing little to combat the traffickers. Many of those arrested were being released and much of the confiscated property was being returned. The judges, still under threat, could only travel under armed guard: in 1989 some 1600 of 4500 judges had received death threats. Mafia bombs were killing and maiming people in the major cities, with attacks on banks, the headquarters of the major parties, schools, trade centres, and the offices of *El Espectador*. On 27 November a bomb killed all 107 people on an Avianca jet, and the drug mafia seemed the likely perpetrator. On 6 December a bomb intended for General Maza Marquez in Bogota instead killed 59 and wounded 500 more, mostly street vendors and bystanders.

By 1990 the Patriotic Union (UP) had lost about 1000 members, murdered since the founding of the UP in 1985. As one example, in March 1990 the presidential candidate Bernardo Jaramillo was assassinated at Bogota airport. One commentator reported that the Party had 'lost some ground in part because so many of its local and regional leaders were killed', at least eighty in the first three months of 1990. In this case the Party has blamed military-backed death squads rather than the drug cartels. Thus Americas Watch, aware of the disappearance and execution of local community leaders, has noted that many Colombians insist 'that army troops often act as though they were an occupation force in enemy territory'. It has been emphasised by Amnesty International and others that the death squads dedicated to the extermination of 'subversives' often worked with the security forces. In one report (Pax Christi Netherlands), it is emphasised that the death squads sow 'an atmosphere of terror, uncertainty and despair', and 'all families in which even one member is somehow involved in activities directed towards social peace' are under constant threat of disappearance and torture.[14] In the same vein the Andean Commission of Jurists, Bogota office, noted that the political killings in 1988 and 1989 averaged eleven a day.

It is also significant that efforts to combat the drug cartels generally ignore the economic links between legal and illegal enterprise; for example, the fact that the large financial corporations are prepared to handle the drug money, and the equally significant fact that the vast bulk of the chemicals needed to process cocaine are exported to Colombia from the United States.[15] The Colombian police have seized vast quantities of such chemicals, many in drums displaying US corporate logos. A CIA study concluded that the United States was exporting these chemicals to Latin America in amounts that far exceed any legal purpose, again suggesting that US companies conspire with the drug barons to make money. One estimate suggested that the traffic of illegal drugs, especially cocaine, from Latin America to the United States throughout the 1980s and 1990s had amounted to as much as $110 billion per year.[16] There is ample scope here for the corruption of many of those people – judicial, police, political, military, paramilitary, corporate – who move close to the drug trade.

Escobar and Others

The illegal production and distribution of drugs has helped to fuel civil war, paramilitary terror and political repression in Colombia and elsewhere. It has also made particular individuals immensely wealthy, to the point that they are assigned a heroic or demonic status in local communities and the wider world, with their entrepreneurial successes signalled in *Fortune* and other journals. The names of the men are known, though there are also various shadowy figures that move through a clandestine world, but few of these criminals come to be arraigned before an effective court. Historically, the two principal Colombian drugs cartels, often in conflict over trade and territory, were associated with particular names: the Medellin cartel was represented by Pablo Escobar Gaviria, the Ochoa Clan and Gonzalo Rodriguez Gacha (alias 'el Mexicano'), while the Cali cartel was led by Rodriguez Orejuela. Through the 1990s, while the role of the leaderships shifted, the power of the cartels continued.

The men who came to direct the Medellin cartel were born between 1947 and 1949, at the start of La Violencia. Jorge Luis Ochoa was the eldest son of a cattle dealer and horse breeder; Rodriguez Gacha was the son of cheese-making peasants; and Carlos Lehder, born to a German immigrant and a beauty queen, was an Adolf Hitler fanatic. José Santacruz Londono, Miguel Angel Rodriguez Orejuela and his brother, Gilberto, all later to represent the Cali cartel began their careers as kidnappers and murderers, and in the early 1970s began refining coca paste from Peru. In 1975 Gilberto ('The Chess Player') was captured in Peru with a plane carrying 180kg of coca paste; and was released soon afterwards.[17] Pablo Escobar began by obtaining small amounts of cocaine in Ecuador and selling it on in Colombia. Then he started buying from Colombian laboratories and in bulk from Bolivia and Peru. Later he began his partnership with the Ochoa brothers.

The trade rapidly expanded through the 1970s, despite brushes with the Colombian police and bouts of political opposition: bribery of public officials and intimidation of witnesses, bombings and assassinations, ensured that the activities of the cartels could not be countered by any police or judicial process. By 1980 it was estimated that 75 per cent of all US cocaine was transported from Colombia, largely through the Medellin network.

According to a US Senate report, the cartel began in 1980 when the M-19 revolutionary group kidnapped a member of the Ochoa clan, known to be producing cocaine. Jorge Ochoa, in response, persuaded the leading cocaine families to contribute $7 million each for the creation of a 2000-man army equipped with the latest weapons. The cartel's army subsequently won a bloody war with M-19 and forced many of its members to work for the emerging cartel organisation. The cocaine families, forced to fight a common enemy, had forged a new relationship that would expand the power of the drug traffickers in the years to come. Thus US Senator John Kerry, committed to exposing the drug trade, headed a congressional investigation where it was concluded that the Medellin cartel had 'perfected the cocaine smuggling business into a high-tech trade based on specialization, cooperation and mass production'. The Escobars managed production, the Ochoas transportation and, until arrests took place, the Lehders distribution.[18] By 1988 the Medellin cartel was earning about $8 billion a year, and *Forbes* magazine listed Pablo Escobar and Jorge Ochoa as among the world's richest men.[19]

By the late 1980s a war had developed between the Medellin and Cali cartels, with some observers suggesting that the Colombian government was giving special treatment to the Cali mafia – either to inflame the rivalries or to protect the cartel that paid the higher bribes.[20] On 13 January 1988 the Cali cartel exploded a bomb against an Escobar penthouse in the exclusive Santa Maria de los Angeles district. Two nightwatchmen were killed, the street was cratered, and houses opposite were flattened, but the penthouse building was scarcely affected. Pablo was absent and family members were unhurt, though his daughter, Manuela, was deafened. The bomb was the first of its kind deployed by the traffickers. It was one incident among many in the escalating war.

The government crackdown, following the assassination of Senator Luis Carlos Galan, targeted the Escobar country estate where 52 people were arrested. In other raids 20,000 police and army personnel confiscated 2000 cows, 100 pigs and a number of hippopotami. It was not obvious why these were connected with the drug trade, and in fact the crackdown accomplished little. One significant cartel figure, Eduardo Martinez Romero, was arrested, but the rest were either abroad or otherwise unavailable. Malcolm Deas, a Colombia expert from Oxford University, England, commented in Bogota: 'The government is seen as doing something, which is important. But laws and decrees are no use unless there is someone they can be used against.' At the same time it emerged that a US plan to kidnap Jorge Ochoa, to snatch him while on holiday in Caracas, had been abandoned because the ambassador to Venezuela, Otto Reich was worried that such an operation would provoke attacks on the embassy.[21]

The government initiative had done nothing to change the situation: President Virgilio Barco had 'launched a war he cannot win'.[22] Washington was agitating for an expansion of its role in Colombia, and welcomed a proposal by the presidents of Colombia, Peru and Bolivia for European involvement in a drug summit. Barco had won President George Bush's 'profound admiration' for his anti-drug campaign, though there were signs that the traffickers had received plenty of advanced warning. Some minor drugs figures had been extradited to face trial in the United States; an Escobar colleague, Gonzalo Rodriguez Gacha, had been killed in a police raid; and early in 1990 the Colombian police destroyed some 17 cocaine-producing laboratories in the southeastern Colombian jungles. Even then, the scale of the trade was so vast that the drug traffic was scarcely affected.

The government had put a reward of $500,000 on the head of Pablo Escobar, and he had been forced to go underground. At the same time the casualties in Medellin were reaching the levels of a conventional war. One local human-rights lawyer, Martha Luz Saldarriaga, noted the scale of the multilayered conflict: 'Beneath the dominant conflict there are scores of secondary wars going on, political conflicts, gang wars and personal vendettas.' Since January 1990 the government, under the terms of its Plan Genesis, was struggling to tackle the drug mafia, some of the established paramilitary groups, and the *sicarios* (bands of young assassins from the shanty towns). Now the authorities were claiming to have broken up 34 gangs of *sicarios*, making 361 arrests, but it seemed likely that the intimidated judges would order their release.[23]

The hunt continued for Pablo Escobar, considered in many countries the most wanted man in the world. Now there was evidence that a former Israeli general was involved with the smuggling of arms to the drug cartels, adding yet another international dimension to the cocaine trade.[24] This Israeli involvement caused concern in the United States, keen to maintain Colombia's support in the confrontation with Saddam Hussein. Thus Ambler Moss, a former US ambassador to Panama, commented: 'The United States has stopped criticising the Soviets, and now Colombia – all of this is the price tag for the Gulf crisis.'

Jorge Luis Ochoa, following his brother Fabio's example, had surrendered to the police on the understanding that he would be tried in Colombia and then quickly released. There were rumours that Escobar was contemplating a similar course of action, though the United States remained hostile to such deals.[25] In December 1990 Cesar Gaviria replaced Barco as president, and then had to address a situation in which Pablo Escobar was still on the run and demanding a cast-iron pardon from the government.

In June 1991, following a carefully negotiated surrender, Escobar gave himself up to the Colombian authorities. Soon afterwards, the armed wing of his cartel, the 'Extraditables', agreed to hand over their weapons. It seemed that the new Colombian administration could take some comfort in such significant developments but no-one believed that the drug wars were over or that the drug trade was at an end. There were also growing concerns at the progressive US militarisation of Colombia, with political, peasant and church leaders fearing that the increasing American involvement would only exacerbate the problems of the region.[26] And it was soon plain that the drugs business was flourishing 'as never before' in the heartland of the Colombian cartels.[27] Escobar, called 'Pablo' by everyone in Medellin, had emerged as a Robin Hood figure, a donor of largesse – including an entire housing estate – to the city's poor, and a model citizen for many. But Medellin remained an inferno. In November 1991 the judges went on indefinite strike, after another assassination of one of their colleagues, and murders were running at an annual rate of 9500, some 25 times the rate in Manhattan. And the powerful Cali cartel, opting to work within the Liberal/Conservative establishment, was operating with little interference.

On 22 July 1992 Pablo Escobar escaped from his custom-built prison outside Medellin, whereupon President Gaviria promised 'to respect his life if he surrenders voluntarily'. Escobar and his men took hostage several senior officials when troops arrived to transport him and his 14 accomplices to a military camp. Five of the inmates were quickly recaptured but Escobar and nine others remained at large. He had denounced the proposed move to the Envigado military establishment on the grounds that he might be sent abroad, whereupon the Colombian cabinet had sat throughout the previous night to discuss the crisis. The escape plunged the government into crisis as comments poured in from all quarters. Thus Robert Martinez, head of the US Drug Enforcement Administration, declared that Colombia 'must take whatever additional steps are necessary to immediately bring Pablo Escobar to justice'.

Nobody believed that Escobar would give himself up. Thus one woman from Envigado commented: 'The government didn't keep its word. Escobar was right to do what he did. Pablo Escobar is a god. It's like he has a pact with the Devil, which gives him the power to disappear. They were going to kill him or send him to the United States.' Again the fear was mounting in the streets of Medellin. Would Escobar again be hiring young assassins to murder his many enemies? Before his escape he had received more than 300 unauthorised visits from wanted criminals and other people.[28] What had they been planning? And what would happen now The United States and Britain were reportedly sending electronic equipment to Colombia to help in the hunt for Escobar Already he had signalled that, granted the right conditions, he would surrender. Would there be another opportunity to track him down?

The United States was becoming increasingly involved in the search for Escobar. Now US military aircraft overflying the Medellin area were being denounced by pro-Escobar politicians as 'a violation of national sovereignty'. At the same time American military personnel and sophisticated surveillance equipment were being despatched to Colombia. Peter Williams, a US Defence Department spokesman, announced the official Washington line: 'At the request of the government of Colombia and in accordance with long-standing US policy, the US government is providing support to the Colombians in their efforts to locate Escobar.' The spokesman refused to detail the extent of the support, while observers were noting that it was the first time that Colombian officials had reported the presence of US military aircraft flying over substantial parts of the country.[29]

Now Escobar's days were numbered. For more than a year the Colombian authorities had failed to locate him, despite extensive US involvement in the hunt. But soon he would grow careless. An era of the Colombian cocaine business was drawing to a close.

FOUR

Drugs, Exploitation and Revolt (Late-1992 to May 1994)

Closing the Net

Pablo Escobar remained in hiding despite all the efforts of the Colombian authorities and their foreign helpers. The most notorious drug baron of them all had somehow found a seemingly safe location, but his days were steadily running to a close. On 15 September 1992 Jorge Eduardo Avendano, an Escobar lieutenant who had escaped with him from jail on 22 July, gave himself up at the prosecutor's office in Medellin, and was immediately transferred to the Itagui maximum security jail. Now it was being rumoured that more surrenders were likely over the coming days provided that there was no 'interference' from the Colombian authorities. A Bogota newspaper reported that even Escobar was close to turning himself in. The ageing priest, Rafael Garcia Herreros, who had helped to arrange the first Escobar surrender 18 months before, said that 'the lost sheep will be returning to the flock' in the next few days.

It seemed plain that Escobar still hoped to negotiate the privileges he had formerly enjoyed in jail, and to avoid the possibility of being killed 'while resisting arrest'. He was doubtless aware also that the US Congress had agreed the principle that foreign suspects could be kidnapped abroad and then taken to the United States for trial. There were many reasons why Escobar was keen to discuss a fresh accommodation with the Colombian authorities. The government had first denied that earlier talks had taken place, but then the authorities had released letters exchanged between Escobar's lawyers and a Justice Department representative, indicating how the initial deal had been negotiated. Now a former senator from Escobar's home state, a man conveniently distanced from the government, was reportedly acting as an intermediary. Some observers were suggesting that Escobar's escape would clearly nullify the earlier plea-bargain accommodation, while the former vice-minister of justice, held at gunpoint during the July escape, was declaring that he would testify against Escobar on a kidnap charge that carried a 9- to 22-year sentence.

On 28 September 1992, following the 10-month Operation Green Ice co-ordinated by the United States Drug Enforcement Administration and the Italian authorities, many leading figures in the Colombian cocaine cartels and Italian mafia families were arrested. Customs officials arrested two US citizens at a house in Queensgate, central London, and seized 43kg of cocaine, worth £7 million at street prices, and some £2 million in banknotes from a lock-up garage. It was claimed that the operation had severed important links between the Medellin, Cali and Pereira cartels on the one hand and the Sicilian mafia, Neapolitan Camorra and Calabrian 'Ndrangheta' syndicates on the other. Among the 34 people arrested in Italy was José 'Tony the Poke' Duran, 38, described by officials as the biggest cocaine distributor in the world for the Colombian cartels. An Italian magistrate, Vittorio Mele, declared: 'I would not hesitate to define this operation as the most important ever carried out in Italy and Europe against narco-trafficking and money-laundering'; while police chief Vincenzo Parisi commented that never before had the mafia 'suffered a blow on such a scale'. In the United States more than 160 people were arrested, including Rodrigo Polonia Gonzales Camorga, head of the foreign office of the Colombian National Bank. George Terwilliger, US Deputy Attorney-General, announced that the arrests had included seven of the top money managers of the Cali cartel: 'Our aim is to drive a stake through the heart of the illegal drugs business by attacking their financial operations.'

A total of 201 people in four countries had been arrested, supposedly decapitating one of the most violent Colombian drug cartels, throwing a suspicious light on prominent Colombian banking, political and military figures. Some 700kg of drugs had been found and about $40 million in New York bank accounts belonging to leading Colombian figures was seized. At the same time some 15 companies used for drug trafficking were closed. In Italy important members of the Corleone family – notorious through *The Godfather* feature films – were arrested.

On 8 October three more members of the Medellin cartel who had escaped with Escobar turned themselves in to the Colombian authorities. There was speculation that the surrender of these three – Roberto, Escobar's brother, and two of the cartel's top gunmen, 'Popeye' and 'Otto' – was a prelude to the surrender of Escobar himself. By now he was under threat not only from the Colombian authorities and the US government ($6.5 million offered for information leading to his arrest) but also from survivors of the Galeano crime family ($1.5 million offered to anyone who killed him), most of whose members had been killed on Escobar's orders. Various criminal groups were hunting for Escobar in the hope of collecting the rewards. On 25 October the Colombian attorney-general's office ordered the jailing of three prison officers who helped Escobar to escape. A month later, Johnny Rivera, one of the men who had escaped with him, was shot dead in Medellin when 200 police surrounded his house. On 5 November six soldiers implicated in the escape were sentenced for up to eight years in prison.

The net was closing on Pablo Escobar but the cocaine trade continued. In October US narcotics agents uncovered evidence that Colombian drug traffickers had developed a method of building glass fibre and plastic products that are infused with cocaine, and can be moulded into any shape. For example, three glass-fibre dog kennels were ground up to yield more than 17kg of cocaine, with a street value of $1.5 million. An FBI agent, Charlie Parsons, commented: 'If anything is made out of plastic or fibreglass, I'm a little suspicious. If it's made in Colombia, I'm a little more suspicious.'[1] Another method of transporting drugs, perhaps more unusual, was detected at Bogota airport. A woman about to board a plane to the United States was found to have bags of heroine, worth $250,000, surgically implanted in her buttocks. But such successes could not disguise the occurrence of the many undetected 'mule' operations, police failures and official blunders. In November 1992 a computer virus, dubbed by officials the 'ghost of La Catedral' (after the prison from which Escobar had escaped), wiped out the conclusions of a US Senate committee that had investigated the jailbreak. It was rumoured that the report had identified top Colombian military officers, ministers and former ministers as Escobar accomplices.

The War Continues

The guerrilla war, intermeshed in many ways with the drug trade, continued unabated. On 21 October 1992, as one incident among thousands in the seemingly endless struggle, leftwing guerrillas blocked the main road east of Bogota, ambushed and killed eleven soldiers – and simultaneously attacked transport and police stations across the country. Sometimes apparently innocent foreigners were caught up in the conflict. In October a British businessman, Peter Kessler, a manager of a banana company who had lived in Colombia for many years, was killed in crossfire after being kidnapped.

On 8 November President Cesar Gaviria declared a state of emergency: 'We are declaring war on the heart and the chequebook of the guerrillas.' Now the government was struggling to respond to a new twin-pronged wave of violence from leftwing guerrillas and narcotics mafias, involving, for example, the recent ambush of 26 policemen guarding a jungle oil installation and the death of another 23 policemen in the Medellin area. The new emergency measures included a ban on the payment of ransom or protection money, the so-called 'revolutionary tax' that farmers, ranchers and businessmen were often forced to pay. The government also outlawed talking to guerrillas, a move against pragmatic local politicians prepared to make accommodations with leftist rebels, and prohibited the publication of interviews or statements that gave publicity to guerrilla factions. Any company violating the new measures would have its government contracts cancelled; any official visiting the camps of armed groups would be fired. At the same time the government was arranging for the photographs of guerrilla leaders to be shown on television, with rewards on offer. Thus attention would be given to such guerrilla leaders as Manuel Marulanda (*Tirofijo*, 'Crackshot') of the Colombian Armed Revolutionary Forces (FARC) and Manuel Perez, commander of the National Liberation Army (ELN).

The guerrillas had secured many 'liberated areas', with many rural inhabitants forced to live alongside the rebel groups. In consequence many local residents often found themselves caught in the firing line between the Colombian army on the one hand and FARC or ELN forces on the other.

Said one Santander resident: 'We are terrified of going out. Recently, all the passengers on a municipal bus were killed in crossfire between the army and the guerrillas.' In such an atmosphere it seemed unlikely that the government would be able to enforce its ban on payment of the 'revolutionary tax', paid not only by ranchers and farmers but also by Colombian and international companies operating throughout the various regions. Nonetheless Gaviria, under mounting business and political pressure, was trying to make a stand: 'There will be no more giving in to narco-terrorism, no more concessions to violence.' In the previous year no less than 980 ranchers had been abducted for ransom money, forcing demands on the government to introduce the death penalty for kidnapping.

Again the legal powers of the army were being extended, allowing the gathering of evidence in contested areas where court officers were under threat of assassination. Properties and bank accounts used for the laundering of rebel funds would be confiscated as a radical attack on the guerrilla infrastructure. Here it was reported that the first targets for expropriation would be six coal mines and a gold mine owned by the National Liberation Army, and a string of co-operatives used for handling food and other guerrilla supplies. Thus Rafael Pardo, Colombian defence minister, judged that these measures would allow the government to choke off the guerrillas' financial and logistical networks; and a government spokesman emphasised that the radical presidential measures were 'totally within the constitution'.

Three days after President Gaviria imposed the 90-day state of emergency three top commanders resigned from Colombia's armed forces, leading to speculation that the new measures had done no more than to generate further dissent and turmoil. In addition, General Farouk Yanine was removed as army chief of staff, despite his reputation as an aggressive commander. There was confusion also in the radical camp. On 22 November Gabriel Garcia Marquez, 1982 Nobel laureate and a friend of Fidel Castro, signed a letter with about 50 of Colombia's most prominent academics, journalists and artists demanding that the guerrillas change their policies. The letter, addressed to certain members of the Simon Bolivar Coordinated Guerrilla Front, which grouped the three main guerrilla organisations, included the words:

> Your actions have created a climate of political and ideological confusion that has turned Colombia into a battleground where taking up arms is the most common form of freedom of expression

... Your war lost its historical validity some time ago. To recognise that would also be a political victory.[2]

On 9 December 1992 bomb attacks on Bogota hotels injured nine people, with another four people hurt when two bombs exploded in the Orquidea Real hotel in the city centre during a ceremony to honour talented students. It was not obvious who had planted the devices but the government blamed leftwing terrorists. The drug traffickers were also running a terror campaign, in part stimulated by the constraints on Pablo Escobar as he continued to lie low to avoid arrest. On 22 January 1993 the Luxembourg High Court of Justice, while upholding the sentences of two drugs traffickers, including the treasurer of the Cali cartel, ruled that $36 million of confiscated assets had to be returned to the Cali drug empire since the particular owner, Heriberto Castro-Maza, was not among the accused. A father-in-law to the Cali godfather José Santacruz Londono, Castro-Maza subsequently died, so the money was released to his wife Esperanza and his daughter Amparo, married to Londono. In such a fashion it proved possible for Cali lawyers to reverse the confiscation of acknowledged cartel funds.

The government and mafia campaign against Pablo Escobar were continuing. In the new atmosphere of terror the Colombian authorities were redoubling their efforts to locate the drug baron, and various factional groups were waging war against Escobar allies and assets. On 1 February a group known as 'People Persecuted by Pablo Escobar' (*Pepes*) claimed responsibility for a series of bomb explosions in Medellin. Escobar, said *Pepes*, would be given 'a taste of his own medicine', and anyone who helped him would face reprisals. In one incident some 15 heavily armed men raided an Escobar ranch near El Penol and blew up the main house after forcing the caretaker to flee. The following day, the government almost doubled the price on Escobar's head to 5 billion pesos (£4.6 million). A Bogota car bomb had just killed 21 people and injured 67, and President Gaviria blamed Escobar. 'We do not just want to encourage those who want to collaborate [with the authorities] but also [to] show that this government will not hesitate in its determination to combat these narco-terrorist organisations,' said interior minister Fabio Villegas.

In early February it was estimated that in recent days dozens of Escobar's henchmen had been murdered while he himself was facing increasing threats to his own security. Among various bullet-riddled bodies found in and around Medellin were those of a city footballer who had played for a team allegedly financed by Escobar, and the chief of a death squad employed by Escobar to carry out contract killings. These were victims of *Pepes*, according to Colombian security sources. At this time Escobar was also being hunted by an élite army and police squad of more than 1000 men, and there were rumours that some police officers were active in *Pepes* and other anti-Escobar groups.

President Gaviria had rejected offers of help from *Pepes*, thought to be supported by gangsters from the Moncada and Galeano families. There were now increasing signs that the net was closing on Escobar. On 14 February General Carlos Arturo Casadiego, former deputy head of the national police force and suspected of taking Escobar bribes, was shot dead in his car. Five days later, the police detained Escobar's mother and eldest son at Medellin international airport as they prepared to fly to Miami. Within a two-week period the *Pepes* group had kidnapped and killed some 37 of Escobar's associates, burned down the El Penol ranch of Escobar's mother, and exploded car bombs outside the apartment blocks where Escobar's wife and brother-in-law lived in Medellin's millionaire El Poblado district. In one attack *Pepes* gangsters poured petrol over Escobar's multi-million pound collection of artistic works by Van Gogh, Dali and Picasso, and after firemen had quelled the blaze returned to the scene to finish the job. Then an art and ceramic gallery owned by Escobar's sister-in-law was destroyed, as was his $5 million collection of classic cars and veteran motorcycles.

Escobar himself was reportedly crumbling under the mounting pressure, seemingly unable to defend his relatives, assets and criminal empire. Now there was growing suspicion that another anti-Escobar group, Free Colombia, supported by leading industrialists and the Colombian security forces, had united with *Pepes* to locate and kill the drug baron. The first *Pepes* communiqué had declared that a reason for using such brutal methods was 'to make Escobar feel in his own flesh and blood his own methods of warfare'. Now Free Colombia was offering a $5 million reward, on top of the government $7 million, for information leading to Escobar's capture. A police officer expressed the widespread view: 'It does not matter who gets him or how, provided the Escobar menace is ended.' What seemed to be the remarkable dismantling of the Medellin cartel was serving to reinforce a common Colombian belief: that only illegal operations could get things done.[3] On 26 February yet another Escobar gangster, Giovanni Lopera, surrendered to the police, the fourteenth cartel member to do so since Escobar's jailbreak. Now the Cali cartel was increasingly able to absorb Medellin business, estimated to be a substantial part of the $30 billion a year cartel trade. And it was judged that the Cali empire would prove to be an even tougher proposition than the Medellin cartel. Thus one Colombian official commented: 'There is no question taking on Cali will be longer, harder and more costly than going after Medellin. They own the city, they have the best intelligence network in the country, and they are socially accepted.' It was acknowledged that the Cali cartel, not averse to the use of pragmatic terror, had created highly efficient networks to process cocaine, to control distribution down to street level throughout the world, and to launder billions of dollars.[4]

On 19 March 1993 the police shot dead Mario Castano, Escobar's military chief, so depriving the drug baron of perhaps the last of his senior lieutenants. Then, perhaps as an Escobar response, massive car bombs exploded in Bogota, killing 11 people and wounding many more, and causing huge destruction and chaos throughout the city. The police defused a third bomb, struggled to bar access to the massive devastation, and were caught up in the general hysteria as a dozen cars blazed, shards of glass tumbled from high shattered windows, and local hospitals reported well over a hundred casualties, many of them serious. It was not known that Escobar was responsible but the police were blaming him. On 23 April the Colombian security forces captured 13 people suspected of organising the car bombings, said by the authorities to have been ordered 'by the fugitive drug baron, Pablo Escobar …'.

A Medellin mausoleum, that of the Munoz Mosquera family, was becoming something of a local tourist attraction, a symbol of the collapsing Escobar cartel. The marble mausoleum contained six brothers, all hitmen for the Medellin organisation, who died young in clashes with rival traffickers or the Colombian security forces. The mother's inscription is dedicated to Brance Munoz Mosquera (known as 'Tyson' because of his build), the most famous of the brothers: 'Brance Alexander Munoz Mosquera, rested in the arms of the Lord on 28th day of October 1992. Son, though you have gone, you will always continue in my heart. Lilia.' A seventh brother, Dandenis, arrested in New York, 'found Jesus' in jail and came to acknowledge the crimes of the Medellin cartel.

On 19 May 1993 a Colombian passenger plane with 134 people on board crashed in mountains near Medellin. Colombian pilots speculated that the crash of the Boeing 727 might have been caused by the loss of radio navigation sites blown up by leftwing guerrillas in the previous year. In one report the pilot had requested permission to reduce altitude, apparently believing he was about 80 miles further along his course; in another he was said to have been flying through a storm. No certain explanation for the crash was found but the speculation continued.

In early June the Colombian police arrested Colombia's international goalkeeper on charges of kidnapping and drug trafficking. He had admitted knowing Pablo Escobar, was said to have received money from the drug boss for his support, visited Escobar in jail, and later praised him for helping young players from the Medellin slums. In August the Cali cartel faced a serious setback when Harold Ackerman, described as the 'US Ambassador' for the Cali drug cartel, was sentenced in a Miami court to life imprisonment. He had attempted to import 22 tons of cocaine into the United States, concealing the drug in shipments of concrete fence posts and frozen broccoli. The value of that quantity of cocaine was said to be 'incalculable'.

The war on drugs, under US pressure, was increasingly merging with the war on the leftwing guerrilla factions. On 28 August guerrillas ambushed and killed 13 Colombian police by attacking a truck with dynamite and automatic weapons some 40 miles south of Bogota. It was one incident among many. In the first eight months of 1993 one person had died violently every hour in the capital alone. Around 5600 people had been killed, 2000 dying of gunshot wounds; 859 had died in traffic pileups, and the cause of death of 1659 further victims was unknown. Such figures compare with the 1087 deaths that occurred in clashes between the security forces and leftwing guerrillas during the same period. Bogota had overtaken Medellin as the most dangerous city in one of the world's most violent countries. In 1992 Colombia's murder rate was 86 per 100,000 population, compared with 9 per 100,000 in the United States.

On 7 October 1993 Alfonso Leon Puerta Munoz, one of Escobar's few surviving accomplices, was shot dead in Medellin, part of a pattern that was commonplace. At the same time General Gustavo de Greiff, the Colombian attorney-general, was declaring the current war on drugs a failure. He pointed out that the United States had set up a naval blockade off the Colombian coast to prevent drugs from leaving the country, destroyed coca fields in Peru and Bolivia and invaded Panama, but none of this had helped to decrease the demand for drugs in the United States: 'We can't keep on fighting against the cartels while the United States is doing practically nothing to diminish consumption. Until we reduce demand, we will only achieve symbolic victories.' De Greiff objected also that traffickers caught in Colombia could not be properly tried because the United States refused to release important evidence. Moreover, there was a growing incidence of US violations of Colombian airspace.

On 16 October a Colombian SAM airline plane with 76 passengers aboard narrowly missed colliding with a US military aircraft. The Colombian civil aviation authorities were investigating how an American plane flying from the Howard military airbase in the Panama Canal Zone had violated Colombian airspace. This was not the first incident of its kind (there were similar occurrences in July 1991 and August 1992, both over Medellin, and an incident a few weeks before over Bogota). The Colombian senators Eduarso Pizano and Samuel Morales announced that they would demand a debate on the risks caused by US flights, and censured the official silence surrounding the incidents. The growing US involvement had done nothing to end the drug trade or to bring the guerrilla war to a close. On 5 November the Colombian senate vice-president, Londono Cardona, was shot and critically wounded in Medellin. The multifaceted civil conflict – fuelled by the commercial ambitions of the drug traffickers, the struggle for human rights, the demands of unyielding ideologies and the characteristic US pursuit of hegemony – was set to continue.

Coal – at a Cost

The drama and horrors of the drug war have tended to obscure the parallel civil conflict that has racked Colombia for decades. The guerrilla war, fuelled in part by drug revenues, has always represented the characteristic struggle of the dispossessed against landowner and capitalist, the poor against the rich. It should be remembered that the people's long struggle in Colombia enjoyed its own growing momentum before the emergence of the drug culture in the 1970s. The 'war against drugs', waged by successive Colombian regimes with increasing US support, is also a war to protect the historical exploitation of the majority of the population by an economic *élite*. This is shown by a brief look at the Colombian coal industry.

The output of coal, important to the Colombian economy, saw a rapid increase in the 1980s and beyond: in 1980 coal output reached 4 million tonnes, in 1990 well over 20 million tonnes. In March 1988 Pedro Galindo, representative of Fedepetrol, the oil workers' federation, stressed in interview how foreign companies rather than Colombia were benefiting from the country's national energy resources. The so-called 'Association Contracts' signed with the multinationals served to damage Colombian sovereignty and to provide the foreign companies with the principal commercial benefits. For example, a coal deal was made with Exxon for the joint development of the coal resource, but Colombia was unable to pay the specified 50 per cent of total costs because that figure amounted to the entire value of the national budget. This meant that Colombia faced penalties under the contract: 'We have to go to the IMF and promise to pay with coal, as we did with the World Bank. The financial organisations of Exxon, Chase Manhattan, the Bank of Japan, Lloyds Bank of Britain, are willing to lend the money and we have to borrow it ... We also have to pay Exxon to take out "our coal". We pay them so much to move it from the mine, so much to put it on the train, so much to move it to the port.' What was the overall result of such a system? – 'We are not obtaining new technology, we do not have a coal products industry, we do not have a research programme.' Moreover, the revenues to Colombia should be balanced against the country's 'share of production costs ... and the financial cost of the debt ... We operate at a loss ...'. In addition, the characteristic open-cast mines put the workers' health at risk in the context of obvious worker exploitation: 'We believe that energy policy can be redesigned to meet social needs ...'[5] The 1990s saw little change in this regard.

In October 1992 the British premier, John Major, was involved in controversy after he promised to help Colombia 'dump' cheap supplies of coal in Europe. It was charged that on a visit to Colombia in June he agreed to help Colombia to fight moves in the European Commission aimed at restricting that country's coal exports to Europe; and that he pledged British investment in the Colombian coal industry – this at a time when British coal jobs were being sacrificed. One of the main objections was that coal developments at El Cerrejon in Colombia, run and half-owned by Exxon, relied upon the exploitation of cheap labour with few rights. Since full-scale mining had begun in 1985 some 17 trade union leaders had been fired by the early 1990s, while some critics were suggesting that the mine should be closed down to avoid the massive pollution of the area with coal dust.

Since winning its international tender in 1976, Exxon had developed El Cerrejon as a self-contained world with its own airports built by the company. Some 700 largely-American managerial and professional staff lived in specially-built new housing in a modern estate, complete with a nine-hole golf course, six-lane bowling alley, supermarket, schools and ecumenical church. The contrast between the living conditions of the estate and the nearby villages was said to be 'stark':

At Calabacita, half a mile from the mine entrance, where many of El Cerrejon's contract labourers live in rented rooms, one storey houses of mud and wattle line the dirt streets. Many lack drinking water and sewerage, and for recreation there is only a street of sad-looking brothels.[6]

'Cheaper labour' was acknowledged as a factor in making El Cerrejon internationally competitive, while workers were complaining also about job insecurity, the threats to health and safety, and other hazards against which there was no worker protection. One complaint was that 140 workers had been incapacitated with job-related illnesses, such as back problems from exhausting 12-hour shifts.[7] Protest strikes were broken and union leaders fired.

There was also growing international awareness of the corporate exploitation of children in Colombian mines. For example, in Boyaca, northeast of Bogota, some of the child miners of Colombia were as young as five years old. According to the Colombian Ministry of Mines, more than 1500 children were working in the area, though such a practice was nominally illegal and a source of some embarrassment to the government. Such children did not attend school, and many were paid nothing for their work.[8] In November 1992 Andrew Cox, editor of UK Coal Review, visited Angelopolis, south of Medellin: 'Coal mining is the only work and the children start working in these unlicensed holes in the ground at the age of seven.' And their parents were equally exploited.[9] Some of the mine owners paid their employees, virtual slaves, wholly or partly in cocaine.[10] It is this sort of Colombia that many of the guerrilla groups are struggling to bring to an end, and that successive repressive regimes, encouraged by the United States, are fighting to preserve.

The Escobar Finale

By March 1993 anti-narcotics agents in Bogota were estimating that the Escobar business had shrunk to around 10 to 20 per cent of what it was the year before. Said one: 'Economically, he's hurting. But it's mostly a cash-flow problem. Even if Pablo comes in, I don't think he's going to live that long ... someone's going to get to him.' Then the Prosecutor-General, Gustavo de Greiff, announced in Bogota that he was investigating a tip-off that the Search Force hunting Escobar had found him but had accepted more than $1 million to let him go. But Fredy Paredes, chief of Colombia's plain-clothes security police, rejected the tip-off as deliberately misleading: 'It's Escobar himself, a disinformation campaign to diminish our prestige. He knows he's surrounded. We've destabilised the financial and military structure of the Medellin cartel. The people here like and support the Search Force.' In early May Escobar signalled by letter that he was ready to surrender if the Colombian authorities would guarantee his safety: 'I am ready to turn myself in if they give me written and public guarantees. I can answer for what I have done.' The letter reportedly carried a fingerprint, that of Escobar, on each of its three pages. But no accommodation was made and the matter dragged on. On 28 November members of Escobar's family, including his wife, 33-year-old Victoria Henao Vallejo, flew to Frankfurt but were said by the German government to be 'undesired' and so were refused permission to enter Germany as a safe haven. Less than a week later, Pablo Escobar was shot dead in Medellin. It was not thought that his death would make much difference to the drug trade.

A brief profile appeared years later in *The Observer* (London) under the line 'Business person of the millennium ... Pablo Escobar Gaviria (1949-1993)'. Here it was suggested, tongue-in-cheek(?), that Escobar had 'truly understood the concept of vertical integration' and had provided an 'end-to-end' solution, enabling the Medellin cartel to become 'the first criminal organisation to mass market the drug [cocaine] in the US ...'. At the end he broke his own security rules by telephoning his wife and children to check on their safety in a hotel where they were under guard. The family had tried to flee overseas several times, and when at last they tried Germany they 'primed the trap that would kill' Escobar.[11] It was known that Escobar's wife had grown increasingly desperate. In a letter to Escobar she had written: 'I don't want you to make errors but, if there is nowhere to go, I feel safer with you. We will shut ourselves in ... Whatever.' But it was too late.

Escobar had sought safety in a two-storey house, heavy iron bars over the windows, in the district of La America, west Medellin. On 1 December 1993, on his 44th birthday, Escobar telephoned his family, now ensconced in the army-owned Residencias Tequendama hotel in central Bogota. The call was too brief for the Medellin scanners to locate him, but on the following day he called again – and this time Escobar spoke too long. A young lieutenant operating the scanners at the Search Force base in north Medellin managed to narrow down the source to about 800 metres. And then Escobar telephoned his family yet again, enabling the exact source of the call to be identified. A heavily-armed assault force took up positions around the house and then five of them broke into the building through the front door.

The operation was quickly concluded. Alvaro de Jesus Agudelo ('the Lemon'), Escobar's bodyguard, was shot dead after racing across the roof of the adjoining bungalow and jumping into the street. Escobar attempted the same route, fractured his shoulder in jumping onto the roof, and then was shot by three bullets in his thigh, his lungs and his head. He died on 2 December 1993 on the tiles of a bungalow roof.[12] His mother and sister subsequently claimed that Escobar had shot himself when he realised he was surrounded by the army and the police. Thus Marina, a sister, mourning by Escobar's grave, declared: 'The Search Force did not kill Pablo, he killed himself'; and his mother, Hermilda Gaviria, observed that the gunshot wound behind his ear was from very close range: 'He did not give them the pleasure of killing or capturing him, he killed himself when he saw that he was surrounded and with no chance of escape.'[13]

Much of Medellin was now in mourning, though on 4 December President Gaviria said: 'Escobar was not a hero. He was a criminal who got the punishment he deserved.' His private armies had succeeded in murdering senior police officers, judges, public prosecutors, a newspaper editor, a television anchorman, an attorney-general, three presidential candidates, more than 300 policemen and hundreds of ordinary citizens.[14] In hiding, Escobar had become grossly fat, while one after another of his henchmen were either killed or captured. For many, Escobar did remain a hero. Soon after his death, thousands of people – many from the poverty-stricken hillside barrios – flooded to the chapel where he lay, in an attempt to gain a last glimpse of the man they had learned to regard as their vital role-model and father-figure. Some smashed down the doors, some broke the windows, and some climbed onto the roof to peer through skylights. Soldiers in the vicinity were forced to abandon the chapel. Young men, wearing gang-member clothes and chanting 'Pablo-Pablo-Pablo' and 'Death to Gaviria', carried the coffin out through emotional crowds to the grave.[15]

At one level it was the end of an era. At another, nothing had changed. Large parts of the drug trade were shifting hands, and the wars would continue. In the nature of things, Pablo Escobar had given a face to the cocaine business and to the violent culture that it inspired. But the wars – for drug revenues and a new social order – would go on. All the main players – traffickers, a repressive regime, guerrilla armies, an exploited people, the US interventionists – were still in place. And the uninvolved men and women, wanting only an end to suffering, had no option but to flee or endure.

Business as Usual

The drug trade had been thrown in high relief by the pursuit and death of Pablo Escobar, but the essential dynamics of the business remained securely in place. It was reported that the Colombian cocaine cartels were paying attention to the single market of the European Union – where the profits were a third higher than in the United States, where the risks of being caught were lower, and where the opportunities to launder the profits were much more varied. By 1994 cocaine was fetching around £26,000 a kilo on the European market, compared to £18,000 in the United States. Cocaine was being shipped from Colombia via Nigeria and Ghana to the European outlets. One method was for a 'mule' to swallow up to 100 drug-filled condoms which would remain in the body for days – unless they ruptured, threatening the person's life. The previous February, 1.2 tons of cocaine were seized near the Finnish-Russian border, revealing the developing relationship between the Colombian drug cartels and the East European crime syndicates.

In Colombia much of the business of the Escobar empire had shifted to the Cali cartel, an organisation with a discernibly different culture. The Cali drug barons had never felt the need to declare war on the Colombian state in the manner of Escobar. They would kill more discreetly, averse to the use of massive car bombs, and preferred bribery to war. It was all a matter of emphasis. In the post-Escobar era about 80 per cent of the world's cocaine supplies were under Cali control, bringing annual profits in the mid-1990s to more than $20 billion. Crime was paying for the skyscrapers going up in the better parts of Cali, for the vast mansions in the suburb of Ciudad Jardin, for swimming pools and polo ponies, for beauty queens and football teams, for telephone taps at Cali's main hotels, for taxi fleets and airport security men, for hitmen and lawyers, and for the continuing bribes to diplomats, politicians, policemen and army officers. In December 1993 Gustavo de Greiff announced that the leaders of the Cali cartel were ready to proceed with their predicted surrender.[16] It seemed a forlorn hope. Francisco Sontura, the Deputy Fiscal, was declaring that in a year's time 'we will have done with the narcotics traffic in Colombia'; but added, 'Well ... perhaps 50 per cent'.[17] And perhaps it would be less than that. In the view of Enrique Perejo, a former Colombian Minister of Justice who had signed extradition orders (and so been targeted for assassination), the reverse was the case: 'This so-called policy of surrender of the traffickers to the state is the opposite. It's the surrender of the state to the traffickers.' The terms of a deal had 'been dictated by the cartels'.[18] In the same vein Gonzalo Guillen, editor of the Bogota-based *La Prensa*, commented:

> Do you really imagine that they are going to give up the most profitable business in the world. They can't give it up. As soon as they lose the profits from the trafficking, they lose their ability to pay the police and army, to buy the politicians, to maintain the apparatus that keeps them alive. Once they stop, they are dead. And if, by some stroke of magic, they did stop, can you imagine that nobody else would take it over?[19]

And he emphasised that mainstream economies had a crucial interest in the drug business: 'Have Europe and America stopped producing the precursor chemicals that you need to refine the cocaine? Have the international banks given up the fortunes in narco-dollars that keep them going? Has the rest of the world got rid of the hundreds of thousands of addicts who buy the stuff?' There were signs also that despite indications that the leaders of the Cali cartel were envisaging a more respectable and secure future the Colombian state was shying away from another drug war. The violence in Cali had begun to spiral: a rate of 50 homicides a weekend and more than 1200 violent deaths in the first nine months of the year. Some Colombians were talking about the 'Medellisation' of Cali. By now, an obvious shift in the Cali culture was plain. The cocaine trafficking would continue. Said one Western intelligence source, speaking of the Cali cartel: 'I seriously doubt they will ever abandon the drug trade.'[20]

In January 1994 British and American drug enforcement officers inadvertently allowed £1 billion worth of cocaine into the United Kingdom in a bungled attempt to combat the Colombian traffickers – a fiasco that led to parliamentary demands for an inquiry.[21] On 17 January, following a more successful operation, British drug investigators were questioning two men after the seizure of 250 kg of cocaine in Manchester. The men, both Colombians, had been arrested as part of 'Operation Begonia', successful in intercepting – according to Pat Cadogan, assistant chief investigator for HM Customs – 'the largest ever consignment of cocaine to be sent to the UK by air'.

There were now growing tensions between the United States and Colombia over drugs policy. In early April 1994 the annual report of the US State Department said that 'widespread corruption' and 'intimidation by traffickers' were undermining Colombian institutions, and that lenient

sentences were being given to traffickers who surrendered. Senator John
Kerry, chairman of the foreign relations sub-committee on terrorism and
narcotics, warned that Colombia was risking 'capitulation to the Cali
cocaine cartel', which he claimed had deeply penetrated the main
Colombian business interests, including banking, shipping, mining, coffee,
oil and cut flowers. Colombia was, declared Kerry, a 'narco-democracy'. In
quick response Gabriel Silva, Bogota's ambassador to the United States,
proclaimed: 'Your frivolous affirmations are an affront to the grave
commitment of Colombians to their institutions'. Washington wanted
tougher measures, including the extradition of convicted traffickers,
whereas Gustavo de Grieff, Colombia's prosecutor-general, had argued that
relaxation of the law was the best way to tackle the drug traffic. In the
Washington Post he had noted that the US 'War on Drugs' had
demonstrably failed:

> Today, cocaine on the streets of Washington is less expensive than it
> was in 1980. What is surprising is that it has taken so long for the
> central fact of the drug trade to sink in – as long as a kilo of cocaine
> changes in value from $500 to perhaps $20,000, by virtue of the short
> flight from Colombia to the United States, there will always be people
> who will be willing to enter the business.[22]

De Greiff also vigorously defended his policy of plea-bargaining with
leaders of the Cali cartel on the grounds that it was virtually impossible to
obtain hard evidence against them. This approach, he suggested, would
enable information to be collected about how Colombian drug trafficking
worked in the post-Escobar phase of the business. But it was clear that the
essence of the trade was the same as ever, just as Escobar had observed: 'You
bribe somebody here, you bribe somebody there and you pay a friendly
banker to bring the money out of the country.'

On 6 May Colombia's constitutional court exacerbated the tensions
with Washington still further by ruling that it was legal to possess small
amounts of both soft drugs (marijuana, hashish) and hard drugs (cocaine,
cocaine base, heroin, crack). The new ruling left drug production,
trafficking and sale illegal, but inevitably fuelled the allegations that the
Colombian drug cartels were helping to shape the law. President Cesar
Gaviria, sensitive to US pressure, was willing to denounce the judgement as
'absurd', but conceded that it would have to be obeyed until either the
constitution could be rewritten or a referendum held. Radio switchboards

were reportedly jammed by ordinary Colombians and specialist drug rehabilitation workers appalled at the decision. The court judgement had been reached by a vote of 5 to 4, with the court president, Carlos Gaviria, saying that the decision to use drugs was 'simply a private matter with no effect on public well-being'. The four dissenting judges described the ruling as deplorable, and a foreign diplomat declared that the judgement 'sets Colombia up to be a country controlled by drug money'.

Then the Colombian government, in response to the mounting US criticism, sent a note to Washington pointing out that the lack of co-operation 'only benefits our common enemy', and expressing hope for an early return to 'dialogue and joint efforts'. Janet Reno, US attorney-general, commented that discussion of drugs legalisation only served to weaken the resolve of the authorities and played into the hands of the drug traffickers. The issue was now creating growing tensions between the Colombian government and the constitutional court. No sooner had President Gaviria announced plans for an emergency decree banning the use of drugs in public places than the court ruled that such a move would be unconstitutional. Some observers were speculating that a number of people with dubious reputations had been given sensitive positions in the prosecutor's off ice: 'De Greiff was told about their background but he still employs them. If he is honest that shows bad judgement or it may mean something worse.'[23]

By the mid-1990s the Colombian cartels were succeeding in expanding the international drug business. Drug use in Colombia itself was increasing (at least half a million addicts), with the government – beset also by the seemingly endless guerrilla war – obviously unable to take control of the situation. In the United States there was growing frustration and alarm at both the expanding drug trade and the successes of the leftwing guerrillas in the field. On 23 May 1994, days before a new presidential election, a large bomb supposedly planted by guerrillas killed five policemen and six other people in Medellin. It was business as usual.

FIVE

The Samper Question (January 1994 to October 1996)

A Congressional Election

As the congressional and presidential elections became imminent in early 1994 the guerrilla factions continued their campaign of social disruption. On 17 January Rudolf Hommes, Colombia's finance minister, narrowly escaped death when a bomb hidden in a lamppost exploded, injuring a bodyguard. This specific targeting of Hommes followed charges by the National Liberation Army (ELN) that he had been responsible for 'policies of poverty'. At the same time the police were reporting that guerrillas of the Colombian Revolutionary Armed Forces (FARC) had kidnapped two US missionaries in Villavicencio, east of Bogota, supposedly as a protest at the slowly escalating American presence in the country.

There was conflict also between rival guerrilla groups. On 23 January at least 35 supporters of the Hope, Peace and Liberty party (EPL), made up mainly of former guerrillas, were massacred in the Uraba region, on the

Caribbean coast, when fired upon by FARC guerrillas. About 1000 people had been killed in the region over the previous year, as various armed groups manoeuvred for control of the rich, banana-growing land before the March local elections. The massacre, in the town of Apartado, was the bloodiest political incident of its kind in five years, and again attempts to sabotage the electoral process were rapidly increasing.

In February it was plain that Colombia's leftwing guerrilla groups had launched a widespread campaign of harassment, sabotage and ambushes in the run-up to the elections. A number of congressional candidates had been kidnapped, with one wounded and one killed; oil pipelines and electricity pylons had been blown up; and there were repeated clashes between army units and rebel groups. The mayors of four towns were taken hostage, and then released a few days later. On another occasion troops of the 16th brigade attacked FARC guerrillas as they were holding a 'revolutionary trial' of a kidnapped candidate in oil-rich Arauca, northeast region. In this incident five soldiers and two guerrillas were killed, with at least a dozen people wounded. Guerrilla raids were being launched close to Bogota, and cars and buses stopped on the main highways were then painted with guerrilla slogans.

On 22 February bombs were exploded in Medellin, injuring four political campaign officers and damaging the Venezuelan consulate. The army seemed powerless to prevent simultaneous guerrilla initiatives in various parts of the country, but there were some army successes: guerrilla plans for more attacks had been discovered, an arsenal of dynamite and anti-tank rockets had been captured, and some losses had been inflicted on the guerrilla forces. It was acknowledged that the quality of the weapons being used by the rebels had greatly improved, while it was assumed by the military that FARC and the other guerrilla organisations were using profits from cocaine and the newer heroin industry to fund purchases of machine-guns, grenades, rockets and other hardware from Europe and Central America. Rafael Pardo, the Colombian defence minister, declared that the guerrillas would not be allowed to interfere with the elections, though it was already plain that the rebel attacks – often in difficult areas that were hard to police – were having a significant effect.

On 13 March Colombians went to the polls to elect a new congress, but it was estimated that around 70 per cent of the electorate, variously indifferent or intimidated, would not vote. Some 200,000 police and soldiers had been deployed to protect the political process, though few observers doubted that the election would be seriously flawed. Two days before the polling stations opened, leftwing rebels kidnapped 31 elections workers near Carcast, 160 miles northeast of the capital; as people went to the polls guerrillas launched a series of attacks, including one on a polling station near Cienaga, 400 miles north of Bogota, wounding one policeman.

It soon emerged that President Cesar Gaviria's Liberal Party was set to retain control over Colombia's senate and house of representatives as a prelude to the presidential election to be held in May. The Liberals had chosen to use the vote as an effective presidential primary with voters, regardless of party affiliation, able to chose among seven candidates to lead the party in the presidential campaign. It seemed likely that Ernesto Samper, a former Liberal economy minister, would be the winner and would be opposed by Andres Pastrana, a son of the former President Misael Pastrana and the candidate of a Conservative coalition. Now the opinion polls were giving conflicting indications of who would win the presidential election: one gave Samper a seven-per-cent lead over Pastrana; another – run by the pro-Pastrana Yankelovich company – gave 31 per cent to Samper and 46.8 per cent to Pastrana; and yet another, the National Survey Centre – financed by the anti-Pastrana Santo Domingo Group – gave Pastrana a one-per-cent lead, within the margin of sampling error. It remained to be seen.

On 10 April, a month before the scheduled presidential election, some 430 leftwing guerrillas handed in their weapons and signed a peace treaty with the Colombian government, inspiring fresh hopes of full negotiations to end the decades-long civil war. But in early May the government declared a state of emergency to stop the release of more than 800 guerrillas, suspected drug traffickers and other prisoners whose pending cases had not been resolved before the legally prescribed time limit. This government move, blocking the mass release just one day before it was due to occur, was yet another attempt to stabilise the situation in the brief period before the presidential election. Colombia remained one of the most violent places on earth. Thus figures provided by Juan Luis Londono, Colombian health minister, suggested that of the 28,000 murders committed in 1993, only eight per cent were the result of the drug trade and the civil war; and that 81.8 per cent were caused by everyday violence that did not have a trafficking or guerrilla connection. The trauma caused by such daily violence was causing a loss in working days per 1000 inhabitants that was running at almost double that of the rest of the world. The presidential election was set to be held in an endemically violent society.

A Samper Presidency

On 8 May 1994 the Colombian people were able to vote for any one of 18 candidates for president – including 'an "ecologist" living in a fire-gutted ruin; a man who never takes off his hat, believes quartz crystals can cure the country's ills, and has a vice-presidential running-mate under arrest for rape; the leader of a "metapolitical" movement whose election symbol, a broom, adds to her reputation for witchcraft; several other unknowns …'[1] In addition, there were four serious candidates, led by the Liberal Ernesto Samper and the Conservative Andres Pastrana. The electorate remained largely indifferent: only about 25 per cent had chosen to vote in the March congressional elections.

On many issues Samper and Pastrana were in virtual agreement, and their neck-and-neck positions suggested that there would have to be a second round of voting three weeks after the first. The economy seemed healthy. More than $1 billion of foreign debt had been paid in the last two years, the peso had been revalued against the dollar, and a sharp rise in coffee prices was set to boost national earnings. International pressures were increasing the degree of foreign access to the Colombian economy, and the lowest income groups were 'a little poorer than before'.[2] The Samper-Pastrana trading policies remained broadly sympathetic to US preferences, while the most intractable problems remained those associated with drug trafficking and the civil war. It was expected that, despite the death of Pablo Escobar, the drug barons would expand their hold on the banking, justice and political systems in ways that would seek to avoid the worst violence of the Medellin era. Both Samper and Pastrana were in favour of negotiated settlements and plea bargaining, allowing drug traffickers to serve relatively short prison sentences and then to enjoy the fruits of their enterprise.

It still remained to address the problems of the guerrilla war, the turbulent civil conflict that had lasted for four decades and drawn the United States into an ever increasing involvement in Colombian affairs. Pastrana professed a belief in negotiation: 'I am asking the guerrillas, tell me what you want and we can sit down together and negotiate a peace process … If that fails then we invest a lot of money in the armed forces to end it that way.' By contrast, Samper proposed social surgery to change 'a culture in which the only way we settle our differences is by killing one another'. He suggested also that there be increased investment to reduce the levels of poverty that generated support for the rebels. It was significant that public services had continued to deteriorate under successive administrations: health care, water supplies, telephones, electricity and transport were all worsening, with Bogota itself suffering from massively increased pollution levels.

The initial results in the presidential election gave Ernesto Samper 45.1 per cent and Andres Pastrana 44.3 per cent, indicating that it was unlikely that either candidate would reach the 50-per-cent-plus-one of votes needed for outright victory. Both the leading candidates began hunting for extra votes and were soon individually claiming victory after it emerged that they were separated by just 18,700 votes. It was also being reported that whatever the final result Colombia had been selected by the foreign ministers of the 109-nation Nonaligned Movement to host its meeting the following year and to take over the three-year chairmanship from Indonesia. Only a third of the electorate had voted in May (fewer than six million out of 17 million potential voters), and the final count had given Samper 45.26 per cent and Pastrana 44.91 per cent. Now some analysts were judging that those who had voted for the third strongest candidate, the former guerrilla leader Antonio Navarro (3.81 per cent), or those who had abstained or returned spoiled or blank ballots amounting to 300,000 possible votes, would tip the balance in favour of the Liberal or Conservative candidates. Other observers expected even more indifference in the second round. Thus Pilar Gaitan, a political analyst from the Institute of International Relations and Political Studies at the National University, commented: 'In the second round, the abstention level could reach 80 per cent.'

On 19 June 1994, with Colombians having voted in the second round of the presidential election, it was found that with at least two thirds of the votes counted Samper had a narrow lead of 1.7 per cent over Pastrana, an advantage of only 107,000 of the 6 million votes counted. In the event, he was finally victorious with a final margin of 126,000 of the 7.5 million votes cast. President-elect Samper, a less than charismatic 43-year-old, was due to take office on 23 August.

Few policy surprises were expected from the new administration. Samper had formerly advocated legalising marijuana, but now had a different attitude. It seemed unlikely that he would change President Gaviria's policies of negotiating surrenders with the drug traffickers and accepting plea bargains, but it was thought he may be more inclined to use the country's wealth to tackle unemployment and deteriorating public services. But for Samper there were problems to come – not least the growing suspicion, voiced by Pastrana on the election of the Liberal candidate, that Samper had accepted drug money and was backed by the traffickers (see *Samper and the Cartels*, below).

The election of Samper did not serve to reduce the level of violence in Bogota and elsewhere. On 9 August, two weeks before he was due to assume his duties, Samper was forced to note yet another political assassination: that of the 60-year-old Manuel Cepeda, a hardline Communist and Colombia's only leftwing senator. Around this time, some 18 telecommunications technicians had been killed in Cali in an apparent attempt by the drug cartel to block official attempts at wire tapping and to use other electronic listening devices. Newly installed devices had been immediately detected and cut off, raising suspicions that some telecommunications technicians were working for the Cali cartel. This was not the most congenial atmosphere for the Samper inauguration.

For the first time in Colombia's history, and on the date of its 175th anniversary (7 August), the assumption of presidential power took place in a massive open-air public ceremony in Bogota's Bolivar Square. Fidel Castro and other invited Latin American heads of state were among the guests on the presidential platform. Juan Guillermo Angel, the president of Congress, and the newly-invested President Ernesto Samper (Colombia's 82nd president) gave speeches to indicate the tone of the new administration, after which the cabinet was installed. Samper spoke about drug trafficking, peace talks with the rebels, the social impact of economic policies, and the development of Colombia's international role. In an assumed reference to US pressures Samper emphasised that no-one had the authority to tell Colombia how it should combat drug trafficking. He indicated also that he would continue to expand the already very favourable relations with Cuba and the other Latin American states, and would promote the efforts of the Nonaligned Movement.

A week later, President Samper was expressing his regrets at the death of Manuel Cepeda, and pledging that the National Security Council would find those who were responsible for his murder: 'We will not lower our guard: on the contrary we are intensifying our fight against all the actions that disrupt the lives of our citizens.' Cepeda, like José Miller Chacon, assassinated the previous November, was one of a number of Communist leaders to receive death threats as part of the 'Coup de Grace' murder campaign. Five years before, Samper himself was hurt in an attack that cost the life of Communist leader José Antequera, one of many party activists to have been assassinated by the death squads. In September 1994 a new paramilitary group, Death to Communists and Guerrillas (MACOQUE), claimed to have a death list of 25 people. One was Hernan Motta, who replaced Cepeda in the Colombian Senate; others were Catholic bishops, senators, guerrilla leaders who had laid down their arms, human-rights activists and trade unionists. By 1995 the leftwing Patriotic Union (UP) coalition had suffered the loss of 2500 members through assassination, among them the presidential candidates Jaime Pardo and Bernardo Jaramillo.

In October, amid signs of national disillusionment with traditional politicians, Samper's Liberal Party lost control of all the big Colombian cities (Bogota, Cali, Medellin and Barranquilla) in the municipal elections. Some 18 million Colombians, half the population, voted for 32 governors, more than 1000 mayors and many local councillors. Military officers were being appointed as temporary mayors in areas where leftwing guerrillas had forced the cancellation of balloting. It was judged that civilians supporting the FARC and ELN guerrilla armies would win power in around 70 villages. Again the elections did nothing to bring the decades-long civil war to an end. On 13 November a police official reported a clash in which paramilitary forces and police combined to repel a leftwing offensive in San Pedro de Uraba, Antioquia province. Some 21 people were killed and three wounded in the five-hour gun battle with FARC guerrillas. On 24 November it was rumoured that President Samper had dismissed General Ramon Gil, commander of the Colombian armed forces, for opposing Samper's efforts to negotiate an end to the guerrilla war; and also General Octavio Vargas Silva, national police chief, because of his links with the drug traffickers. In December coca growers and leftwing guerrillas trapped Colonel Leonardo Gallego, Colombia's anti-drug chief, ambushed troops, and attacked an airport in protest against the eradication of drug crops. For a week thousands of peasants filled the streets of San José del Guaviare, 180 miles southeast of Bogota, demanding a halt to the coca eradication programme. FARC guerrillas fired machine-guns at helicopters, killing one officer and damaging three machines. Then 11 soldiers were wounded in a FARC ambush.

The question of corruption was also receiving attention. According to Major-General Rosso José Serrano, Colombia's new police chief, honour was the best weapon to use against the drug traffickers: money does 'not last but honour endures'. A survey conducted by *Semana* magazine indicated that corruption was costing Colombia $40,000 per day in public funds, with 90 per cent of recipients never going to prison or repaying one cent. A *Prensa Latina* analysis suggested that current trials of 180 state officials and ex-officials who had illegally obtained some $15 million in a 30-month period indicated that stolen state funds could amount to more than a thousand times that figure. Official research showed that 88 per cent of Colombians were convinced that financial corruption was widespread and that 95 per cent of crime went unpunished. Perhaps there was some comfort to be gained from a relatively peaceful New Year period with some 79 people killed (58 murdered and 21 killed in road accidents, compared with 74 and 22 the previous year). On 8 January 1995 guerrillas attacked a prison in southern Colombia, freeing 93 inmates; and on the same day six Colombians were murdered with exceptional brutality in their apartment in the New York borough of Queens (a seventh victim, left for dead, jumped from a balcony). A Colombian victims' organisation was reporting that kidnapping remained a virtual industry: one person was abducted and held for ransom every six hours, with 90 per cent of kidnappings going unpunished.

Many of the murders and kidnappings in Colombia were linked to the immensely lucrative drug trade that the Samper presidency and US intervention were doing nothing to curtail. The drug barons were continuing to consolidate their international links – through the Carribean and Latin America, in Africa and Asia, and throughout the countries of the European Union. One report indicated how a dozen British crime families had seized control of the country's drug trade, in one estimate worth more than £3 billion a year, and strengthened their links with the Colombian cocaine cartels and the Turkish heroin syndicates.[3] The Samper administration was having little impact on the Colombian drug traffic, though Samper himself was now popular in the country (82.9 per cent support, according to *El Espectador*). The civil war continued and drug traffickers were either in prison with negotiated sentences or continuing with their profitable business. It seemed unlikely that Samper would be able to achieve a significant breakthrough that would radically change the situation. In early February gunmen burst into a Colombian farmhouse in Caldas, where a family was praying for a murdered relative, and sprayed mourners with bullets, killing all nine. Three of the gunmen and a policeman died in the subsequent confrontation.

Wars – and a Peace?

On 27 February 1995 Hernando Pizarro, a former guerrilla leader (whose brother was assassinated in 1989 while running for president), was murdered by gunmen. A week later, about 500 heavily-armed FARC guerrillas raided the town of Ituango, killing more than a dozen people. In March tens of thousands of Colombian doctors and nurses went on strike in protest at low wages and poor working conditions, and in Cali a prison riot involving 1600 inmates was brought to an end by troops and police firing tear gas and water canons. Elsewhere a plot by imprisoned drug traffickers to assassinate senior government officials, including the prosecutor-general, was uncovered by Colombian intelligence agents. In Medellin, five teenagers were killed and one seriously injured when gunmen on bicycles fired on a group of youths in a park. The violence continued, much of it inexplicable in the obvious terms of mafia, death-squad or guerrilla objectives. On 26 April about 200 rebels attacked a police base in southern Colombia, killing a woman and wounding five other people. At the same time, there were some signs that peace talks might be possible between the government and the guerrilla groups.

On 3 January and 16 February 1995 the Simon Bolivar Guerrilla Coordinating Committee, combining the FARC and the EPL, sent letters to Carlos Holmes Trujillo, the Colombian high commissioner for peace, indicating the guerrilla willingness to enter into talks and specifying the conditions for such a dialogue. Holmes then responded by detailing the government's position, following President Samper's declared willingness to enter into negotiations 'within the obligatory principle of constitutional order being maintained by government institutions'. It was significant also that Gerardo Abreu (alias Francisco Galan), one of the main ELN chiefs, was declaring from his prison cell his organisation's readiness to enter into fresh talks with the government.[4]

The FARC organisation then made the goodwill gestures of releasing Danny Applegate and Tommy Tyrving, two Swedish technicians held hostage since December 1994, and of sending a further message to the government via Bernardo Hoyos, the Galician priest and former mayor of Baranquilla, emphasising FARC's willingness to begin new talks on the condition that the Colombian army withdrew from La Uribe, Meta region, site of the FARC general command. In response, President Samper subsequently announced in Bucaramanga that the government was prepared to begin immediate and separate talks with the various guerrilla groups, then calculated to include about 17,000 members.[5] He warned that acts of violence such as kidnapping, laying mines and attacking oil installations could not be considered acts of war, as opposed to terrorism, and that the guerrilla forces must be prepared to observe the Geneva Protocol specifying the humanitarian obligations binding on the parties to a conflict. But government minister Horacio Serpa Uribe stated that the envisaged peace process would not extend to the paramilitary groups, still intent on assassination, since the government was not prepared to tolerate the existence of such groups operating outside Colombia's military and security institutions .

The government seemed to be acknowledging that the guerrilla forces could not be defeated in the field. If peace were to be secured it would involve government and guerrilla compromises on territorial and other issues.

A Cali Surrender

Through 1994 Gilberto and Miguel Rodriguez Orejuela, two of the world's leading drug barons, tried to make a deal with the Colombian government: they would give themselves up in return for a minor punishment and immunity from later arrest. The government seemed prepared to negotiate but buckled under intense US pressure to ensure that the drug traffickers would be denied the deal they wanted. It had seemed that in the light of Washington's attitude an agreement would not be possible. Then in October, in an interview with *Time*'s Tom Quinn in Cali, Gilberto Rodriguez restated his proposal but in an expanded form: he and his brother would surrender, and also bring along hundreds of other Cali traffickers. There would be a negotiated surrender under the reformed penal code, a lenient prison sentence, and a pledge that the brothers would get out of the drug business. The drug trade was facing a new situation. Rodriguez commented:

> Most of the new generation are under 30 and have no criminal record. They're not known by Colombian authorities, much less the DEA [US Drug Enforcement Administration]. These people are interested in legalising their situation, but they will go to jail only if there is real evidence against them ... they'd have to get out of the business and stay out, and dismantle their infrastructure, their labs, their routes. We have to be serious about that.[6]

President Samper had decided that there was no point in having the drug barons in jail if they continued with the trafficking. By contrast, the surrender scheme promised a reduction in the scale of the drug business.

Thus a senior Colombian law-enforcement official called the plan 'verifiable, manageable, politically salable, and it should be attractive to the US too'.[7] There had been no fresh consultations with the United States, but it seemed likely that there would be a hostile American response, with US officials highly sceptical about the idea that the Cali bosses would simply abandon their global cocaine interests.

The Colombian government was arguing that it would be foolish to ignore the surrender option. Gustavo de Greiff, prosecutor-general, had decided that the country could no longer afford the violence and social disruption that attended the endless war against the traffickers. In the event, a surrender date had been set for 23 March 1994, before the plan was aborted following the hostile DEA response. The Gaviria government reverted to its tough line, but Samper, while prepared to continue with the crackdown, was equally keen to explore the surrender option. A senior Colombian official commented that US policy would create another drug war and leave the Colombians 'holding the bag'. This would do nothing to end the drug trade: 'The gringos only want to punish narco-trafficking, not eradicate it.'

A principal problem was that the Colombian government had no confidence in its ability to defeat the Cali cartel. Fernando Botero Zea, defence minister, had acknowledged the 'amazing' intelligence capability of the cocaine barons, able to use a sophisticated telecommunications system to tap into police operations. In Cali alone, the cartel was said to employ 1500 taxi drivers, 1500 street vendors and an equal number of security guards to warn the traffickers of any impending move against them. Prosecutors, judges, witnesses, jurors and the police were still being bribed and intimidated, making it virtually impossible to bring court cases against the cartel. The Colombian charges against Miguel and Gilberto Rodriguez were open to negotiation, but the many US indictments against the brothers were a different matter. In particular, both were charged with running a 'continuing criminal enterprise', a crime that carried a life sentence.

On 9 June 1995 Gilberto Rodriguez was arrested in Santa Monica, an affluent neighbourhood of Cali, following mounting US pressure for the Colombian authorities to take a firmer line against the traffickers. The 56-year-old Gilberto was found crouching in a cupboard behind a television set in one of the Cali 'safe houses'. When the police, having located the secret compartment, confronted the billionaire drug boss he reportedly shouted: 'Don't shoot me. I will surrender.' Then he handed over money and handguns, and was flown to Bogota to be charged with drug trafficking.

President Samper spoke of a 'great victory', and US ambassador Myles Frechette declared: 'This is a great triumph for the Colombian police and the government of Colombia.'[8] In April the Colombian police had offered rewards of $1.25 million for help in capturing the two brothers. Now it seemed that a mortal blow had been struck against the Cali cartel.

Gilberto Rodriguez, nicknamed the 'Chess Player' for his shrewdness and skill in evading arrest, had made no move for the three pistols beside him and given himself up with a whimper ('Take it easy, boys … I'm a man of peace'). The daily *El Tiempo* carried the headline 'Checkmate' over the report of the arrest, but it was soon obvious that there was no room for complacency. On 10 June a devastating cluster bomb exploded at a music festival in Medellin, killing at least 30 of the revellers and wounding hundreds. President Samper had been celebrating 'the beginning of the end of the Cali cartel', but the style and timing of the bomb suggested that Cali gangsters were sending a plain message. Almost as the bomb was going off, Samper was saying to a reporter that Gilberto might be treated leniently 'if he is willing to collaborate' – the sort of language that Washington did not want to hear.[9]

On 19 June Armando Sarmiento, the Colombian director of prosecutions, predicted that Gilberto Rodriguez might spend nine years or less in jail, despite being regarded by some officials as one of the world's most dangerous men. Sarmiento explained the government thinking: 'There was no negotiation. He could face two separate sentences of 12 years for a 24-year maximum total. But there are automatic reductions. If he collaborates by confessing, it saves the state two of three years of trial. He can get time off for that. Then there's an automatic one-third reduction if he studies or works in jail. And when he's 65, a judge can decide if there is no danger in releasing him.' It was likely that he would be held in a newly-built jail at Palmira, near Cali, though the prosecutor was emphasising that the *Catedral* mistake would not be made again. (Escobar's *Catedral* prison had included Jacuzzi, fax, cellular phones, champagne, women visitors – and inadequate security.) However, a prison guard admitted that there had been 'a rush to ensure that *Don* Gilberto had enough pillows' (my italics). When Sarmiento was asked about his meeting with 'Don Gilberto', he responded with the same terminology, and then added after a pause, 'as you call him'.[10] Then he said: 'We had coffee. He said spontaneously that he would confess to all crimes. All I guaranteed was due process … He spent a lot of time asking me not to go after his children, swearing they were not criminals.' But three of his grown-up children, and his wife Mariela, were in hiding, wanted on trafficking charges.

President Samper was now saying that the Cali cartel, thought to control about 80 per cent of the world's cocaine supply, could be destroyed within months, but that another mafia group might be poised to take over. He told a group of journalists in Cartagena that the government was concentrating on a cartel run by Henry Loaiza Ceballos, known as the 'Scorpion' (because of his murderous reputation). Some 15 farms belonging to the 'Scorpion' (*el alacran*) had been seized, but Loaiza had eluded capture. Already $1 million had been paid to (unnamed) people instrumental in the capture of Gilberto Rodriguez; now some $2 million was being offered for Loaiza, a one-time leader of the military wing of the Cali cartel. Loaiza, whose ruthlessness brought him immense power, was said to have been involved in the 'chainsaw massacre' of 107 peasants who had refused to work for the cartel. Within days, the net closing, Loaiza had surrendered and was in custody.

On 5 July 1995 another leader of the Cali cartel, José Santacruz Londono, was arrested after a bodyguard for the national police chief spotted him dining in a Bogota restaurant. Santacruz Londono, known as 'Chepe' and *El Estudiante* (The Student), was the fourth of seven Cali cartel leaders to be imprisoned in less than a month. Then another billionaire, he started his criminal career as a car thief and kidnapper, after dropping out of a university engineering course. A few days later, Phanor Arizabaleta, another Cali boss, became the fifth drug lord to be taken into custody in the period. Ramiro Bejarano, director of the Colombian secret police, commented: 'Arizabaleta surrendered voluntarily. He plans to submit himself to the government's leniency policy.' A short time later, Arizabaleta confirmed his acquiescence when, in handcuffs, he spoke to the waiting journalists: 'It is my will and my desire to submit to justice.' By now he had no other option. The Cali cartel was being systematically stripped of its leaders, but the drug business was set to continue under new control.

Samper and the Cartels

The massive revenues from the cocaine trade over decades had led to corruption of Colombian politics at every level. Thus drug money had found its way into the pockets of municipal officers, mayors, congressmen, presidential candidates – and even presidents. Some observers were charging that Samper was far from immune to the general corruption that had infected every aspect of public life in the country. Throughout the 1994 campaign that led to his victory, Samper was often accused of accepting financial support from the drug barons, and when Pastrana conceded defeat, five hours after the close of polling, he could not resist a final accusation: 'I campaigned against political machinery, corruption and drug trafficking. That is why I assure the country that a president who has received money from drug trafficking has no moral right to lead the nation.'

A few days after the June election, fresh charges were fuelling the growing political scandal. Now it was being said that Cali cocaine bosses had offered the Samper campaign $3.6 million on the assumption that Samper would be willing to advocate cartel-friendly policies. On 22 June, Andres Pastrana called on Samper, a mere seven weeks before his inauguration, to resign if it were proved that drug traffickers had financed his campaign. Tapes were then released of telephone conversations between a cartel-linked journalist, Alberto Giraldo Lopez, and the cartel leaders, Miguel and Gilberto Rodriguez Orejuela, where they discussed multi-million-dollar contributions to Samper; and where evidence emerged of cartel meetings with campaign officers of both the major parties. At a subsequent press conference Pastrana said that his own campaign finance chief had rejected an offer of cartel money, just as Samper denied that his campaign had receive support from the drug traffickers.

The tapes were damaging also to the outgoing Gaviria administration, smarting under US accusations that the government had been too lax with the drug cartels, allowing Colombia to become a 'narco-democracy'. Samper, just weeks away from assuming office, was struggling to limit the harm to his own party. The content of the tapes was plain, but it remained unclear at this stage whether money had changed hands and why Pastrana was trying to exploit the revelations when his own officials seemed to be equally implicated.

It was reported that the tapes had come into the possession of US officials before the June vote, with their decision to take no action causing 'a behind the-scenes flap' in Washington.[11] A State Department official commented that the US 'can't interfere with elections', while DEA officials were furious: 'No-one did anything. They allowed this travesty to take place. Everybody, including the US government, is participating in this cover-up.' Robert Gelbard, the Clinton administration's Assistant Secretary of State for International Narcotics Matters, judged that the news from Bogota was 'the worst kind of information we could receive', and that 'if these accusations are true, it will definitely affect bilateral relations'.[12] One DEA official suggested that the Colombian government had lost its stomach for the battle against the drug traffickers: 'Colombia ... is willing to let the

Cali families launder their money, legitimize their wealth and their names so their sons and grandchildren can someday run for President.' To some Colombians such remarks were slanderous. In *El Tiempo* the columnist Enrique Santos Calderon wrote that the only thing that the tapes proved was that the Cali cartel wanted to finance the campaigns but 'not that it succeeded'.[13]

The Colombian vice-president-elect, Humberto de la Calle, due to be inaugurated with Samper on 7 August, did not want to appear 'naive or angelical'. He believed that there was 'some flow of money from narco-traffickers to the congressional level ... there are congressmen who listen to drug dealers ... that is what obligates Colombia, and particularly the next administration, to be on guard'. So here it was acknowledged that drug money was finding its way to the Colombian congress, a fact that angered Washington. At the same time the United States had a clear interest in maintaining a working relationship with the Colombian authorities. Thus Michael Skol, the principal deputy assistant secretary of state at the US Bureau for Inter-American Affairs, emphasised that it was the future that should be considered: 'We don't want to lose the co-operation with Colombia, and we have been told it will not be lost.'[14]

In mid-July charges were also being levelled at General Octavio Vargas Silva, the Colombian national police chief, now said to have received narco-funds. In response, or as part of a US pressure campaign, the DEA head, Thomas Constantine, abruptly cancelled a planned courtesy meeting with Vargas in Washington, whereupon an indignant Vargas denied he had ever taken drug money: 'I swear on my honour as a policeman, I swear to God, I swear on my family's honour, I have never broken my oath to serve my country.' It seemed unlikely that the US State Department would be prepared to believe him, just as it appeared to be highly sceptical about Samper's denials. Now the US Senate was calling for a freeze on $40 million in antidrug aid to Colombia unless Samper, not yet inaugurated, could show that he was pursuing vigorous antitrafficking policies. The Colombian foreign minister, Noemi Sanin, declared in response: 'We won't accept unilateral criteria on how we should run our narcotic interdiction program.'[15] It was also emerging at this time that the US State Department had prepared a document criticising Bogota's role in the war against cocaine. President Gaviria quickly denounced the American attitude and the criticism that Colombia was failing to meet international agreements in the fight against drug trafficking. Colombia, he declared, was a sovereign nation, a solid collaborator in this fight, and one that had made more sacrifices than others.

The crisis over Samper's possible involvement with the drug traffickers was continuing to escalate. Thus Enrique Pajero, a former Liberal presidential candidate, seemingly assumed Samper's guilt: 'It is one of the worst crises to occur in the history of Colombia. The president of the republic must resign'. It was 'very serious' that he had 'committed himself to an alliance with a criminal organisation ...'. In the same spirit, Alvaro Gomez, a leading Conservative, urged Samper to resign ('The country is suffering a crisis of credibility'), but at least one political analyst, Eduardo Pizarro, thought that a resignation would have a 'devastating effect' and only encourage the Marxist guerrillas to intensify their struggle against the state. A public opinion poll revealed that 77 per cent of Colombians thought that Samper had benefited from drug money, though 41 per cent believed that he had not known about the mafia contributions made to his campaign.

The defence minister, Fernando Botero, had been forced to resign; and Samper's former campaign treasurer, Santiago Medina, had provided a detailed testimony – thus increasing the pressure on the Samper administration. Medina testified that on 24 April Botero told him that the campaign needed cartel money, and that when he told Samper of this the president-elect said 'very nervously that he wanted to be out of the loop on this and that I should co-ordinate it with Fernando Botero'. According to the Medina confession, allegedly stolen from the prosecutor-general's office and then published, he conveyed various points to the Cali leadership:

- Samper appreciated the cartel's help to gain the presidency;
- Samper backed the surrender policy and negotiation to overcome drug trafficking and violence;
- Samper backed Gustavo de Greiff, now ambassador to Mexico, who supported negotiation with traffickers and the legalisation of drugs;
- Samper committed himself to the surrender of the Cali cartel;
- Samper would work to achieve the best solution.

On the strength of these assurances, according to Medina, some $1.2 million was raised for the first round of the presidential election in May, and $4.9 million for the second round. After the election Miguel Rodriguez repeatedly called Medina to request a meeting with president-elect Samper.[16]

This was not a version of events that Samper was prepared to recognise.

Days before his inauguration he talked with reporter Tom Quinn in Bogota. When asked if he had contact with the drug cartels, Samper replied:

> The only contact I have with drug traffickers is the four slugs I've still got in my guts from the time they tried to kill me. Kill me! This country knows I am a victim of the narcos, not a buddy of theirs.

The US concerns, in Samper's view, could be put down to the end of the Cold War: 'Journalists and conspiracy-theory government officials are looking for truculent situations to exploit. They're people looking for another war, and they'd love to see Colombia made into a Vietnam against the druggies.' The cartels had gained 'a degree of power', but 'they don't run the country'. They may have 'five or six congressmen on their payroll', but it was nonsense to say that such influence could force the Government 'to name crooks to key positions' or to suggest that Colombia was 'in effect a narcodemocracy'. [17]

The prosecutor-general, Alfonso Valdivieso, was now declaring that he would continue with his investigations 'even if the president has to fall'. Samper, for his part, was denouncing what he regarded as a conspiracy of slander and lies aimed at discrediting the government, the president and his family. Some pro-Samper commentators judged that the plot had been hatched in Washington. Thus legislator Carlos Lucio stated on Radio Caracol: '*This conspiracy originated in the United States ... The United States is gunning for the Puerto Ricanization of Latin America*'; and even Jaime Arias, leader of the opposition Conservatives and no friend of Samper, denounced the participation of Myles Frechette, the US ambassador to Colombia, in the anti-Samper campaign. On 24 August 1995 Noemi Sanin, Colombia's ambassador to Britain, tendered her resignation, citing the allegations of drug-related contributions to Samper's 1994 campaign.

In September President Samper was questioned about the allegations, and denied all links with the drug traffickers. A day later, gunmen in Bogota wounded Antonio José Cancino, Samper's lawyer, and killed two bodyguards. The political situation remained highly unstable and the anti-Samper allegations were continuing. On 2 November the 76-year-old Alvaro Gomez Hurtado, a former Conservative candidate for the presidency, was gunned down near the entrance to Sergio Arboleda University in Bogota. An aide was also killed. The Colombian government deplored the shooting as 'an attack on the nation as a whole'.

In late-November President Samper rejected the option of a plebiscite to determine whether he should continue in office, and discarded also the idea of a further commission to investigate the accusations that he had received drug money. Andres Pastrana's proposal to create an 'impartial' commission was, according to Samper, unconstitutional; and in any case the president still had a good popularity rating. The Attorney-General's Office was then announcing that the first stage of the investigation into bribery charges against three of the president's advisors would close in the first half of December, whereupon the evidence would be assessed. In early December it seemed likely that Samper himself would be cleared of all charges.

The Colombian relationship with Washington still appeared to be a crucial factor in whether the Samper presidency would survive. In a televised speech in late December Samper minimised the importance of the US threat to withdraw Colombia's certification as a partner in the war against drugs. Hopefully, he said, it would be possible to avoid permanent US-Colombian tensions over the drug issue. Already it was plain that the United States was unhappy that Samper was surviving the charges against him. Thus Robert Gelbard, US under-secretary of state for international drug matters, backed by the State Department, even went so far as to question the 'seriousness' of the exoneration of Samper by the parliamentary commission investigating the drug allegations. Samper affirmed that, whether or not the United States withdrew certification, Colombia would 'continue to combat drug trafficking because it is a national commitment'.

On 12 January 1996 José Santacruz Londono ('The Student'), alleged No. 3 in the Cali cartel, calmly escaped from jail by unscrewing the one-way mirror from the prison interrogation room, climbing into the empty viewing room, and driving past guards at Bogota's maximum-security La Picota prison, politely waving as he did so. It seemed unlikely that such an escape could have happened without inside help, reinforcing the widespread belief that the cartel's tentacles reached into the highest levels of government. A US diplomat expressed the common attitude: 'There's something rotten here.' Carlos Medellin, a new justice minister, had just been sworn in and was promising swift trials of the alleged cartel bosses, but the Londono escape was an obvious blow to the Samper administration. On the following day there was a further setback. Marta Elena Sanchez, a lawyer who ran the Palmira prison on the outskirts of Cali, was shot dead by gunmen who opened fire on her from a car. Londono had apparently escaped in an official vehicle, and the government had been powerless to protect Sanchez.

The Samper administration could scarcely claim that it was winning the drugs war.

The exoneration of Samper had done little to quell the accusations or to stabilise the political situation. There was growing pressure for Samper to resign, though he continued to deny all the allegations. The accusations were, he said in a brief televised response, 'infamous'; if any drug money had been used by his 1994 campaign it had been 'behind my back'. Opponents noted that the commission exonerating Samper had been stacked with Liberals, with more than half of them also under investigation for cartel links. According to Enrique Parejo, the president would have to resign 'because the country now knows he is a liar'. At the same time Pastrana was continuing to agitate for a change of regime: it was not just that the Samper campaign had been infiltrated by drug traffickers, it was worse than that – Samper, said the Conservative leader, 'went to ask the Cali cartel for money'. On 25 January Senator Fabio Valencia, a Conservative leader, announced that the opposition party was withdrawing all support from the Samper government (four Samper ministers were connected with the Conservative Party): '... it has been decided that the Conservative Party would pay a better service to the country by withdrawing from the administration ... whoever stays in the government does so in his own name ...'.

It now seemed that Samper's days were numbered. Santiago Medina had charged that Samper had personally organised financial contributions from the Cali cartel, and also met a Cali drug baron during a Latin American summit in Ecuador. In response, Samper called the allegations 'absurd and libellous'. Some 2000 students marched to the presidential palace in Bogota, wearing stickers carrying the word 'Resign!', and office workers gave them a ticker-tape welcome. Housewives, bearing similar stickers, joined in by banging saucepans and shouting slogans. Gabriel Garcia Marquez was predicting that Samper might fall from power as a result of the scandal. Then General Ricardo Emilio Cifuentes, a senior military commander, declared that he was resigning because he felt Samper was 'not worthy of the presidency'. And there were reports that Samper's lawyer, Antonio José Cancino, was preparing to leave the country after receiving anonymous death threats.

In late-January 1996 it seemed that the Colombian congress might pardon Samper as part of a deal to secure his resignation. An opposition congressman commented that the president had to be given 'a way out'. Now a communiqué supposedly from the jailed cartel leaders was claiming that Samper had been given millions of dollars during the 1994 campaign. The communiqué, believed by *El Tiempo* to be authentic, included the words: 'Because we have been threatened with extradition in order to keep us quiet behind bars, we have decided to follow the example [of Fernando Botero, the Samper defence minister]. We want to help save the nation and all the citizens who are being deceived ...'. On 30 January Colombia's congress went into emergency session to tackle the growing crisis, and Samper demanded an immediate investigation: 'I ask the Congress to investigate me quickly in order to reach a definitive end of this crisis. The only thing I ask is due process. Let me be judged quickly, but with the guarantees that the constitution and the law provide me.'

On 6 February Alfonsio Valdivieso, the Colombian prosecutor-general, was quoted as saying he expected to file criminal charges against President Ernesto Samper. Again Samper was refuting the allegations as 'odious'. If there had been any drug money in the campaign it had been without his consent and it had not led to any commitment to the traffickers, 'as is clear from the successes obtained against the drug cartels in my administration (sic)'. On 14 February the public prosecutor presented Congress with charges against Samper that were judged likely to lead to impeachment proceedings. Valdivieso denounced Samper for illicit enrichment, electoral fraud, falsifying documents and complicity. The so-called Accusations Committee of the House of Representatives would decide whether to pass the case on to the full House, which would then vote to clear Samper or to pass the case on to the Senate. The Committee was weighted heavily in favour of Samper's Liberal Party.

The Colombian 'Sampergate' case reopened on 23 February 1996, with the determined prosecutor, Alfonso Valdivieso, backed by an increasingly angry public. There was now a growing view in Colombia that Samper would have to go. Perhaps a deal would be struck to facilitate his exit from power. Perhaps the general election, scheduled for 1998, could be brought forward. Perhaps the vice-president, Humberto de la Calle, could take power. The Conservatives were hostile, the Liberals were disenchanted, Church leaders were demanding resignation, and Congress would be likely to yield to the mounting public pressure. 'Congress is opportunistic,' said Ingrid Betancourt, a Liberal congresswoman, 'If they feel that the president is going to fall in the end, they will probably abandon him.' It was hard to see how President Ernesto Samper could survive.

A Hostage Released

The guerrilla war had continued through the Samper crisis. On 16 August 1995 the president had declared a state of emergency in an effort to combat a wave of rebel violence. The body of a British student, captured on 24 June, had been found on the outskirts of Bogota. The 22-year-old Trevor Catton, taken hostage for an initial half-million-dollar ransom, had been tied up, shot repeatedly, and then dumped in a river. In late-August a soldier working at the British embassy in Colombia was captured by guerrillas after being stopped at a roadblock. Negotiations to free the 32–year-old Staff Sergeant Timothy Cowley were so sensitive that the Foreign Office kept news of the kidnapping secret for a fortnight until it leaked out. A third British citizen, a security advisor to a British company, was held for about five days until he managed to escape, killing several of his captors. Sergeant Cowley had failed to take any precautions to protect his security, according to General Camilio Zuniga, head of the Colombian armed forces: 'He was a functionary who, according to what I've been told, liked to watch birds and went to the area without taking any security measures.' It was thought that the negotiations to free him would not be helped by the fact that British instructors were helping to train Colombian special-forces personnel. Moreover, the British government was opposed to the payment of a ransom, a ploy designed to discourage further kipnappings. It was acknowledged that rebels from the Jaime Bateman Cayo band had contacted the British embassy in Bogota, but details of their demands were not released. On 29 August it was reported that guerrillas had killed at least 16 people in a banana plantation, the third massacre is less than a month in the northwestern Uraba region.

On 8 December 1995 Colombian soldiers, working closely with the SAS and Scotland Yard, rescued Sergeant Cowley after 119 days in captivity. Alberto Villamizar, who headed the Colombian government's anti-kidnapping campaign, said that the FARC rebel group had carried out the kidnap and that no ransom had been paid, though £1.3 million had reportedly been demanded. Cowley, speaking in Spanish, subsequently said he felt 'very well' and had become accustomed to the environment he was in – 'which is living in the middle of the wood surrounded by people who have got guns. The guns are all pointing at you and you haven't got one to point at them. It's very worrying ... I wrote a book, which I've lost, and I watched birds'.[18] During much of the time Cowley had been blindfolded, bound hand and foot, and tied to a tree. On 8 February another British citizen,

Philip Halten, was seized by three armed men at a roadblock near San Luis and taken hostage along with a Colombian, a Dane and a German. Villamizar commented that the lives of the men were not in danger: 'Usually Colombian guerrillas give good treatment to kidnapped people.'

The conflict continued. On 14 March 1996 guerrillas used a donkey loaded with explosives to kill 11 policemen in Chalan, Sucre. Two days later, the Colombian army was put on maximum alert after a rebel ambush killed 31 soldiers and wounded 18 near the border with Ecuador, 350 miles southwest of Bogota. Juan Carlos Esguerra, the Colombian defence minister, commented that the government might need to call up some reservists to combat the rebels. On 5 May at least 16 people were killed by FARC guerrillas during raids on two towns in Uraba, northwest Colombia. These were a few incidents among hundreds over the period. There seemed to be no end in sight.

Samper Secure?

The multifaceted Colombian war was continuing on many fronts. Thus in the 'banana belt' of northern Colombia guerilla forces were fighting against the self-styled defence groups – paramilitaries (*parracos*) – for control of the territory. Some 20,000 people had fled, some leaving the region altogether. Throughout the country the death rate was soaring. In May 1996 the National Forensic Institute reported that 39,375 people had suffered violent deaths over the previous year, most of them not fully investigated. Near the Bucaramanga airport, northeast Colombia, justice officials found eight skulls and other human bones, possibly those of street children and other poor people killed by the paramilitaries.

On 23 May the congressional investigating committee recommended that President Samper be cleared of all charges. A few days later a terror group, 'Dignity for Colombia', threatened to kill the kidnapped brother of former president Cesar Gaviria if Congress were to finally clear Samper of the corruption charges. It now seemed that the public prosecutors had decided not to arrest three cabinet ministers also involved in the scandal – interior minister Horacio Serpa, foreign minister Rodrigo Pardo, and communications minister Juan Manuel Turbay. Now the official mood was swinging in Samper's favour.

Colin Crawford from Strathclyde, the only foreign-born member of Colombia's House of Representatives, was suggesting odds of 2–1 on that

Congress was about to clear Samper of all corruption charges, not least because the 165-member house was dominated by Samper's Liberal Party. Crawford judged also that the evidence was too weak to convince anybody beyond reasonable doubt; and he pledged that he would vote to exonerate the president ('Samper is an extremely intelligent man, a fantastically intelligent man, and he's a great politician'). The drug problem went back a long way and Samper was no more than a scapegoat.[19]

On 13 June the Colombian congress voted more than two to one (154 total) to end the impeachment proceedings against President Samper. To congress members such as Ingrid Betancourt the vote came as no surprise: 'Those who absolved the president are politicians who received money from the cartels and committed the same crimes as the president.' Some 24 members of the congress were under investigation over links to drug trafficking, and seven were already behind bars. Samper, declaring himself 'satisfied' with the vote, was then faced with the task of rebuilding his political legitimacy. A week later, Jesus Angel Gonzalez, a state governor, was assassinated while trying to secure the release of a congressman held by rebels for more than a year.

President Samper was now threatening to sue anyone who questioned the congressional vote absolving him of all the corruption charges. On 28 June Luis Guillermo Nieto Roa, Samper's lawyer, issued a statement saying that a team of lawyers had been instructed to take legal action 'including any lawsuits that are deemed necessary to demand total respect for the good name' of the president and his family. The issue was not dead but it increasingly seemed secondary to the exigencies of the war. On 30 June some 18 people were killed and 10 hurt when gunmen opened fire near a bus station in Medellin. Police suspected that this fresh massacre was carried out by a criminal gang called *Los Victorinos* which was feuding with leftwing militias. In another incident, gunmen killed four men and wounded two women on a farm near Medellin. On 9 July a dozen FARC rebels died in fighting with government troops, and the ELN killed five members of a rancher's family. On 2 August the Colombian army fired at striking coca farmers protesting at government plans to destroy their crops, wounding ten people.[20] Some 50,000 people were now protesting in four southern provinces.

On 19 August 1996 the *Semana* news magazine revealed that a military *coup d'état* against President Samper had been aborted the previous year only days before it was due to take place. The plot, scheduled for 11 November, was aborted when, on 2 November, Alvaro Gomez Hurtado – a former presidential candidate then singled out to head the *coup* government – was assassinated. His death, on a Bogota university campus, remained a mystery. There was some ambiguity about the role of Myles Frechette, US ambassador, in the *coup* plot. He admitted in a televised interview that the *coup* idea had been brought before him, but there are differing accounts of his reaction. Did he reject the idea 'out of hand'[21], or were the plotters able to sell him the plan to depose Samper and bring an end to the political crisis?[22] In any event it was bizarre that an accredited ambassador should keep such information secret for more than a year and then announce it to the public via a television broadcast. In one estimate there were more than 50 assassination attempts against Samper 'between the day he took office in 1994 and late-1996'. And the opposition to the Samper presidency was far from over.

On 6 September 1996 vice-president Humberto de la Calle called upon President Samper to resolve the country's political and economic crisis by resigning: 'Colombia looks like it's falling to pieces.' Four days later, the vice-president resigned, saying that Samper should do the same because he lacked legitimacy. The Samper administration had known nothing but continued crisis, an unwinnable war, and persistent US interference – including an escalating military presence – in Colombian affairs.

SIX

War by Various Means (September 1996 to October 1997)

Rebels, War and Cocaine

In September 1996 the Colombian government was facing an escalating guerrilla war. As one incident among many, about 500 leftwing rebels attacked a military base in the jungle at Las Delicias, close to the Ecuadorean border (34 soldiers killed, 20 wounded, 59 missing). The army unit had been in charge of destroying cocaine-processing laboratories, and, according to defence minister Juan Carlos Esguerra, the attack was in retaliation. At the same time the guerrilla forces launched attacks in 12 other states, killing around 100 people in what was the bloodiest and most widespread rebel initiative in years.

A nationwide alert was declared, with the security forces ordered to remain in their barracks and military patrols stepped up. President Ernesto Samper stressed that the rebels were wrong if they thought that the government would be distracted from its 'eradication' operations in the south of the country. Nonetheless the guerrilla attacks were an obvious setback to government policy. After the attack at Las Delicias, 340 miles south of Bogota, the bodies of the soldiers were not discovered immediately, and the rebel fighters had ample time to escape before army reinforcements arrived. In recent weeks, tens of thousands of peasants had gathered in southern Colombia to protest at government plans to destroy the coca plant, the main source of income for the poor farmers in the area. More than a dozen civilians had been killed in the demonstrations, encouraging the peasants to support a rebel response. It seemed clear that the guerrillas were also protecting their own economic interests. Thus Holdan Delgado, chief of the armed forces, said that the rebels were defending their interests in the coca cultivations: 'This is truly revenge for the number of laboratories destroyed and crops affected.'

The guerrilla war continued to grow, with both sides claiming victories in their campaigns. On 23 September the authorities reported that police and soldiers had destroyed more than a tonne of cocaine and cocaine paste after a raid on a drug laboratory in the southeast province of Guaviare, while rebel forces continued to mount attacks that were largely unpredictable. Now President Samper, on his way to New York to deliver an anti-drug speech to the UN General Assembly, was embarrassed to learn that 3.7 kg of heroin had been found aboard his aircraft. It was not known who had planted the drug on the Boeing 707, or whether this was a deliberate attempt to discredit Samper who was widely assumed to have received $6 million in cartel contributions to the 1994 election campaign.

The escalating war had caused food prices to rocket in Bogota, according to an *El Tiempo* survey carried out in late-September 1996. Guerrillas from FARC and the ELN had attempted to place a stranglehold on the major cities and towns by burning trucks, creating physical obstructions and establishing manned roadblocks. It was found that food prices had risen by more than 10 per cent, and that the effects of the rebel campaign were reaching as far as ports on the Caribbean coast and the northeast provinces. The military and the police were forced to escort some traffic, so eroding the protection of other sensitive sites. In October the various guerrilla factions launched a series of attacks on military and other targets, on one occasion freeing 41 prisoners from a jail in Mocoa in the southwest province of Putumayo.

The government campaign against the drug trade was continuing, but in conditions of growing national instability. Gilberto Rodriguez Orejuela, the Cali drug lord, had agreed to pay a fine approaching $100 million in a plea-bargain deal that was set to allow his early release. An anonymous ('faceless') judge heard Gilberto Rodriguez confess to the charge of 'illicit enrichment' – in addition, according to Alfonso Valdivieso, to 19 counts of fraud in using bank accounts to launder the massive drug revenues. Gilberto also confessed to financing electoral campaigns, following the charges that Samper had been funded by drug money. But now Cali was counting the cost of the government anti-drug campaign. The inhabitants of the city were relieved that perhaps fewer bodies, cartel victims, would float down the Cauca river, and no-one mourned the passing of the *traquetos*, the cartel thugs who habitually roamed nightclubs picking out women to gang-rape and murder. But the *calenos* (Cali inhabitants) were likely to miss the billions of dollars that the traffickers had invested in the city, pouring massive funds into property, construction and general financial assistance.[1]

The cartel barons reportedly provided low-interest loans to anyone who asked. Thus Guillermo Londono, a retired soldier living in Cali, commented: 'My friend went to the mafia and said "I need 20 million pesos (£12,000) to set up a hardware shop," and the boss just said "Okay, no problem, here's the cash".' In this vein Gustavo Alvarez, a novelist and politician, observed that drug money 'had a capacity for redistribution that no other money has had'.[2] Then, when the state moved in, the cartels rushed to liquidate their assets to prevent massive confiscations, causing prices to plunge. The inevitable consequences were an increase in private debt, a drop in the level of construction, and a rapid growth in unemployment in the city (15 per cent in October 1996, one of the highest rates in country).

In late-1996, with the Samper administration able to point to various successes against the Cali cartel, blocks of flats in the city were standing empty, some construction projects had been abandoned half way through, floors in mafia-owned apartment blocks were unoccupied, and restaurants and bars – seeing a collapse in trade – were up for sale. Alejandro Rincon, owner of a Cali bar, commented: 'Business is bad, bad, bad. Security is worse – I had to get one of these' (he brandished a revolver loaded with dum-dum bullets).[3] No-one in Cali believed that the local economy would improve in the short term. Perhaps the Cali cartel had been fatally wounded, but the drug trade continued to thrive.

The Colombian police were now claiming that more of the cocaine business was now being conducted in Brazil, Peru, Venezuela and Ecuador, though much of the drug traffic was being blocked. Colonel Benjamin Nunez, head of the Cali anti-drug task force, said: 'We are seizing the majority of the cocaine shipments. When the Cali cartel existed, we didn't seize one kilo of their cocaine because a whole organisation existed ... and they bought everyone.' Myles Frechette, US ambassador, was less sanguine: 'But what we don't know is how much more is being produced.' It remained uncertain how much business the Cali drug barons were conducting from prison. In October 1996 the Ecuadorean police seized 6.3 tonnes of cocaine heading for Mexico, a shipment that may have belonged to Victor Patino, a cartel leader then in jail. Colonel Hector Escamilla, director of La Picota prison where Gilberto and Miguel Rodriguez were then held, noted that the jailed cartel leaders could still communicate by public telephone: 'It's difficult for us to try to intercept or control their conversations.' Security was lax: lawyers could visit the jailed bosses six days a week, conjugal visits were allowed, and most packages sent outside by inmates were not searched. All this suggested that the illegal cocaine business was being conducted by other means. In any event there were still massive volumes of drugs on the streets of the United States.[4]

The uncertainties about the cocaine traffic remained. Few observers doubted that the cartels had been seriously damaged, perhaps fatally, and equally there was little doubt that the cocaine Colombians remained internationally active.[5] The main question was not whether the drug business remained intact, but who – after all the anti-drug efforts and campaigns – was running it. In Colombia the Samper administration continued to govern as well as it could – waging an endless war against the guerrilla insurgency, doing deals with drug barons, struggling to cope with an expanding US presence, and introducing constitutional and other changes in domestic politics.[6] It seemed obvious that drug money was still finding its way into Colombian politics, and that Washington would have a growing interest in an enlarged US intervention to combat both the drug trade and leftwing guerrillas. The scene seemed set for unending social and political turmoil.

Conflict as Usual

On 24 November 1996 three guerrillas were killed in a gun battle with the army in southern Colombia, bringing to almost 40 the number of people killed in political violence in three days. In this case, according to General José Miranda Garcia, FARC rebels had fought with the army in a jungle region of Putumayo province, following the murder by rightwing death squads of dozens of people in northern Cesar, Magdalena and northwest

Antioquia province. On the following day, Luis Eduardo Iglesias, a pilot whose helicopter had crashed, was missing in the mountains after falling out of another army helicopter that had rescued him. This was not the only controversial rescue attempt ...

The arrest in late-November of Werner Mauss, a German secret agent, and his wife ended hopes that there may be German mediation in peace talks between the Colombian government and the ELN guerrillas. Mauss and his wife were arrested at Medellin airport trying to smuggle Brigitte Schone, previously kidnapped by the ELN, out of the country. He had reportedly obtained the $1.3 million ransom in Germany and paid three-quarters of this amount to the ELN to secure the release of the 40-year-old Brigitte, wife of Ulrich Schone who had worked as a BASF manager in Colombia. These events had alarmed the Colombian authorities.

In September Mauss had managed to secure the release of the kidnapped engineer, Karl-Heinz Tresser. In response to this and the second case the Colombian public prosecutor Alfonso Valdivieso declared: 'In that Mauss has attempted to smuggle a kidnapped person out of the country, he is a threat to our national security. It would be bad news should it emerge that foreigners in our country endorse kidnappings.' It was now possible to argue that German kidnap money, amounting to millions of pounds, was linked to the revival of ELN fortunes. Over the previous two years Mauss had purchased the release of no less than seven foreigners held by ELN guerrillas, and had thus violated the Colombian anti-abduction law. And there were further complications ...

In 1990 the Mauss couple had tried to interest Siemens in the commuter train Metroproject in Medellin, until a minister blocked their approach. At the time Alvaro Uribe, governor of Antioquia province, accused Mauss of illegally taking a commission. Then President Samper met Mauss in Madrid and decided to support a possible Siemens involvement in Metroproject, after which the company won the tender for a $60 million modernisation. Then it emerged that Eduardo Mestre, a former senator who was serving a prison sentence for involvement with drug money, and Jorge Serpa had been involved in the deal; and that Horacio Serpa Uribe, the interior minister and Jorge's cousin, had stayed at Mauss's house near Bonn in Germany. Hence links had been established between guerrilla kidnappings, drug money, German ransom money, bribery, corruption, other illegal activities, a senior Colombian minister – and President Ernesto Samper. Was this another nail in Samper's political coffin? He had survived an almost continuous political scandal since his 1994 election. Could he survive the new revelations?[7] It seems that he was scarcely touched by them.

On 5 December some 24 peasant farmers, including a pregnant woman, were killed in the jungle region of Sucre, northern Colombia. Here a rightwing death squad, the self-defence force of Cordoba and Uraba, mutilated the bodies to prevent any identification and then dumped the remains on the streets of Coloso and Tolo Viejo. In the previous week the paramilitaries had carried out further massacres, bringing the total of dead over a few days to about 60 men and women, accused by the Colombian security service of having possible leftwing sympathies. In Boyaca province an entire family, including three children, was hacked to death by men wielding machetes.

In Bogota many survivors of the death squads ('My father was killed by paramilitary forces when I was six months old') and the rest of the urban poor continued to live in squalid shacks or on the streets, suffering further abuse and persecution. Some 50 per cent of all Bogotanos live below the poverty line.[8] And to such privation was added all the brutalities and horrors of one of the most violent societies on earth. On 16 December a car bomb exploded outside the home of Juan Gomez Martinez, a prominent opposition leader living in Medellin. A gunbattle between police and paramilitaries had preceded the blast which killed one man and wounded 48 people. The next day, the Colombian security forces arrested a man at Bogota's city hall just before President Bucaram of Ecuador was due to meet the Bogota mayor, Antanas Mockus. The man, carrying a suitcase packed with explosives, was presumed to be involved in an assassination attempt. Only weeks before, Bucaram had survived a 'suspect' fire on board his helicopter.

The war against the drug barons was intensifying, following the persistent US pressure. In January 1997 it was plain that the new Law for Property Confiscation would in theory be applicable to those properties of suspicious origin acquired by or through the drug cartels. Almost as soon as the new law was adopted, the Search Brigade and the Attorney-General's Office began operations designed to confiscate 77 estates, mansions and luxury apartments. In the first stage of such operations, according to the Ministry of Justice, the government hoped to confiscate goods worth 200,000 million pesos (about $200 million) belonging to the drug traffickers. The Special Commando, appointed by the government to carry out the expropriations, was initially targeting properties in Valle del Cauca, Risaralda and Cordoba, and in some parts of the Atlantic Coast and the centre of the country. Such initiatives were not likely to end the drug trade, or even to seriously erode its commercial attractions. The most probable outcome was that the cocaine business would suffer significant setbacks before the trade began expanding again under new auspices, under the management of a fresh set of ambitious entrepreneurs. Cocaine would continue to be supplemented in the market by other drugs: for example, crack variants, heroin and *yage*, this latter becoming increasingly popular in mainstream Colombian society.[9] And the revenues would always be sufficient to blunt the zeal of the authorities.

In mid-January 1997 Samper announced an economic state of emergency designed to reduce Colombia's $2.6 billion budget deficit, and asked all Colombians to unite behind a policy of austerity. Some estimates suggested that 19,000 state jobs would be cut over the coming days. Luis Eduardo Garzon, leader of the Colombian Workers' Federation, commented that the government's plans would give the current wave of popular protest 'greater justification'. President Samper was now resorting to a 1968 law, used by former presidents Gaviria and Betancur, granting presidential power to enact decrees that bypassed congress at times of national economic need. The coffee and banana markets had collapsed, exacerbating problems caused by peso overvaluation against the dollar. The Colombian financial institutions were buying dollars, leaving the central bank with a massive foreign currency reserve and pushing up inflation (already at 28 per cent). Oil helped to redress the balance-of-payments deficit, but also encouraged the influx of foreign currency. Nor did the oil industry contribute much to the employment of Colombian nationals. The analyst Carlos Alberto Esteban observed that the majority of the workers in the oil sector were 'blue-eyed blondes' (that is, foreigners). Some $600 million was to be trimmed from public spending – a move that would worsen the already desperate plight of the poor and lend added support to the guerrilla campaign.

On 16 January President Samper indicated that the government was ready to talk with the FARC rebels to secure the release of 60 soldiers held since 30 August. The gesture did nothing to discourage the guerrilla attacks throughout the country. At the end of January, as one of many incidents, leftwing rebels detonated 155lbs of dynamite in a building in Medellin city centre, according to General Luis Ernesto Gilibert, an officer in the national police. The targeted building was known to house a leader of one of the government-backed death squads. The guerrilla war, intermeshed with drug bribery and business, was set to continue. The Samper administration was under growing threat from various quarters.

Samper Surviving

In early February 1997 the Samper administration was preparing for talks with the FARC guerrilla group to secure the release of 70 captive soldiers, perhaps as a prelude to more extensive peace talks. The soldiers were reportedly lower-class conscripts whose plight had been largely ignored for months. At the same time there were signs that the drug traffickers were taking fresh initiatives to develop the cocaine business. One extreme case concerned efforts by the cartels to import a Piranha-class atomic-powered submarine from the Russian military to help the drug trade. Officials from the US Drug Enforcement Administration (DEA) arrested Ludwig Fainberg, then facing 30 indictments, after three years of covert surveillance. A DEA spokeswoman commented on the intentions of the drug cartels: 'These guys were negotiating with military officials in the ex-Soviet Union for the purchase of a submarine they were going to use to take narcotics to California and other places.' The sale – in this case by the Kronstadt naval base near St Petersburg – would have given the drug smugglers a new advantage in a fresh arms race. Thus Lieutenant Gary Bracken, of the US Coastguard, commented: 'Our vessels are not equipped with sonar.' The discovery of the projected deal led to speculation that the traffickers were already using methods that were unknown to the Colombian authorities or DEA officials.

President Samper was as usual facing serious problems on several fronts. In addition to the obvious guerrilla successes and evidence of new trafficker moves in the drug war, the Colombian government was being forced to confront the consequences of the new austerity measures. On 9 February the Samper administration was bracing itself for a nationwide strike by 800,000 state workers, after talks to avert the stoppage broke down. The Colombian army was stationing troops in strategic areas in anticipation of nationwide civic protests. In neighbouring Ecuador, President Abdala Bucaram, having survived the assassination attempt in Bogota, had been deposed after a general strike.

The Colombian stoppage, called by the United Confederation of Workers (CUT), originated in a dispute over a government public-sector pay offer, about 9 per cent below inflation. The working-classes, formerly pro-Samper, were beginning to desert the government, with public-sector employees now also winning the backing of private-sector workers. Enrique Calderon, a political analyst, noted that with labour minister (and former CUT leader) Orlando Obregan failing to retain worker support 'the president has very few friends left'. The United States, angry at the former drug scandals, had withdrawn Samper's entry visa – which in turn had prompted further controversy, mounting criticism of Samper, and the worsening economic situation. Samper's popularity had plummeted but, as a spectator at Bogota's bullring shouted when a hapless bull fought desperately for survival: 'That bull is harder to fell than Samper.'[10] On 13 February the president's opponents resorted to new tactics: a 44lb bomb exploded at Barranquilla airport near the runway where Samper's jet landed minutes later. In such a political climate it was not difficult to understand why in early-1997 one enterprising company was netting $300,000 a year marketing bullet-proof tuxedos, business suits, ball gowns and cocktail dresses.

The violence, as always, was stimulated by peasants' revolt, worker agitation, guerrilla struggle, trafficker turf conflicts, death squad criminality – and the endless government attempts to keep a lid on the cauldron. The war against the traffickers had inevitably merged with the war against the leftwing rebels, and government sorties into the Colombian jungles and savannah generally had many purposes. The peasants, relying on coca revenues, typically co-operated with the guerrillas and the traffickers, all with an interest in the production and distribution of cocaine. The coca plantations of Guaviare, Meta, Caqueta, Putumayo and Amazonas – despite the government crackdown – were still supplying 80 percent of the world's cocaine. The guerrillas continued to take their percentage and in return to protect the supply lines and the laboratories hidden deep in the Colombian jungles. In one version of this scenario, 'Yesterday's freedom fighter is today's narco-guerrilla and tomorrow's trafficker'.[11]

In one typical police operation, SAS-trained Colombian troops were using grenade launchers and heavy weapons to attack a located cocaine laboratory deep in the jungle, little more than a shack where the coca leaves were being turned into the characteristic paste. Freshly-picked coca leaves were fermenting in petrol – the first stage in the production of cocaine: some ten 20-gallon barrels were filled with the choking mixture. Then the troops, commanded by General Rosso José Serrano, set fire to the laboratory and continued their hunt for the main laboratory in the area and the production network – landing strips, storage areas, routes through the jungle. The soldiers were set to uncover a production line 'more lucrative than that of Ford or General Motors – at the cost of one of their lives'.[12] In 1996 Thomas Constantine, DEA director, presented Serrano, 'America's favourite policeman', with a citation. But he looked to his future with trepidation, declaring that on retirement he would have to leave Colombia, 'until the drug lords and the traffickers forget what I have done to them'.[13]

The United States was fond of General Serrano but less than enthusiastic about President Samper. In late-February 1997 Washington was again deciding whether to certify Colombia as an effective ally on the war on drugs, and so to reverse the decertification (1 March 1996) caused by the Samper drug-money scandal. Robert Gelbard, US secretary of state for narcotics affairs, remained convinced that Colombia should not be granted certification status: President Samper was 'truly corrupt, with a clear history of co-operation with drug traffickers and receipt of their money since 1982'. In response, Colombian interior minister Horacio Serpa called Gelbard 'arrogant, aggressive and lacking in objectivity'. It was not surprising that General Barry McCaffrey, the White House drugs chief, backed Gelbard: 'Coca production is up over the last five years, and opium production is up dramatically. Criminal organisations continue to run their enterprises out of jail, and reintroducing extradition has gone nowhere.' Prominent Colombians had visited Washington, lobbying for certification and the economic and other benefits that it conferred; but US hardliners were pressing for sanctions against Colombia, including the withdrawal of US landing rights for Colombian airlines and increased tariffs on Colombian exports to the United States. Alfonso Valdivieso, Colombia's chief prosecutor, had denounced the certification process as 'odious', saying that it interfered with Colombian independence.

The Samper administration seemed to be surviving, despite the wars and the usual American hostility. On 27 February a bomb in the banana-growing region of Uraba, supposedly planted by FARC guerrillas, killed seven people and wounded 40 more; while at the same time it was being reported that Gabriel Garcia Marquez, Colombia's Nobel laureate novelist, had abandoned his country for exile in Mexico: 'The situation has become unsafe and turbulent. I'm off, because I have to have somewhere that is conducive to writing.' The degree of violence in both the urban and rural areas seemed to be escalating. In late-February the body of Frank Pescatori, an American geologist kidnapped in Guajira, was found. The 40-year-old scientist, snatched by five unidentified gunmen on 10 December 1996, had been shot through the head.

On 28 February the United States decided that Colombia should be maintained in a decertification status; that is, Washington was not prepared to acknowledge the country as a partner in the drug war. A week later,

Myles Frechette, US ambassador, stated that the decision had put his life in danger. Interior minister Horacio Serpa had called Frechette a 'nasty gringo', and a Colombian senator declared that if Frechette failed to provide proof that Samper had been linked to drug money the ambassador was a 'son of a bitch' and should leave the country. Myles Frechette responded: 'Frankly, the comments that have been made about me in the past few days have put my life in danger.' The imposition of decertification now implied that US aid would be stopped and that punitive sanctions might be imposed. But while US-Colombian relations deteriorated, American encroachments on the territory and sovereignty of Colombia continued to increase.

Killing, Refugees and the US

On occasions foreign tourists were victims of the Colombian wars. In early March 1997 two European tourists, a German and an Austrian, died in a clash between troops and leftwing guerrillas. The two men had been captured by FARC rebels after wandering over the unmarked and densely forested frontier between Panama and Colombia, the area known as the Darien Gap. Then a Colombian army patrol stumbled upon the group and, according to the defence ministry, the two Europeans were shot by their captors as the rebels retreated, losing four of their own men at the same time. Two other tourists, captured in early February, survived the clash.

The murders and the FARC presence were seen as serious blows to Colombian plans to develop one of the country's poorest and most remote regions as an eco-tourism destination. Only weeks before, the presidents of Colombia and Panama, keen to stimulate economic growth in the area, had announced the creation of a two-million-acre joint 'biopark', combining national parks on either side of the border. In an effort to encourage tourism and to improve environmental protection the leaders had chosen the old Cana mineworkings (on which Joseph Conrad based the San Tomé silver mine in *Nostromo*) to launch their project. But the high rate of kidnapping was a great handicap to the scheme. In 1996 some 1439 people, among them 44 foreigners, were reported kidnapped, most of them contractors working on remote mining, oil or hydro-electric projects. One British engineer employed by a Danish company had been held for seven months before being released, and nationals of various countries were being warned not to travel unaccompanied in Colombia. One consequence was that travel companies were giving the Darien Gap wide berth, particularly after the Colombian government was warning that it could not guarantee the safety of travellers in the region.[14]

Throughout Colombia the violence was continuing, in some areas at an unprecedented rate. In 1997, by mid-March, about 100 police officers had been killed, with 82 guerrilla attacks and 261 people known to have been kidnapped. Some members of the Colombian government were now arguing that the rebels should be given 'belligerent' status – which would open the way for a dialogue with the guerrilla forces but also give them international recognition. On 25 March police used teargas to calm a riot by more than 2000 prisoners in Bogota's La Modelo jail. The authorities agreed to fire the prison director and to ease the appalling jail conditions. On 30 March a bomb exploded at La Picota maximum security prison, which housed Cali cartel leaders, killing William Infante who had been convicted of murdering a presidential candidate. At the same time the rampant three-decades of rural violence had forced 180,000 people to flee their homes.

The United Nations and human-rights organisations had released figures showing that an average of 500 people were being displaced from their homes every day, giving Colombia more internal refugees (*desplazados*) in 1996 than Rwanda. Gilberto Echeverri, Colombia's new defence minister, having offered to talk with 'anyone, anywhere' to end the violence, declared himself shocked 'by the lack of enthusiasm for peace'. The *desplazados* were being ignored, forcing one human rights worker to observe: 'The world is neglecting one of the world's largest population migrations on the planet.' In March, as one example, 3500 inhabitants of the jungle town of Riosucio were fleeing from their homes – the third massive exodus in 1997 – in order to escape the factional fighting for territorial control.

Land reform, virtually ignored by successive Colombian administrations, was a crucial problem. The leftwing guerrillas were fighting to return control of the countryside to small-scale farmers, while the Colombian army and the paramilitaries were intent on preserving the large landowners' grip on much of Colombia. In Bellacruz, hooded men, death-squad paramilitaries, executed peasants in front of their families, and threatened others with clubs and machetes until the entire population was forced to flee. A survey in *El Tiempo* suggested that 35 per cent of refugees were fleeing the paramilitaries, 14 per cent the army and 29 per cent the rebels. Thousands of dispossessed peasants were pouring into Colombia's squalid and overcrowded shanty-towns every month, inevitably swelling the levels of urban violence. More than one million people were living without sanitation, health care, education provision or income – an inevitable recipe for violence, disease, prostitution, theft and social disaffection. Thus Cecilio Adorna, the UNICEF representative for Colombia and Venezuela, commented: 'The fact that even one family has to live in such conditions is enough to warrant rapid and effective action by the state.' In 1994 President Samper had promised ambitious spending plans to improve the living conditions of the refugees, but Colombia's economic plight had worsened and now there was a fresh phase of imposed austerity.

The United States had blocked most of its aid to Colombia following the 'decertification' decision – a decision that inevitably hit the Colombian poor. Now the UK was providing some of the help that might formerly have been offered by Washington. In April 1997 Britain was supplying aid to some 7000 Colombian refugees fleeing the military conflict, despite the recent kidnappings by guerrillas of BP workers. In one view, the United States was playing politics over Colombia – 'its embassy in Bogota regards itself as a kind of *de facto* government'[15] – while British diplomats were quietly trying to influence events on the ground. Britain was the first country to provide food, medicine, tents and mattresses to the Colombian refugees along the northwest coast, and to offer various other forms of help. Some years before, the British government had turned a Medellin rubbish dump into an open-air theatre, and now it was establishing a 'distance learning programme' to provide education to young Colombians via new computer technology.[16] The violence continued.

On 3 April rioting inmates in a Valledupar prison took eleven hostages and then demanded negotiations with the authorities. On the following day one of the hostages was released and the prisoners demanded bulletproof vests, parachutes and helicopters before they would free the rest. The talks dragged on until, on 13 April, the remaining hostages were released under the terms of a deal negotiated with the prisoners. The released hostages were then taken in an International Red Cross vehicle to a hospital in Valledupar before being returned to their homes. José Noe Rios, the government deputy minister who had led the talks, told reporters that the prisoners would lay down their arms and that the authorities would retake control of the prison. The inmates, according to the deal, would be transferred to another jail, their conditions would be improved, and financial aid would be given to their families.

At the end of April President Samper was again coming under mounting criticism – this time for beginning a 10-day trip to Africa and the Middle

East, a journey that opponents were calling a useless 'safari'. Samper was not travelling alone: an 87-strong party – derided by critics as a 'needless delegation that insults the poor' – was scheduled to travel to Brazil, South Africa, Kenya, Egypt, Israel, Algeria, Morocco and Spain. And in early May there were again growing tensions with the United States. On 7 May 1997 Colombian legislators failed to back the government's call for an end to the country's ban on extradition. Thus the constitutional affairs committee of the Colombian senate voted 8-8 on whether to approve a draft law to lift the ban. Senator Luis Guillermo Giraldo, keen to see Colombia's drug lords tried in US courts, declared: 'The bill has sunk. This is a defeat for the whole country.' President Samper had proposed the bill eight days before, under intense pressure from the Clinton administration, but now it seemed likely that Washington would be quick to denounce the Colombian refusal to authorise extradition. Then Alfonso Valdivieso, Colombia's top prosecutor, resigned fuelling speculation that he was at odds with the Samper administration and was preparing to stand for the presidency.

On 19 May a rightwing death squad smashed its way into a Bogota apartment and killed three people, including two human-rights workers. A one-year-old boy, who had escaped death by hiding in a closet, was found sitting between the bullet-riddled bodies of his parents, Mario and Elsa Calderon and his grandfather, Carlos Alvarado whose wife suffered multiple bullet wounds but survived. It was also reported that jailed Colombian drug barons had placed President Samper and US ambassador Myles Frechette on a hit list of assassination targets, as a reprisal for recent attempts to end the six-year ban on the extradition of drug lords. A police spokesman commented: 'The drug traffickers' goal was to assassinate a nationally and internationally known figure to press against the approval of extradition.' Other figures on the assassination list included General Rosso José Serrano, the national police director, and Carlos Medellin, an outspoken proponent of extradition who had recently stepped down as justice minister. The murder plot had been discovered through wiretaps on telephone lines in the maximum security wing of La Picota prison. On 23 May the supreme court in Caracas ruled that Justo Pastor Perafan, an alleged Colombian drug baron arrested in San Cristobal in April, could be extradited from Venezuela to the United States to face trial. Janet Reno, US attorney-general, praised the extradition decision and accused Perafin of smuggling 30 tons of cocaine into the United States.

On 15 June the FARC guerrilla group freed 70 soldiers, captured in combat and held for months, after President Samper agreed to temporarily demilitarise a 5200-square-mile jungle zone, including the remote southern town of Cartagena del Chaira, where the captives were released. Weeks later, rightwing paramilitaries tortured and murdered some 30 peasants when about 100 death squad members stormed the village of Mapiripan in Meta province. Three of the victims were decapitated and one of the heads was mounted on a lamppost; other victims were mutilated before their bodies were dumped in the River Guaviare. Alfonso Ortiz, Meta's governor, declared: 'It was a blood act, a terrible thing.' Luis Fernando Perez, a police inspector, said that at least 200 people had fled the village since the killings began. FARC rebels had killed 50 police and soldiers in the region, disrupted transport routes, and crippled oil production in the Cano-Limon field. Now the death-squad paramilitaries were venturing into the guerrilla strongholds. Colombia's internal conflict looked set to escalate.

The civil war had already displaced up to one million people, and by August 1997 the turmoil was spreading into Panama, where paramilitary groups were beginning terrorising and murdering civilians accused of collaborating with the Colombian rebels. Months ago a few people had been killed, with others kidnapped or raped, and now the situation seemed set to deteriorate. Thus Monsignor Romulo Emiliani, Bishop of Darian, Panama, reported that more than 40 paramilitaries had seized the town of Yape on 23 June: 'Among their weapons were hand-grenades, bazookas and flamethrowers. Behind them, in the mountains, was a larger group awaiting their orders.' The death squads searched the town for four days, hunting for rebels, and then, according to human-rights groups, beheaded a 58-year-old health worker. The Peasant Self-Defence Organisation of Cordoba and Uraba (ACCU), the most powerful of the local death squads, had also been responsible for the killing of about 30 peasants in southeast Colombia a few days before. There were reportedly about 2000 ACCU members, led by Carlos Castano, a landowner and graduate of the hit-squad schools set up in the 1980s by British and Israeli mercenaries and funded by the drug cartels. ACCU had 'cleansed' much of the Gulf of Uraba before moving to the west to murder selected civilians. President Samper had often defended the 1994 government decree authorising the formation of 'self-defence groups' (paramilitaries, death squads) to fight the guerrillas and their sympathisers ('subversives'). The United Nations and human-rights groups have condemned the paramilitary factions and called for them to be disbanded.[17] It seemed clear that the campaign of ACCU and the other death squads against the rebels and 'suspect' civilians would continue. Almudena Mazarrasa, the representative in Colombia of the UN High

Commissioner for Human Rights, said in August 1997 that Colombia was becoming a 'feudal nation' where everybody sets up their own 'private army'.

The escalating Colombian refugee crisis was affecting such neighbouring states as Ecuador and Venezuela and countries far afield, such as Britain. Government statistics showed that thousands of Colombians had fled the fighting to seek asylum in Britain, and that nearly all had been refused entry. Organisations in Britain working with refugees were expressing concern that innocent Colombians refused asylum were being put at risk of assassination, simply because officials had turned down asylum applications because of a lack of understanding of human rights issues in Colombia.[18] A report (*Caught in the Crossfire*, September 1997), researched by Tony Kay and produced by the Refugee Council, showed that Colombian refugees had been refused asylum on the mistaken ground that groups such as M-19 and Union Patriotica (UP), as legitimate parties, enjoyed official protection in Colombia. But UP had already lost 3500 activists to political assassination, and, as Juan-Carlos Lema (member of the Colombian support group, Open Channels) had emphasised: 'The fact that M-19 became a political party does not mean they are not at risk. A lot of people want to have revenge and the government is too weak to give protection.' Amnesty International had commented that government forces often co-operated with rightwing paramilitary groups responsible for a dramatic escalation of 'torture, political killings and disappearances'. In 1996 more than 1000 civilians were extrajudicially executed by the Colombian security forces and paramilitary groups.[19]

The British government had decided to clamp down on the influx by introducing a new visa requirement for all Colombians coming to Britain. In this context, Mike O'Brien, the immigration minister, warned of the 'increasing and alarming' numbers of Colombians making 'unfounded' claims for asylum. After the change in the British law, the monthly asylum applications from Colombia fell from almost 250 to about 15. At this time refugee support groups were commenting that there were many people fleeing persecution among the one million displaced Colombians, and that they were often unable to provide evidence of a home and a job, details usually required for a visa. Another concern was that Colombians in London were being stigmatised by police fears that the Colombian drugs cartels were active in Britain. The Refugee Council then held a series of meetings with Home Office officials in an attempt to make the treatment of Colombians more 'fair and efficient'.[20]

Rebels, Politics and Weather

On 22 August 1997 President Samper again expressed his willingness to demilitarise agreed parts of the country in order to facilitate talks with the FARC guerrillas. He also called on the rebels to halt their campaign to sabotage the forthcoming (October) municipal and provincial elections: 'The government I represent is willing to create the conditions and guarantees for an eventual meeting, including the creation of demilitarised zones if the guerrilla shows its clear desire to talk.' The FARC rebels acknowledged the offer as a 'substantial first step', but indicated that a number of other conditions would also have to be met.

Such overtures were doing nothing to reduce the levels of violence in most parts of the country. In one reported incident, a single case among thousands, three more corpses were found in a small clearing in the jungle. The men, face down in the dirt and with their hands tied behind their backs, had been hacked to death with machetes – further victims of the paramilitary *machacabezas* (headcutters), a local name for death-squad members. By September about thirty mayors had already been assassinated in the year, with many local officials resigning because of death threats. Some 298 councillors in Cesar province were threatening to resign, while Jairo Florez, their president, described the situation as 'critical, chaotic and desperate'. Both the guerrillas and the death squads had warned that traditional partly candidates campaigning in their areas would be targeted for assassination. In August FARC and ELN guerrillas kidnapped the nine town councillors of Simiti and also 23 electoral candidates, and forced them to withdraw from politics.

In Putamayo province the entire electoral process was under threat. Thus governor Jorge Fuenbringer commented that if the situation became any worse the voting might have to be suspended. It was plain that the Colombian army, with undisguised links to the paramilitaries, was failing to protect the public; and indeed many of the worst human-rights abuses were being perpetrated by army units. In one case, that of the jungle town of Riosucio, many of the 4000 people who fled the area were driven out by army attacks. In addition, many troops were being deployed to protect oil installations and other economic assets, giving very few opportunities for army units to pursue the guerrillas into their strongholds. Alfredo Rangel, political analyst, commented on the growing success of the rebel campaign: 'On the one hand the guerrillas reap the fruits of long-term planning and a clear strategy. On the other, the army is hobbled by disorganisation and lack of clear objectives.' He concluded that the bullet was undermining the ballot throughout much of rural Colombia, putting the entire democratic process under attack: 'The outlook is bleak.'[21]

In September Tony Lloyd, Britain's Foreign Office minister, was observing a Colombian crop-spraying plane during the destruction of an opium poppy field when suddenly the aircraft was riddled with bullets fired from the ground. A British diplomat commented that the plane had been about a mile out when the pilot, hit in the foot, said that he was being shot at by guerrillas: 'This incident clearly shows the dangers that law enforcement agencies are up against in tackling the scale of the illicit drugs trade in Colombia.' The incident, trivial by Colombian standards, at least acquainted the British group with the sort of hazard being encountered by public officials working in a country that had lived with an escalating civil war for more than thirty years.

President Samper, forced to cope with the endless drug scandal, US hostility, the cocaine wars, economic crisis and the escalating guerrilla war, was now being forced to confront extreme weather conditions – in the shape of the El Nino effect. In October 1997 half of Colombia's provinces were suffering droughts in a worsening economic situation. Some three months of drought had destroyed 200,000 hectares of staple crops and caused a 23-per-cent drop in cotton production. The Colombian agriculture ministry was estimating that the losses to the milk and beef sectors would exceed £75 million in the year. Forest fires had raged over 60,000 hectares, denuding the hillsides and increasing the likelihood of landslides when the rains began again. Predictions of unusually low rainfall in the short term meant that coffee and flower production – two of Colombia's main exports – would be threatened. In some regions nearly three-quarters of the rivers had run dry, and with many reservoirs already 30 per cent down on seasonal levels there was a growing chance of water rationing.

SEVEN

Human Rights, Terror and Law

The Framework

The history of Colombia, like that of many countries, is steeped in blood. The Spanish conquest, the long servitude, the liberation wars, nationalist victors gnawing on the body politic – all preparing the unstable ground for the unimaginable horrors of the 20th century. Then the injustices of feudal Colombia stimulated the popular appetites for reform and revolution until, in the post-WW2 world, the country collapsed into civil war, the brutalities of an exploding drug culture, and all the pressures and tensions of an escalating foreign intervention.

In this context, any human-rights profile of Colombia was (and remains) a nightmare. Intimidation, forced displacement, terror, extrajudicial execution, torture, kidnapping, massacre, government repression, death squads, bombing, chemical warfare – social chaos and suffering that continue to rack a country and to spill over into neighbouring states (Panama, Ecuador, Venezuela).

The problems have been exacerbated by domestic and external economic pressures. Thus Latin American peasants have turned to cocaine production as subsistence agriculture and profits from traditional exports have declined under the impact of US and other commercial policies. For example, in July 1988 the United States, sensitive to alleged fair-trade violations, suspended the international coffee agreement, which within two months ruined the economics of Colombia's leading export. The US 'Food for Peace' program had already undermined the Colombian production of crops for domestic use, unable to compete with US exports. With the increasing peasant reliance on cocaine production came the massive growth in rural and urban violence, the corruption of politicians and police, the development of paramilitary and rebel factions able to tax drug revenues, and the growing interference of a United States intent on consolidating and extending its regional hegemony.

In these circumstances it was inevitable that human-rights groups, struggling against social abuse and injustice, would come to be targeted by the paramilitaries and other factions. Thus in mid-September 1989 some 28 staff members of the Popular Education Institute (IPC) were captured in a raid by the Colombian security forces and accused of being leftwing guerrillas hired as terrorists by the Medellin drug cartel. The event received much publicity, though little attention was given to the conclusion of the Andean Commission of Jurists that the charges against the IPC workers were 'clearly a set-up by the military forces which are looking to discredit the popular work' of the Institute. The staff workers arrested, including the director, were held incommunicado and were all tortured, according to the Andean Commission – a growing trend as new US aid began flowing to the Colombian military. Human rights groups were warning that such developments were inevitable as the United States worked to consolidate its links with the Colombian armed forces, known to have an appalling record of human rights violations.[1]

In the late-1980s and through the 1990s the United States became increasingly committed to providing support for what many observers were acknowledging was Colombian state terrorism. Thus Alfredo Vasquez Carrizosa, president of the Colombian Permanent Committee for Human Rights, declared: 'Behind the facade of constitutional regime, we have a militarised society under the state of siege provided' by the 1886 Constitution. Here the national constitutional rights had no relation to reality since 'poverty and insufficient land reform have made Colombia one of the most tragic countries of Latin America'. Legislation for land reform had been ignored by the powerful landowners, and the decades of violence had been caused 'by the dual structure of a prosperous minority and an impoverished, excluded majority, with great differences in wealth, income, and access to political participation ... violence has been exacerbated by external factors. *In the 1960s the United States, during the Kennedy administration, took great pains to transform our regular armies into counterinsurgency brigades, accepting the new strategy of the death squads.*'(my italics)[2]

This is what was happening in Colombia, before the pretext of the 'war on drugs' was used to justify the escalating US intervention. The aim, in the context of the growing popular disaffection with successive repressive regimes, was 'to make the military establishment the masters of the game ... it is the right to fight and to exterminate social workers, trade unionists, men and women who are not supportive of the establishment ... And this could mean anyone, including human rights activists such as myself'.[3] The Kennedy administration had encouraged the emergence of militarised National Security states in Latin America, dedicated to achieving 'internal security' by such methods as assassination, torture and mass murder; and had promoted the Alliance for Progress, a 'social catastrophe'.[4] The Reagan administration continued the support for state terror in Colombia and elsewhere, with the 'drug war' simply providing 'another modality for pursuit of these long-term commitments'.[5]

The Colombian human-rights record has been judged the worst in the hemisphere, 'not an easy prize to win' (Chomsky). In 1981 Lars Schoulz, an academic specialist on human rights in Latin America, found a close correlation between US foreign aid and torture: US aid 'has tended to flow disproportionately to Latin American governments which torture their citizens ... to the hemisphere's relatively egregious violators of fundamental human rights'. In the same vein Edward Herman, an economist at the Wharton School of the University of Pennsylvania, noting the relation between torture and foreign aid, observed also the correlation between US aid and the climate for business operations. Noam Chomsky and others have explored these connections and concluded that US leaders have not supported torture because they enjoy it. Torture is a matter of indifference to them, but it happens to correlate with profits for US investors – so torture is indirectly rewarded, in Colombia and elsewhere. US profits can be helped 'by torturing union leaders and human rights activists, murdering priests who are trying to organise peasants, and so on'.

The assassinations, disappearances, extrajudicial executions, massacres and the rest have run on over the decades, for the full period of the Cold War and beyond. On 4 July 1990, as one incident among thousands, Alirio de Jesus Pedraza Becerra, a 40-year-old lawyer and human-rights worker, 'disappeared' following his detention by armed men in Bogota. He was seized by eight heavily-armed men and pushed into a waiting car. An investigation was initiated but Dr Pedraza was never found. Soon after his disappearance a number of human-rights workers began receiving death threats, urging them to stop their activities or to suffer the same fate as Pedraza. Thus on 10 July Elvia Uran de Beltran, a long-time member of a human-rights group in Medellin, received a death threat by telephone, as did Martha Luz Saldarriaga Velez, a human-rights lawyer.

Dr Pedraza was a well-known 'subversive' in that he belonged to the Political Prisoners Solidarity Committee (CSPP) and was investigating human-rights violations attributed to the Colombian armed forces. He had represented families of peasants massacred by troops in May 1988 in Llano Caliente, Magdalena Medio; and was working also on behalf of trade unionists who had been detained and tortured in Cali. The army and the police continued to deny that Pedraza had been detained. In May 1991 a delegation from Amnesty International visited Colombia in an attempt to highlight the continuing human-rights violations in the country. Ian Martin, AI General-Secretary, declared to the National Constituent Assembly: 'In the case of Colombia the need to enshrine clear and unequivocal safeguards in the Constitution clearly acquires particular relevance and urgency in view of the dramatic and escalating levels of human-rights violations in recent years.' The Colombian interior minister, Humberto de la Calle Lombana, called the speech 'unilateral' and 'exaggerated'.

In December 1991 some 20 Paez Indians, including women and children, were massacred by about 40 heavily-armed men, some in military uniform. Members of the Paez community had gathered to celebrate a religious feast near the town of Caloto when the men burst into the building and told the victims to lie down before shooting them in the back of the head. On 8 January 1992 two lawyers investigating the massacre and helping the survivors were killed at their homes, while an anthropologist also involved in the enquiry disappeared. On 29 May Oscar Elias Lopez, a lawyer and advisor to the Regional Indigenous Council of Cauca (CRIC), was killed in circumstances that suggested an extrajudicial execution. Officials were saying that members of the National Police were involved in the massacre, though no warrants were being issued against them.

It was now plain that President Cesar Gaviria, visiting London in July 1993, had been unable to stem 'horrific human rights violations by his security forces'.[6] Colombian and international human-rights groups were charging that the incidence of 'political' murders was far greater than cocaine-related killings. Since the founding of the opposition Patriotic Union (UP) in 1985, some 777 party activists had been assassinated, with more than 100 trade unionists killed during President Gaviria's first year in power. An Amnesty Report stated that in 1992 at least 1000 people had been 'extra-judicially executed by the armed forces, or by paramilitary groups' operating with the military's support or acquiescence. According to the Andean Commission of Jurists, during an 18-month period of Gaviria's rule, only one per cent of 'politically motivated killings' could be attributed to the drug traffickers, while the state security forces were responsible for almost half the killings, paramilitary groups nearly one third and leftwing rebels about one-quarter. About 300,000 people had become refugees as a result of political violence in the past decade.[7]

In July 1993 the Labour MP Michael Meacher, then the British shadow minister for aid and development, drew attention to the human-rights situation in Colombia, 'one of the most violent countries in the world'. Colombia had 'over 70 murders a day, and a rate higher than 70 per 100,000 inhabitants (compared with less than 1 per 100,000 for many European countries)'. This was a situation for which government and government-supported forces were mainly responsible:

> Analysis of the perpetrators of political killings in 1992 shows the guerrillas responsible for up to 25 per cent but that the armed forces and government security organisations and paramilitaries were behind nearly 75 per cent of the political violence.[8]

The number of political murders, 'still rising, reached 4430' in 1992 – 'as many in a single year in Colombia as all the political deaths during the whole 16 years of the Pinochet dictatorship in Chile'. With all the factors taken into account, political killings were running at an average of 8.4 per day, more than twice the average 3.9 deaths per day from combat operations: 'The victims are largely trade union organisers, human rights lawyers, peasant leaders and political figures ... of the 264 trade union leaders who were murdered worldwide between January 1990 and March 1991, 138 were Colombian ... more than half.' (On 12 February 2001 the British MP Eddie McGrady, noting that 1336 trade union officials had been killed in Colombia over the last decade, called on the Blair government to urge the Colombian authorities to provide better protection against the 'violence ... perpetrated by paramilitary organisations, aided sometimes openly by the armed forces'.) In 1993 Michael Meacher, as an opposition MP, had suggestions for the then Tory government; in 2001 the Blair administration seemingly had no interest in Colombian human-rights abuses.

In January 1988 a Medellin death squad, *Amor por Medellin* (Love for Medellin), kidnapped the 26-year-old José Castano, bound his hands and feet with wire, dragged him behind a moving car, beat his head for four days with a metal bar, raped him with it, and then left him for dead on the stinking Guavaval rubbish tip. After two months in a coma, he regained consciousness, but was paralysed and unable to speak. The death squad had thus served a warning to Oscar, José's brother, the leader of a public service union whose name had already appeared on a death list. In September Oscar Castano was granted refugee status in Britain, though he had plans to return to Colombia and to press for the creation of a 'truth commission' to attribute blame for political violence.

Since 1980 there had been about 16,000 political killings in Colombia, not including the deaths in the guerrilla war. *Amor por Medellin* was only one of 140 groups responsible for a large proportion of the 3080 political murders in 1992 alone. The Bogota-based magazine *Utopias* put the murder toll at more than 9000 since Gaviria became president in 1990 and promised change. Again it was said that the principal targets of the armed forces, the security units and the death squads were 'trade unionists, peasant and indigenous leaders, politicians, human rights activists and even primary school teachers ...'.[9] Amnesty International judged that the lives of 150 trade unionists, human-rights workers and community leaders listed by military intelligence as rebel sympathisers were in danger. It was now possible to suggest that President Gaviria was himself linked to the high incidence of political murders. Thus Oscar Castano declared that Gaviria's inactivity made him an 'accomplice', a political beneficiary of the bloodshed: 'The problem is not a lack of laws to care for human rights. The problem is a lack of political will by the government, its silence, and its inability to control the military.'[10]

In March 1994 Amnesty International claimed that the Colombian government was primarily responsible for the country's human-rights catastrophe, which had seen more than 20,000 politically motivated deaths in the past eight years: 'There are many myths about political violence which the government uses to obscure its responsibilities. In reality the vast majority of political killings are perpetrated by the Colombian armed forces and their paramilitary protegés … successive governments have hidden behind a skilfully constructed public image, while bureaucratic trappings that are supposed to safeguard human rights do little to protect anyone.' In response, Rafael Pardo Rueda, Colombian defence minister, declared on television that Amnesty was attempting a 'malintentioned statistical manipulation'. The human-rights organisation was now identifying the wide range of targets whose lives were under threat: opposition activists, human rights lawyers, judges, trade unionists, community activists, indigenous leaders, peasants, homeless children, homosexuals and drug addicts. No attempt was made to exonerate the guerrillas or the drug cartels from their share of the carnage, but Amnesty charged that the state was responsible for the bulk of the killings. It remained to be seen whether international pressure would be exerted on the Colombian government to live up to its democratic pretensions.

In May there were signs that the Colombian regime was planning to take Amnesty International before a UN forum, the first time that any country had attempted to take legal action against a foreign human-rights organisation. The Colombian government had its Western allies: the British MP Tristan Garel-Jones, a former Foreign Office minister, was accusing Amnesty of exploiting the situation in an attempt to raise funds. Fernando Brito, the director of the Colombian Department of Administrative Security (DAS), announced on 26 May that he intended to sue Amnesty for claiming that his department was preparing secret lists of people for execution: 'DAS is very concerned to avoid human rights violations in Colombia.'

An Amnesty newspaper advertisement, placed in the *Observer*, *Times*, *Guardian* and *Financial Times*, to which Garel-Jones took exception, had followed up the March report (*Colombia: Political Violence – Myth and Reality*) and summarised the situation.[11] The advertisement included the words: 'This ad will upset the Colombian government … The Government wants you to believe that most of the murders are committed by drug-dealers, guerrillas or rogue soldiers. In fact most are the work of the armed forces and police … the chaos in Colombia is spiralling out of control – it has become a struggle between those who support human rights, and those who suppress them …'

In early 1995 President Ernesto Samper startled the Colombian military and won praise from human-rights groups when he admitted the state's guilt in massacres of peasants in the southwestern town of Trujillo between 1988 and 1990. Here peasants were dragged from their homes, burned with blowtorches, tortured in various other ways, cut up with chainsaws and then dumped in a river. The incidents, among the worst in Colombia's bloody history, caused international outrage, though no-one had been found guilty of the crimes. Then Samper declared: 'I accept as president of Colombia and in defence of international humanitarian law, the corresponding responsibility for the grave crimes committed by servants of the state.' Perhaps it was too soon to celebrate. Robin Kirk, Human Rights Watch, said she was 'surprised and pleased' by the Samper admission: 'I hope the government takes concrete actions to prevent things like this from happening again.'

In January 1992 Blanca Cecilia Valero, who had worked for many years as secretary of the Barrancabermeja-based Regional Human Rights Committee, despite constant intimidation, was shot dead by two men as she left the office. Three police men reportedly watched the incident but did nothing. In January 1994 a Colombian newspaper reported that two naval officers had told the Attorney-General that their naval intelligence unit had assassinated the woman, and also about 100 trade unionists, teachers, journalists and other human-rights workers. As women were increasingly taking on leadership roles in Colombian local communities and organisations, they were facing growing risks from the armed forces, the death squads and armed opposition groups – all of which were carrying out human-rights abuses with impunity.[12]

Suffer the People

In July 1997 various human rights groups[13] placed a newspaper advertisement to highlight the continuing human-rights abuses in Colombia:

> On Human Rights Day in 1994, President Ernesto Samper declared his support for Colombia's human rights organisations, and promised to protect the lives of their members. Yet three years on, human rights defenders are continuing to be killed, 'disappeared', or forced into exile; others live in hiding, or endure death threats, harassment and surveillance. The violence cannot be laid at the door of Colombia's infamous 'drug wars', but is carried out in the context of an increasingly vicious armed internal conflict, in which all sides – army, paramilitary and guerrilla – are abusing human rights and international humanitarian law.

The government had said 'all the right things', but 'empty promise follows empty promise'. It was clear that 'No protection program has materialised, no progress into the "special investigation" has been reported, and paramilitary groups have neither been abolished nor controlled ... human rights defenders are losing their lives ... Their enemies are desperate to silence them, and their government can't or won't protect them'.

The human-rights defenders were being attacked (see *Targeting Rights Workers*, below), as were many other sectors of Colombian society – by the paramilitaries (death squads, 'self-defence' groups, etc), the guerrillas and other armed factions. Human Rights Watch noted that there were 'at least seven [paramilitary] groups allied under the name United Self-Defence Groups of Colombia (Autodefensas Unidas de Colombia, AUC).[14] The AUC was a descendant of Muerte a Secuestradores (Death to Kidnappers, MAS), the alliance formed in the 1980s between the military, the police and Middle Magdalena businessmen and landowners. By 1983 MAS had been responsible for more than 240 political killings – of elected officials, small farmers, community leaders and others. Here the main MAS objectives were to identify and target anyone who might be depicted as 'subversive'. Massacres were commonplace – which led to people abandoning their villages and land, so enabling the paramilitaries to become new landowners. On one occasion, some 42 people from the Uraba town of Pueblo Bello were kidnapped and killed, the AUC leader Carlos Castano claiming that this was 'an error' due to poor training: 'Our military force had grown enormously, and sometimes the men used the weapons for bad purposes.'

On 30 August 1988 armed men commandeered a bus and killed five passengers; ten more El Tomate residents were later dragged from their homes and executed; some 22 houses were burned down, with the public bus set on fire after the driver had been shackled to the steering wheel. A Jesuit priest, Sergio Restrepo, regarded as suspect because he worked with the poor, was shot dead outside the Jesuit parish house. The Castano gunmen have admitted that some of those killed were bystanders, shot by mistake. In 1997 the AUC units carried out at least 155 massacres, with the Colombian Attorney-General's Office formulating accusations in 271 cases implicating AUC members, many involving massacres. Castano himself has declared that the strategy of massacring civilians thought to be aiding the guerrillas was a useful one that the AUC has energetically pursued: 'We realised that we could isolate [guerrillas] and saw that this was a strategy that had very good results. Today, we continue to apply the same mechanism ... with the same excellent results ...' The sociologist Alejandro Reyes pointed out in the daily *El Espectador* that the massacres of civilians achieve a definite purpose: 'The massacre ... serves as an efficient notification to the population to sever any ties of support they may have with the guerrillas. Many of those who may have sympathised with guerrillas get scared and flee the region. Then the self-defence groups organise their own local support network, preferably of families who have lost members to the guerrillas. As a result, the self-defence groups consider the region recovered from their enemies.'

On 12 April 1996 the National Police withdrew from the town of Caicedo, after suffering one casualty, despite desperate pleas from the local authorities urging them to stay. Police officials then commented that since the residents supported the guerrillas they did not deserve protection. Eight days later, the ACCU paramilitaries, one of the AUC groups, seized the town and forced its residents to assemble in the central square. Then the armed men, working from a list of names, selected four people – Dario Restrepo, Caladino Gonzalez, Jorge Eliecer Castro and Isaias Gonzalez – and executed them. In a subsequent interview the ACCU claimed responsibility for the killings. In the same fashion the ACCU carried out massacres in Media Luna (October 1996; 60 ACCU men executed seven villagers and forcibly disappeared another six); in Coloso, Fichilin and Varsovia (December 1996; 30 ACCU men killed a police inspector and others, leaving bodies on the road); and in Mapiripan (July 1997; dozens of ACCU men killed 13 people and threatened others with death; 200 ACCU members rounded up villagers and executed some in the local slaughterhouse by cutting their throats). In this last case, judge Leonardo Ivan Cortes reported hearing the screams of the people the ACCU men brought to the slaughterhouse to interrogate, torture and kill over a five-day period: 'Each night they kill groups of five to six defenceless people, who are cruelly and monstrously massacred after being tortured. The screams of humble people are audible, begging for mercy and asking for help.' At least two bodies – those of boatman Sinai Blanco and airstrip manager Ronald Valencia – were decapitated. Antonio Maria Herrera was killed and hung from a hook before the ACCU members quartered his body and threw the pieces into the Guaviare River.

The authorities arrived days after the ACCU men left Mapiripan. Five bodies were located, though there were reports of perhaps another 20 thrown into the river. Judge Cortes had made eight telephone calls for help, along with calls from other desperate villagers, but neither the police nor the army's Joaquin Paris Battalion nearby were prepared to react until the

ACCU men had left town. The army subsequently admitted that it had not registered the arrival at San José airport of a chartered aircraft used by the ACCU members, despite the clear policy of registering every arriving plane and passenger.

Individuals were being killed in their homes, in addition to the mass murders of selected villagers in central square, public buildings and slaughterhouses:

- On 21 February 1996 Edilma Ocamo and her daughter, Stella Gil, were seized by ACCU paramilitaries, and were then bound, beaten and decapitated;

- On 11 June 1996 Hector Hernan Correa, a mentally retarded man, was in his home in La Granja when about 20 ACCU men arrived. A paramilitary smashed his way into the house, dragged Correa into the living room and shot him dead. On the same day the ACCU men dragged a teacher from a sports centre and executed him, and shot a man from a ladder where he had been painting a house. The paramilitaries then reportedly said: 'This is just the beginning';

- On 13 June 1996 two professional drivers were taken from their homes in the Choco hamlet, El Sierte, and then tortured beneath an image of the Virgin Mary before being executed. When another man refused to hand over his keys, he was dragged out of his vehicle and shot dead. Then his vehicle was burned;

- In November 1996 Eli Gomez Osorio registered a complaint with General Alfonso Manosalva that soldiers working with paramilitaries had raped local women. Gomez then began receiving death threats. On 26 November ACCU men intercepted him in town and shot him dead;

- On 27 February 1997 about 60 heavily armed ACCU men arrived in Vijao, Choco, set up three machine guns and began indiscriminately strafing the town. Then the paramilitaries searched the houses, found a uniform and some munitions in the home of Marino Lopez, took the man to a local river, decapitated him, and then cut off an arm and a leg before throwing his body into the river.[15]

Other villagers were killed in La Victoria de San Isidro (24 March 1997; seven residents kidnapped, two executed after torture); in Rio Viejo (25 April 1997; Juan Camacho Herrera, a street vendor, decapitated: 'This is to give you an example of how guerrillas should be killed'); and near Betulia, Antioquia (17 May 1997; people forced off a bus and executed).

In addition, the paramilitaries typically took hostages, attacked medical workers and ambulances, and made repeated threats against civilian populations. Government officials investigating massacres were terrorised into leaving the country for their own safety. Civilians were told that if they travelled to certain places, they would be declared 'military objectives' and killed. And in October 1997 the AUC notified pilots and charter air companies that if they flew to Puerto Alvira or Barranco de Mina their aircraft would be 'destroyed or brought down by any of our units'. Airline companies immediately suspended the 33 daily flights to the region, causing shortages in food and medicine and prompting residents to flee.

Colombian civilians suffer also under guerrilla campaigns. The FARC leadership, for example, has claimed to respect international law, but a substantial body of evidence has implicated the rebels in massacres, murder, torture, hostage-taking and attacks on such targets as medical workers and ambulances.[16] Thus in August and September 1995 the FARC group and its urban militias carried out at least five massacres, with many of the victims having nothing to do with politics or the conflict. Human Rights Watch cites 'the massacres of six people at La Heladeria "La Campesina" on August 12; Churido, with four victims, and Mapana, with five victims, both on August 19; Finca Los Cunas, with fifteen victims, on August 29; and Bajo el Oso, with twenty-four victims, on September 20. Often, victims were bound and beaten before being executed'.[17] The FARC commander Marulanda, interviewed in *Resistencia Internacional*, recommended attacks on 'any civilian factories and trucks', claiming that such attacks destroy the source of the government's wealth, 'so that they will be unable to maintain this war over a long period'.[18] Human Rights Watch has cited also the FARC massacres at:

- Finca Osaka (14 February 1996; ten men and one woman taken from a bus and executed at the side of the road);
- Alto Mulatos and Pueblo Bello (4 and 5 May 1996; seven people tied up and then executed, with bodies left inside burning houses; seven more peasants killed, with the bodies severely burned and only identified months later; a woman, her two young daughters and her daughter-in-law burned alive in their home);
- San José de Apartado (8 September 1996; four local community leaders killed, including Maria Eugenia Usaga, who was pregnant);

- El Hobo, Huila (21 June 1997; rebels detonated a five-kilo bomb packed with screws, pieces of chain, staples and nails at the entrance to a bar, and then opened fire from a nearby park – four women and the bartender killed; one civilian killed and three more wounded in the rebels' escape);
- Milan, Caqueta (20 July 1997; five Koreguaje Indians killed; five days later, seven men separated from women and children, then bound, forced down a path to the cemetery, and executed – bodies later found lying face down in a circle with the feet at the centre).

Killings by FARC guerrillas have also taken place at Medina, Cundinamarca (16 June 1996); Labranzagrande, Boyaca (11 March 1996); Caqueta (20 June 1996, 17 February 1997); San Vicente del Caguan (4 January 1997); La Guajira (February 1997); Caracoli (4 May 1997); Canas Gordas (6 August 1997); Sabanalarga (10 August 1997); Anza, Antioquia (14 November 1997); and many other places. Human Rights Watch has compiled a similar catalogue of massacres, killings and hostage-taking for the ELN guerrillas force (which in 1987 merged with the Union Camillista, UC, to form the UC-ELN). The UC-ELN has declared its sensitivity to the demands of international humanitarian law (the ELN adopted a 'Guerrilla Code'), but this has not been reflected in guerrilla behaviour 'in the field'.

Suffer the Children

Children have always suffered in war – by losing parents and other relatives, through trauma, by losing the means to survival, by being forced into military service, by being targeted as perceived elements in a conflict, and in many other ways. The wars in Colombia have caused a massive onslaught on the health and survival prospects of millions of children.

The pressures of poverty and conflict have forced tens of thousands of children onto the streets of Colombia's towns and cities, where the country's most vulnerable young people are targeted for exploitation and murder. When, in 1993, a bloody massacre of street urchins occurred in Rio de Janeiro, the United Nations Children's Fund (UNICEF) announced that, although 1000 children were being murdered every year on the streets of Brazil, in Colombia – with a quarter the population – twice as many children were being killed. Through the 1990s Colombia had one of the world's worst records for the killing of children, mostly carried out by self-proclaimed 'clean-up' groups. In August 1993 posters were being plastered up along block after block of Bogota's grimy central streets, inviting the public to attend the burials of the children scheduled for extermination. A frightened 14-year-old looked at the posters with their black crosses: 'They mean us. We are just dirt. They can kill us whenever they want.'[19]

A conference was being staged in Bogota on violence and cruelty against children, and volunteers from the Renacer Foundation, dedicated to helping young vagrants, were touring the area, urging children to get off the streets at night. Stella Cardenas, a psychologist with the Foundation, commented on the street posters: 'We take this very seriously. Two teenage girls were shot down earlier this week. We fear this is a public call for a massacre.' Martha, a 14-year-old prostitute, noted the trouble that someone had gone to: 'They have paid to print all these posters and stick them up. That means they are organised and serious, and mean to kill us.' In fact the organisers were blatant: the death notices were signed by industrialists, shopkeepers and civic groups in Bogota, pillars of the community frustrated at the levels of child destitution and crime in the city. One boy commented on his resort to mugging: 'How else are we going to live? If I had a home to go to, if someone would give me work, I wouldn't steal'. Another boy flaunted himself by baring his chest to a group of passing policemen: 'Shoot me then, come and kill me.' Four weeks before, his friend Emilce, a teenage prostitute, was shot dead. In another incident a security guard in a Bogota shopping centre, ordered to clear out young males, simply pulled out his gun and shot a 17-year-old youth in the leg in front of dozens of shoppers. The guard was not charged. On the streets of Bogota and other Colombian cities the children were being killed by shopkeepers, the police, 'clean-up' gangs, paramilitaries – with impunity. In Bogota alone, four children were being killed every day.

They were also dying in other ways – since the guerrillas, the paramilitaries and the security forces were routinely recruiting children for combat.[20] The guerrillas have dubbed the child combatants 'little bees' (*abejitas*), able to sting before their targets realise they are under attack; paramilitaries call them 'little bells' (*campanitas*), noting their use as early-alarm systems. One report (May 1996) by Colombia's public advocate claims that up to 30 per cent of some guerrilla units were made up of children, with other evidence suggesting that some guerrilla militias were 85 per cent children.[21] The UC-ELN was believed to have the largest proportion of children in its ranks, with one testimony indicating that it was common to see a rebel unit with 15 adult commanders leading up to 65 child soldiers.

The FARC and the EPL also included children in their ranks. Francisco Caraballo, an EPL leader, has commented that the group accepts children into its ranks if they are family members of militants. The FARC organisation has even gone so far as to carry out recruitment campaigns in elementary schools and children's homes, promising to send families a regular salary. Thus Valle del Cauca, the Cali public advocate, has commented: ' Guerrillas have presented themselves in schools and the homes of children offering to take the children to war, enticing them with stories about fighting and offering to sign them up, as a kind of adventure. They have offered the families money and guarantees of security in exchange for allowing their children to join the guerrillas.'

Some children have joined the guerrillas by choice, while others have been forcibly recruited. Human Rights Watch has suggested that FARC forcibly recruited children as young as twelve, with families often not daring to report such events. One 14-year-old girl related how she had been brought to the guerrillas by her mother, forced to cook and carry a shotgun, and later imprisoned after refusing to work, before she managed to escape. Children have been used to collect information, to make and lay mines, and even to ambush enemy patrols. One child guerrilla told how he and the other children drank milk mixed with gunpowder to give them 'more energy', and he noted the desire to kill troops: 'You say to yourself: I hope they come my way, and then you load up and shoot off a round and feel more capable, with better morale.'[22] One former child guerrilla, recruited at thirteen, told how she had used pistols, AK-47s, Galils, M-16s, R-15s, Uzi submachine guns, Ingrams and a 357 Magnum: 'In the organisation, you understand that your life is your weapon, it is your mother, it watches out for you day and night.'

The child soldiers can be executed for desertion or for passing information to the enemy, and can be killed in juvenile detention centres after capture (often by other child guerrillas in the same facilities). It is clear that children have been (and still are) regarded as a valuable war asset in the rebel campaigns, and that the government forces and paramilitaries are equally keen to recruit children. Human Rights Watch found in 1998 that 7685 children (under 18) were serving in the National Police, 7551 in the army, 338 in the air force, and 83 in the navy. Some 22 per cent of the 15,657 total were 15 and 16 years of age. The Colombian police have recruited seven-year-olds to work as 'little patrollers', and many of the children are expected to work in war zones. It has been found also that up to 50 per cent of some paramilitary units are made up of children. One former child paramilitary testified to the Public Advocate's Office that he had been forcibly recruited at nine: 'There were more children like me, about eleven, and my same age. Another five were between ten and fifteen years of age. We were all serving two years.' Eight-year-olds were seen on paramility patrols in the Middle Magdalena region, often a compulsory form of service that families oppose only at risk of their lives.

In June 1999 Olara Otunnu, the UN Special Representative of the Secretary-General for Children and Armed Conflicts, reported progress after meetings in Colombia. He had talked with government and FARC representatives, and received a government pledge to raise the minimum age of recruitment from 15 to 18, and a FARC pledge that children under 15 would not be recruited (and that ways to demobilise any under-age children would be explored). The UC-ELN had already recognised that 'some children have been killed or wounded as a result of our acts of war and we feel that it is an imperative to recognise these as serious errors of lack of foresight or crossfire in the midst of conflict ... We will make an effort to avoid repeating this type of regrettable action'. It still remains to be seen what practical effects this admission and the pledges negotiated with Olara Otunnu would have in the real world of the Colombia wars.

Forced Displacement

The Colombian wars have led to one of the largest population displacements of modern times. People have been terrorised, dispossessed, kidnapped, wounded and killed – and, in often desperate attempts to survive, they have fled their homes and their land. Typically, peasants have abandoned their villages after soldiers or paramilitaries have executed selected men and women. Thus in the town of El Salado, Bolivar, a teacher, Doris Maria Torres, and five farmers were forced to lie down in the town square before being executed by ACCU members. Over the next week in March 1997 some 320 families abandoned the town, leaving behind their houses, furniture, schools and fields. Journalists subsequently reported only 'empty streets, lined with mute houses ... and travelled only by the wind and an occasional starving dog that seemed to be searching for its masters'.[23] All the parties to the Colombian wars have forced such displacements, causing a vast humanitarian catastrophe.

The estimates suggest that more than one million Colombians have been forced to flee their homes. A 1997 study, by the Consultancy for Human

Rights and the Displaced (Consultoria para los Derechos Humanos y el Desplazamiento, CODHES), a research and humanitarian aid group, showed that since 1995 the scale of forced displacement had almost tripled. In 1997 some 257,000 Colombians were newly forced to flee. In mid-2001, according to the US Committee for Refugees, Colombia had the fourth largest displaced population in the world, after Sudan, Angola and Afghanistan. The reasons are well known. There are massive human-rights and laws-of-war violations, and also a powerful business factor: some influential business interests have allied themselves with the paramilitaries to force poor farmers from land that would then be occupied or bought for paltry sums.[24]

In 1996 humanitarian aid officials in Tierralta, Cordoba, had registered the arrival of 567 families, many saying that they had been told to abandon their homes by FARC guerrillas. The rebels evidently judged at that time that their conflict with the ACCU paramilitaries would be aided by a mass displacement of civilians and the better access to provisions that such a substantial displacement would provide. For similar reasons, the FARC rebels forced the displacement of an estimated 3000 people from 27 villages around Currulao to Apartado, Antioquia, in June 1996. Here families were fleeing with no more than they could carry on their backs, while their children were suffering from serious food and water shortages and an almost total lack of adequate shelter and medical care. Most of the displaced had been poor farmers, but all sectors of society were affected: professionals, elected officials and business families were made to flee their homes, these people with at least the resources to set up a new household elsewhere. Among all the parties to the wars, only the AUC publicly accepted responsibility for a displacement policy. Thus Carlos Castano, in an interview with *El Tiempo*, acknowledged that his forces had 'a lot of responsibility' for making people abandon their homes, since armed conflict produced forced displacement 'as it develops'.[25] This is easy to understand. When people witness atrocities and are threatened with the same, they are inevitably too frightened to remain.

The displaced people have not always been able to remain in Colombia. There are today thousands of Colombian refugees in Ecuador, Panama, Venezuela, Costa Rica, Sweden, Spain and the United States (we have seen also that Colombians refugees have exercised the minds of British officialdom). It remains the case that most displaced Colombians continue to live in misery and fear. Many have witnessed atrocities, and the thousands of refugees forced to exist in Colombian urban poverty have found themselves trapped in an underworld of crime, exploitation and violence. Others are struggling to survive in Colombian camps for the displaced. At the end of 1997 more than 4200 internal refugees were housed at the Pavarando camp, 3000 at the Turbo stadium, and an estimated 3000 divided between parks in Ituango and Puerto Valdivia, all in Antioquia. In a 1998 report, the UN High Commissioner for Human Rights pointed out: 'The situation of the displaced population, both in collective settlements and on the outskirts of cities, is critical in the extreme and takes the form of lack of access to basic health, food, housing and education services, and serious overcrowding.' For example, one displaced man in the Pavarando camp commented: 'Many children have hepatitis or malaria. Families are disintegrating.' In the Turbo sports coliseum, vast and unventilated, the people lived 'like pigs on the floor'. Many were depressed. A father is quoted: 'When I see the bad life I am living, I feel like I want to take poison and kill myself and my family. I sometimes think I should have died as a little child so that I wouldn't have to be living like this.'[26]

There has been a serious insufficiency of government aid to the displaced families, forcing them to survive in dire circumstances as best they can. Many of the refugees continue to lack adequate food, clean water and basic medical care. On one occasion the Public Advocate's Office found that 79 people, including 43 children, relocated to a farm, had received no drinking water for over a month. In other cases the government forced refugees to return to their villages, even when no security could be guaranteed. When ACCU paramilitaries were carrying out massacres in and around Riosucio, Choco, the former home of many of the displaced families, the government denied that such killings were taking place and told the refugees to return. Some Colombian refugees in Panama, having fled from the likelihood of assassination, were rounded up by Panamanian police and forcibly returned to Colombia. And even in the Colombian camps the displaced families are often under the threat of murder by paramilitaries that control the area. One official Colombian enquiry found that the displaced faced 'constant danger ... not a single judicial, police, military or government representative has attempted to stop these murders, torture, or forced disappearances that the inhabitants of these places have been subjected to'.

On 28 February 2000, as one example, 2500 people of the Cacarica River Basin began to return home almost three years after having been forced to abandon their homes and land. Paramilitary groups, acting in unison with government forces, had moved into the area of Riosucio, northwest Colombia, killed dozens of people and forced 3800 residents to flee. Now the people were asking the security forces to protect them, and demanding that the murderers be brought to justice. Said one of the displaced: 'How can I live in peace if my oppressors remain free?' By 2001 the situation remained insecure. Refugees and other families being threatened with displacement could ask the authorities for protection, but the Colombian government continued to focus on other priorities. The displaced families survived in the urban shanty towns, in remote jungle sanctuaries, in the massively under-resourced camps or beyond Colombia's borders. In late December 2000 Maria Rodriguez, one desperate mother among thousands, gathered up her six children, trekked through a Colombian drug-producing area, and arrived at the Lago Agrio frontier town in Ecuador: 'We brought almost nothing. We wanted to be discreet.' A neighbour who had made the same journey focused on his reasons: 'The paramilitaries say if you have one brother in the guerrillas, they have the right to kill everyone in your family.'[27]

Father Edgar Pinos, working with Colombia's displaced, reckoned that the worst was still to come. US military aid – including powerful Blackhawk helicopters – to the Colombian military would be bound to exacerbate the conflict in war-ravaged Putumayo: $800 million-worth of weapons and munitions was not intended to reduce the scale of the armed struggle. The paramilitaries were strong in the area of Putumayo, leading to further FARC initiatives – and more displacements. Soon the coca pickers, caught up in the turmoil, would be fleeing or otherwise jobless, if they survived. The refugees and the drug culture were spilling over into Ecuador, and the rebels were often slipping across the frontier for rest and recreation.[28] How long would it be before the escalating Colombian conflict led to military confrontation in Ecuador?

Targeting Rights Workers

Any society's attitude to its human-rights workers is a useful index of that society's moral status. Human-rights activists are invariably under-resourced (military matters are a greater priority for most countries) and often dismissed as 'bleeding hearts', 'do-gooders', etc. (In Iraq, US officials notoriously abused humanitarian workers as 'bunny-huggers'.) Colombia is a special case, not the only one. There, human-rights workers are not just under-funded or insulted, but threatened and killed.

Some human-rights organisations – such as *Corporacion Regional para la Defensa Humanos* (CREDHOS, Regional Committee for the Defence of

Human Rights) and *Asociacion de Familiares de Defenidos-Desaparecidos de Colombia* (ASFADDES, Association of Relatives of the Disappeared) – were forced to close their regional offices in Colombia after staff were repeatedly threatened with assassination. In the same way, workers from a variety of other non-governmental organisations (NGOs) have been forced to seek refuge outside the country.[29] Offices have been raided and staff have been given death threats. On 27 February 1998 Jesus Maria Valle Jaramillo, director of *Comité Permanente por la Defensa de los Derechos Humanos de Antioquia* (CPDH, Antioquia Permanent Committee for the Defence of Human Rights), was shot dead in his office. The Colombian government had taken some steps to provide greater security for human-rights workers but these were largely inadequate. Some organisations now have bomb-proof doors and security cameras, and human-rights workers have been offered bullet-proof vests: such measures 'afford very limited protection ... where human rights defenders and their families may become the victims of human rights violations at any time of the day or night'.[30] Official investigations have been carried out into the wounding and killing of some human-rights workers, but these have been inconclusive. A presidential order to respect human-rights defenders has been rendered ineffective by a countervailing message from the Colombian security forces that human-rights workers are in effect the covert political wing of the rebel opposition.

The security forces and army officers have denounced human-rights workers, so inviting the death squads to target them for threats, harassment, abduction and extrajudicial execution. Influential rightwing groups have accused human-rights organisations of supporting the 'subversive process' in Colombia by attacking the rule of law and encouraging the guerrilla war. One 94-page military intelligence report named 50 members of human-rights and social organisations across Colombia as being involved in terrorism and acting as fronts for armed opposition groups. In 1996 one of the targeted organisations, *Colectivo de Abogados*, working to defend political prisoners, received two international prizes for its human rights activities. (Colombian military intelligence denounced the organisation, a lawyers' collective, for its work in 'campaigning for bandits'; while one of its staff, the lawyer Miguel Puerto Barrera, was declared to be an '*objectivo militar*', military target, of the notorious XVI Brigade).[31]

Amnesty International has identified three different types of campaign conducted against human-rights workers: intensive and intimidating surveillance, often accompanied by death threats; extrajudicial execution, abduction, harassment ...; and detention and prosecution in 'regional justice' courts on the basis of 'evidence' provided by Military Intelligence.[32] Human-rights workers have been followed, photographed, verbally abused, threatened, bombed, kidnapped, beaten, detained, denied due process of law, denounced, raided and assassinated. Amnesty has concluded:

> A coordinated strategy exists within the security forces to represent national and international human rights organisations as subversive and acting on behalf of the armed opposition. The government ... has taken no effective action to step this propaganda war ... The government's unwillingness or inability to confront those behind the strategy encourages further attacks on human rights defenders. A consequence of this strategy has been the criminalisation of many human rights defenders for carrying out their legitimate activities ... the judicial process that the accused are subject to, does not meet international fair trial standards.[33]

Amnesty International has continued to urge the Colombian government to provide proper protection for human-rights workers, to investigate attacks and other abuses, and to reform the system of 'regional justice' (in accordance with the International Covenant on Political and Civil Rights, ICCPR, of which Colombia is a signatory). For example, following the killing of Josué Giraldo (of the Civic Human Rights Committee of the Department of Meta) on 13 October 1996, a sustained Amnesty campaign urged proper investigation by the Colombian authorities. At the same time the Inter-American Court of Human Rights issued a resolution requiring the Colombian government to protect all members of the Meta Civic Committee, to investigate the murder of Josué Giraldo and other acts against members of the committee, and to bring those responsible to justice. The government condemned the killing and opened an inconclusive investigation. This case, and many others, showed that human-rights defenders work in Colombia at their peril.

The Rape of Barrancabermeja

On 16 May 1998 a heavily-armed paramilitary force moved unhindered through the city of Barrancabermeja, Santander – rounding up residents, forcing some onto trucks and killing others. Seven bodies were later discovered, with at least 25 people forcibly abducted. Gunfire was heard in the city and the victims reportedly cried out for help, but the Colombian security forces took no action to confront the paramilitaries or to track them down as they left Barrancabermeja. There was evidence also that a security force check-point, established on the orders of a local military commander, had been abandoned shortly before the arrival of the paramilitary group.[34]

Barrancabermeja, an oil-refining river port, is the heart of the Magdalena Medio region. The city, with more than 250,000 inhabitants, is wholly dependent on the oil industry and the headquarters for the state-run Ecopetrol (*Empresa Colombiana de Petroleos*, Colombian Oil Company). The Barrancabermeja refinery supplies 60 per cent of Colombia's gas and other fuel needs, and is considered to be a stronghold of the FARC and ELN guerrillas, and to a lesser extent the EPL rebels. For years the paramilitary groups have been working to take control of the city, its population swollen by peasant refugees now living in extensive shanty towns. In 1995 the CREDHOS human-rights group warned of the paramilitary advance in the region, while the *Comité de Derechos Humanos de Sabana de Torres* (Sabana de Torres Human Rights Committee) was repeatedly denouncing the murders and 'disappearances' being committed by the paramilitary groups. On 23 December 1997 an assassination attempt was made against Mario Humberto Calixto, the president of the Committee, forcing him to flee the area. The paramilitaries were continuing a campaign of threats, torture and murders – including the extrajudicial execution of at least eight people in the municipality of Yondo between 21 and 30 December 1996 – but the security forces, with a heavy military presence in the region, took no action. In fact, there were repeated reports of collaboration between the Colombian security forces and the death squad paramilitary groups.[35] The paramilitaries had been allowed to tighten their grip around Barrancabermeja and to begin their comprehensive attack on the city.

The incursion on 16 May 1998 began with heavily-armed gunmen – some wearing hoods, some wearing bullet-proof jackets – moving into the southeastern areas of the city. Customers were forced out of a bar, one reportedly beaten unconscious and left for dead. Two local residents, Juan de Jesus Valdivieso and Pedro Julio Rondon, were forced onto trucks (when the identity of Juan de Jesus was confirmed a paramilitary spoke on a walkie-talkie radio: '*aqui encontramos a este hijo de punta*', 'here we have this son-of-a-bitch'). In the nearby Campestre district the paramilitaries captured several people, slitting the throat of Pedro Julio Rondon who had tried to escape. In the Divino Nino district the gunmen surrounded 500 local residents attending a street party. Many were beaten with rifle butts and kicked, and several were forced onto the military trucks. Elsewhere the paramilitaries forced people to the ground, beat them, shot one man in the legs, and shot another three times in the head, killing him instantly. The police and the security forces, later informed of the killings and abductions, 'made no discernable attempt to pursue the gunmen or track them down'.[36]

The oil workers union, *Union Sindical de Obreros* (USO), Colombia's most powerful union, subsequently denounced the military for allowing the killings and abductions to take place and declared that they had warned the Ecopetrol management of the imminent paramilitary attack on the city. The USO, with the support of many religious and civic leaders, then launched a strike which forced the Colombian government to set up a Commission of Enquiry. On 3 June President Samper received a statement from the AUSAC paramilitaries declaring that the 25 abducted people were 'subversives'; and in August Camilio Aurelio Morantes, the AUSAC commander, stated in an interview by the magazine *Semana* that the detainees had been killed between eight and 15 days after they were abducted because of their links with the Barrancabermeja urban militias. The paramilitary commander said that some of the bodies had been incinerated whilst others had been thrown into the Magdalena River, and he pledged that the offensive against Barrancabermeja would continue.

The Commission of Enquiry was predictably ineffectual. Many of the witnesses and investigators were terrorised by AUSAC death threats; an implicated corporal, initially the only person under investigation to be detained, was freed on a derisory $150 bail bond; the Colombian armed forces, as expected, denied their involvement in any of the atrocities; and in the months after the attack on Barrancabermeja the AUSAC paramilitaries issued death threats against the civilian population of the city, declaring various named individuals to be 'military targets'. Amnesty International concluded:

> Despite the international and national outcry caused by the Barrancabermeja massacre of 16 May 1998, the Colombian Government has still not taken decisive measures to fully investigate the forced 'disappearance' of 25 people and the extrajudicial execution of a further seven. The failure to fully investigate the attack and bring to justice all those responsible has encouraged continued human rights violations in Barrancabermeia and the surrounding regions by paramilitary forces acting with the support or acquiescence of the armed forces.[37]

Barrancabermeja was (and remains) part of a pattern of abduction, murder and massacre that successive Colombian administrations have been unwilling or powerless to combat with firm resolve. Part of the answer is that there is official complicity in many of the horrors of the Colombian wars.

Killings, Disappearances, Massacres

It is plain that the Colombian turmoil has generated a plethora of human-rights abuses, including (as noted) murders, disappearances and massacres – a situation that has persisted for decades. In March 1997 the UN Human Rights Committee was expressing deep concern about evidence that the paramilitary groups were receiving support from members of the military, and that legalisation of the armed vigilante groups (*convivir*) would further aggravate the human-rights situation. The Committee recommended that members of the armed forces and police accused of human rights abuses should be tried by independent civilian courts, that the support given by the military and security forces to the paramilitaries should be investigated, and that the paramilitary groups should be disbanded.[38]

Death threats were being received by human-rights workers and many other types of 'subversives' (trade union leaders, civic officials, community leaders, etc), and 'disposables' were being killed by police-backed paramilitary groups (death squads) in towns and cities throughout Colombia. The urban victims included drug dealers, vagrants, homosexuals, children and suspected delinquents of all sorts. In May 1997 three detainees – Juan Carlos Herrera, Fabian Gomez and Andres Escobar – were abducted from the Valle de Lili juvenile detention centre in Cali, Valle del Cauca, by heavily armed and hooded men. The three were not seen again. In May three detainees were abducted and later found shot dead. In 1997 at least 140 people 'disappeared' after detention by the Colombian security forces of the paramilitary groups. Ramon Osorio Beltran disappeared in April in Medellin when he was seized, together with his young son, by heavily-armed men. The boy was later released but the whereabouts of his father, a leader of the Agricultural Workers Trade Union, remained unknown.[39] In August the Colombian Constitutional Court concluded that human-rights violations such as murder, 'disappearance', torture and rape could not be considered 'acts of service' and should therefore fall within the jurisdiction of the civilian justice

156 Colombia: A Brutal History

system. This was a potentially important Court ruling and it soon brought a military condemnation. General Manuel Bonett Locarno declared that *military* jurisdiction was the 'lifebelt' of the military and that 'if society sends us to fight it has to give us legal protection'.

In June Fidel Castano Gil, a paramilitary leader, had been convicted and sentenced *in absentia* to 30 years' imprisonment for the 'disappearance' and murder of 43 men from Pueblo Dello, Uraba in 1990. Only two of Castano's gunmen were in custody and he remained at large. In September Carlos, brother of Fidel Castano, was charged with the murder of Senator Manuel Cepeda Vargas in 1994, but Carlos too remained at large and continued to operate in various parts of the country. Hundreds of civilians were being killed every year, including the leaders of human-rights groups, trade unionists, politicians, electoral candidates and members of indigenous communities. FARC guerrillas reportedly killed 20 members of the Koreguaje indigenous communities of El Cuerazo, San Luis and Aguas Negras between July and September 1997. In November the FARC rebels dragged Mario Domico and his son David from a meeting and shot them both dead. In March the ACCU paramilitary group killed 30 members of the San José de Apartado 'peace community' in response to its claimed neutrality.[40]

The ELN abducted and killed Jorge Cristo Shaiun, a Liberal senator, in Cucuta in August, and threatened to kill other political figures in North Santander. Then the ELN dynamited a farmhouse in La Union, Antioquia, killing the eleven year-old twins Santiago Andres and Mario Alejandro Lopez. Over the period, at least 600 people were kidnapped and held hostage, mainly by the FARC and ELN guerrilla groups; the victims included politicians, international observers, landowners, businessmen, journalists and judicial officials. Most were released alive, but others were killed when ransom demands were not met or during rescue attempts by the security forces.

In April 1998 Eduardo Umana Mendoza was executed, following the killing of Jesus Maria Valle in February – two of Colombia's most prominent human-rights lawyers. On 4 May a 200-strong paramilitary force killed at least 18 residents of Puerto Alvira village in the municipality of Mapiripan, Meta. A further eight disappeared, and four others were badly injured. Despite repeated warnings from the National Ombudsman that an attack was imminent, the Colombian authorities took no steps to protect the residents. On 16 May the paramilitaries launched the onslaught already described on the city of Barrancabermeja. Of 2104 serious violations of international humanitarian law in 1998, recorded by the *Centro de Investigacion y Educacion Popular*, some 1479 were carried out by the paramilitaries, 531 by the guerrillas and 92 by the army. Through the 1990s political violence was accounting for between 3000 and 4000 deaths a year, with the Permanent Committee for the Defence of Human Rights in Colombia estimating the deaths in 1998 alone at 3832 people killed by political assassination, social cleansing and massacre. Another estimate suggested that 1512 combatants had fallen in battle over the same period. In addition, there were kidnappings, disappearances and the victims of forced displacement.

The pattern was sustained through the 1990s.[41] Thus Amnesty International reported for 1999:

> More than 1000 civilians were killed by the security forces or paramilitary groups operating with their support or acquiescence. Many victims were tortured before being killed. At least 150 people 'disappeared'. Human rights activists were threatened and attacked; at least six were killed. 'Death squad' style killings continued in urban areas. Several army officers were charged in connection with human rights violations; many others continued to evade accountability. Armed opposition groups were responsible for numerous human rights abuses and the taking of hundreds of hostages.[42]

In the same vein the Amnesty International *Report 2000* noted the 'continuing escalation in the long-running armed conflict' and an increase in 'serious human rights violations'. Again the principal victims of political violence were the civilians, particular community leaders in disputed areas – and trade unionists, political and social activists, academics, human-rights defenders, judicial officials, church workers and journalists. It was recorded here that progress had been made in preparing peace talks between the various guerrilla groups (FARC, ELN, EPL) and the government, but many factions were working to prolong the conflict: 'Those working for peace continued to face serious dangers; "death lists" containing the names of prominent peace activists and human rights defenders were publicly circulated in September. Several were killed.'

On 14 January 2000 rightwing death squads shot and killed eight people in the northern Colombian cattle-rearing town of Valledupar, and reportedly killed another seven in the Carribean region of Guajira. The paramilitaries had been responsible for many of the 35,000 civilian deaths over the past decade, with FARC deciding to walk out of the November (1999) peace talks in protest at the government's failure to confront this paramilitary-inspired carnage. On 30 June 2000 the UN World Food Program (WFP), addressing the Colombian situation and fearing an escalation in the conflict, launched an appeal concerning 'the worst humanitarian situation in the western hemisphere'. On 27 July the UN Secretary-General, Kofi Annan, expressed his concern at the human-rights situation in Colombia, particularly the high incidence of kidnappings and massacres of civilians. In the same vein, Human Rights Watch (*World Report 2001*) judged that the paramilitary groups were responsible for 78 per cent of the human-rights violations in the six months from October 1999, and that Colombia's armed forces often collaborated with the paramilitaries.[43]

On 15 August 2000 soldiers launched an attack on children on a school field trip near Pueblo Rico, Antioquia. The adult chaperones screamed as they watched adults and six of the children shot dead. General Jorge Mora, the Colombian army commander commented: 'These are the risks of the war we are engaged in.' Two months before, troops of the Rebeiz Pizarro Battalion had fired on a car, wounding all the six adults and two children returning from a party. More atrocities were committed by the Calima Front, set up by the Third Brigade in Cali in July 1999: in the first year of its existence the Front carried out some 200 killings and displaced more than 10,000 people.[44] On 18 February 2000 the ACCU paramilitaries set up a kangaroo court in the village of El Salado, Bolivar, and for the next two days 'they tortured, garroted, stabbed, decapitated, and shot residents'.[45] One six-year-old girl was tied to a pole and suffocated with a plastic bag; a woman was gang-raped; the authorities later confirmed that 36 people had been killed. A survivor told *The New York Times*: 'To them, it was like a big party. They drank and danced and cheered as they butchered us like hogs.'

During the same period the FARC guerrillas were continuing to murder civilians, to execute captives, to take hostages, and to force thousands of Colombians to flee their homes. During 2000 the group was maintaining 70 battle fronts with an army of around 17,000 trained, uniformed and armed members. The guerrillas were now using weapons that were bound to cause civilians casualties – such as gas canisters packed with gunpowder and shrapnel, and launched as bombs. The use of such devices against Vigia del Fuerte, Antioquia, in March left the town a virtual ruin and caused many civilian casualties, including the town mayor. The FARC rebels executed 21 police agents, among them some who were receiving medical help in the local hospital. Simon Trinidad, a FARC commander, declared in an interview with Human Rights Watch that humanitarian law was 'a bourgeois concept'. At the same time all the groups worked to displace people from their homes and land. In a report released in 2000, Francis Deng, UN representative on internally displaced persons, described Colombia's situation as 'among the gravest in the world ... Displacement in Colombia is not merely incidental to the armed conflict but is also a deliberate strategy of war.' By now there were, in some estimates, at least 1.8 million forcibly displaced people in Colombia with between 80,000 and 105,000 Colombian refugees in Venezuela, Ecuador and Panama. During the first six months of 2000, another 134,000 Colombians were forcibly displaced, most by the paramilitaries.[46]

The abuses continued. On 25 May 2000 Jineth Bedoya, an *El Espectador* reporter, was abducted from the lobby of La Modelo maximum security prison in Bogota, in full view of the guards. She was then drugged, bound, gagged and driven to a city three hours away, where she was beaten, tortured and raped by four men. She was told that the men had plans to kill journalists, before they finally abandoned her at a local garbage dump. In early 2000 paramilitaries attacked La Modelo prison and after a day of fighting the authorities counted 32 dead, including one dismembered prisoner, and dozens of wounded. On 12 February 2001 the British MP Eddie McGrady called on the Westminster government to urge the Colombian authorities to provide better protection for trade unionists from the murder campaigns of the death squads. He noted that the 'violence is perpetrated by paramilitary organisations, aided sometimes openly by the armed forces', and he added that aid to Colombia should not support the armed forces at the expense of trade unionists. It seemed unlikely that the British government would respond to such an appeal. Human rights in Colombia were not a British or a US priority.

Law

There is a substantial body of international humanitarian law that relates directly to the human-rights abuses profiled in the present chapter. Human Rights Watch, for example, has focused on:

> *Article 3 common to the Geneva Conventions of 12 August 1949*
> *Protocol Additional to the Geneva Conventions of 12 August 1949,*
> *and relating to the Protection of Victims of Non-International*
> *Armed Conflicts (Protocol II), 8 June 1977* [47]

The essential difficulty is not in locating relevant international law but in finding ways of enforcing its provisions. Law, domestic or international, without an associated capacity for enforcement is largely impotent, though the *moral* pressures exerted by unenforcible legislation can sometimes produce a worthwhile practical effect. It can be emphasised, with Human Rights Watch, that violations of international humanitarian law 'are not abstract concepts in Colombia but the grim material of everyday life':

> War bursts into the daily activities of a farm, a village, a public bus, or a school with the speed of armed fighters arriving down a path or in four-wheel drive vehicles. Sometimes, armed men carefully choose their victims from lists. Other times, they simply kill those nearby, to spread fear ... a willingness to commit atrocities is among the most striking features of Colombia's war.[48]

The many parties to the conflict are aware of its character, since they are active in shaping it, and equally aware of the rules of war specified in international humanitarian law. But all the parties are committed more to the continuing armed struggle than to law enforcement – a situation that renders the humanitarian problems of Colombia intractable, and the search for justice little more than a fanciful dream. In this context it is useful to stress again the relevance of specific legal instruments which have gained – in theory – an important degree of consensual international support. *Common Article 3*, cited above, addresses armed confrontations between relatively organised armed forces occurring exclusively within the territory of a particular state. *Protocol II Additional*, above, applies to non-international armed conflict where insurgent forces are highly organised and where there is a need to protect civilians and capture combatants. In addition, there is customary international law, the growing and consistent body of relevant legal obligation that has acquired weight through theory and practical effect. It is possible also to cite the general principals of law recognised by 'civilised' nations, and the teachings and judgements of prestigious jurists – as specified in a different context in the Statute of the International Court of Justice (Article 38, c & d).[49]

In the Colombian conflict there is a vast gulf between words and deeds, with all parties manipulating 'the concept of international humanitarian law for perceived political and tactical gain ... much of the opposition to the full compliance with laws of war in Colombia is a cynical justification for continued, deliberate, and atrocious violations of the minimum standards necessary to protect human life'.[50] The parties, all cynical in their calculation of *realpolitik* advantage, have varied in their response to legal obligation. For example, the FARC guerrillas have advertised their observance of international humanitarian law when they have perceived a political advantage in so doing. On many other occasions, highlighted by Human Rights Watch, Amnesty International and other organisations, they have blatantly violated the laws of war, even denying such violations when the evidence is overwhelming. The UC-ELN rebel group has carried out internal discussions of international humanitarian law, and urged negotiations to 'humanise' the political conflict, but this group, like the FARC rebels, continues to commit countless violations in the field. And the same is true of other rebel factions and the dozens of paramilitary groups, all indifferent to the constraints and remands of international humanitarian law in their conduct of the war.

There are legal obligations on all the parties to the conflict.[51] Many of the activities of the guerrillas and the paramilitaries are prohibited in international law, as is much of the behaviour of the Colombian government. Moreover, the United States has particular responsibilities in view of its close relationships with the Colombian security forces and the Colombian military.[52] In reality *all* the parties to the Colombian conflict are acting in violation of international humanitarian law, though in varying degrees according to their respective interests and strategies.

The Continuing Nightmare

In the first seventeen days of 2001 the paramilitaries of the rightwing United Defence Forces of Colombia (Autodefensas Unidas de Colombia, AUC) carried out 23 massacres, one of these (on 17 January in the village of Chengue, Sucre) involving the slaughter of 26 people. It was widely known that the paramilitary death squads were working with the army, sympathetically viewed by Washington. The 24th Brigade of the Colombian army was scheduled to receive US aid and training, despite its well established links with paramilitaries commanded by Carlos Castano.

On 13 February ten gunmen attacked and killed Ivan Villamizar, repeatedly threatened for his work in documenting massacres carried out with army collusion in the La Gabarra region. Again this illustrated the escalating terror that was forcing so many people to flee their homes. In 2000 some 317,000 Colombians became displaced, with 15,000 crossing Colombia's borders to face an uncertain future as refugees. Human rights groups estimated that more than 600,000 people had become displaced since President Pastrana took office in August 1998.

The United States was now actively encouraging the abuse of human rights, not only because of the US ideological accord with the regime and the armed forces that sustained it but also because Washington was overtly easing the pressure for an improvement in the Colombian human rights record. Thus the Clinton administration waived the human rights conditions contained in Public Law 106-246, giving the Colombian military carte blanche for its strategy of active collaboration with the paramilitary death squads. Since the Clinton waiver was invoked on 22 August 2000 the human rights situation had further deteriorated. Human Rights Watch addressed the issue of the waiver (which made the supply of US arms to the Colombian military independent of human rights abuses), and asked President George W. Bush whether he supported the Clinton policy: 'Please explain how requiring the Colombian military to uphold human rights protections threatens the national security interest of the United States.'

On 21 March 2001 three Colombian soldiers, including a lieutenant colonel, were accused of having ties with rightwing death squads responsible for several massacres. The formal accusation, one of several previous cases, was judged by human rights groups to be totally inadequate – in their view only a suspension of Plan Colombia, including more than $1 billion of US military aid, would properly address the scale of human rights violations throughout the country.

On 31 May rightwing death squads in northern Colombia killed eight people, including five young children: about 35 men in camouflage fatigues had entered the village of San Diego, Cesar, and hurled grenades into two homes where terrified children were seeking refuge.

The United States was well aware of the scale of atrocity throughout Colombia. On 11 July José Miguel Vivanco, an executive director of Human Rights Watch, stressed the problem when testifying before a US Senate subcommittee:

> We urge this subcommittee to press Colombia's leaders for real progress on stopping attacks against human rights defenders and ensuring accountability for past murders. Even as Colombian

authorities continue to provide bullet-proof glass for the offices of threatened human rights groups and bullet-proof vests and bodyguards for human rights defenders who receive death threats, these brave individuals continue to be murdered by experienced killers who continue to count on impunity for their crimes.[53]

Human Rights Watch continued to highlight abuses committed by the rebels and a Colombian army prepared to 'promote, work with, support and tolerate' the rightwing paramilitary groups, 'treating them as a force allied to and compatible with their own'. The Clinton waiver was criticised as contributing to a situation in which 'the [Colombian] military appears to have a virtual carte blanche for continued active coordination with paramilitary groups responsible for most human rights violations in Colombia'.[54]

In October 2001, a week after Human Rights Watch had accused the Colombian army of failing to crack down on the paramilitary death squads, at least 62 civilians and three drugs officers were found murdered in various places. In one incident some 60 heavily armed men marched into the village of Alaska, near Cali, rounded up the villagers, separated the men from the women, and then slaughtered all the men. The Human Rights Watch report commented: 'Even as President Andres Pastrana publicly deplores successive atrocities, each seemingly more gruesome than the last, the high-ranking officers he commands fail to take the critical steps necessary to prevent future killings'. On 15 October the rightwing AUC group admitted that it had murdered two Colombian congressmen, claiming that they had links to rebel factions: 'The AUC capital city front, fulfilling in Bogota orders from our organisation's chiefs of staff, killed Octavio Sarmiento and Alfredo Colmanares Chia, both recognised bandits.' On 26 November the rightwing death squads murdered Luis Angel Charrua, a prominent Indian activist, founder of Valbuena's National Organisation of Indigenous Peoples of Colombia (ONIC); two other men were killed at the same time. In the first six months of 2001 about a dozen Indian leaders were murdered and many more received death threats or disappeared.

Paramilitary atrocities were occurring every day.[55] On 29 November paramilitaries massacred 12 people in the village of Montebello, Antioquia. Two days later, the death squads kidnapped Aury Sara Marrugo, regional president of the oil workers' union (USO); his body was found on 5 December.

On 10 January 2002 President George W. Bush signed Public Law 107-

115 which then covered most foreign aid, including $625 million (mostly for Colombia) intended for the Andean region. Section 567 of the law detailed the specific human rights conditions for military assistance to Colombia. The US Congress had removed the waiver option but there were no signs that the Colombian government was working to meet its human rights obligations. In early 2002 Amnesty International, Human Rights Watch and the Washington Office on Latin America (WOLA) issued a joint document to highlight aspects of the US human rights certification provision, and the extent to which the Colombian government was failing to meet its human rights obligations. Many high-ranking officers known to be associated with paramilitary abuses were identified.[56]

The Colombian government had taken no action against these officers: they remained on active service and in some cases, after the perpetration of atrocities, the men were promoted. The armed forces characteristically ignored evidence against senior officers, and prosecutors were often too afraid to conduct effective investigations. In fact it was part of the paramilitary role to eliminate government prosecutors, investigators and crucial witnesses in key cases. Hence the following individuals were assassinated in 2001 and early 2002: Juan Manuel Corzo, director of the attorney general's investigative unit (shot dead as he drove with his mother); José de Jesus Geman, town council member (killed in Bogota hotel); Yolanda Paternina, in charge of the Chenque massacre investigation (shot dead in front of her home); Maria del Rosario Rojas Silva, investigating paramilitary activity in Norte de Santander (shot six times as she left a health clinic); Miguel Ignacio Lora, investigating paramilitary finances (shot dead); Fabio Luis Coley Coronado and Jorge Luis de la Rosa, investigating the Chenque massacre (kidnapped and presumed dead); a former paramilitary pilot, witness in government case (shot dead); and Ivan Villamizar, former public advocate and president of Cucuta Free University (shot dead by ten gunmen).

The joint report also lists specific massacres and more than two dozen specific assassinations regarded as 'benchmark' challenges for investigation by the Colombian authorities. This material also represented a serious challenge to the United States government. Did it really care whether or not the repressive Colombian regime took effective measures to address the rapidly deteriorating human rights situation?

On 19 March 2002 Mary Robinson, UN human rights commissioner, condemned the far-right Colombian death squads for the upsurge in kidnappings, torture and murder, a deterioration that was 'grave, massive and systematic'. In a report to the US human rights commission Robinson declared:

> Unfortunately, throughout 2001 there was a significant deterioration in the human rights situation. The activities of paramilitaries constituted the main cause of these violations and the state cannot ignore its responsibilities.

The pledges made by the Colombian government to combat the paramilitaries had been 'weak and inconsistent' – 'The impunity that those responsible for paramilitary actions enjoy and the limited effectiveness of the state in combating them explain to a great degree the increasing strength of these groups.' The United States, having signalled to the UN that it did not want Mary Robinson to serve another term as human rights commissioner, forced her to step down.

In April human rights groups were reporting a further increase in kidnappings and assassinations of unarmed civilians by rightwing death squads working with the Colombian military. One incident involved paramilitaries working with Fifth Brigade intelligence agents entering a pool hall in the Cecilia Castro neighbourhood of Cucuta, Norte de Santander, and killing four men and a woman. In the first few months of 2002 the death squads had killed more than one hundred people in the area, with the regional security forces not only declining to offer protection but actively participating in the bloodbath. In a separate incident paramilitaries entered the rural area around Palimira and executed four local peasants including a 15-year-old boy. On 13 April two union leaders, Hernan de Jesus Ortiz and José Robeiro Aineda, were shot dead while dining together in a restaurant. On 22 May the United Nations issued a report denouncing the obvious collaboration between the Colombian armed forces and the rightwing paramilitaries.

The nightmare continued through 2002 and into 2003, with the United States, then preoccupied with planning its fresh aggression against Iraq, having no active interest in Colombian human rights – or in human rights elsewhere. On 31 May 2002 Amnesty International again blamed the army and their paramilitary allies for the 'vast majority of extrajudicial executions and "disappearances"', noting that many of the victims 'were tortured before being killed'. Amnesty recorded also that the paramilitary activities had intensified in several regions where 'US-funded units were operating'.

On 17 July Amnesty International representatives met President-elect Alvaro Uribe Velez in London and urged reforms to improve the Colombian human rights situation. There were few signs that useful progress would be made. A 2002 report on abuses of trade unions rights, published by the International Confederation of Free Trade Unions (ICFTU), suggested that workers would remain vulnerable: 'Yet again, activists in public service trade unions were the most frequent targets, primarily because of their recalcitrance in debates about the country's fiscal readjustment policies and privatisations.' In the first seven months of 2002 more than 100 trade unionists were killed – teachers, lecturers, public-sector workers, journalists, workers in health and agriculture, construction workers, food workers, workers in manufacturing energy and science – 'Colombia accounts for 90 per cent of the total number of trade unionists murdered or disappeared in the world.'[57]

American military involvement in Colombia was growing and there was also a developing British involvement, this latter largely kept secret. In 2001 John Spellar, defence minister, said in a written answer to a parliamentary question that releasing such information 'would be harmful to national security, defence or international relations'; in August 2002 the British ministry of defence repeated this evasion.

In September the Colombian government clamped down further on human rights, giving free rein to the security forces to carry out raids and arrests without the need for a warrant. Decree 2002, formerly thrown out by the constitutional court, would allow legal 'disappearances' and the creation of 'rehabilitation zones', under the authority of a military commander, to restrict the free circulation of citizens. It meant that a military dictatorship had been formally established in law.

The nightmare continued. The inhabitants of San Vicente del Caguan and other cities in Colombia's formerly demilitarised zone (DMZ) were suffering from increased violence and human rights abuses, with Amnesty International blaming the guerrillas, the Colombian army and the paramilitary groups. Very few killings were reported in the DMZ before the collapse of peace talks on 20 February 2002, but more than one hundred politically motivated killings had occurred since that time. Paramilitary forces were increasingly perceived as the fastest growing illegal armed group in Colombia, responsible for thousands of murders every year. The government was doing nothing to address the worsening human rights situation, while US military aid continued to escalate.[58]

Amnesty International was expressing further concerns, with

Washington preoccupied with its alleged 'war on terrorism' and the coming onslaught on Iraq. The US-linked companies, intent on oppressing and exploiting the Colombian people, remained sympathetic to the paramilitary death squads and encouraged violence to protect their assets. And the situation was continuing to worsen. Correa commented on the situation in early 2003:

> Because the workers continue to resist this oppression, the paramilitaries now try to kidnap family members. They've burnt union headquarters and destroyed whatever evidence they can so that we are unable to bring a case against them.[59]

On 20 January 2003 some 150 paramilitaries descended on Kuna Paya village and assassinated village leaders Ernesto Ayala, San Pascual Ayala and Luis Enrique Martinez. Luis Caicedo, a local witness, said: 'We found three corpses chopped up by machetes with bullets in their head in the mountains so we couldn't take the corpses back because the land was still being guarded by the paramilitaries.' The mayor of Vasquez, Gilberto Vasquez, was also murdered, his body found with a bullet in his head inside his house in the village. One villager said that the indigenous people had tried to use bows and arrows to confront the paramilitaries because there had been no police in the place for two years. No police had arrived to help the villagers, and two days after the attack there had still been no response from the border patrol.[60]

Elsewhere the paramilitaries were escalating the terror, in some cases targeting women as largely defenceless. Thus the Popular Women's Organisation denounced the most recent killings in Barrancabermeja: 'We reject the violent and criminal wave that is assaulting our city, and in particular violence against women, victimised for being the mother, wife, daughter or lover of an actor in the war, or for defending human rights, or for being a social leader.' Recent assassinations, highlighted by Women's Voices of the Organisation, included:

> Maria del Carmen Cristancho Sanchez, a 40-year-old saleswoman, killed at night on 21 January 2003 in the district of Pozo Siete; left with a sign which said 'For being informant and collaborator of the 24th Front of the FARC';
>
> Diocelina Sanchez Restrepo, 42–year-old lottery ticket seller, taken from a taxi in the Barranca district and killed on 20 January 2003;

Gloria Munoz Lopez, 46 years old, killed at night on 20 January 2003, allegedly by a stray bullet from the gun of a paramilitary.

In early 2003 the leftwing guerrillas were resorting to suicide car bombs, and the paramilitaries continued their assassinations and massacres. In the first ten days of January rightwing assassins killed 57 civilians in the eastern town of Cucuta; with one incident involving unarmed civilians, including a pregnant woman, dragged into the streets and shot. Then US troops were arriving in Arauca on an express anti-guerrilla mission, committed to the training of a 1000-strong Colombian 'Critical Infrastructure Brigade' for the protection of Occidental assets.

On 28 January 2003, on the day that George Bush delivered his state of the union address, General Carlos Ospina, head of the Colombian army, shook hands with his American counterpart and settled down to discussions on US military aid to the Colombian armed forces. It was of interest, though not to Washington, that the Colombian attorney general office had documented the behaviour of troops under Ospina's command on 25 October 1997. On that day Ospina's regular troops and a paramilitary force threw a cordon around the village of El Aro in a region considered sympathetic to the rebel guerrillas. Then the paramilitaries moved in the village:

> They captured a shopkeeper, tied him to a tree, gouged out his eyes, cut off his tongue and castrated him. The other residents tried to flee, but were turned back by Ospina's troops. The paramilitaries then mutilated and beheaded 11 of the villagers, including three children, burned the church, the pharmacy and most of the houses and smashed the water pipes. When they left, they took 30 people with them, who are now listed among Colombia's disappeared.[61]

This multifaceted atrocity, one of thousands, was better documented than most. The reputations of Ospina and his like, close friends of Washington and immune to the demands of law and natural justice, were not in doubt.

The Colombian army – and so the paramilitary death squads – continued to receive lavish US aid, and continued to put it to good use. On 4 February 2003 it was time for the paramilitaries to assassinate Rosario Camejo, private secretary to regional governor Oscar Munoz. They waited until she left her home for work on a Tuesday morning, and then shot her dead – just one more death in tens of thousands.

EIGHT

Looking to Washington (October 1997 to May 1998)

War on Politics

In October 1997 the leftwing guerrillas were escalating their campaign to disrupt the scheduled municipal elections. At the same time the paramilitaries were continuing to target the police, community leaders, trade unionists, key human-rights activists, suspected 'subversives' and others. Two separate attacks – one blamed on the rebels and one on the paramilitaries – had left 28 police, soldiers and prosecutors dead. The second of the attacks, blamed on the guerrillas, wiped out 17 officers in Alto de Bodega. On 6 October President Samper held an emergency 'war council' of Colombia's military top brass to consider the carnage caused by the rebels and rightwing paramilitaries over a 24-hour period. Now the armed forces were on maximum alert.

Some 30 mayors had been killed, and around 1200 candidates had withdrawn in the face of kidnappings and death threats: in some areas there was no-one left to vote for. President Samper was warning the armed factions that their campaign of disruption would not succeed ('We will defeat them'), but most independent observers doubted the ability of the government to establish sufficient order for the electoral process to take place. In September Samper had proposed peace talks with the rebels, but then the military had launched an offensive against rebel strongholds in the south of the country. A 3000-strong force fired a million rounds of automatic fire in Los Llanos de Yari: nine Indian casualties were then reported and the army was accused by congressmen of bungling the operation. The FARC guerrillas responded to the Yari offensive by detonating explosives, hidden in discarded tyres, under the car of General Manuel Bonett, the armed forces commander. He escaped unhurt. At this time, following two official reports, there were repeated charges that the Colombian army was complicit in a wide range of paramilitary atrocities.

Most of the guerilla violence was being directed at political and military targets, but on 15 October three members of the so-called 'peace community' of San José were shot dead, apparently by FARC gunmen. Ramiro Correa and two colleagues had tried to defy the rebels by refusing to sell them food, a posture in line with the community's self-assumed neutrality in the armed struggle. This incident again illustrated San José's vulnerability in the absence of government or international protection. Despite such events, the Colombian authorities remained committed to the elections. Thus Maria Emma Mejia, foreign minister, announced that the vote, scheduled for 26 October, would be overseen by 50 foreign diplomats and observers.

Again there was ample evidence that the conflict was spilling over into areas of Panama. In mid-October Panamanian policemen, with M-16 assault rifles slung over their shoulders, arrived by helicopter in the jungle town of Yaviza at the end of the Pan-American Highway. Over the past year the rightwing Colombian paramilitaries had been conducting a cross-border offensive against leftwing Colombian guerrillas – an escalating confrontation that had brought terror and economic strangulation to the frontier provinces of Darien and Kunayala. The local people doubted that the police would be able to offer effective protection. One resident of Yaviza, not wanting his name to be mentioned, expressed the common view of the Panamanian police: 'They don't do anything.' In fact, after shootouts with the various Colombian forces, which had left one policeman dead and several wounded, the police were under orders not to engage any armed group in the Darien region. The Panamanian army had been disbanded after the United States invasion of 1989, and so far the conflict had cost eight lives and created hundreds of refugees in the area.

The conflict was also causing substantial social disruption. Robberies were now commonplace, and the indigenous Embera, immigrant Colombian farmers and Panamanian colonisers, were afraid to sail down the rivers that served as the principal transport link with the outside world. Health workers had stopped visiting the villages, the crops were going untended, and agricultural projects had come to a standstill. The Panamanian police were finding it convenient to blame the growing conflict on the robbers, but in fact there was a growing confrontation between the ACCU paramilitaries and the FARC guerrillas. The FARC, present in the Darien forests for the previous 30 years, had never terrorised the local communities or launched attacks on the Panamanian police. Instead, the Colombian rebels had preferred to keep a low profile in the region, perhaps kidnapping a few people but mainly using the Darien for resupply, recuperation, and the cultivation and smuggling of cocaine. Some estimates suggested that around 300-400 ACCU troops were advancing towards the Pacific coast in an attempt to trap the FARC rebels in a 'pincer' movement, with 5000 Colombian soldiers in the Choco region of northwest Colombia aiding the ACCU campaign.[1]

The United States was now becoming increasingly concerned at the escalation of the Colombian civil war. On 21 October Barry McCaffrey, President Bill Clinton's drugs tsar, ended a two-year freeze on contact with the Colombian government and began a three-day visit. He arrived in Bogota as the campaign of disruption by the various armed groups against the imminent municipal elections was growing in intensity. Death threats were being received by electoral candidates, forcing some to flee the country. Thus Hernan Motta, the lone senator of Colombia's radical leftwing Patriotic Union (UP) party, left the country after being threatened with assassination (since the party's founding in 1985 around 3500 members had been murdered). On 23 October ELN rebels killed a political candidate and kidnapped two election observers from the Organisation of American States (OAS). Maria Emma Mejia, the Colombian foreign minister, made a radio appeal to the ELN to release the two men, Raul Martinez of Chile and Manfredo Marroquin of Guatemala, and to take her hostage in their place. In a separate incident, the ELN demanded that the 51-year-old Nain Bayona quit the race for the mayor's office in Norte de Santander. She refused to withdraw from the election, whereupon the ELN rebels kidnapped her and then shot her dead.

By the time of the scheduled election (26 October 1997) for mayors, governors, municipal and state bodies, more than 2000 candidates had withdrawn following death threats from leftwing guerrillas and rightwing paramilitaries. More than 50 candidates had been murdered. On 24 October a police officer and an army captain trying to defuse a bomb in Puerto Santander on the Venezuelan border were killed when it exploded. In the days before the elections more than twenty bombs had exploded, targeting police stations, electoral offices and buses in six cities. On 26 October urban Colombians voted in large numbers, despite the continuing risks of bombs and bullets, but in the rural areas, where voters were likely to face greater hazards, few people were prepared to defy the leftwing guerrillas and the rightwing paramilitaries. As usual, the Colombian army seemed incapable of providing a secure environment for the election process. Josue Ancizar, mayor of Cabrera, south of Bogota, reported that not one of the 3500 registered voters had turned out: 'One day the security forces are here and the next day the guerrillas come through. Nobody wanted to risk their lives by voting.' In Cartagena del Chaira, southern Caqueta province, a stronghold of the FARC rebels, only ten of an estimated 4000 eligible people voted.

By any reckoning, much of the election process had been reduced to the level of a fiasco. The death threats had resulted in mass abstentions, and many candidates for local office were elected with only a handful of votes. Thus regional officials were reporting that at least nine mayors were elected with fewer than 20 votes each. Pablo Antonio Hernandez, a mayoral candidate shot dead in Saravena, northeast Colombia, more than a week before the election, won 4870 votes. At the end of October a Colombian court fined the government £135,000 for failing to prevent the assassination of Jaime Pardo Leal, UP presidential candidate, in October 1986. The money was to be paid to his widow and children.

Killers and Cocaine

The successes of the Colombian government in combating the drug cartels had done nothing to end the cocaine traffic. The business remained 'alive and well' and although the notorious drug barons were out of the picture 'their lower-profile successors' were proving elusive to the law enforcement agencies.[2] In the United States there was a massive and growing demand for cocaine and other drugs – which provided a great incentive for business enterprise. New production sites were set up, new smuggling routes developed, and new players came upon the scene. Some of the trade was shifting from the Colombians to the Mexicans, who formerly had been content to move cartel cocaine across the US border. In the same way, Peru and Bolivia, once prepared to serve the Colombians, were by 1998 developing a range of autonomous operations. Some observers were suggesting that the new cartels were becoming as brutal as the Colombian cartels of earlier times. The Russian mafia, including former KGB experts in clandestine operations, were now doing business with Colombian traffickers – to the point that Russian anti-narcotics officials were being given permission to work in Colombia as part of an accord signed on 27 November 1997 by President Samper and Yevgeny Primakov, the Russian foreign minister.

There were still uncertainties about the actual successes of the authorities in tackling the Colombian cartels. The monolithic empire had been severely damaged, if not shattered, but some anti-narcotics specialists suspected that much of the drug trade remained in Cali hands. One Colombian source suggested that lopping the head of the Cali cartel was like taking a hammer to a blob of mercury: 'Hit it with a hammer and it splatters into tiny drops which are much more difficult to spot, but it doesn't stop being mercury.'[3]

The machinations in the drug business were, as always, enmeshed with or running alongside the bloody events of the Colombian civil war. In late-November 1997 a rightwing death squad perpetrated yet another massacre – the fourth in ten days – in the rural area of Dabeiba, Antioquia. Some 14 peasants were killed in this latest atrocity, 22 homes were burned, and 300 more people were forced to flee into nearby mountains in northwest Colombia. President Samper called yet another emergency meeting to discuss the escalating violence. In early December the death squads were reportedly out of control, with 59 people killed in six massacres in the past two weeks. In one incident nine people were dragged from their homes and then summarily shot, while hundreds of men, women and children were being forced to flee.[4] William Parra, President Samper's press secretary, had been kidnapped – presumably by drug traffickers opposed to the Congress vote lifting Colombia's ban on extradition.[5]

The Colombian government responded to the new wave of violence by offering rewards ($385,000 to $770,000) for information leading to the capture of six paramilitary leaders, the 'most wanted' being Carlos Castano, the charismatic and widely-feared leader of the so-called 'headcutters'. President Samper said on television that the killers would be pursued 'to hell if necessary', and he pledged to establish a special police unit to hunt down the death-squad leaders. Already Arnulfo Castillo-Agudelo, Leader of the Black Snake group, had been jailed for 21 years for murder and organising hired assassins, but many observers were sceptical. The army was known to collaborate with the paramilitaries, and the army's support was essential for President Samper's survival. A source at Amnesty International in London, noting that a law establishing a police unit to combat paramilitaries had been passed as long ago as 1989, commented: 'It's just talk. The paramilitaries have a free rein.'[6] Another human-rights activist observed that Carlos Castano, secure in a heavily-guarded jungle base in northern Colombia, was 'Mr Untouchable'.[7]

Human-rights groups were saying that the paramilitary successes against guerrilla factions had led the army and the government to ignore the death-squad killings, and even to help the paramilitaries by supplying intelligence. Some reports were suggesting that the Colombian army and the paramilitaries often worked together on joint operations, with death-squad members sometimes being sent into villages to do the army's dirty work. Castano himself, though funded by large landowners and drug barons, had reportedly distributed 14,000 hectares of farmland to the peasants in order to consolidate his popular support.[8] When the Castano farm was raided by police in 1990, two dozen decomposed corpses were found, many of them showing signs of torture.

On 16 December 1997 President Samper signed an act legalising the extradition of Colombian citizens, but with loopholes to protect the Cali drug barons held in Colombian jails. This meant, from the US perspective, that Samper was not prosecuting the anti-drug war with sufficient commitment, just as he was failing to crush the insurgent forces. In late-December guerrillas captured 18 soldiers after an attack on a mountain-top army base in the south, according to official intelligence sources. An intercepted radio conversation had revealed that hundreds of FARC rebels had overrun the remote Cerro de Patascoy communications base in the Andes, southwest Narino province. In early January 1998 two dozen people were killed in a wave of politically-related violence in northern Colombia, and in Popayan, southwest Colombia, hundreds of rioting prisoners took 585 people – including visiting women – hostage in an overcrowded jail. The 1100 inmates, in a prison designed for 900, were demanding better conditions.

Losing the Battle

In early February 1998 Amnesty International closed its office in Bogota after receiving a 'series of threats', and after the murder of two human-rights workers a few weeks before. On 9 February Shell announced it was selling its 25 per cent stake in the Cravo Norte oil fields and its 37.5 per cent share of an exploration contract in the Samore block. The company denied it was being frightened off by any guerrilla intimidation, even though the Cravo Norte field had been subjected to repeated pipeline bombings causing millions pounds worth of damage and frequent interruptions in production: 'This is a change in strategy in the portfolio and we're going to focus on offshore gas and oil opportunities in Colombia.' The Shell announcement came just days after BP had declared that it was pulling out of large swathes of territory because of security concerns. The ELN guerrillas, led by Manuel Perez, a former Spanish Roman Catholic priest, were targeting Colombia's oil infrastructure as a way of protesting at excessive foreign involvement in the industry.

At the same time a death squad was killing 48 people, burning some alive, in a 10-day orgy of murder in Puerto Assis, Putumayo province. A week later, an official of the International Committee of the Red Cross reported a further massacre – this time of 40 peasants in the villages of El Anzuelo, Puerto Chiare and Rincon de Indio. The government took no specific action to address these massacres, though continuing to wage a war against the guerrillas and the drug trade on several fronts. On 19 February José Nelson Urrego, a presumed heir to the jailed leaders of the Cali cartel, was arrested in Medellin. The Colombian authorities were happy to regard this capture as the effective end of the Cali empire but minister of defence Gilberto Echeverry was urging the community to help the authorities prevent Medellin from regaining the status it had enjoyed in its Escobar days. Now there was speculation that Colombia's new extradition law might cause Urrego to end up in a US jail.

In early March FARC rebels inflicted on the Colombian army one of its bloodiest defeats in more than 70 years of war. General José Sandoval, second-in-command of the Colombian air force, admitted that the fate of 120 soldiers from an élite counter-insurgency unit attacked by guerrillas was unknown, while the rebels were claiming to have killed around 70 and to have captured eight more. One day later, FARC was announcing that 80 troops had been killed, 50 wounded and more captured. General Fernando Tapias, the army's second-in-command, acknowledged that 'more than 100 men', soldiers and rebels, might have died in the fighting. Soon after the attack, about 1000 Colombian troops were reportedly combing the jungle for a 400-strong FARC force. In the last week of March it was reported that troops had killed 12 leftwing guerrillas in western Colombia; that the rebels had killed three people, injured 14 and captured 20 more when troops moved in to dismantle a roadblock in Meta province; and that among the people recently captured by FARC guerrillas were four Americans and an Italian.

President Samper's ruling Liberal Party had won the congressional elections, but with massive abstentions and with at least 19 people killed. Ingrid Betancourt, the prominent critic of the president, was the biggest individual vote-winner in the Senate. The profile of the drug trade had shifted, but Colombia remained one of the most significant suppliers of cocaine to the US market; the government was not winning its war against the leftwing guerrilla organisations, despite army collaboration with the paramilitary death squads; and the scale of the human-rights violations continued to be the worst in the hemisphere. These circumstances were highly conducive to the escalating US involvement in the sovereign affairs of Colombia.

Seeking US Help

On 28 February 1998 Madeleine Albright, the US Secretary of State, said that the Clinton administration had decided to waive the two-year-old sanctions that had been imposed on Colombia. Washington was recognising that the Colombian police and counter-narcotics forces had carried out an 'effective eradication and interdiction effort' against the drug trade. For example, Colombia – with US assistance – had destroyed 160 square miles of coca and 27 square miles of opium poppy in 1997, though the coca crop rose 18 per cent over the period. The United States seemed to be less concerned at such activities as death-squad murders and similar atrocities committed by the Colombian armed forces.

Three days earlier, on 25 February, Victor Carranza, the world's richest emerald dealer, had been arrested on accusations of sponsoring paramilitary death squads. The 63-year-old businessman was arrested at night at the end of a government-run congress in Bogota intended to establish order in the marketplace. The use of 40 heavily-armed special agents in the arrest led to speculation that the Colombian authorities were about to take control of the world's largest emerald industry, long known to be linked to drug trafficking and the paramilitary gangs. Pablo Elias Delgadillo, a Carranza aide, commented that the arrest was not serious: 'In Colombia, everybody who does not get kidnapped or refuses to pay war taxes to the guerrillas is accused of being a paramilitary.' Human-rights activists were reminding people that Carranza's 2000-strong private army, the Black Snake, had killed hundreds of leftists and driven peasants off their land as he built his business empire in Boyaca and the eastern plains. Carranza had also been arrested in the early 1990s after a mass grave had been found on his land.

The Colombian military authorities, reliant on the private armies in the war against the guerrillas, were now admitting for the first time that they were not equal to the task of fighting the Colombian rebels. A military high-command source told the country's parliamentarians: 'In view of the territories involved, the population and the subversive force that we confront, it is clear that our forces are insufficient.' It was clear that the announcement was preparing the ground for more US military assistance and involvement, and that it derived from a visit to Bogota by General Charles Wilhelm, head of the Miami-based US Southern Command, responsible for Latin America. '*The Colombian military is preparing the ground for what they hope will be a greater US involvement in Colombia as soon as the government, which the US views as utterly corrupt, leaves power after the elections in May,*' said one US diplomatic source.[9]

General Wilhelm had urged the Colombian government to strengthen its army while at the same time laying the foundation for a possible political settlement with the opposition forces. The massive defeat earlier in the month of the Third Mobile Brigade had stunned the nation, demoralised the army and heartened the guerrillas. The élite Brigade had supposedly been a highly-professional unit in a largely conscript army, and yet had been comprehensively out-classed by the FARC military force. It was then estimated that there were about 15,000 FARC fighters, well-trained and well-equipped, controlling large areas of forest, moving freely and levying 'taxes' on the cocaine trade. It was plain that the United States was becoming increasingly concerned about an impressive leftist army, benefiting in various ways from the seemingly indestructible drug trade, which the Colombian authorities seemed unable to defeat or even to contain.

The current US aid to Colombia was officially about $37 million, intended mainly for use in the southern half of the country where there seemed to be an obvious alliance between the rebel forces and the drug traffickers. The Pentagon claimed that the aid was mainly spare parts, communications equipment, ammunition and maintenance, but the FARC and other rebel groups reckoned that the US involvement was much deeper. Thus Fabian Ramirez, a FARC commander, commented: 'The claim that the United States is combating drugs in Colombia is a sophism. All the military and economic aid it is giving to the army is to fight the guerrillas, and most army battalions have US advisors.' US ambassador Curtis Kamman had pledged that America would continue to help Colombia by supplying military aid, but had suggested that there would be no increase in the US military presence.

At the end of March the FARC rebels threatened to kill four kidnapped Americans if they were found to have links with the US intelligence agencies. Otherwise, according to Commander 'Romana', head of the FARC 53rd Front, a ransom would be demanded. According to the US State Department, the four men were on a bird-watching trip and were kidnapped at a rebel roadblock on the road running east from Bogota to the town of Villavicencio. Two dozen Colombians and an Italian were also seized as government troops moved in to dislodge the guerrilla forces. On 3 April Thomas Fiore, one of the Americans, set free to deliver a message to the United States government, was found after wandering in the jungle for seven hours. (In another report, the 43-year-old Fiore managed to escape.[10])

The death of 'Father' Manuel Perez Martinez, ELN leader, in February had raised new doubts about any prospect of an early end to Latin America's longest guerrilla insurgency. Nicholas Rodriguez, the new leader, was quick to declare: 'On Father Perez's grave, the ELN swears it will never abandon the oppressed and exploited. It will never give up the revolution.' Over the past four years, more then 22,000 people had been killed, more than half of them civilians, and 500,000 people had fled their rural homes. It seemed that this grim process was set to continue, with the government powerless to control the situation. Alfredo Rangel, a former national security advisor to President Samper, said: 'While the guerrillas go from strength to strength, the state has become a spectator to a confrontation between leftwing guerrillas and rightwing paramilitary groups.' President Samper had recently hailed the inauguration of the National Peace Council, an advisory group comprising 200 mayors, governors and businessmen, as a crucial step towards bringing the rebels and the government together for talks. Five days before Perez died, the ELN and the government signed an accord to begin peace talks in June. Then the rebels withdrew from the agreement, accusing the government of political opportunism in the run-up to the elections. It now seemed clear that the guerrilla forces were gaining in strength, and that the Samper administration had no strategy to contain their advance. The various rebel groups were moving to consolidate their links – with the prospect of a FARC/ELN/EPL union representing an even more daunting challenge to a corrupt and demoralised army.

In mid-April Terry Waite and Terry Anderson, both once held as hostages in Beirut, arrived in Colombia with the support of Nobel Laureate Gabriel Garcia Marquez, in an attempt to secure the release of three American missionaries kidnapped more than five years before, even though it was not known whether the men were still alive. At the end of April 1998 the FARC rebels released two American hostages who had been held for 32 days. Thomas Fiore, the Italian Vito Candela and the 63-year-old Louise Augustine, an American Roman Catholic nun, had been released earlier in the month. In return, the Colombian news media agreed to broadcast a six-point communiqué from the FARC guerrillas denouncing what it described as the long history of United States intervention in Colombia's guerrilla war.

Drugs and the War

On 6 May 1998 the Independent Television Commission (London) announced an inquiry into an award-winning documentary, *The Connection*, that claimed to have penetrated the Cali drug cartel.[11] The film claimed an exclusive interview with the 'number three' in the cartel, tracked an alleged heroin 'mule', and claimed to expose a new heroin route from Colombia to Britain. Allegations had been made that the so-called documentary was no more than a fake exposé of the Colombian drugs trade. On 17 May the Colombian police, seeing a Dutch woman struggling with a heavy suitcase at Bogota's airport, arrested her and found 22 lb of liquid cocaine in shampoo bottles. Commentators speculated on the 'mules' and smuggling that was not being detected.

The bloody wars in Colombia, rooted in drugs and political ideology, continued to swell the human toll of misery and murder. Early in May rightwing paramilitaries had marched into the town of Puerto Alvira, Meta, gunned down 23 people, and then burned down their homes and businesses. Most of 1500 families were forced to flee. The Colombian authorities, knowing that the attack was imminent, had done nothing. Six months before, the paramilitaries had sent 45 letters and faxes, warning of their plan to move out of their northern power base and to penetrate the leftwing guerrillas' strongholds in the coca-growing southeast regions of the country. It was known that three ministers, seven generals, two senior policemen, two local governors and the civil aviation authority had been alerted – and yet the Colombian authorities had left Puerto Alvira undefended.[12] In addition, more than 20 local councils had received similar notification of forthcoming massacres by the paramilitaries, with little prospect of protection by the state. Attacks elsewhere (see *The Rape of Barranca-bermeja*, Chapter 7) had revealed the extent of army involvement in paramilitary atrocities.

The 'headcutters' were running rampage in many areas, while local community leaders and human-rights activists struggled to alert national and international opinion to the impending massacre. Carlos Eduardo Zatizabal, a local activist, said: 'In the absence of an official response to the announcement of future massacres, we are trying to prevent a repeat of Puerto Alvira.' Even the National Ombudsman, José Fernando Castro, was claiming that the Colombian army was negligent in its failure to respond to paramilitary threats, while minister of defence Gilberto Echeverri was acknowledging that the military 'did not have the capacity or the resources to answer every call'. And the minister had denied all charges of conspiracy between the army and the rightwing death squads: 'All manner of things can happen within armed forces as large as Colombia's.' In mid-May some observers were suggesting that the 20th Intelligence Brigade was responsible for a series of death-squad-style assassinations, and Washington went so far as to withdraw the right of General Ivan Ramirez, the unit's commander, to enter the United States – while Washington continued to equip and train the Colombian army. It seemed likely that the massacres would continue, while army chief Mario Hugo Galan denied all charges of conspiracy and refused to take effective action: 'We categorically reject defamatory and irresponsible declarations. We are grateful for all the solidarity expressed against attacks mounted by the enemies of Colombia.'[13]

On 19 May 1998 thousands of Colombians joined hands and waved white flags and handkerchiefs as they marched through major cities to protest against the mounting violence of the civil war. In Cali, a television reporter was shot dead. Now, according to a leaked police report, the rebels had formed as many as 300 guerrilla cells in Bogota's poorest areas, where the police had little presence and where lawless gangs roamed the streets. The report suggested that an estimated 110 rebel sub-commanders were organising training centres in Bogota, along with weapons warehouses and recruitment offices. The rebels already controlled 40 per cent of the rural areas of Colombia, with the US Defence Intelligence Agency now warning that the Colombian army was so ineffective that the leftwing guerrilla groups could seize control of the entire country within five years.

NINE

Pastrana and Power (May 1998 to October 1999)

Voting for Change

On 24 May 1998 heavily-armed leftwing guerrillas attacked the San Isidro jail near the southwestern city of Popayan, releasing a third of the 970 inmates. In the attack 320 prisoners escaped (35 later recaptured) and two inmates and a guard were killed. It seemed that the rebels would again try to undermine the presidential elections scheduled for 31 May, but then the FARC guerrilla chiefs pledged not to use violence to sabotage the 'villainous and deceitful' elections in which Ernesto Samper would no longer be the Liberal Party candidate. At the same time the rebels called on voters to abstain and to forge grass-roots democracy by setting up 'people's councils' at the local level. In many regions of Colombia, with half the total territory outside government control, the FARC pledge seemed worthless.

The intimidation of voters, by both rebels and paramilitaries, appeared to be well entrenched as a permanent feature of the Colombian political process. For example, early in May a FARC guerrilla force moved into the barracks in Puerto Ospina, abruptly abandoned by a Colombian army regiment. Some 200 people, including the village priest, fled up-river in boats – leaving 400 villagers, mostly women and children, to contemplate their future with dread. One mother said: 'I know that one day soon the paramilitaries will come. And they will kill us all.' The village was one of thousands of communities terrorised by the endless war between leftwing rebels, rightwing paramilitaries and the Colombian army.[1] Thus in the town of La Jagua, in the northern oil area of Cesar, mayor Ana Alicia Quinzo was surveying the guerrilla-bombed wreckage of the town hall where the elections would have been held: 'I guess we'll have them somewhere else.'[2]

It seemed likely, despite the war and all the associated impediments to the electoral process, that Colombia was destined for a political shift. It was now clear that Andres Pastrana, heading the conservative Alliance for Change, was leading Horacio Serpa, Liberal Party, who had served as interior minister in the Samper government. In addition, Noemi Sanin, the former foreign minister, was enjoying a huge last-minute wave of support in Bogota and elsewhere in her independent bid to become Colombia's first female president. She had improved trade links with Venezuela, while serving in the Samper administration, but was now rejecting both the Conservative and Liberal Parties – a posture that had appeal for many Colombians disillusioned with decades of ineffectual political leadership.

In many towns and cities throughout the country, especially in Bogota, the intending voters were searched for arms as they approached the voting stations. At least 16 people were killed in election-related violence, and it was hard to estimate precisely how many thousands had been intimidated into abstention. In the event, the Liberal Party's Horacio Serpa won 34.6 per cent of the vote, the Conservative Party's Andres Pastrana 34.4 per cent, and the independent Noemi Sanin a surprising 27 per cent, the best ever result for a Colombian presidential candidate without traditional party support. The result achieved by Sanin, seen by many observers as a significant moral victory, had signalled a fresh element in Colombian politics. It seemed that the traditional parties would no longer be able to dominate the political scene, and already there was speculation about what might happen in a future presidential election. The columnist Ernesto Cortes commented: 'An independent third force has been established ... The strength of Ms Sanin's support will succeed in shifting the agenda of both traditional parties.' And Sanin herself was keen to emphasise that three million Colombians had 'voted in protest and made clear their desire for change'.[3]

The run-off ballot scheduled for 21 June would be between Horacio Serpa and Andres Pastrana, with many voters regretting the exclusion of Sanin. Thus Aleida Montoya, a housewife, noted the 'sad day for the Colombian people – the only candidate to put our interests ahead of those of the ruling élite is out of the race'. And now there was mounting evidence that the electoral process had been deeply flawed. Some 250,000 soldiers and police had been on the streets to safeguard the polling, but – despite the FARC pledge – leftwing guerrillas had allegedly forced the cancellation of voting in 27 towns and kidnapped around two dozen election officials. Some estimates suggested that, despite a 48 per cent abstention level, the 10.6-million-vote represented the highest level of participation ever in a Colombian presidential election. Only 26,878 votes separated the first two candidates. It was plain that Noemi Sanin's Option Life supporters would be crucial in the run-off election.

President Ernesto Samper, soon to be out of power, was now reportedly considering moving to Britain or Spain with his family because of fears for his life.[4] He considered himself to be 'Colombia's most threatened citizen' and judged that a period in Oxford, England, might be prudent until it was safe to return home. The United States had revoked Samper's visa two years before, blocking access to one possible sanctuary, and it was obvious why Samper would have been keen to find some alternative refuge. The leftwing guerrillas in Colombia were stronger than ever; government troops were powerless – or unwilling – to prevent the many death-squad massacres, kidnappings alone were averaging around 50 a week, and the drug trade was thriving. José Fernando Bautista, minister of communications, was well aware of the dismal Samper legacy: 'Everything is destroyed. It's hell. It's going to take four years just to rebuild half of what was ruined in the past four years' – but Samper was continuing to insist that the guerrillas had been weakened ('delegitimised politically … economically weakened in that we have continued to fight against their sources of income'). Ominously, a report issued in March by the US Defence Intelligence Agency (DIA) declared that if the Colombian military did not receive assistance, and did not reorganise and build up its combat effectiveness, Colombia could become a 'narcostate' run by guerrillas, within five years. The scene was being set for increased US involvement in many aspects of Colombian affairs.

The United Nations was already developing a multi-billion-dollar plan to combat the international drug trade, but Washington was judging the scheme to be too expensive and unrealistic.'[5] Washington preferred an escalation of US military involvement, including the use of mercenaries that could be deployed against the leftwing guerrillas.[6] A principal element in the UN scheme was that if Colombian farmers could be given economic incentives to grow maize or potatoes instead of coca then a significant blow would be struck against the cocaine traffic. But here little attention was given to the fact that American agribusiness had already eroded staple production in Colombia and elsewhere. Moreover, US corporations were happy to supply the chemical products needed for the drug trade, just as US banks were keen to profit from the vast injections of narcodollars. The UN plan failed to address many aspects of US corporate philosophy in the real world. In Colombia itself, Colonel Leonardo Gallego, intent on cocaine eradication, knew where his priorities lay: 'We need new American helicopters, Black Hawks, to be able to fly further and longer.'[7] There were plenty of men in Washington who would be keen to oblige.

Many observers, while noting the general relief at the Samper exodus, judged the two presidential candidates in the 21 June run-off to be 'rather uninspiring'[8] – a situation that was not uncongenial to US ambitions (who in Washington would have liked to have seen a charismatic Fidel Castro campaigning in Bogota?). The runoff election was being viewed with widespread apathy – in addition to intimidation another reason for not voting. Well over a million Colombians had been driven from their homes, largely by the rightwing paramilitaries, because the *campesinos* were regarded as an obstacle to the mining and agricultural schemes being pursued by the landed élite. In 1997 the rightwing paramilitaries carried out most of the 185 massacres perpetrated to further the commercial ambitions of businessmen and large landowners. Few Colombians believed that the election would 'do much to mitigate the violence or excise the rottenness at Colombia's core'.[9] Serpa and Pastrana (or 'Serprana' and 'Pasta') were both promising change, radical reform, an end to corruption, economic revival, a close to the civil war. At the same time, the 'headcutters' were becoming more active as the mercenary thugs behind the politicians, mainstream businessmen, the drug traffickers and foreign interests.

Pastrana, supported by Nobel laureate Gabriel Garcia Marquez, was widely seen as a privileged candidate, out of touch with the poor. Serpa, by contrast, was eager to emphasise his working-class roots. In the Colombian cauldron of social chaos, political corruption and rampant violence, the differences between the two men did not amount to much. Hernando Gomez Buendia, a political analyst, saw Pastrana as 'a light person, in all that implies, for a country that doesn't necessarily have light problems'.

Pedro Rodriguez, a peasant farmer driven from his land by soldiers and paramilitaries, judged that Pastrana was 'conservative ... against the poor'. Perhaps Serpa was better: 'He is closer to the people and has made interesting statements about the massacres. But he is also like Samper, and Samper's record was appalling.'[10]

Pastrana Elected

The war was continuing, a greater coca acreage than ever before was now being planted, and the Colombian military seemed as reluctant as ever to confront the excesses of the death-squad paramilitaries. The Medellin cocaine cartel had been crushed, and also the Cali cartel – but then, according to many commentators, Medellin was again assuming its prime position at the heart of the Colombian drug trade. The former Medellin middlemen were taking control of the business, now that the drug barons were either dead or in jail, and the new controllers of the trade 'have a great deal more sense' than Pablo Escobar and the rest of the former cartel leadership.[11] The new bosses were representing the third round of the cocaine enterprise, after the Escobar and Cali phases – and the trade was set to continue. Thus a one-time drug smuggler, asked about whether it would be possible to destroy the drug traffic, replied: 'Not while it brings in so much money.'[12] This was one of the traditional features of Colombian culture against which Andres Pastrana was elected president on 21 June 1998.

After 97 per cent of the votes had been counted, Pastrana had won 50.5 per cent of the vote, and Horacio Serpa 46.4 per cent. The new Conservative president noted that Colombia had 'really voted for a change', and he pledged to make peace with the leftwing rebels and 'to improve the quality of life of 18 million Colombians who live in poverty'. On the night of the run-off election, hundreds of Pastrana's supporters danced and sang outside his campaign headquarters, some shouting 'Andres, Andres'. Jimmy Camargo, Pastrana's campaign advisor, was rejoicing that his candidate had won by more than half a million votes: 'It's incredible. People have rejected business-as-usual. The horrible night is over.' The rebel attacks, it was claimed, had been relatively few – even if there had been a number of deaths, including two police fatalities in an attack on two helicopters near the southern city of Neiva. Pastrana greeted his victory with a predictable declaration: 'Today's result is a victory for all Colombians. Tomorrow begins the fight for reconciliation, for reconstruction, and for peace.' One voter, Carmen Rios, expressed the general mood: the people had wanted change but had finished up with the options of traditional right and left, which, in the hard world of Colombian politics, implied very little change at all: 'I voted for Pastrana, but only for lack of any other option.' The political analyst Andres Riveros noted that the new president had some major obstacles to overcome and that 'a broad spectrum of society' were pinning their hopes on him: '... he has the opportunity to go down in history as the man who picked Colombia up off its knees'.[13]

It remained to be seen whether the 44-year-old Pastrana would have anything new to contribute to the Colombian political scene. After graduating in law at the Rosario University in Bogota he spent time as a magazine editor and a television reporter – on the *Guion* periodical and TV Hoy, respectively (both family businesses). In 1988 he became the first elected mayor in Bogota, having been kidnapped by drug traffickers during the mayoral campaign – an incident that did much to boost his popularity. Pastrana was elected to the senate in 1991, and was defeated by Ernesto Samper in the presidential elections three years later. The new (1998) president was said to believe in market economics and the politics of the centre-right. Some observers judged all this to be a respectable, if unremarkable, pedigree. Perhaps the multifaceted Colombian predicament needed a president with more exceptional talents.

President Andres Pastrana was soon advocating a ten-point program, under the slogan of 'An Alliance for Change'. The ten proposals consisted of a job-creation plan, reductions in the cost of living, support for the agricultural sector, a construction program for housing and infrastructure, moves towards equal opportunities, guarantees for adequate nutrition and good education, an anti-drug plan, making the streets safe, a battle against corruption (through the 'Only Clean Hands on Public Funds' program), and a strategy for domestic peace. Commentators remained doubtful that the new administration would be able to tackle the problem of the paramilitaries sponsored by the landowners, and the fact that the congress would be dominated by the Liberal opposition. Even with the support of dissident and independent Liberals, President Pastrana was still faced with the need to consider the opinions of the five million voters who supported Horacio Serpa in the run-off election. Pastrana confirmed that he would not agree any United States request for the extradition of Ernesto Samper, Colombian president until the new inauguration on 7 August 1998. Samper, for his part, invited Pastrana to 'neutralise hatred', while wishing him 'more loyal and worthy adversaries' than he had encountered during his own administration. Before long, the Pastrana administration was giving cause for concern: for example, analysts noted that plans to merge state agencies as a means of reducing costs would be likely to increase the unemployment level, already standing at 14.5 per cent; and the traditional Right was concerned at Pastrana's evident enthusiasm for early negotiations with the guerrilla leaders.

On 9 July, even before his inauguration, President-elect Pastrana announced that he had held face-to-face talks with Manuel Marulanda Velez, the legendary FARC leader (and, born on 13 May 1928, the world's oldest guerrilla leader). At a secret location outside Bogota, Pastrana and Marulanda had agreed to begin full peace talks by the end of the year. On 12 July Colombian leaders met representatives of the National Liberation Army (ELN) for secret talks in Mainz, Germany, as another tentative step towards ending more than three decades of conflict. In early August president-elect Pastrana met with President Bill Clinton and proclaimed 'a new beginning' in relations. After meeting in the oval Office with Bill Clinton, Attorney-General Janet Reno and General Barry McCaffrey, US drug tsar, Pastrana said: 'The years of mistrust are now behind us'; but noted that he and Clinton had not discussed the lifting of the US sanctions imposed on Colombia. At the same time, death-squad paramilitaries had again moved into the Colombian oil port of Barrancabermeja and fired indiscriminately into bars and discotheques, killing at least eight people and wounding four.

In early September the Pastrana administration's economic proposals were stirring up domestic controversy. For example, one controversial recommendation was the extension of value-added tax (VAT) to goods that served primary needs. Some trade unions supported the moves, while others perceived that the changes would hit the most vulnerable social sectors. The government was also proposing more severe punishment for tax evasion and smuggling, the national expansion of an energy consumption surcharge, budget cuts in non-essential areas, and close monitoring of public expenditure, in order to prevent corruption. Horacio Serpa, amongst others, pointed out that Pastrana had promised to reduce VAT by 4 per cent while the bill in question reduced VAT by only one per cent and extended it to other items – a change that leaders of the United Federation of Workers (CUT) opposed because, by targeting consumer goods, 'it will hurt the working class'.

President Pastrana had now created a 'peace cabinet' and begun to consider the guerrilla demands for a withdrawal of troops from a vast region in conflict and for the creation of a prisoner-exchange process. Already there were plans to demilitarise five municipalities before the end of November 1998. In response, the ELN and the EPL had agreed to free dozens of congressmen and mayors, already held for several months. The ELN had called a unilateral halt to armed operations in August, and was accepting government participation in preparations for a national convention to introduce wide-ranging political reforms, not least the creation of a constituent assembly. Pastrana had stated that the armed forces were ready to participate in the peace process. It remained to be seen where such moves would lead – whether a genuine peace could be achieved, or whether a host of powerful factions, not least the United States, would judge that accords negotiated between an elected Colombian government and leftwing guerrillas would damage their interests.

War and Peace?

On 5 October 1998 guerrillas clashed with Colombian soldiers at Riofrio, west of Bogota, and Apartado, north of the Colombian capital, leaving 16 rebels and one soldier dead, according to the army. A week later, there was a significant move towards possible peace negotiations. The ELN, after a four-day conference in the mountains, Antioquia, agreed to prepare for peace talks with the Colombian government. Yago Pico de Coana, the Spanish ambassador, who had helped oversee the preliminary discussions, commented: 'I sense a strong will for peace and this agreement opens up the possibility of real progress.' Two ELN leaders – Francisco Galan and Felipe Torres – had been briefly allowed out of the Itagui maximum security jail, near Medellin, to take part in the talks. Torres, after a tearful reunion with colleagues after nearly five years in prison, and during a meal of fried pork and plantains, said: 'I feel like I am in heaven. I have returned to embrace the cause which I have always fought for, and had the chance to ride a horse and swim in the river again.'

The government's high commissioner for peace, Victor Ricardo, pledged to evaluate the agreement against the Colombian constitution and the laws that regulated the government's handling of the peace process. The Pastrana administration was also preparing for peace talks with the FARC guerrillas, scheduled to begin on 7 November, giving the ELN an incentive to agree a favourable accommodation with the government. Manuel Marulanda, the

FARC leader, had agreed to become involved in peace talks, provided he was allowed to wear military fatigues. Still, the prospects of a negotiated peace, while the death-squad paramilitaries were waging a terror campaign across the country, seemed remote.

In early November FARC guerrillas stormed the town of Mitu in the southern Amazon jungle, killing 80 policemen and 15 civilians. At the same time, Helmer Pacho Herrera, a former leader of the Cali cartel and one of the world's most powerful drug traffickers, was shot dead while playing football in his Bogota prison yard. Having headed the Cali empire for more than 20 years, he had surrendered two years before, and have begun to give information about his former colleagues in an attempt to win a lenient sentence. Known as 'the man of a thousand faces', Herrera was the last of the seven Cali drug barons to be captured; but then, because of plastic surgery, he could be identified only by fingerprints. His prison assassin, caught after the act, was nearly lynched by pro-Herrera prisoners.

The murders, kidnappings and massacres were continuing, despite preparations for peace talks and Pastrana's declared commitment to negotiated agreements. In early November, Ed Leonard, a 60-year-old worker for a goldmining company, Terramundo Drilling, was kidnapped by FARC guerrillas and offered for ransom, whereupon Norbert Reinhart, the 49-year-old owner of the company, agreed to take the place of his employee. The guerrillas, delighted at the prospect of gaining a more valuable property, agreed the deal – and immediately increased the ransom demand from $500,000 to $800,000. Sophie Legendre, a spokeswoman for the Canadian government, commented on 11 November: 'As far as we are aware it was purely human nature – a compassionate gesture by Mr Reinhart. However, the exchange of hostages is against our government's recommendations.' One estimate suggested that the FARC and ELN guerrilla groups earned together about $250 million from kidnappings in 1997. Most victims were Colombians, but foreigners attracted international media attention and higher ransoms.[14]

In mid-November the remains of 25 murdered children were found in Pereira, western Colombia, possibly caused by the 'social cleansing' of suspected juvenile delinquents in urban areas. It was known that children were being killed in the towns for various reasons. Four children and seven adults were killed and some 66 other people were injured when a natural gas pipeline exploded at Arroyo de Piedra, Atlantico state, 400 miles north of Bogota. The pipelines were frequently being targeted by the guerrillas, but on this occasion officials were suggesting that the explosion was accidental.

Rafael Bohorquez, a health official, commented: 'The blast was so great it sent rocks flying and brought down power and telephone lines. The nearby houses caught fire and their inhabitants have lost nearly everything.' In late-December Pedro Pablo Ramirez, suspected of murdering more than two dozen children and then burying them, often with body parts missing, in ditches in Pereira, was captured.'[15]

Again, the prospect of peace talks was doing little to mitigate the levels of violence. When FARC forces staged an attack on the mountain stronghold of the United Self Defence Forces of Colombia (AUC), the rightwing alliance of paramilitary groups, more than 30 people were killed, including children. The FARC rebels were claiming also that Carlos Castano, the AUC leader, had been killed in the fighting – a claim disputed by Alberto Morales, self-appointed paramilitary spokesman: 'It's been said that he's alive ... that he's still in the area and that he hasn't spoken for security reasons.' In any event the confrontation had been a bloody affair. Burned and dismembered bodies littered the villages around the AUC base at El Nudo de Paramillo, though it was unclear who had caused such carnage. Army commander General Victor Alvarez commented: 'The villages have been completely destroyed. There is only desolation and death.' A local health worker preferred not to believe that men were capable of such 'pure barbarism'. Now it was being suggested that the paramilitaries, bitterly opposed to any accommodations between the Pastrana government and the guerrillas, were committed to sabotaging the forthcoming peace talks.

On 7 January 1999 President Andres Pastrana and Manuel Marulanda, FARC leader, were to have met at the jungle town of San Vincente del Caguan to begin talks intended to end four decades of civil war. Whatever the outcome, the meeting was expected to be historic – the first time that a serving Colombian president had ever met the commander of the most powerful guerrilla army in the country. The talks were intended to be no more than preliminary. President Pastrana had already declared that full-blown negotiations would follow initial agreement on the participants, location and agenda.

All the signs were that the preliminary talks would have been a momentous affair. The FARC leadership had drafted in 5000 peasant farmers, as a show of solidarity, while the Colombian air force was flying in dignitaries from at least 20 countries. A region the size of Switzerland had been turned over to the rebels for 90 days to allow them to assemble without fear of attack. President Pastrana had arrived on 6 January with 60 bodyguards, and FARC guerrillas had combed every inch of San Vincente and set up a ring of checkpoints. All the interested factions – including the United States – were preparing to scrutinise the historic encounter. Washington was already pledged to pump $290 million into the Colombian armed forces through 1999, but Pastrana was declaring, at least in public, that Colombia was on the road to peace: 'There is growing mutual trust which we will continue to nurture, and for the first time a genuine will on all sides to seek a negotiated settlement.' It remained to be seen whether such overt optimism was justified.

In the event Manuel Marulanda failed to show up for the meeting, leaving a dejected Pastrana to speculate on why he had been snubbed by the legendary FARC leader. The president was left sitting beside an empty chair, under the guns of several hundred vigilant FARC guerrillas. Joaquin Gomez, a rebel negotiator, tried to explain: 'Peace is not made with a photo opportunity. We felt our leader's life was in danger. The very fact that we are here is a sign of our commitment to constructing peace with social justice.' At the same time there were reports that the FARC rebels had arrested two gunmen before the peace talks were due to begin. Pastrana declared his continuing commitment: 'I have come here today to keep an appointment with history. We come to the opening of talks with an open agenda, with no intention to veto or to impose issues.' The upshot from this first unsatisfactory encounter was a joint statement indicating the willingness of both sides to negotiate an end to a war that had cost 30,000 lives and left well over a million people homeless since abortive peace efforts were launched seven years before.

More meetings were planned, with no hint about whether Marulanda would attend. The FARC rebels had a radical agenda, and their accumulating military victories in the field suggested that they were not about to abandon their ideological ambitions. Part of the problem was the rural economy, dependent to a large extent on coca cultivation. Paul Reyes, FARC commander, emphasised that the peasants were involved in the growing of coca and poppies 'because they have no other option' but that it was important to search for alternatives. Pastrana had confirmed his offer to implement a $3 billion development plan for Colombia's poor rural areas, when a peace agreement was reached, but there was much more to the FARC vision than that. Marulanda and the rest of the FARC leadership had a comprehensive philosophy of social justice, against the self-interested capitalism of indigenous businessmen, large landowners and international corporations. It seemed unlikely that Pastrana, relying on mainstream political opinion, would be able to square the circle.

In mid-January 1999 Norbert Reinhart, who had traded places with one of his employees taken as a hostage, returned to Canada after having been released by the FARC rebels. He had reflected that hostage-taking was a fundraising matter, not a political statement: 'They killed hostages, but in less than 2 per cent of cases. It wasn't unlike going camping.' Reinhart declared himself out-of-pocket by about C\$230,000. Reinhart's personal initiative had succeeded where a heavy-handed official response would probably have ended in failure.

On 7 January the peace talks between the government and the FARC rebels had been inaugurated, only to be abandoned twelve days later. The rebels declared on 19 January that the peace 'conversations' with the government would be 'frozen' since the Colombian army and police were not doing enough to combat the rightwing paramilitary groups. On 25 January the FARC rebels announced that the peace talks would be frozen for three months, until 20 April, to allow the government enough time to make progress towards eliminating the paramilitaries, perceived as a key element in the government's counter-insurgency strategy. It was now clear that the paramilitary death squads had launched a vicious killing spree, doubtless with the intention of undermining the talks. In a six-day period, from 7 to 12 January, the paramilitaries had killed 160 civilians – an unusually high rate of murder, even for the death squads, that brought no response from the Colombian armed forces. On 13 January Carlos Castano, having evidently survived the earlier FARC attack on the AUC base, sent a letter to President Pastrana announcing an end to the murder campaign and proposing a dialogue with the government. Pastrana, at a press conference during a trip to Cuba (16-17 January), indicated his willingness 'to begin negotiations with the paramilitaries at a different table, separate from the process we are engaged in with the FARC and the one we will soon begin with the ELN'.[16]

The Pastrana response, seemingly agreeing to give the paramilitaries the same status as the rebels in the peace talks, angered the FARC leadership and led to the FARC communiqué of 19 January: 'We are demanding that you, the government, take efficient action to stop the murder of defenceless people. We consider it necessary to freeze the talks and leave our proposals on the table until we see satisfactory results in the fight against the paramilitaries.' It was clear that the freezing of the talks did not mean that the guerrillas were leaving the table. Joachim Gomez commented that the FARC dialogue with the government was 'like a piece of meat, which instead of being put in the oven is left in the freezer to be prepared at a more appropriate moment'. Pastrana responded immediately by postponing a separate series of discussions about a FARC proposal to exchange 452 jailed guerrillas for about 320 army and police personnel then in FARC custody.

The government had wanted to combine the prisoner-exchange talks and the peace discussions in the same negotiating process, but the FARC leadership had insisted on 'separate tables' for the two topics. Victor Ricardo, high commissioner for peace, was now defending the government's efforts to defeat the paramilitaries (despite the widespread assumption that the death squads meshed with official policy). He declared in a letter (20 January) that the government had 'not rested on rhetoric' and emphasised that there had been 'concrete results', with 370 members of the paramilitaries currently in government custody. If the FARC rebels chose to break off talks, declared Ricardo, they would 'place Colombians at risk of being frustrated once again'. President Pastrana too was expressing frustration. In a radio interview (21 January) published in *El Espectador* he commented: 'What we want to know is whether we're going to sit down and negotiate or not. Every Colombian knows we're not going to do away with paramilitarism from one day to the next.' And now Pastrana was also rejecting the FARC demand for a law allowing a blanket prisoner exchange, arguing that those who had committed serious 'crimes against humanity', such as murder and torture, could not be released under any circumstances. Perhaps lesser crimes could be treated differently: 'It depends on where and how, the way the crime was committed.' This suggested that about 100 of 450 FARC members in Colombian prisons might be freed.

The prisoner-exchange discussions took place on 24 January and lasted eight hours, the third and longest official encounter between the two sides. The talks, like the earlier sessions, took part in San Vincente, part of the 'clearance' (*despeje*) zone created as a demilitarised five-municipality region to meet the FARC precondition for talks. The discussions (24 January) were interrupted for 40 minutes when a Colombian air force jet flew loudly over the clearance zone. The Air Force subsequently denied that such an overflight had occurred, but Ricardo acknowledged that the overflight had 'delayed the meeting'. The prisoner-exchange talks quickly moved to the question of the paramilitaries, an issue of primary concern to the FARC rebels. Here a key FARC demand was that the government should end its support for the paramilitary groups – a level of continued support that was fully described in a 19-page document, *Paramilitarism as a State Counter-Insurgency Policy*, submitted by the FARC representatives to their government counterparts.

The report listed a large number of government and military officials whom the guerrillas regarded as paramilitary backers and collaborators. These included ten army generals, five congressmen, one governor, two ex-governors, two former cabinet ministers and Major Royne Chavez, a police official who then headed the president's security unit. General Rosso José Serrano, head of the national police, reacted angrily to the report: 'I will not accept that the FARC become judges of my men.' In the same spirit General Eduardo Herrera Verbel of the army's Fourth Brigade declared that 'as a general and a Colombian' he would not 'respond to accusations from criminals'. And General Rafael Ruiz, commander of the Sixth Brigade and named in the report, condemned the document as 'another pamphlet from those in the FARC who wish to place obstacles before the peace process'. So the peace discussions were suspended until 20 April and the prisoner-exchange talks until 26 April. The entire discussion process had stalled.

The FARC rebels had an obvious interest in government action against the paramilitaries. The paramilitaries would be weakened, so facilitating rebel ambitions for military expansion; and the Colombian army would be forced to deploy troops away from the guerrilla-controlled areas, again aiding the FARC military ambitions. If the FARC leadership had been able to force government action against the paramilitaries, it would be like, according to the *Semana* news magazine, 'killing two birds with one shot, without even firing a shot'. And the FARC leadership also had an interest in a prisoner-exchange agreement – not only because of the desire to free their comrades (very few high-ranking FARC members were in prison), but because such an exchange would grant the rebels the status of 'belligerent force' under international rules of war. In this case, the FARC guerrillas would derive various advantages. The *Semana* magazine (25 January 1999) explained:

> Few understand the implications of this recognition for a guerrilla movement. International law establishes that if a state agrees to a 'change of prisoners of war', it is tacitly accepting the belligerent character of the group taking part. As a consequence, the armed conflict stops being internal and becomes an 'international armed conflict'. This entails a prohibition on punishing prisoners from both sides ... In other words, Colombian prosecutors and judges will be unable to accuse or judge guerrillas who have been captured. The penal code will not apply to them ... the recognition of belligerency automatically means accepting the fact that the guerrillas are seeking

to establish a state ... the sovereignty of the state will be put in serious doubt, and the international community would be obliged to remain neutral until the 'dispute of legitimacies' is resolved through arms.

These are not the only consequences of a 'recognition of belligerency'. It implies also that a state territory may come to be separated to facilitate the establishment of a new independent state or to allow annexation to another state. Moreover, the belligerent group can thereby solicit and obtain diplomatic privileges and immunity, sign international treaties, and trade legally – including for weapons – with other states. There is no need for an official document to exist to confer belligerency status. It is enough, for example, for imprisoned guerrillas to be granted the status of prisoners of war – a principal objective, for obvious reasons, of FARC policy.

There was also the matter of the demilitarised *despeje* zone. Perhaps it would be maintained beyond the original 90 days, a period scheduled to end on 7 February. In his interview (21 January), President Pastrana said that he had not decided whether to extend the period, though there was speculation that this might happen, though for a reduced geographical area (say, from five to three municipalities). And there were other considerations. Pastrana had said also that the discussions could be moved overseas or to neighbouring countries, not least to ease the guerrillas' security concerns. Costa Rica had agreed to host the Colombian peace talks, even to the point that paramilitary groups would be allowed to participate. President Pastrana had also mentioned the options of Venezuela and Spain. For the moment, the peace talks were not going anywhere.

Earthquake and Politics

On 25 January 1999 an earthquake, measuring 6.0 on the Richter scale and the worst in Colombia since 300 people were killed in 1983, ripped through the central coffee-growing region of the country. At least 250 people were killed and 3000 injured; telephone communications were disrupted; and buildings were brought crashing down in at least five provinces. In Bogota tall buildings swayed under the shock, and fractured gas pipes caused fires throughout Pereira where a church and scores of houses collapsed. Television viewers were treated to pictures of a flattened taxi and the body of a woman under concrete. In the city of Armenia, Quindio state, the earthquake demolished a six-storey building, a hotel, a theatre and a police station. By the night, more than 150 bodies had been found in Armenia, 50 in Pereira, 30 in Calarca, and 17 in Circasia. President Pastrana cancelled his planned World Bank meeting in Munich, and flew to Pereira. Late trading in the New York coffee market was reportedly unaffected, but traders had yet to respond to the damage.[17] Rescue teams were sent from Britain, the United States, Russia, Japan, France and other countries.

In the absence of adequate relief supplies, the survivors were looting shops and supermarkets in a desperate battle for food and other essentials. President Pastrana declared that 2000 soldiers and 700 police would be brought in to the town of Armenia to combat the gangs of armed looters: 'I have come to impose order ... We will work to resolve the problems and distribute food adequately to avoid what happened today.' Security forces in Armenia struggled to disperse a crowd of 5000 angry victims, just as baton-wielding police in Calarca tried to stop scores of people looting the local supermarket. One protester commented: 'If nobody else will look after us, we will have to look after ourselves. This is the first food we have seen in three days' (as he carried off a sack of vegetables). A young mother of three, threatened by a policeman, shouted: 'Since Monday [four days before] we have had no homes, no tents, no plastic sheeting, no blankets, no drinking water, no food, no electricity and no medicines. What are we supposed to do?'[18]

The poor administration had aggravated the lack of money and supplies. In the capital, air force officers had failed to prioritise the tons of supplies flooding into Bogota's airport. One aid worker in Armenia judged that the emergency services had no more than 5 to 10 per cent of the material needed.[19] And he criticised also the lack of co-ordination between all parties to the relief effort: 'Those dispatching supplies seem not to be fully aware of the type or quantity of assistance we need. There have been rescue teams teasing certain corpses out of the rubble in the centre while there are still hundreds buried, maybe alive, in outlying areas.' Everywhere there was a lack of essential equipment. And the early casualty estimates were now seen to be wildly optimistic: by 30 January it was known that almost 900 had died, with more than 3500 injured and about 200,000 homeless.

The organised gangs were quick to exploit the situation. Some gunmen had been infiltrating Armenia from Cali, taking advantage of the chaos to loot on a massive scale. By now, President Pastrana had ordered 4000 soldiers and police to the area, but they were unable to guarantee security. Looters were shooting at aid workers,[20] the death squads were exploiting the chaos by continuing to kidnap and murder,[21] looters were posing as relief workers, and human-rights workers were again being targeted by the rightwing paramilitaries.[22] On 2 February an Oxfam official claimed that the death squads were exploiting the effects of the earthquake as a smokescreen to attack human-rights organisations.[23] Thus Oxfam's Richard Hartill judged that the rightwing paramilitaries had killed seven human-rights workers and kidnapped seven more over the previous few days, with other reports suggesting that the death squads had specifically targeted such human-rights organisations as the Instituto Popular de Capacitacion (IPC) in Medellin.[24]

Talking Peace or Not?

On 16 February 1999 Nicolas Rodriguez, the ELN leader, said that the National Liberation Army was breaking off talks with the government because of President Pastrana's failure to withdraw Colombian troops from four municipalities in the northern Bolivar province to allow the negotiations to proceed in a secure environment. The FARC leadership had already suspended their discussions because of the government's unwillingness or inability to crack down on the paramilitaries. It seemed obvious that the peace talks were foundering.

The United States, unenthusiastic about peace talks, was now viewing Colombian affairs with increasing alarm. There was no prospect that the leftwing rebel forces would be defeated by a demoralised and corrupt Colombian army, and the FARC and ELN leaderships seemed able to dictate terms to the Pastrana administration. Nor did it help when three American hostages were killed by a group of FARC guerrillas. The three – 41-year-old Ingrid Washinawatok, 24-year-old Terence Freitas and 39-year-old Lahe'ena'e Gay – had been kidnapped by FARC guerrillas while working with the indigenous U'wa tribe. Later, their bodies, hooded and bound, were found dumped across the border in Venezuela. Each had been shot in the head and chest at least four times, and the bodies showed signs of torture. The Colombian army then released what it claimed was an intercepted radio conversation between German Briceno, a FARC commander, and another rebel: 'Let the bitch die. She's nothing to us.' At first a FARC official denied involvement in the affair, but then Raul Reyes, one of the FARC leaders, admitted the guerrilla responsibility: 'We condemn the abominable assassination of the three Americans' – and implied that the guilty squad leader, the 6-year veteran 'Gildardo', would face rebel justice in Colombia ('We will not turn over our fighters to any state').[25] The FARC leadership appeared keen to placate American opinion, now viewing the rebel statement with caution, though it was plain that the incident had fuelled the hawkish line in Washington.

The paramilitaries were continuing to threaten peasant communities, particularly those judged to be living in guerrilla zones of influence. And even a group of British and Irish organic farmers, maintaining the 3500-acre 'Atlantis' community (in part with income derived from astrology readings), was considering moving into caves to escape from the promised arrival of the 'headcutters'.[26] Community leaders had been concerned that their acceptance by the FARC rebels would render Atlantis a likely target of the death squads. Similar events were unfolding elsewhere throughout rural Colombia. The paramilitaries, with or without government complicity, would target a region and then terrorise local communities into fleeing the area. Then the leftwing guerrillas, aware of the failure of the Colombian army to act, would respond with its own attacks on paramilitary positions – so inevitably causing further casualties, more destruction of property, and further human suffering. On 12 April ELN guerrillas hijacked a Fokker-50 turboprop of the domestic airline Avianca en route to Bogota, taking 35 passengers and crew hostage. The rebels later released some of the hostages, including a three-month-old baby.

On 20 April the peace talks between the Colombian government and the FARC rebels resumed as planned. Again, San Vicente del Caguan was the meeting-place, though there was no assumption that the resumed talks would be any more successful than the first encounter on 7 January. The FARC leadership was continuing to insist that the government take action against the paramilitaries, and earlier in the month President Pastrana had gone so far as to demand the resignations of two army generals known to have collaborated with the paramilitaries in committing atrocities against the civilian population. Analysts were suggesting that the government was responding to FARC pressure and was desperate for progress that would bring an end to the civil war. It seemed that Pastrana had begun to tackle the paramilitary question, that the pact on the demilitarised (*despeje*) zone would be extended beyond its expiry date of 7 May, and that some progress would be made on the prisoner-exchange issue.

On 2 May President Pastrana met Manuel Marulanda for six hours – the first time that a sitting Colombian president had talked face-to-face with a guerrilla leader. The encounter was widely seen as breathing new life into

Pastrana's efforts to achieve a negotiated peace. Four days later, the government and FARC representatives reached a negotiation agenda intended to address a range of political, military, economic and social issues, as the FARC negotiators pressed for the implementation of a broad leftwing agenda. It was agreed that the twelve topics to be negotiated would include military reform, land tenure, distribution of oil wealth, anti-drug programs that would involve crop substitution, political reforms to strengthen democracy, reform of the judicial system, and effective action to combat the rightwing paramilitary groups. The arrival at an agenda did not lead to immediate negotiations, and again it seemed that delays would erode the momentum of the talks.

The two sides had agreed that an international commission would be invited to 'accompany and facilitate' the talks and to help 'overcome any problems that might arise'; and both sides declared that they would organise public hearings around the country to involve civil society in the peace process. The Colombian government announced that it would add a retired general to its five-member negotiating team, as a ploy to increase the chances of armed-forces support for whatever agreements might be reached. There was no talk at this stage of a ceasefire, though it seemed likely that both sides would refrain from any major offensives that might destabilise the peace talks. It was agreed that the FARC guerrillas would maintain control over the five-municipality demilitarised zone in the Meta and Caqueta regions – a situation that now seemed likely to continue indefinitely. The FARC negotiators had quietly dropped an earlier request that a sixth municipality be added to the *despeje* zone as a 'laboratory' for testing new drug-fighting strategies.

Few observers doubted that the May talks represented a ground-breaking event. For example, José Fernando Castro, Colombian public ombudsman, commented: 'This is a huge step forward. It breathes new and very positive air into the peace process.' Pastrana and Marulanda had met for the first time, embraced warmly, and shared a barbecue. But the talks had not yet yielded peace, the paramilitary Carlos Castano was promising a new offensive, and the United States was closely observing developments and working out its own strategy from the sidelines. Pastrana and Marulanda both wanted peace, as they individually defined it, but there were powerful players on the scene who saw no advantage in a Pastrana/FARC agreement and who were intent on escalating the Colombian conflict.

The crucial peace talks were scheduled to be held on 19 July at the stronghold village of La Uribe in the foothills of the Andean eastern cordillera, part of the area that President Pastrana had cleared of Colombian security forces to allow the FARC rebels to negotiate in conditions of security. But then, days before the talks were due to begin, the planned negotiations were postponed because the Colombian government and the FARC rebels were unable to agree on the team of international observers. The guerrillas had launched a nationwide offensive and President Pastrana had adopted a new hardline tone. Both sides, wanting to begin negotiations from a position of strength, were doing no more than eroding the fragile goodwill that had been created in early May. Washington, doubtless much relieved, blamed the FARC rebels for the breakdown in peace talks – and announced plans to increase military aid to the Colombian government, and so to the death-squad paramilitaries.

Politics by Other Means

The preliminary talks, although not leading to the full multi-topic negotiations, had served to consolidate the FARC control of the demilitarised regions. On 8 November 1998 FARC guerrillas had descended on the towns of Mesetas, Vistahermosa and Uribe and set up their barracks under the slogan 'Opening pathways to a new Colombia'. Then they had decorated the towns with metal billboards of Jacobo Arenas, a late commander, and Che Guevara. Slogans in red paint were daubed on walls, urging all teenagers to join the Communist Party. The rebels had taken control, and hostile observers talked about the creation of forced labour camps and gulags.[27] Other commentators were prepared to acknowledge the benefits that the guerrillas had brought to the region.

Order had been restored to an area which, a short time before, during the boom in timber and cocaine, had been ravaged by vice, looting and violence. One man said: 'The guerrillas have managed to end corruption. In one year, FARC has fired five different mayors for embezzlement.' And in the same vein Ricardo Lorenzo Cantalapiedra, a local priest, declared: 'For the past five months, this has been a paradise of peace. Tell the paramilitaries that we're fine.' The FARC rebels were 'showing the government that we can run our own state', even if the local people had to be coerced into support: 'Everyone here has to contribute whether they like it or not.'[28] Elsewhere the familiar modes of conflict continued.

In early May some 300 Colombian police officers fought a day-long battle in an attempt to close a huge cocaine producing complex, deep inside the paramilitary stronghold of Magdalena Medio province. Colonel Leonardo Gallego, head of the Colombian anti-narcotics division, said: 'This is a serious setback to paramilitary groups involved in drug trafficking, and it is only the first. My men will be continuing operations to dismantle other paramilitary laboratories.' On 22 May the AUC paramilitary death squad kidnapped Piedad Cordoba, a member of the opposition Liberal Party and head of the Colombian Senate's human-rights commission. In a radio broadcast the AUC group accused her of supporting leftwing rebels, whereupon a government presidential spokesman demanded her immediate release: 'Acts of force or violence can never be used to sway decisions made about the affairs of state.' Now there was some government disquiet about the demilitarised zone ceded to the FARC guerrillas. On 26 May Rodrigo Lloreda, Colombia's defence minister, resigned in protest at Pastrana's willingness to allow the rebels full control of an area the size of Switzerland. Lloreda was joined by 14 of the country's 30 generals and 200 officers, all opposed to the government's moves to negotiate peace with the rebel groups. Four days later, ELN guerrillas kidnapped more than 100 churchgoers, many of them children, during a children's mass in Cali. Lilliana Cortes, a political analyst, commented: 'It is ironic that while President Andres Pastrana struggles to breathe life into his peace process, the civilian population has been subjected to new heights of terror and abuse.'

On 7 June 1999 hundreds of thousands of Colombians took to the streets of Cali to protest at the new wave of mass kidnappings. The ELN rebels had escaped with 59 churchgoing hostages to a mountain hideout in cattle trucks, a fresh complement of hostages to add to the 25 still held from the Avianca hijack. FARC rebels were also holding civilian hostages, as well as 271 soldiers and 220 policemen, intended for exchange for rebel prisoners held by the government. (In 1998 some 2137 Colombian civilians, six a day, were kidnapped – with 1000 still held in captivity a year later.) The ELN guerrillas were now agreeing to release 30 of its church hostages if the government was prepared to call off its troops for 48 hours.[29]

The peace process and the overall social situation seemed to be permanently mired in violence and confusion. Indigenous tribes (the Embera-Katios) were now demanding a seat at the peace negotiations; the comedian Jaime Garzon was killed on his way to work, generating a 60,000-strong Mass in Bogota's central square; and the government seemed powerless to address Colombia's worst economic recession for 50 years.[30] In mid–June the ELN released 33 bedraggled hostages to an international commission, the first victims to be freed after the recent spate of mass hostage-taking. Most of the hostages, cold and exhausted, refused to talk to the press.

The peace talks, scheduled to recommence on 6 July, were again postponed when the FARC rebels claimed that the United States was preparing to escalate its military intervention in the Colombian civil war. A US State Department spokesman quickly denied the charges but everyone knew that Washington was providing millions of dollars of extra funding to the Colombian military on the pretext of the 'war on drugs'. The Colombian government peace commissioner, Victor Ricardo, read from a joint government/FARC communiqué indicating that the full negotiations would now be rescheduled for 20 July. President Bill Clinton had offered his support for the peace talks, but in response US Republicans had criticised the White House for 'coddling narco-terrorists'. President Pastrana, noting that Colombian fortunes remained a preoccupation of American politicians, observed that 'we are the ham in the US sandwich'. Already Benjamin Gilman, the Republican chairman of the House international relations committee, was supporting Pentagon voices suggesting that it was time for the United States to launch military action against the FARC guerrillas.

On 9 July FARC rebels launched a surprise attack on the Colombian army in the mountains 16 miles east of Bogota, leaving at least 85 people dead and 96 troops missing. Some 500 rebels, commanded by Henry Castellanos ('Romana'), had fought through the night against five army battalions supported by helicopter gunships and air force combat planes. General Fernando Tapias commented that the army had detected rebel movements by satellite over the previous week, and that they had set out from Uribe, the northern Colombian village where the peace talks were due to resume. The Colombian defence minister, Luis Ramirez, said: 'This rebel group thinks the way to arrive with strength at the peace negotiation table is by escalating violence in the zone, but this strategy is absolutely mistaken.' President Pastrana was now decrying the 'demented war' being waged by the rebels, opining that the peace process would be adversely affected. After the bloody attack on Colombian troops near Gutierrez, the FARC leaders were proclaiming that the 'first great offensive' against Bogota itself was being planned, despite the prospect of early peace negotiations.

There were now ample signs of FARC's growing ambitions. On 10 July the rebels launched attacks in more than 20 towns throughout the country, bombing bridges, banks, army bases and oil installations, blocking roads and assaulting police barracks. The clashes near Bogota left about 80 people dead, with the military claiming that air strikes had killed up to 200 guerrilla fighters. President Pastrana then ordered a curfew over 30 per cent of the country. Nestor Humberto Martinez, Colombia's interior minister, announced the curfew: 'The measure basically covers 10 departments of the country. The army and security force presence in other zones is sufficient. The measure also covers the north-east of Cundinamarca.' The curfew was clamped on all travel between nightfall and sunrise for an indefinite period in 10 of Colombia's 32 provinces in the east and south, and in 10 towns on the southern and eastern edge of Bogota. The authorities claimed that the radical measure had been imposed because the guerrillas were preparing to storm regional capitals and might even attempt an assault on Bogota. The FARC and ELN rebels, now in control of half the country, were now judged to be capable of attacking and occupying mid-sized regional centres. By 12 July it was clear that the guerrillas were advancing towards Bogota, in some regions using 'tanks' made from tractors wrapped in steel sheets, and missiles made out of gas canisters. On 13 July the United States expressed its 'outrage' at the rebel offensive and ordered fresh talks between the government and the guerrilla forces.

There were now fresh revelations. The *Cambio* magazine, edited by Gabriel Garcia Marquez, was claiming that rightwing death squads had planned to assassinate President Pastrana during a visit to Muzo earlier in July. The reason was the president's failure to invite the paramilitaries to share the peace table with the FARC rebels. In the event, Pastrana had cancelled his journey by road to the emerald-mining region because of bad weather. The president had fortuitously avoided a possible ambush, but violence was continuing to escalate throughout the country. On 30 July a powerful bomb, at least 45 kg of explosives packed in a lorry, ripped through the Medellin offices of the Colombian army's anti-kidnapping squad, killing at least nine people and wounding 30 more. The squad, Gaula, was devastated and it was not at first clear whether there had also been civilian casualties. The facades of at least a dozen houses were shattered, and vehicles had been flipped over by the force of the explosion. In later reports it was acknowledged that the bomb had flattened four city blocks and was one of the most devastating attacks in Colombia in recent years. General Victor Alvarez, a Colombian army chief, said: 'We've had reports from our helicopters that the town of Narino, 100 miles northwest of Bogota has been partially destroyed, with 40 homes and businesses wrecked.' It was now clear that the rebels were equipped to launch simultaneous attacks on a massive scale.

The death-squad paramilitaries were now also intensifying their operations, in late-August killing 29 people ever a three-day period and forcing hundreds of terrified civilians to flee into neighbouring Venezuela. One of the worst massacres occurred in La Gabarra, when a paramilitary gang marched into the small border town, selected 19 men and women at random, and shot them dead. About a dozen more people had been killed in northern Cesar province and in the southeast region of Huila. The Venezuelan president, Hugo Chavez, commented: 'The Colombian government is in no position to guarantee us security along our frontiers. We have decided to open conversations with the Colombian guerrillas, first, to seek to contribute to the process of peace and, second, to assure Venezuelans greater safety and to keep the conflict on the other side of the border, because it is not a Venezuelan fight.' The UN High Commissioner for Human Rights in Colombia was now condemning the government following another AUC massacre by death squads linked to the military. The Colombian government 'has not taken the measures and actions necessary to guarantee the life and safety of the inhabitants ... The office reminds the Colombian state of its international duty to thoroughly investigate these acts and take action in respect of possible omissions by public officials'. Carlos Castano, AUC leader, admitted on local radio that he had ordered the new wave of killings: 'I can't wait for the guerrillas to put on their uniforms before I kill them.'[31]

On 1 September 1999 more than a million Colombian trade union members, involving both the public and private sectors, and supported by thousands of peasant and grassroots social organisations, took part in a massive general strike to protest against government austerity measures and free-market economic policies. Military sources declared that FARC guerrillas were launching attacks to coincide with the protest. Public transport in Bogota came to a virtual standstill, and most shops and businesses remained closed. Some 200 people were arrested in the capital alone as protesters clashed repeatedly with riot police in working-class neighbourhoods. The demonstrators managed to block several main roads across the country, including a main route through the central coffee-growing area. President Pastrana had urged the workers to call off the strike, saying that it could complicate talks with the International Monetary Fund (IMF) for a $3 billion loan.

The strike was called off when the government agreed to hold month-long talks on privatisation and economic policy. Some 400 FARC guerrillas had fired gas cylinders packed with explosives at the police barracks and a bank in Hato Corozal, Casanare province, with 50 rebels killed as they tried to flee the town. Elsewhere, in the town of Yolombo, northwest Antioquia, a rightwing death squad murdered at least 15 peasants, forcing other villagers to flee. And in another action carried out in solidarity with the general strike, a FARC unit took over a hydroelectric plant in Buenaventura on the Pacific coast.

The peace talks were imminent, though viewed with little optimism. In early September President Pastrana sacked Brigadier-General Alberto Bravo, the third dismissal in the month, for allegedly ignoring the death-squad atrocities in Yolombo, La Gabarra, Tuba and other villages. On 17 September a Colombian peace team met with ELN representatives in Venezuela in an attempt to secure the release of dozens of hostages, and to breathe life into the stalled peace process. Jaime Bernal, Colombian attorney-general, said: 'I don't want to generate expectations and hopes which are baseless.' There were few hopes around.

Again the conflict was intensifying. The death-squad paramilitaries were now conducting a new campaign to derail any realistic chance of useful peace talks. Much of the population was suffering under terror, insecurity and gross economic hardship. And the United States, increasingly angry at Pastrana's failure to roll back the mounting guerrilla successes, was more than ever contemplating the characteristic US option of a heavy military intervention against a popular people's movement.

TEN

The US Involvement

Roots

The growing US involvement in Colombian affairs is far from an isolated or unusual phenomenon. For all of two centuries Washington has assumed the right to intervene in Latin American states whenever it was judged that US interests were at stake. This imperialist posture, rooted in the instincts of economic expansionism, evolved first in competition with 19th-century European colonialism, then under the global challenges of a 70-year Cold War with the Soviet Union, and finally in the context of threats, real or imagined, to US ideological hegemony.

On 2 December 1823 President James Monroe (1758-1831), in his annual address to the US Congress, outlined the principles that would come to shape American policy to regional states for the rest of the 19th century and after. Here the American continents 'are henceforth not to be considered as subjects for future colonisation by any European powers'; 'any attempt' by the nations of Europe to encroach on 'any portion of this hemisphere' should be considered 'as dangerous to our peace and safety'. The lofty principle of *Manifest Destiny* had been invoked to justify the breaching of the so-called 'permanent Indian frontier' in North America, with the genocide of the native Americans that this policy entailed. Now the Monroe principles, dubbed the *Monroe Doctrine* in 1853, were being used to extend the reality of a North American imperialism to the entire hemisphere.

It was easy (and still is) to see the Caribbean as the 'American Mediterranean',[1] and the whole of Latin America as the US 'backyard'. The American imperial impulse slowly gained momentum through the 19th century, briefly diverted in the 1860s by the turmoil of the Civil War but thereafter impacting on the national affairs of states in Latin America and beyond. In 1872 the British prime minister, Benjamin Disraeli, observed that the New World was 'throwing lengthening shades over the Atlantic' and creating 'vast and novel elements in the distribution of power'. It had been noticed that by the end of the Reconstruction period America had begun to evince a marked interest in the Pacific islands and 'even before the Civil War, her interest in such Caribbean territories as Cuba had been intense'.[2] Britain was now dreading 'the rise of a great American maritime empire based on the Caribbean'.[3]

The period saw dozens of US imperial interventions in Latin America (here only a few examples need be given). US Marines landed in Buenos Aires in 1852 to protect American interests; Nicaragua was invaded in 1853, 1854 and 1894; Uruguay in 1855. In 1898 the United States invaded Cuba to give 'the American capitalists what they wanted'.[4] The newly 'independent' Cuba, despite its effective victory over Spanish colonialism, was denied a seat at the US-Spain peace talks in Paris. Cuba was converted into a *de facto* US protectorate, with American forces granted the 'right' to invade again whenever they chose, and with the United States achieving a permanent 'legal' naval base (Guantanamo) on the island. Such events set the pattern for the bloody US interventions in the region in the 20th century – in the interests of strategic and commercial advantage. It was no accident that the brutal dictator General Gerardo Machada Morales, who terrorised Cuba from 1925 to 1933, was an executive of the John Pierpont Morgan financial empire; or that the US military and economic interventions in Latin America would continue to multiply over the decades.[5]

The growing US involvement in Colombia has been associated with a massive deterioration in that country's human-rights record, allowing Colombia to be regarded as the 'champion human rights violator in the hemisphere'.[6] It is significant – in the context of such human-rights abuses (see Chapter 7) and the exposure of the entire political process to kidnappings, terror and assassination – that the United States has chosen at times to depict Colombia as a stable democracy (such enthusiasm has waned in recent years because of the guerrilla successes in the conflict). What the United States meant of course was that Colombia offered good business opportunities where an ineffectual two-party system was unlikely to impede entrepreneurial initiatives and investment returns. At the same time the United States acknowledged that it would be necessary to crush any Colombian groups that showed a commitment to human rights and social justice. Noam Chomsky, activist and academic, notes:

> the constructive advice of a Kennedy military mission to Colombia: 'As necessary execute paramilitary, sabotage, and/or terrorist activities against known communist proponents' (a term that covers peasants, union organizers, human rights activists, etc). The pupils learned the lessons well, compiling the worst human rights record of the 1990s in the hemisphere with increasing US military aid and training.[7]

It is obvious that the US involvement in Colombia predated the 'war on drugs'. A main concern of the United States was to maintain a political framework that would remain reliably supportive of US corporate ambitions. The war on drugs was to be shaped in such a way that this principal concern would be addressed.

In the event, the United States proved unable to arrest the expansion of the leftwing guerrilla movement or to end Colombia's role in the production and distribution of cocaine to the American mainland and elsewhere. In December 1976, the year of the bicentennial celebration of the start of North American independence, Octavio Gonzalez, the head of the US Drug Enforcement Administration (DEA) office in Bogota, was shot dead by Thomas Cole from New York state. The killer was trapped whereupon, according to Washington sources, he committed suicide. But his motives were never made clear, and the Colombian police were reportedly sceptical. Cole's body was found 18 feet from where he died, a rib was shattered, and the two bullets that had penetrated his skull came from different guns. One suggestion was that Cole had been sent to kill the DEA chief because Gonzalez was threatening to expose Central Intelligence Agency (CIA) operations that were undermining the anti-drug campaign.[8] The CIA has always had its own drugs agenda, motivated not least by the need to obtain substantial unauthorised funds for covert operations.[9]

There were other early US setbacks. In May 1976 the square-rigged yacht *Gloria*, the Colombian navy's flagship, set sail from Cartegena on the Caribbean in order to participate in the bicentenary celebrations in New York. Later, the yacht came under US surveillance after four suspected Colombian drug traffickers, arrested in Mexico, admitted to collaborating in a cocaine shipment on the *Gloria*. The ship was searched, and a sailor and a non-commissioned officer were detained aboard after 6kg of cocaine were found in the ventilation system. (One problem was that the *Gloria* enjoyed diplomatic immunity.) It soon emerged that the yacht was carrying vastly more cocaine. On 19 June it was reported in Colombia that a total of 30kg of cocaine had been seized aboard the ship, some of it disguised as coffee. Another 10kg was found under the deck a month later when the Gloria was anchored at Boston. Julio Cesar Turbay Ayala, Colombia's former president and ambassador in the United States, spoke as the yacht sailed up the Hudson River for the bicentennial parade: 'I feel very proud of the *Gloria*'s participation in this celebration.'[10]

The United States was learning about the problems of tackling the Colombian drug trade. There was evidence that the ship's captain had known in advance about the cocaine; that the US authorities had found as much as 150 kg; and that the matter had been hushed up by all sides. It was obvious that Colombian drug trafficking penetrated the highest echelons of the government and the armed forces, and that US–Colombian relations would be threatened if Washington pushed too hard. Hence the United States preferred to maintain Colombia as a staunch ally in its anti-Communist crusade in the region. Successive Colombian governments, contending with their own leftwing guerrillas, could be relied upon to oppose the regional influence of Cuba's Fidel Castro and the Nicaraguan Sandinistas. For the United States the drug trade was a minor matter in the light of such political considerations. The 'war on drugs' would always be sacrificed 'in order to fight Communism in Central America or to protect US control of the Panama Canal', with the option of coupling drug trafficking with leftwing rebels and governments in order to give grounds for US intervention.[11] This was the approach that was set to shape US policy on Colombia over four decades.

With the expansion of the Colombian drug trade in the 1980s, there were signs that the traffickers were exploiting CIA covert operations to ship cocaine into the United States. In fact, the expansion of the Medellin cartel's trafficking activities coincided with the CIA's second largest operation of the decade, aid to the contra guerrillas trying to overthrow the

Sandinista government in Nicaragua. It is remarkable, in this context, that all the major US agencies involved in these matters have stated on the record that the Medellin cartel used the contra forces to smuggle cocaine into the United States. Thus the US State Department reported in July 1986 that 'available evidence points to involvement with drug traffickers by a limited number of persons having various kinds of affiliations with, or political sympathies for, the [contra] resistance groups'.[12] David Westgate, DEA assistant administrator, testified before the US Senate that people 'on both sides' of the Nicaraguan war were drug traffickers 'and a couple of them were pretty significant'.[13] And the head of the CIA's Central American Task Force stated in May 1986 that Eden Pastora, the contras' Southern Front commander, was surrounded by people 'involved in cocaine … His staff and friends … were drug smugglers or involved in drug smuggling'.[14]

Hence the United States, in supporting anti-Sandinista contras known to be involved in cocaine smuggling, was directly complicit in the drug trade.[15] The US State Department preferred to play down the contra link with drug smuggling, but the DEA and the CIA were prepared to admit that leading contra commanders were major traffickers. The Senate subcommittee, chaired by John Kerry, concluded that systematic cocaine smuggling by US-supported contras had become a major element in the regional corruption that had facilitated the expansion of the drug trade. The subcommittee stated that 'individuals associated with the Contra movement' were traffickers; cocaine smugglers had taken part in 'Contra supply operations'; and *the US State Department had made 'payments to drug traffickers … for humanitarian assistance to the Contras, in some cases after the traffickers had been indicted … on drug charges'* (my italics).[16]

It was found also that John Hull, an American expatriate rancher in Costa Rica who was involved with the CIA, had played a leading role in the cocaine traffic across Central America.[17] Moreover, the Christie Institute, a Washington legal advocacy group, lodged charges in a private indictment that CIA agents and former agents had played major roles in the Central American cocaine traffic.[18] In short, the United States – via the CIA and other organisations – was directly complicit in the Colombian cocaine trade that relied on various conduits through Central America. At the start of the US-fomented Nicaraguan war, Honduras and Costa Rica were already well-established transit points for the flying of Medellin-cartel cocaine to the United States.[19] The contras and their CIA backers were quick to see the advantages of tapping into the Medellin cocaine traffic.

In 1982 the United States issued a visa to Pablo Escobar, even though the

US State Department had been informed a year earlier by the DEA that Escobar was among the 'top ten' Colombian cocaine traffickers. Errol Chavez, the first resident DEA agent in Medellin, had risked his life in obtaining information about the cartel. Six of his informants had been murdered – one of them, a cousin of Escobar, found naked with six bullets in his back. Another informant, a member of the Ochoa family, was discovered with his eyes gouged out. On one occasion a human tongue was found thrown into Chavez's garden.[20]

The character of Escobar was well known, rooted as it was in Medellin culture, and yet the US embassy in Bogota decided to give the known drug baron a visa. The decision invited speculation and was never fully explained. Was it merely a bureaucratic blunder, or was Washington protecting relations with Colombia where Escobar held considerable sway? Or was it significant that the US-supported contras in Nicaragua were deriving useful revenues from the Medellin cocaine traffic – even if there was evidence that the Sandinistas were also obtaining drug revenues?[21]

The Colombian drug trade was providing the United States with a fertile pretext for developing its penetration of the region in many different ways. Thus, when Colombia requested that the US install a radar system near its southern border to monitor cocaine-shipment flights, the United States responded by installing a radar system on Colombia's San Andres Island, far from the drug flights, 500 miles from mainland Colombia but only 200 miles off the coast of Nicaragua. The Colombian government charged that the Pentagon was interested primarily in monitoring Nicaragua, not in fighting the drug trade, a charge that was confirmed by other sources. Thus Senator John Kerry's foreign affairs aide appeared to share the Colombian assessment, and the British embassy in Costa Rica, noting that country's request for radar assistance in combating the cocaine traffic, advised that a Pentagon proposal had no relevance to the drug trade but was designed to monitor the Sandinistas.[22] The Kerry Senate Subcommittee reported that the US war against Nicaragua was interfering with 'the US's ability to fight the war on drugs' – which in reality meant that the Reagan administration was exploiting the cocaine traffic 'in pursuit of its international terrorist project in Nicaragua and other imperatives, a standard feature of policy for decades'.[23] Again, the general principle was clear: the 'war on drugs' was a useful pretext for an expansion of US hegemony in the region, and one moreover that could provide helpful covert revenues in particular circumstances. This principle would continue to be central in the shaping of US policy through the 1990s and after. In addition, there was now evidence of blatant Western support for the running of the Colombian cocaine trade.

In July 1988 a Colombian intelligence report noted that at the training camps of the 'hired assassins and drug traffickers in the Magdalena Medio' region 'the presence of Israeli, German and North American instructors' had been detected.[24] The report acknowledged that trainees at the camp, supported by cattle ranchers and farmers involved in coca production and by the Medellin cartel, had 'apparently participated in peasant massacres' in a banana region. In August 1989 British and Israeli trainers were reported, with the *Washington Post* citing another DAS document stating that the men in the training centres were believed to be responsible 'for massacres in rural villages and assassination of left-leaning politicians'. The report further indicated that some of the instructors had gone 'to Honduras and Costa Rica to give training to the Nicaraguan contras'.[25]

The Israeli mercenaries, led by Yair Klein, a former Israeli Defence Force colonel, staged their first, three-week training session in March 1988, while Klein claimed that Colombian military officers knew of their involvement with the paramilitaries and that he was unaware of any drug-trafficking connections. The Israeli press reported that Colonel Klein and his associates used a network of ultra-orthodox American Jews to launder the money they received in Colombia. One Israeli reserve general suggested that the Americans wanted to remove Israel from Colombia 'so that the US can run the arms supply there without interference'.[26] Menachem Shalev, a columnist in the *Jerusalem Post*, asked: 'Why the moral outrage? Is it worse to train loyal troops of drug barons than it is to teach racist killers of Indians, Blacks, Communists, democrats, et cetera?'[27]

In August 1988 a team of eleven British mercenaries led by Peter McAleese, a former SAS member, flew to Colombia and met Colombian military officers who supplied them with full intelligence data and introduced them to former rebels who had surrendered under an amnesty programme. One plan, which never materialised, was to attack the Casa Verde, the mountainous headquarters of the FARC guerrillas in the Meta province. The mercenaries were in no doubt that the Colombian authorities knew of their existence and their activities.[28] Here was a case where Israelis, Britons, Germans and other mercenaries were prepared to carry out 'dirty work' for the United States, including the training and supply of rightwing paramilitaries involved with the drug cartels and peasant massacres.

Drugs, US and Cartels

The United States has often seemed uncertain how to confront the linked problems of the Colombian drug trade and the decades-long civil war. It was not clear how the drug barons could be rooted out without upsetting influential elements of Colombian society (some commentators remembered the *Gloria* fiasco), and there was the perennial problem – which the US had already failed to solve in Cuba, Vietnam and elsewhere – of how to provide effective support for a demoralised army that was being beaten by highly-motivated guerrillas in the field. The plan (already mentioned) to kidnap drug lord Jorgé Ochoa in Venezuela was abandoned in August 1989 when the US State Department began to have doubts, and there was always the vexed issue of extradition (how could Washington induce Colombia to surrender suspected traffickers for trial in US courts?). How, above all, were the guerrilla gains to be reversed?

In the late 1980s all the US Joint Chiefs of Staff were reluctant to send combat units into Colombia to confront the private armies of the cartels and the leftwing rebels accustomed to military struggle as a way of life. Seized weapons shipments had shown the cartels to be as well-equipped as modern infantry battalions – thus making 'the Mafia look like a kindergarten', according to General Alfred Grey, commandant of the US Marines. And if US troops were sent to Colombia they would be sure to come into conflict with the guerrilla armies accustomed to deriving 'tax' revenues from the coca growers. At the same time it was against all the characteristic US instincts to stand by and watch what was – from Washington's perspective – a deteriorating situation. Already US satellites and surveillance aircraft were being used to monitor events in Colombia, and a new military group, Joint Task Force 4, had been sent to the region to track developments. President George Bush had already signalled his decision to send military advisors to Colombia to provide training in counter-insurgency warfare. And there was talk also that a policy applied to Bolivia two years before – US military helicopters transporting police squads on raids – might be used in Colombia.[29] There were the usual anxieties on Capitol Hill that already the United States was becoming too deeply involved in the Colombian turmoil. The US attorney-general had suggested that US combat troops should be sent to Colombia, while others preferred an extension of covert action. In September 1989 President Bush unveiled a $5 billion 'anti-drugs' programme for Colombia. No-one doubted that most of the allocated funds would be used to support the

Colombian armed forces and their paramilitary allies in their endless war against the leftwing rebels.

It now seemed cleared that US policy in the region was in disarray. US and Panamanian drug enforcement officials were warning in the early 1990s that only a short time after the US invasion of Panama in December 1989 – ostensibly to break the grip of the drug traffickers and money launderers – the country was falling back under the domination of the Colombian cocaine cartels. The cartels were flooding Panama with dollars and drugs in an effort to open new shipment routes to Europe and the United States. If Operation Just Cause – involving some 24,000 troops, tanks, aircraft and helicopter gunships, later supplemented by a further 12,000 troops – had failed to suppress drug trafficking in Panama, what sort of US force would be needed to suppress the drug trade in the vastly more inhospitable environment of Colombia? Panama's erstwhile President Manuel Noriega, long-term CIA asset, had been an easy opponent (though the US forces had managed to incur 23 fatalities and 200 wounded by 'friendly fire'), but the battle-hardened troops of the Colombian guerrilla armies, accustomed to fighting in jungle and mountainous terrain, would be an entirely different proposition.

The administration of George Bush (1988-92) was making efforts to develop an anti-drug strategy by concentrating US attention on 'source countries' where the coca leaves were grown and processed into cocaine. By 1990 the US Southern Command, responsible for all US military activities in Latin America and the Caribbean, was declaring the anti-drug campaign its 'number one priority'.[30] But the debate continued about what the precise US role should be. In a telephone interview with Human Rights Watch on 16 March 1996 Colonel James Roach, US military attaché and the Defence Intelligence Agency (DIA) country liaison in Bogota, noted the 'very big debate' about how the United States should have been allocating money for anti-drug operations in Colombia: 'The US was trying to help. But if you're not going to be combatants, you have to find something to do.' One ploy was to provide intelligence.

Colonel Roach described a 14-member team, led by a US Navy captain, which had made recommendations to the Colombian Defence Ministry for the reorganization of their military intelligence networks. The team had included representatives of the DIA, the CIA, US Southern Command and the US embassy's Military Group. A later Defence Department letter (17 March 1996) to Senator Patrick Leahy confirmed the perceived role of the Department as attempting to make Colombia's military intelligence networks 'more efficient and effective'. Roach acknowledged that it was known at the time – even from Colombian military reports – that the Colombian army was working with the rightwing paramilitary groups, despite their appalling human-rights record.[31]

The former Colombian defence minister, Rafael Pardo, in interview with Human Rights Watch (8 February 1996), told how the Defence Ministry, in addition to receiving US recommendations, was soliciting opinions from British and Israeli military intelligence. 'The decisive US input yielded Order 200-05/91, issued in May 1991 by the Colombian Defence Ministry. It is significant that the Order had 'little if anything to do with combating drugs ... throughout its sixteen pages and corresponding appendices, the order ... makes no mention of drugs'.[32] Instead, the Colombian military, following US recommendations, was presenting a plan 'to better combat what they call "escalating terrorism by armed subversion"'.[33] It was plain, as amply demonstrated by Human Rights Watch, that Order 200-05/91 was – amongst other things – laying the basis for a continuation of the covert partnership between the Colombian military and the paramilitaries, a partnership rendered illegal by Decree 1194 which prohibited such contact. In short, the US armed forces had recommended that the Colombian military develop its relationship with the illegal death squads – and the advice had been heeded.

The consequent reorganisation of Colombian military intelligence yielded a number of networks, one based in Barrancabermeja and run by the Colombian navy. This network, deriving from the US recommendations, oversaw dozens of informants and death-squad assassins who were ordered to monitor and attack selected targets throughout the zone. A former Colombian intelligence agent, Saulo Segura, revealed in an interview with Human Rights Watch (18 September 1995) the sorts of targets that would be attacked. These included: the Oil Workers Union (*Union Sindical Obrero*, USO); the San Silvestre Transportation Workers' Union, the Regional Committee for the Defence of Human Rights (*Comité Regional para la Defensa de los Derechos Humanos*, CREDHOS) and the Patriotic Union (UP). The same groups were included in a death threat circulated in January 1992 by the Ariel Otero Command, a paramilitary group.

Hence the United States, under the convenient pretext of the 'war on drugs', was working to develop a counter-insurgency strategy that involved encouraging the collaboration between the Colombian military and the death-squad paramilitaries. Put bluntly, US taxpayers were funding Colombian assassins.

There was also a gradual escalation of the direct US military involvement in Colombia. In early 1994 there was controversy over the announcement that some 150 members of the 46th Battalion of the US Army Engineers Corps, stationed at Fort Rucker, Alabama, would soon be arriving in Valle del Cauca, Colombia, to implement 'civilian aims' (in connection with a joint operation: 'Strong Roads in the South 94'). Commentators were noting that 'civilian aims' implemented by the US army – as in Somalia – inevitably had a military dimension. On 7 January General Octavio Gnecco, commander of Colombia's marines, revealed that the 150-strong US engineer contingent, based 190 miles southwest of Bogota at Bahia Malaga, were not the only US troops in Colombia. A second group of US military personnel was building a naval base on a river in a guerrilla-controlled region: 'In Puerto Lopez we have received the support of the United States government, of the navy, which is helping us to build an advanced river post.' On 9 February President Cesar Gaviria declared that a Colombian court that had accused him of violating the constitution by allowing US troops and military aircraft into Colombia was playing into the hands of drug traffickers and criminals. The high court had concluded that the Colombian president had trampled on national sovereignty.

The issue of US troops in Colombia remained controversial. The Colombian press had commented that the American presence had a possible military objective, with the opposition daily *La Prensa* pointing out that the US troops were not in the country just to build a school and a health centre, and to repair roads – since such tasks could easily have been performed by local labour. Perhaps, opined the press, the real objective was to establish a US-manned radar system on Colombia's Pacific Coast, where the troops had set up camp illegally (that is, without the approval of the Colombian senate or the Council of State, as stipulated in the constitution). Commentators were noticing that 600 US soldiers and policemen had recently arrived in Costa Rica, extending the US capacity to monitor Nicaragua and other states in the region.

The United States was continuing to pressure Colombia into effective action – against drugs and against leftwing guerrillas. A senior US official had commented that diplomatic niceties no longer applied when it came to drug questions (though he refrained from mentioning the rebel successes in the war): 'The whole point is to get the Colombians to do things. These people lie. Three years from now we'll still be hearing about their plans.'[34]

The US war against the drug trade sometimes yielded unexpected results. In early June 1995 three former members of an anti-drugs task force were charged, along with 56 others, for activities associated with the Cali cocaine cartel.[35] One of the accused was Michael Abbell, former chief of the justice department's Office of International Affairs under the Reagan administration. During the 1980s Abbell led efforts to extradite Cali drug barons to the United States, but once he had left the department in 1984 he began work as legal counsel to the Cali cartel, committing criminal acts that went far beyond the legitimate services of a defence lawyer. Donald Ferguson, a former federal prosecutor, was accused of paying 'hush money' to cartel members; while Joel Rosenthal, another former prosecutor, was pleading guilty to money laundering.

The 161-page indictment, the result of 10 years' work, depicted the Cali cartel as a vast organisation managed like a global trading corporation. It was revealed, amongst other things, that 40ft cocaine-filled containers were concealed among timber, coffee and frozen vegetables to elude the US radar planes and ships patrolling the Caribbean. The US lawyers were accused of various criminal acts, including passing on death threats to jailed traffickers and their families to ensure that the cartel leaders would not be embarrassed by unhelpful court testimonies. Joel Rosenthal was quoted as reminding one Cali agent 'what would happen if he did co-operate' with the US authorities. In response, the accused lawyers claimed that the FBI had committed many serious violations of 'attorney-client privilege', carrying out raids on offices and seizing records – some relating to clients not involved in the Cali case.[36] The lawyers also claimed that the FBI was effectively blaming the attorneys for their clients' alleged crimes.

The investigation had included the 'Broccoli Bust' three years before, when a total of six tons of Colombian cocaine had been found buried among frozen broccoli in the port of Miami. George Weise, US Customs Service, acknowledged that the Cali cartel was not about 'to throw in the towel but I think we've had an impact here'; while in Miami US attorney Kendall Coffey declared that the indictment was taking the battle 'against the Cali cartel as far as it can go without multinational co-operation and assistance' – a supposed reference to Bogota, seen by the US as foot-dragging in the anti-drug campaign. However, the Colombian authorities had arrested two senior administration officials – prosecutor-general Orlando Vasquez and comptroller-general David Turbay – under investigation for alleged links with the Cali cartel.[37]

At the same time various practical steps were being taken, however ineffectual, to destroy the drug supply at source. In 1991 Colombian pilots trained by the United States had begun a campaign of crop-spraying, using aircraft supplied by the US government to destroy fields of opium poppies and coca plants by means of the chemical glyphosate, which supposedly disappeared into the soil within a period of ten days. It was claimed that by the mid-1990s thousands of hectares of crops (12,000 hectares in the first half of 1995 alone) had been eradicated in this way. (There were no reports of ecological studies of the impact of vast amounts of poisonous chemicals being dumped on the Colombian countryside.) Still, Washington judged that the Colombians were not doing enough to support the much-hyped 'war on drugs'.

In early 1996 the United States was threatening to withdraw Colombia's certification as a partner in the anti-drug campaign – a move that would seriously affect that country's entitlement to US aid. In a televised speech President Ernesto Samper minimised the threat, saying that he hoped it would be possible to prevent US-Colombian relations from heading into a permanent state of tension. But the scene was set for a new phase of US hostility. Robert Gelbard, US under secretary of state for international drug matters, was questioning the decision of a Colombian parliamentary commission to exonerate President Samper following allegations that he had accepted drug money in his electoral campaign. At the same time US ambassador Myles Frechette was declaring that it would be difficult for Colombia to retain its certification status in 1996. In fact, if the statistics were accurate, the Samper administration had achieved much in its proclaimed battle against the drug trade.[38] It seemed obvious that the US had an interest in demonstrating Colombian failures: if the Bogota administration could not cope with domestic problems that were threatening American interests, then the United States would have no choice but to intervene.

On 1 March 1996 President Bill Clinton declared Colombia an unco-operative nation in the struggle against the drug trade, and accompanied the announcement with sharp economic and aid restrictions against the country. Colombia was not alone: Clinton also denounced Afghanistan, Burma, Iran, Nigeria and Syria for lack of co-operation. By contrast, Mexico, Peru and Bolivia were judged to have won the right to certification, so bringing a variety of aid entitlements. The consequences for Colombia and the other non-co-operative states were potentially serious, since the United States was now committed to voting against them in the international financial institutions. A block on access to international finance could seriously damage domestic economies accustomed to foreign loans.

The Colombian government responded by redoubling its efforts to recover assets from the drug barons, by moving to sign pending anti-drug agreements, and by taking steps to ensure that existing agreements were enforced. A campaign was launched to advertise the effectiveness of the Colombian anti-drug policies, while Rodrigo Pardo, minister of foreign affairs, informed the Colombian press that the battle against drugs would continue with added determination. The US 'decertification' had concentrated the Colombian mind, but perhaps the Bogota administration should not have bothered. It was obvious that Washington was working to its own agenda.

In June 1996 there were persistent rumours, denied by US Southern Command, that the United States intended to invade Colombia along the area that borders Panama. With many Colombians encouraged by press speculation to believe that the US had cast its eye on the Uraba banana-growing-region, Conservative senator Fabio Valencia declared that the United States was 'just a metre away from invading'. Some commentators were even going so far as to suggest that UN peacekeepers should be invited to occupy the area, to prevent the United States from invading one of the most strategically important zones in the Western hemisphere. Uraba, a town of 700,000 inhabitants, was already a focus for violence, drug traffickers, leftwing guerrillas and rightwing paramilitaries (in 1995 there were almost 1000 violent deaths), so Washington – ever keen to preserve what it liked to call 'regional stability' – had ample grounds for a military intervention (to restore peace – and to further the ambitions of US banana distributors). Above all, there was the disturbing matter of the leftwing guerrilla advances. This alone was giving impetus to US plans – and there were many other reasons for American concern.

Marco Tulio Gutierrez, head of Colombia's secret police and a close ally of President Ernesto Samper, was forced to resign following allegations that his agency had been trailing the US ambassador, Myles Frechette, and tapping his phones. On 18 June 1996 Gutierrez dismissed the charges as 'false, ridiculous and slanderous', and then resigned. The United States was now threatening Colombia with economic sanctions, whereupon President Samper commented: 'Relations between our two countries are going through a crisis of mutual confidence. We have a trade balance of almost $10 billion, which is distributed equally. If there is a trade war, they would also be hurt.' On 11 July the United States revoked President Samper's visa because of his alleged links with the Cali cartel. According to Nicholas Burns, State Department spokesman, the administration had decided that

President Samper was 'ineligible for a visitor's visa under US law'. The issue was straightforward: 'Our message today is clear and it is simple. People who knowingly assist narco-traffickers are not welcome in the United States. He is not welcome in the United States.' Washington was now trying to isolate the Colombian president while attempting to maintain co-operative relations with Colombian law-enforcement officers.

The United States remained unconcerned that its aid to Colombia was facilitating the perpetration of atrocities. In October Amnesty International was urging Washington to stop its arms shipments because the Colombian army was using American equipment to commit gross violations of human rights. Amnesty was now accusing the army of widespread killing of innocent *campesinos*, community leaders and human-rights activists over the previous ten years. In September President Clinton had agreed a $40 million military aid package and the sale of seven Black Hawk helicopters, while repeatedly denying that any of the American weapons fed to Bogota had been used to kill civilians. William Schulz, Amnesty's executive director in Washington, declared: 'There are strong reasons for believing that the United States equipped bandits in uniform who killed, among others, people who were inconvenient for the Colombian government.'

While the US government was prepared to arm the death squads, American staff at the US embassy in Bogota were willing to accept bribes from drug traffickers. In October 1997 a convicted Colombian drug trafficker testified to the United States Congress that the Medellin drug cartel had bribed US officials to obtain visas for travel to the United States. The hooded witness, 'Mr Rodriguez', said that an illegal US visa cost $5000 at the time of his arrest three years before. A US government spokesman admitted that the allegations were being taken seriously. At the same time there was growing disquiet about how American military equipment was being used in Colombia. The Clinton military aid package was now being shipped to the Colombian army, with General José Bonett, commander of the Colombian armed forces, acknowledging that the weapons could be used against leftwing rebels, whether or not they were engaged in cocaine operations: 'It's the same organisation, and everyone in it is responsible. You can't say this guerrilla front is good and this one is bad.' President Clinton had not explained his decision to supply the Colombian military with equipment, except to say that the shipments were important to America's national security.

The arms were being shipped, the human-rights abuses were mounting, the steady increase in US involvement continued, and the fields and jungles of Colombia were being sprayed – in scenes reminiscent of Vietnam and Agent Orange – with 'toxic rain'.[39] American officials in Bogota – against the advice of Greenpeace, the Worldwide Fund for Nature, and even the manufacturers, Dow Agrosciences – were saying that tebuthiuron was their choice to accelerate the aerial destruction of coca leaf cultivation deep in Colombia's southern rainforests. The tebuthiuron herbicide ('Spike 20P') carried a label: 'Caution – Do not apply near desirable trees or other woody species. Exposure of even a small part of a plant root system may cause severe plant injury or death.' Even with such a potent weapon the herbicidal campaign seemed futile. About 20,000 acres of coca leaf had been destroyed since 1994 but cultivation was continuing to rise. One report, by the National University in Bogota, even claimed that the programme was essentially counterproductive. Growers under threat moved deeper into the jungle and planted more to absorb the losses; prices were pushed up, adding incentives to the drug traffickers.[40]

While US officials were praising tebuthiuron, in preference to the problematic glyphosate, the manufacturer, Dow Agrosciences, was urging caution: 'It is our desire that tebuthiuron not be used for coca eradication. It could be very risky where the terrain has slopes, rainfall is significant, desirable plants are nearby, and application is made under less than ideal conditions.' All the signs were that the United States was being drawn into another jungle war. US officials were continuing to deny the accelerating pace of the escalation, but in April 1998 the Pentagon was acknowledging that already it had 200 military and civilian personnel in Colombia.[41] The growing US involvement in Colombia's wars seemed obvious to independent observers. Was this a blind drift into a massive military commitment, or part of a planned strategic agenda?

The Growing Involvement

The growing US involvement in Colombia through the 1980s and 1990s was essentially a military matter. In the mid-1990s Cuba offered free medical help to Colombia to fight the encephalitis and dengue epidemics which were devastating the country's coastal regions. There was nothing of this approach in US initiatives. Rather, Washington preferred to pour in an ever increasing volume of armaments to fuel the endless civil war, the plethora of gross human-rights abuses, and the prodigious suffering of a people.

Through the 1990s it was plain that US weapons, *matériel* and training were going to army units with links to the paramilitaries and involvement in human-rights abuses, 'a fact that the United States is aware of but has not made public'.[42] Since the waning of US military support for El Salvador, Colombia had emerged as the hemisphere's top recipient of US aid (through the first half of the 1990s the US provided $322 million in military aid, nearly all on a 'give-away' basis[43]) and much of this was linked to human-rights abuses that Washington preferred not to acknowledge. Colombian officers linked to abuses were being trained by the CIA, and some were themselves even working as instructors at the School of the Americas and the Inter-American Defence College in Washington DC. US arms sales to Colombia through the 1990s were reaching record levels.

In September 1996 the Clinton administration notified Congress of its intention to supply a further $169 million worth of military equipment to Colombia, including 12 Black Hawk helicopters, 24 M60 machine guns, 920,000 rounds of 7.62 mm (M80) ammunition and many other items. The administration was admitting that the military aid was not specifically allocated to the 'war against drugs'. Thus when congressman Lee Hamilton asked if the helicopters could be used '100 per cent for counter-insurgency' if the Colombian army wished, Robert Gelbard, assistant secretary of state for international narcotics matters, replied: 'Theoretically, they could.' It was subsequently announced that President Clinton, using his special drawdown authority, would be donating a further $40 million-worth of military aid, including nine river patrol boats, 32 helicopters, five C-26 observation aircraft, aircraft spare parts, communications gear, field equipment, and various training and utility vehicles. Moreover, it was expected that this massive and escalating supply of military equipment would be supplemented by commercial arms sales.

Throughout this period the Clinton administration seemed largely indifferent to the human-rights abuses being perpetrated by the Colombian army and their paramilitary allies. In 1994 Amnesty International urged the US government to suspend military aid to Colombia until the human-rights issue could be properly addressed. A subsequent memorandum, from staff judge advocate Colonel Warren D. Hall III to his superiors, acknowledged that the United States might be open to criticism for human-rights violations committed by Colombian military personnel trained by US staff; and that US-supplied equipment might be used in operations 'during which human rights violations might occur'. But it was 'unrealistic', noted Hall, for the Colombian military 'to limit use of the equipment' to operations in the war against drugs.[44] In short, the Colombian military was free to use US

training and US-supplied equipment however it wished, even if this involved
selected essentially political targets and committing human-rights abuses.[45]
The links between US involvement in Colombia and such abuses are well
documented by human-rights organisations and other groups. In November
1996 Human Rights Watch commented:

> The United States has taken some steps to address human rights
> violations by the [Colombian] military ... However, we believe that
> the United States should increase pressure on the Colombian military
> by also suspending the visas of officers with records of human rights
> abuses. Even now, officers implicated in serious crimes travel freely in
> the United States ... the United States should screen not only
> individuals, but also units engaged in a pattern of human rights
> violations, including the Luciano D'Elhuyar Battalion. Such units
> should not receive US training or supplies until the Colombian
> government can supply convincing evidence that not only have past
> abuses been fully investigated and those responsible punished, but
> also that there is effective oversight preventing similar abuses from
> occurring.[46]

Such pressure from human-rights groups was not without effect. In 1997 the
US State Department concluded a human-rights report by noting that the
Colombian armed forces had committed 'numerous, serious human rights
abuses'; and that 'the Samper administration has not taken action to curb
increased abuses committed by paramilitary groups, verging on a policy of
tacit acquiescence'.[47] At the same time some Republicans in the US Congress
were complaining that concern about human-rights was hampering the war
against drugs (which they identified with the counter-insurgency
campaign), and urging appropriate action against FARC and the other rebel
groups, now achieving significant successes in the field. On 31 March 1998
General Charles Wilhelm, head of US Southern Command, called
Colombia 'the most threatened country in the United States Southern
Command area of responsibility',[48] and later declared that criticism of
human-rights violations by the Colombian army was 'unfair'.[49]

In late February 1998 the United States decided to lift a range of
sanctions on Colombia, originally imposed because of the country's alleged
lack of co-operation in the anti-drug campaign. Colombia was not being
certified as in full compliance with the US war on drugs, but the decision
meant that it would be easier to supply the country with aid, particularly

military aid that could be used in the counter-insurgency war. It was now plain that Washington was becoming increasingly alarmed at the guerrilla successes against the Bogota regime, and was searching for a policy that would rollback the leftwing advances throughout Colombia. In April the Colombian army – in some assessments, facing collapse – was being described by US advisors as 'vulnerable and incompetent', causing the United States to double the number of military advisors in the country and to supply more Black Hawk helicopters. It was now being reported that the leftwing guerrillas were increasingly well equipped, with access to cargo planes, heavy weapons and even surface-to-air missiles.

The Colombian army was responding by urging ever-increasing US military aid. Thus one veteran soldier in the élite counter-insurgency Battalion Five commented (addressing a British journalist): 'The Americans, even you the British, you should all be fighting this war with us. We are fighting the world's war. It is your war, too.' In the same vein, army commander Manuel José Bonett judged that the Americans were beginning to understand 'the unholy alliance between the drug lords and the guerrillas' and that they knew 'our war is their war'; and Bonett added that he was happy to accept US military aid – even 'atomic bombs'.[50]

Many US policy-makers were urging a greater militarisation of the Colombian war – a persistent pressure to which the Clinton administration seemed keen to respond. In October 1998 the US Congress appropriated a further $280 million to fight the drug war (and so the war against the rebels). In December defence secretary William Cohen announced support for the creation of a joint anti-drug battalion with the Colombian army, including 1000 Colombian soldiers trained and equipped by the United States. And in March 1999 Senator Dewine introduced the so-called Drug Free Century Act to authorise the provision of $1 billion in anti-drug aid for the Western hemisphere over the following two years, a package designed to include massive extra military aid to the Colombian armed forces.

The United States remained broadly unsympathetic to the degree of conciliation that the Colombian government was showing to the rebel organisations. For example, US policy makers were highly critical of the *despeje* (demilitarised zone) scheme, which seemingly allowed the guerrillas to consolidate their grip on much of rural Colombia. Why, it was asked, should the leftwing rebels be allowed to build up their strength in a 'safe' zone and to expand the production of drugs? It was known that the FARC guerrillas were 'taxing' drug production, and that coca cultivation was common in the five municipalities of the *despeje* zone. It seemed obvious in these circumstances that the insurgents could only gain strength by being allowed to produce, distribute and tax cocaine in a wholly safe environment. With such considerations in mind, US congressman Benjamin Gilman, chairman of the House international relations committee, had proposed a bill prohibiting aid to Colombia if the *despeje* policy was implemented, but President Pastrana had managed during a state visit to Washington to convince enough US senators to support a 90-day amendment to the bill to allow a 'grace period' for the *despeje* without a block on US aid. When the FARC guerrillas subsequently proposed a freeze on the peace talks, an advisor to the international committee commented: 'We're not surprised by the FARC decision. What incentive could they have to negotiate when the drug business is going so well for them?' Similarly, Roger Noriega, chief of staff of the Senate Foreign Relations Committee, chaired by Senator Jesse Helms, told *El Tiempo*: 'Everyone recognises President Pastrana's effort and nobody doubts his good intentions. However, these guerrillas are not trustworthy and it's difficult for them to commit to peace when they have so many economic incentives from extortion, kidnapping and narco-trafficking.'

The US State Department, judged *El Tiempo*, 'is more patient than the Congress, invoking the theory that peace processes tend to pass through difficult moments and, for the moment, it is best to give Pastrana room to manoeuvre'. But now the US State Department was facing congressional criticism for allowing a mid-level diplomat to meet with a FARC representative in Costa Rica in December (1998), in circumstances where the Department had possibly lacked the legal authority to agree the meeting. The dispute, relatively trivial, served to highlight the tensions in the Clinton administration over US policy on Colombia. Washington was increasingly disturbed by the drift of events, but what was to be done – apart from continuing the flow of military aid? US aid for Colombia's security and armed forces was scheduled to reach about $300 million in 1999. On 22 January the US ambassador to Colombia, Curtis Kamman, attended the inauguration of the $20 million (US-funded) radar post at the San José del Guaviare military base: 'The hole in Colombian air space, which existed before, is closing. Now there are no holes. There are no places where there is no control.' The radar installation was hyped as an additional weapon in the drugs war, but plainly it could be used for any appropriate surveillance or military purpose.

On 6 July 1999 the leftwing guerrillas in Colombia were warning the United States to stop its military build-up in the country or be enmeshed in a Vietnam-style war. Thus Jorge Briceno, the chief FARC military strategist, declared: 'This isn't Yugoslavia for them to just come in and do whatever they want. Those kinds of troops wouldn't last long here, given all the discomforts and the harshness of the tropical climate.' He had no doubt that the United States was gearing up for direct military intervention in Colombia: '*The north Americans have been intervening here for more than 50 years, but now they want to do it more directly. We're alerting world public opinion to oppose this, because it's no good. Look what happened in Yugoslavia. The north Americans talk about human rights while they bomb a nation and destroy it. They're the world's worst terrorists.*' If the US adopted a direct military role in Colombia's civil way, said Briceno, the conflict would spill over into neighbouring countries: 'If you're attacked at home, what do you do? You have to go where your neighbour is.' Already Washington was sensitive to FARC 'threats' against Panama. General Charles Wilhelm, head of US Southern Command, had admitted that a direct United States intervention, 'either cooperatively with Panama or unilaterally if conditions dictate', was an obligation: '*We are conducting contingency planning to that end.*'[51]

With fresh peace talks between the Colombian government and the FARC rebels scheduled for 19 July, the United States was admitting that it was sharing intelligence with the Colombian security forces – if, according to State Department spokesman James Rubin, such information was critical to protecting either the Colombians who were fighting the drug trade, US personnel or contractors who were providing 'technical assistance'. Rubin was keen to emphasise the 'explicit guarantees' from the Colombian government that the shared information would only be used for the intended purposes: 'If information comes to our attention that this intelligence is being misused or passed to others, we will reconsider. To date, we have no such information.' On 25 July the United States military increased its presence in Colombia to search for a de Havilland surveillance plane that had disappeared in the mountainous region of Putumayo. Lieutenant-Colonel John Snyder, Southern Command, emphasised the scale of the US operation: 'We're bringing more resources into the area and using everything from Navy and Air Force craft to Customs planes. A ground search is a consideration, but this is extremely mountainous terrain.'

On 5 August the United States and Colombia launched a new élite 3000-strong navy unit equipped with gunboats, designed to fight leftwing rebels along the country's extensive river networks. President Pastrana and General Wilhelm attended the ceremony to inaugurate five Colombian

battalions in Puerto Leguizamo, a remote Amazon town close to the border
with Ecuador. US government reports had indicated that US Special Forces,
including Navy SEAL teams, had been training Colombian and Ecuadorian
soldiers in river warfare to fight the leftwing rebels. Said General Wilhelm:
'The guerrillas have a political agenda and drug traffickers have an agenda
which is profit. They are different people, but their agendas have come
together and create a unique challenge for Colombia and the United States.'
It was now clear that Colombia was becoming a top US priority for military
intervention. On 10 August a Washington team that included Thomas
Pickering (State Department), Peter Romero (State) and Brian Sheridan,
head of US Special Forces operations, visited Colombia, just two weeks
after a visit by Barry McCaffrey, drug tsar, and General Wilhelm, Southern
Command head. McCaffrey was now calling for the US military aid
contribution to be increased four-fold to $1 billion in 2000.

In August 1999 it emerged that US embassy staff in Bogota had been
using the Air Force Postal System to ship cocaine to the United States. Eight
embassy staff and family members were being investigated, while Laurie
Hiatt, wife of Colonel James Hiatt, the US military attaché in Bogota, had
been charged with conspiring to send at least six packages of cocaine, each
containing about 2.7lb of the drug (with a total value of $235,000) to the
United States. Observers were noting that, despite all the efforts of US
personnel – including the 200 Special Forces and other troops directed by
Colonel Hiatt, coca production had risen more than 50 per cent in the
previous two years.[52] US policy, according to critics, had gone awry.

By now there was a growing clamour of US opinion urging military
intervention to win the 'war against drugs' and to rollback the leftwing
guerrillas. Thomas Pickering, under-secretary of state, declared on
returning from Colombia that the deployment of US troops was 'a crazy
idea' – just as a thousand US marines were arriving in Colombia for a
'training exercise' and McCaffrey was urging a rapid build-up of the US
military involvement: 'Colombia is in a near crisis situation. This is an
emergency.' Jorge Suarez, FARC deputy commander, warned that if the
United States intervened 'it will see blood flow'.[53] And Cuba's Fidel Castro
was warning that a US military intervention in Colombia would be 'a
colossal disaster' for the world, 'a massive, incredible mistake'.[54] On 26
August the US State Department James Foley announced that Washington
was planning to intervene more heavily in Colombia.

Aid, War and 'Plan Colombia'

The Clinton administration, sensitive to the growing Colombian crisis, was now reconsidering the entire aid policy. One likely consequence was a much enlarged flow of military aid to the armed forces, previously constrained because of tacit but largely ineffectual human-rights considerations.

Washington was also inviting the Colombian government to submit its own estimates of the country's aid requirements – in view of the drugs crisis, the social needs of Colombia, and the war against the well-trained and highly-motivated guerrilla armies. During his visit to Bogota in August 1999, US Under Secretary of State Thomas Pickering asked President Pastrana to provide Washington with a 'plan' for ending the country's spreading conflict, for eliminating drug trafficking, and for dealing with Colombia's other social ills. The intention was for Pastrana to present the 'plan' on 21 September, during a visit to New York for an opening of the UN General Assembly.

The Clinton administration already knew the gist of what would be in the new 'plan'. Fernando Ramirez, Colombian defence minister, and General Fernando Tapias, armed forces chief, had already asked for $500 million in aid over the next two years, a figure that was being reflected in the comments of Washington hawks. According to *The New York Times*, the total aid to Colombia over the following three years was likely to be between $1 billion and $1.5 billion, most of which would be military aid. On 15 September Guillermo Fernandez, Colombia's foreign minister, said that he was hoping for at least $1.5 billion over that period of time. This was all creating tensions in Washington. Liberal congress members were reluctant to underwrite the growing US involvement in Colombian affairs, with the Indiana Republican Dan Burton dismissing aid to the Colombian military as a 'pet project' of Barry McCaffrey.

On 26 August 1999 the United Nations rebuked Colombia over yet another massacre, this one costing 36 lives; and on the following day the columnist Jonathan Power, writing in *The Miami Herald*, commented that the United States could go to war in Colombia 'on the wrong side'. On 2 September it was reported that six 'Super Huey' helicopters – dubbed 'anti-drug helicopters' (in some accounts) – had been delivered to Colombia. Before long the Pastrana 'plan' would propose a massive increase in military aid to the country.

In the event the Pastrana 'plan' proposed expenditure of $7.5 billion over the following three years, with $3.5 billion coming from the United States and other countries. More than half of the funds specified in the proposal would be spent on the Colombian military and police, which meant that $500 million a year would be directed at these targets, compared with the $300 million that the US donated to Colombia's security forces in 1999. The Clinton administration had concluded that more should be spent on Colombia's army than in previous years. This all seemed a recipe for escalating the conflict, for plunging Colombian society into even more violence, and for more human-rights abuses.

The rebels were soon signalling their response to the new proposals. Thus the FARC general secretariat declared: 'The alliance between President Pastrana and the US to step up the war against FARC, under the pretext of fighting drug trafficking casts doubts on the government's will for peace. These factors are not signs of the government's commitment to a long-lasting peace but of a warlike attitude that could lead to a civil war of unforeseeable consequences.' Again the FARC rebels were complaining that the government had done nothing to crack down on the ultra-right death squads or to negotiate on the release of jailed rebels. Such failures were an obstacle to the resumption of peace talks between the Colombian government and the guerrillas.

In his address to the UN General Assembly, during his five-day visit to the United States, President Pastrana called for patience and stressed the need for international aid to make peace with the rebels, to fight the flourishing drugs trade, and to pull the country out of its worst recession for 70 years. On 21 September Pastrana met President Bill Clinton for the second time since taking office the previous August. It now seemed plain that the Clinton administration was endorsing Pastrana's attempt to link the fight against the drug trade with the war against the leftwing rebels. Already the FARC guerrillas were claiming that the United States had at least 10 times the number of military personnel in Colombia than it was saying. Washington was admitting to perhaps 250 military personnel in the country, but FARC commander Ivan Rios was suggesting that there were many more:

> In Colombia, we calculate that there are around 2000 north American military personnel. Some of them are involved in espionage, while others serve as delegates to the various security forces, such as the DAS [state security police] or the police. Still others are training battalions or piloting military spy planes such as the one which crashed [with a number of US fatalities].[55]

Commander Rios warned that Washington's 'spiral of intervention' in Colombia was a dangerous policy: 'It's possible that this isn't going to be like some little Vietnam, but that it will turn out to be a big Vietnam.'

In early October 1999 Colombian troops rescued more than 50 people, including schoolchildren, who had been kidnapped by EPL guerrillas. Two hostages were wounded and a female rebel killed in the fighting. At the same time death-squad paramilitaries were dumping the bullet-riddled bodies of ten peasants in the central square of the small farming village of Guadalupe, and then scrawling in blood on the wall: 'Rebel sympathisers face execution.' Young men had been dragged out of their homes during the midday siesta, then beaten, 'tried' and shot dead as other villagers watched. The Colombian police and a handful of journalists arrived two days later – to find the bodies still on the cobbled-stone square. It was a common event. Over a four-year period more than 5000 people had been killed by the paramilitary group headed by Carlos Castano: 'We will stamp out the guerrilla plague even if it means killing innocent people.'[56] A wave of massacres in the Catatumbo river valley, Norte de Santander, in which more than 70 people were murdered a month before, had been taken as further evidence that the death-squad militaries were operating with the support of the US-supplied Colombian army.[57] On 7 October various human-rights groups condemned the United States for its plan to increase aid to the Colombian military. Thus Carlos Salinas, spokesman for Amnesty International, said: 'Sending US military aid to Colombia is the same policy that backed death squadrons in El Salvador in the 1980s.' It seemed unlikely that such commentary would affect US intentions. Jesse Helms, chairman of the Senate Foreign Relations Committee, emphasising that the leftwing guerrillas were threatening neighbouring countries, declared that without US help 'Colombia could lose this war – or seek to appease the narco-guerrillas'.

Fresh peace talks were scheduled for 24 October, though few observers expected them to achieve much. A communiqué, signed by the Colombian government chief negotiator, Victor Ricardo, and three prominent FARC commanders, was read over a local radio network. The declared goal, in getting the talks back on track, was 'to reach an agreement to find peace for Colombians'. But such developments did nothing to constrain US plans for a massive military intervention in Colombia.[58] Already hundreds of US 'green beret' trainers were working with the Colombian army, massive supplies of military equipment were being shipped in, and the US Congress was likely to approve an overall military aid package that could reach $2 billion over the next two years – Washington's largest military commitment in Latin America for a generation.[59] Colombian Colonel Carlos Suarez commented: 'We need helicopters, maybe 300 of them, we need long-range howitzers. By the sounds of it, we are going to receive much of what we need.' Pastrana was trying to keep the peace option alive, but he had talked with the Americans – who preferred war: 'I've been to the jungle, I've met with the guerrilla leaders, there is a peace process, however fragile … now I've been to Washington, too, and, obviously, we need to conduct war as well.'[60] The United States had little interest in the matter of human rights, which President Pastrana admitted was causing 'big problems'.

On 22 October Guillermo Fernandez, Colombian foreign minister, reported on the talks with the FARC negotiators: matters 'of mutual interest' were discussed 'in a very positive and cordial meeting'. Other talks were planned. In late October General Barry McCaffrey visited Britain to drum up additional support for the US campaign in Colombia (members of the SAS were already working with La Jungla, General José Serrano's paramilitary police unit[61]), while on 29 October some activists picketed the US embassy in London to call for an end to Washington's interference in Colombia. Oscar Silva, spokesman for the Campaign Against US Intervention in Colombia, noted the strategic importance of Colombia to the United States because it had to give up the Panama Canal. Moreover, the country was 'also very rich in oil' and was valuable because of its long Pacific coastline: 'The US has given over $1 billion to the Colombian government and it's not being spent on finding a social solution.' Now there were anxieties that Washington was trying to mobilise an international force for intervention in the civil war: Britain was already involved, and Peru, Ecuador and Argentina had already indicated that they would support a multinational intervention force. It seemed clear that the Clinton administration, in escalating the war, would accomplish no more than to expand the violence and human suffering in a country that was already facing deepening social problems, economic recession and an unprecedented level of human-rights abuses.[62]

There was continuing debate about President Pastrana's 'plan', now dubbed 'Plan Colombia', for the solution of the country's many problems (see Appendix 2). At the same time the Clinton administration, perhaps 'cherry-picking' the Pastrana proposals, was focusing on the *military-aid* elements in Plan Colombia in order to serve Washington's primary task of defeating the leftwing guerrillas. It was proposed that during 2000 and 2001 the Clinton package would add about $1.6 billion in new military and police assistance, most going to Colombia but with small allocations going to Colombia's Andean neighbours (see Appendix 3).[63] The Clinton plan had five goals: (1) to equip the police with 30 Black Hawk and 18 Huey helicopters and to deploy counter-narcotics battalions and police in southern areas where much of the coca and heroin poppy was being grown; (2) to strengthen the interdiction capacity by supplying local and regional radar facilities; (3) to enhance coca eradication with more spray planes and base facilities; (4) to promote crop substitution; and (5) to improve the administration of justice to reduce violence and improve human rights observance.

The scheme (compared with Plan Colombia) was criticised from every political perspective. It was easy to see the Clinton proposals as yet another boost to Yankee imperialism, with massive military aid being supplied to suppress a host of legitimate political demands (see Appendix 1). Some rightwing commentators judged that the aid package was insufficiently robust, arguing that even more could be done. The Clinton administration was calling for 'emergency appropriations', but it was reckoned that the first Black Hawk helicopters might not arrive in Colombia for 18 months, and some pundits remembered that past deliveries of aid had been bungled. Over the previous year the US State Department had sent outdated ammunition to the Colombian police, and there had been other supply problems that encouraged scepticism about the new proposals. Moreover, the question of alternative-crop production had not been thought through. The Andean Trade Preferences Act was due to expire in 2002, but the Clinton plan made no provision to ensure markets for Colombia's new crops, should they ever be produced. In the event the $1.6 billion aid package was cut to $1 billion in the US Senate, though this still meant that massive military aid would be injected into the Colombian civil war. Now Washington had involved Japan and the European Union in discussions on how the Clinton package might be given significant international support. Britain's prime minister Tony Blair had predictably expressed enthusiasm for the plan and offered to mobilise European support, heedless of the plain fact that Washington was intent only on creating an international consensus for military intervention against a popular people's movement.[64] Already it was being suggested that Britain's contribution to the war would be £150 million.[65]

It was not long before specific US-supported aspects of the war, to be boosted by the Clinton proposals, were attracting detailed criticism. For example, some commentators were saying that the campaign of spraying coca and poppy plants was akin to biological warfare against human beings. Here particular attention was given to the increasing use of the mycoherbicide fusarium EN-4, the basis for many of the biological weapons developed by the United States, the Soviet Union, Britain, Israel, France and Iraq. The English mycotoxicologist Jeremy Bigwood, a researcher into fusarium derivatives used in biological warfare, has commented that the use of fusarium in Colombia would damage crops other than cocaine, and also develop mutations that could kill people with immune deficiencies. Animals or human beings eating plants poisoned by fusarium could themselves be affected. Bigwood and the Latin American expert, Sharon Stevenson, have together published details of the many adverse affects of fusarium spraying. In addition, Eduardo Posada, president of the Colombian Centre for International Physics, found the substance fusarium to be 'highly toxic', noting a 76 per cent mortality rate among immune-deficient hospital patients who had been infected by the fungus: *'To apply a mycoherbicide from the air that has been associated with a 76 percent kill rate of hospitalised human patients would be tantamount to biological warfare.'*[66]

The 'ghost of Vietnam' was now haunting Plan Colombia:

> In the 1960s, the mission was called 'Search and Destroy'. Today, it's Plan Colombia, the objective of which is to eradicate cocaine drug lords, leftist and rightist guerrillas, rightwing paramilitary vigilantes, thugs and thousands in between. In Vietnam, the enemy was identified as communists. In Colombia, everybody seems to be a potential enemy.[67]

The Plan, in its Pastrana version or with added Clinton 'spin', was increasingly, seen as a plan for war rather than a plan for peace. Plan Colombia was now being rejected by some 60 Colombian groups: social organisations, non-government organisations, human-rights groups, and Peace for Colombia movements. While keen to support the need for international aid to address Colombia's many problems, the groups rejected the Plan:

> We reject Plan Colombia because it uses an authoritarian concept of national security exclusively based on a strategy against narcotics. It will lead to an escalation of the social and armed conflict. It fails to provide real solutions to drug-trafficking. It endangers the peace process. It attacks the indigenous populations by destroying their

culture and their way of life, and it will seriously affect the Amazon eco-system. It will worsen the humanitarian and human rights crisis, increase forced displacement and aggravate the social and political crisis.

In June 2000 some of the hundreds of thousands displaced by the war descended on Bogota and displayed their slogan: 'With hunger, there is no peace.' But Washington was gearing up for an escalating war, funded in large part by the American tax-payer, that could only bring more poverty, more hunger, more despair and more gross human-rights abuses. Now even Europe was in danger of sleep-walking its way into the Colombian civil war.[68] On 21 August General Fernando Tapias, Colombia's armed forces chief, declared: 'What is clear – there will be peace, but, first, there will be war.' He judged that Plan Colombia was creating 'a point of no return in the peace process'; the rebels would 'have to accept a negotiated solution from the government' – just as the Vietnamese 'rebels' were forced to capitulate to American power? Raul Reyes, chief FARC negotiator, commented: 'If they implement the Plan Colombia in practice, they will have the worst conflict that this country has ever seen. And we will be ready for it.'

The United States was urging Colombia to observe its human-rights obligations,[69] while such observance did not seem to be a condition of massive military aid.[70] Some observers were already claiming that Plan Colombia had produced its first victims: six schoolchildren shot dead by the US-backed Colombian military on 15 August 2000 in the northern town of Pueblo Rico.[71] On 30 August President Clinton, meeting with Pastrana in Cartagena, was urging Colombian co-operation with the US plans (two FARC rebels were arrested as they assembled a bomb close to a building that Clinton was due to visit later in the day). Protests, guerrilla attacks and blockades of major roads greeted Clinton's arrival – perhaps inducing him to declare that the United States would not become involved in a 'shooting war' – 'This is not Vietnam, neither is it Yankee imperialism.' In Bogota, some 5000 protesters wearing Uncle Sam hats and skeleton masks shouted 'Yankee go home!' and 'Imperialism out of Colombia!' as they thronged outside the heavily-fortified US embassy building. At Bogota's National University, a crowd of hooded students, opposed to the US president's visit, clashed with baton-wielding security forces, and an 18-year-old policeman was killed. Over the previous few days there had been rebel attacks throughout the country: 11 civilians, three guerrillas and six police officers were reported killed.

Plan Colombia, then being applied in characteristic US fashion, appeared to have no chance of achieving its proclaimed objectives. There was no doubt that American money would escalate the bitter decades-long conflict[72] – already shaped in large part by US intervention. It seemed unlikely that the leftwing guerrillas – battle-hardened, well motivated, competently led, copiously equipped, and controlling half the country – would be defeated in their own land. And the drug farmers and distributors, feeding the reliable appetites of American and other consumers, would not be deterred.[73]

Another Vietnam?

President Clinton had declared that Colombia 'is not Vietnam', recalling the potent symbol that hung like a shadow over all America's intended or actual military adventures. Ernesto 'Che' Guevara, the Argentinian revolutionary, had wanted to create 'two, three or more Vietnams'; in 1981 US policy in El Salvador was again evoking images of Vietnam;[74] on 10 August 1996 the influential Moslem cleric Sheikh Mohammed Hussein Fadlallah warned the United States of a 'new Vietnam' if it attacked Iran; and the US-led wars against Afghanistan (2002-) and Iraq (2003-) yet again generated comparisons with Vietnam. It was inevitable that America's enduring sensitivity about the US defeat and humiliation at the hands of the Vietnamese in the 1960s/early 1970s should evoke similar comparisons in connection with the growing American involvement in Colombia.[75]

From the mid-1990s the Colombian anti-drugs forces, with the help of the United States, had sprayed toxic chemicals in an attempt to eradicate coca-growing in the southern jungles. In 1998 the sprayers moved from glyphosate, difficult to use in strong rain or wind, to tebuthiuron – analogous to the Agent Orange sprayed in Vietnam. Dow Agrosciences, supplying the highly toxic product (Spike 20P), had gone so far as to emphasise the hazards of tebuthiuron usage, seemingly reluctant to see it sprayed on the Colombian rainforest. The chemical could kill desirable trees as well as coca crops, and it was 'very risky' to apply Spike 20P 'where the terrain slopes, rain-fall is significant … and the application is made under less-than-ideal circumstances'.[76]

The use of toxic defoliants in Colombia became a potent symbol of the growing US 'Vietnamisation' of the war: 'While in Colombia [August 2000], Clinton did his best to dispel the notion that the US is about to slip into the morass of another jungle war such as El Salvador, or worse, Vietnam.'[77] But all the signs were there – the pledges of US aid, military support, tolerance of government corruption and army human-rights abuses, the slowly escalating US military presence in the country, and a powerful indigenous guerrilla movement. Independent observers were saying that the most likely result would be stalemate, complete with corrupt officials, black marketeers, drug traffickers and no visible US exit strategy – an exact rerun of the Vietnam fiasco. Already doubts were being voiced in the United States about the growing American involvement. Thus Professor Abraham Lowenthal, University of Southern California, commented on the possibility of new US aid to the Pastrana regime:

> The strongest case for approving the requested Colombian appropriation rests on the argument that there are some real, if limited, prospects that the Pastrana government could modestly advance its approach if it had US assistance. The fact that the US has the resources does not mean that it has the right answers. Washington should make security and economic assistance available while focusing on how to minimise the risks of more direct US military involvement.[78]

The new aid package, heralded by the Clinton visit to Cartagena,[79] was designed to include the services of a senior American general and more than 300 US military advisors – 'the largest number since the Vietnam war'[80] – to train the Colombian armed forces in their fight against leftwing guerrillas. The plain intention was for the United States to facilitate the destruction of the guerrilla movement – to secure American interests in Colombia and to intimidate neighbouring states. But it seemed obvious that the growing US involvement would devastate the rural and urban poor in Colombia and provoke further upheavals in the region.

At a meeting of twelve Latin American presidents in September 2000, the major countries refused to endorse Washington's Plan Colombia, rebuffing appeals from Clinton to support a general US military and police offensive against drug traffickers and opposing further US incursions in the region. One report noted that looming over the meeting was concern at what President Hugo Chavez of Venezuela described as 'the Vietnamisation of the entire Amazon region'.[81] Chavez, then well aware that Plan Colombia would generate 'combat activities that could complicate our situation', called for the creation of a 'South American NATO' that would organise its own policing of drug traffickers.[82]

In late 2000 it was reported that Peter Face, a Vietnam veteran and US Southern Command top official, had visited Bogota several times and that the Pentagon was 'considering boosting its "in-country" supervision of the Colombian army's counterinsurgency offensive'. Already the 'drug-eradication' regiments were being trained by US personnel, despite the Colombian army's appalling human-rights record. Thus Benjamin Gilman, leader of the US House of Representatives international relations committee, had withdrawn his support for Plan Colombia, urging that the Colombian army be cut out of the scheme and replaced by less tainted police. In early 2001 it was becoming increasingly obvious that the United States was becoming bogged down in an unwinnable battle, with the word 'Vietnam' still haunting policy-making in Washington.[83] In March the Colombian governors of the provinces most affected by the toxic spraying – Putumayo, Narino, Cauca and Tolima – called for an end to the crop destruction and more social programmes to encourage the farmers to turn to other activities. Thus Governor Ivan Gerardo Guerrero talked of a 60 per cent increase in stomach upsets and skin rashes in Putumayo since the spraying began, and pointed out that deformed babies were being born in the rural municipality of Puerto Guzman: 'The fumigation arrived in 30 days in enormous quantities, but the social aid has only begun to arrive drop by drop.'

On 14 June 2001 the Colombian authorities subpoenaed three US citizens for apparently passing on coordinates to facilitate a Colombian bombing attack that killed 17 civilians, including five children, and injured dozens more. The three American pilots were said to have been flying surveillance aircraft for AirScan International Inc., the company responsible for monitoring the Cano Limon pipeline in north-eastern Colombia. Investigations had shown that the killings had resulted from US-made cluster bombs dropped from a Colombian air force helicopter. It seemed obvious that US-based Occidental Petroleum, operating the Cano Limon oil field, was using American personnel and US-supplied weapons to protect its assets.

In July it emerged that President George W. Bush was seeking to deploy a private army – unanswerable to Congress – in Colombia by securing a congressional vote to lift the cap on the deployment of privatised military personnel. Congress had insisted that no more than 500 such personnel, in a purely training role, could be deployed; and that no more than 300 non-military personnel largely working for firms such as DynCorp as coca-spraying pilots, could operate in Colombia at any one time. But the new

$676 million programme – the Andean Counterdrug Initiative – was designed to deploy an unlimited number of former servicemen in the country.

The new legislation also contained provisions to allow State Department contractors to purchase weapons and ammunition from federal funds – for 'defensive purposes'. At the same time there was growing pressure in the United States for Washington to focus more on counter-insurgency and less on counter-narcotics schemes. Jan Schakowsky, a US congresswoman, commented on the new Bush legislation: 'It's a back-door way of escalating our involvement in the Andean region and providing additional money to private military contractors who have not been effective.' On 30 July a Colombian judge, Gilberto Reyes, ordered the government to suspend aerial spraying with glyphosate herbicide and to provide evidence of the chemical's impact on human health and the environment. Anne Patterson, US ambassador, noted the failure of the programme: 'Everywhere we look there is more coca than we expected.'

On 8 August 2001 a group of Colombians in Australia took over the nation's consulate in Australia for several hours to protest against 'the United States invasion' of Colombia and the US-backed military plan to wipe out the leftwing rebels in the country. After five hours the occupation of the building in the north of the city, surrounded by 100 heavily armed police, ended peacefully. Men, women and children were driven away in police vans and released without charge. A spokesman for the Bolivian Movement for a Second Independence of Colombia demanded an end to US involvement in Bogota:

> We are protesting against Plan Colombia, we are protesting against the Yankee invasion of Latin America and the American invasion of Colombia.

At the same time the US House of Representatives was approving an extra $700 million in aid to Colombia on top of the more than $1 billion approved the previous year as part of the former President Clinton's effort to support the Plan. On 20-22 July more than 350 delegates from 35 countries and 50 organisations had met in El Salvador to build a world movement against US involvement in Colombia.

Even in the US Congress there were human-rights opponents of Plan Colombia, seeking to derail the growing American involvement. In this context it was clear that a primary reason for the Bush commitment to the

Colombian government was the US energy interest: Colombia remains one of the main sources of coal burned in American power plants. But this interest was continuing to have serious consequences for human rights: 'In Colombia, US energy, military and trade policy are becoming intertwined with devastating consequences for the country's labour movement.'[84] John F. Tierney, Massachusetts Democrat, emphasised the impact of US support for a Colombian regime determined to suppress workers' rights: 'These are innocent people trying to make Colombia a safer and more prosperous place, like Cristobel Uribe Beltran of the Association of Workers and Employees in Hospitals, Clinics and Organisations, who was kidnapped on June 27 and assassinated the very next day.'[85]

Organisations such as Human Rights Watch and Amnesty International were producing substantial evidence that aid provided by Plan Colombia was supporting rightwing militants determined to target trade union leaders. At the same time the privatisation of Colombian mines and oil fields, urged by the US-dominated International Monetary Fund (IMF), was facilitating increased control of the Colombian economy by US corporations. Trade union leaders were being assassinated in the interest of American corporate profits while, despite Colombian legal objections, the US-supported toxic fumigation of peasant land was continuing *as a means of clearing the areas coveted by American multinational corporations.*

Thus Liz Atherton, Colombia Peace Association, commented in October 2001 on the US policy of spraying toxic chemicals on peasant land in Colombia's southern states:

> ... in spite of overwhelming evidence that Amazon biodiversity is being seriously damaged; that adults and children are being made sick with diarrhoea, vomiting, skin rashes, eye and respiratory problems; that livestock and fish in contaminated waters are dying; that food crops are being destroyed and all means of subsistence are being removed; that people are showing signs of severe malnutrition and thousands have been forced to leave their homes ...[86]

This US 'terrorism by proxy' had various aims: to clear the *campesino* population from areas rich in coveted natural resources for development by US corporations; to eliminate popular resistance by killing community leaders and displacing the population; and to expand US hegemonic control in the region.

On 20 February 2002 the Colombian president, Andres Pastrana, announced the end of the peace process with the FARC, a move prompted by the Bush administration. The scene was now set for an escalation of the developing US war against the Colombian people.[87] Washington would continue to pour billions of dollars into the maelstrom, to use chemical and biological warfare against peasant agriculture, to facilitate human-rights abuses, and to encourage the endless slaughter of those human impediments to corporate profit. It is the American Way.

Expanding the Conflict

President Bush was now considering a massive expansion of the US involvement in Colombia. The peace process had collapsed and Washington was looking for further excuses to extend its so-called 'war against terrorism'. Observers suggested that the number of military 'advisors' available to the Colombian regime would soon be increased – a feature of the progressive 'Vietnamisation' of the conflict. Already influential Pentagon officials were arguing that FARC should be made a priority target because of its links with the IRA and other terrorist groups. One option being considered was to use Black Hawk helicopters for transporting Colombian troops into battle against the guerrilla factions. And it was oil, not drugs, that the earlier Bush aid package ($98 million) had been intended to address. It was no accident that Occidental Petroleum, with substantial oil interests in Colombia, was a generous donor to the US Republican and Democratic parties.[88]

After the election of Bush – and 11 September 2001 – a new 'anti-terror' focus quickly developed in US policy towards Colombia. Thus John Ashcroft, US Attorney General, declared that 'the State Department has called the FARC the most dangerous terrorist group based in the Western hemisphere' who have 'engaged in a campaign of terror against Colombians and US citizens'. The anti-drug policies were rapidly fading into the background: the US priority was military action against leftwing guerrillas. Washington had already given Colombia $1.3 billion in 2001-2 and another $700 million was made available in 2003 – all of this support finding its way into the hands of the Colombian military and the repressive government. In 2003 the United States was instructing the Colombian military to concentrate its war against the FARC insurgents in the southern parts of the country – what American strategists called the 'Southern Push'. By now it was proving difficult to tar the guerrillas with the drugs brush.

Thus Klaus Nyholm, director of the UN drug control agency in Colombia (UNDCP), was observing that the local guerrilla fronts were quite autonomous: in some areas they were instructing the farmers not to grow coca, and prior to the Colombia military offensive against the guerrilla territories the FARC were co-operating with a $6 million UN project to replace coca crops with new forms of agricultural development. It seemed plain that the 'narco-guerrilla' charge was little more than US propaganda designed to justify an expanding American intervention. In fact, the rightwing paramilitaries, terrorist factions supported by US aid, have remained the biggest drug traffickers in Colombia:

> The US ... has clearly participated in strengthening the ties between the leading terrorists in Colombia, the Colombian military and their paramilitary allies, who are responsible for over 80 per cent of all human rights abuses committed in Colombia today ... the paramilitaries, as stated by the US's own agencies, are amongst the biggest drug traffickers in Colombia today ... US military aid is going directly to the major terrorist networks throughout Colombia, who traffic cocaine into US markets to fund their activities.[89]

The United States had helped to make such terrorist activities more effective by creating what Human Rights Watch termed a 'sophisticated mechanism ... that allows the Colombian military to fight a dirty war and Colombian officialdom to deny it'.[90]

The Bush policy on Colombia was being driven by the familiar US instinct to protect the interests of the major American corporations, especially oil companies such as Occidental but also a host of commercial groups with interests in the region. Paul D. Coverdell, a US Republican senator, commented that any destabilisation of Colombia could spill over into other countries: 'In fact the oil picture in Latin America is strikingly similar to that of the Middle East, except that Colombia provides us with more oil today than Kuwait did then [1990]. This crisis, like the one in Kuwait, threatens to spill over into many nations, all of which are allies [of the US].'

The issue was simple. Washington would take all necessary measures to protect the US corporate interests in Colombia, just as the US had prosecuted the massive 2003 aggression against Iraq in pursuit of the country's oil resource. In this context any American talk of 'democracy', 'terrorism' and 'human rights' was no more than public-relations camouflage for a US-supported war of terrorism, murder and displacement.

In August 2002 the Colombian military launched a new offensive against the FARC guerrillas, carrying out bombing raids on leftwing camps. This followed Bush's decision to loosen US aid law, enabling American military aid to be used directly against rebel groups engaged in 'terrorist' activities. The new US law, signed by Bush, allowed US-supplied attack helicopters and other equipment, including satellite technology, to be used for the first time directly in counter-insurgency operations. In response, a leading FARC commander reportedly ordered his men to target Americans in Colombia: 'We must find where the gringos are, because they all have declared war on us.'[91]

The Corporate Agenda

Military and economic aid from the United States is one of the principal elements enabling the repressive Colombian oligarchy to survive. The Colombian economic élite colludes with US militarism and multinational corporations to make massive profits while the people and the environment are devastated. In this fashion the United States and the drug cartels, enjoying a symbiotic advantage, prevent the Colombian people from overthrowing a regime that kills 5000 to 10,000 people every year.

Today more than half of all legal Colombian exports travel to the United States; and the US receives 80 per cent of all exports if cocaine and heroin are included. The levels of violence and ecological destruction have enabled Colombia to become a highly lucrative profit centre for the United States, and the Bush administration is determined to preserve this congenial state of affairs. The oligarchy is heavily involved in many US business enterprises in the country and remains an ally of Washington and a supporter of US foreign policy. The inevitable corollary is that many of the US-linked companies are involved in environmental destruction and gross human-rights abuses – a situation that the rightwing President Alvaro Uribe remains determined to protect.

On 9 September 2002 the Bush administration approved a further aid package, worth more than $35 million, focused directly on the Colombian military – after deciding that the armed forces were doing enough to protect human rights in the country. An aid package of more than $60 million had already been donated to the military earlier in the year. These fresh donations of military support were only a small part of total US aid to

Colombia, the third largest recipient of aid from Washington after Israel and Egypt. At the same time minimal funds were being made available for social programmes.

Military expenditure was going abroad to purchase expensive weapons and equipment, largely from the United States. Colombia, like many other countries, was being forced to open its economy to US corporate penetration, and this was doing nothing for small Colombian businesses forced to compete with multinational organisations. President Uribe was taking over the granting of oil concessions, allegedly to discourage regional corruption while, conversely, local 'agrarian institutes' were being freed up in the hope of reducing central corruption. Many independent observers perceived the situation as highly unstable, presided over by an insecure regime that would be forced to rely increasingly on US-supported repression.

By 2003 the Bush administration wanted to boost the aid package to $2 billion, most of it as aid to the Colombian military. Richard Armitage, US deputy secretary of state, was claiming that al-Qa'ida and other terrorist groups were operating on Colombia's border. In the same vein the Pentagon's Rogelio Pardo-Maurer, former aide to the head of the Nicaraguan contras (who waged a successful terrorist war against the democratically-elected Sandinista government), was urging increased US spending on the Colombian military. But again Washington's motives in expanding military aid were plain. Thus Ron Paul, a Republican congressman and member of the House international relations committee, commented:

> Pretending that the fighting there [in Colombia] is somehow related to our international war on terrorism is to stretch the imagination to breaking point. It is unwise and dangerous. It has nothing to do with our national defence or our security. It has more to do with oil and we know it.

In October 2002 US Green Berets were reportedly training and equipping Colombia's 18th Brigade in Arauca province, one of the most dangerous regions in the country. The Brigade had been promised eleven American Huey helicopters, and further weapons and equipment were anticipated. On 30 October Oliver Houston, writing in *The Guardian* (London), was predicting with others: 'We could soon be seeing the "Vietnamisation" of the whole Amazon region.'

The Growing US Commitment

Colin Powell, US secretary of state, visited Colombia on 3-4 December 2002 and pledged continued US commitment to work with Colombia on common goals – such as 'democracy' and 'the war on terrorism'. He made no mention of oil or the protection of American corporate interests, suggesting only that the creation of an attractive investment environment would be good for jobs. The United States, declared Powell, was 'very impressed' with President Uribe's efforts to destroy the coca crops: 'This is a partnership that works and a partnership we must continue to invest in.' Powell further congratulated Uribe on Colombia's presidency of the UN Security Council, having no doubt that Washington would be able to rely on Colombian support over the US confrontation with Iraq. The Secretary of State was confident that Colombia, as temporary head of the Council, would ensure 'an open, full, comprehensive debate on the nature of the [Iraqi] declaration' (according to Security Council resolution 1441), concerning its-alleged weapons of mass destruction.[92]

Powell had applauded Uribe's willingness to continue spraying toxic chemicals over large tracts of Colombia but failed to address the growing concerns about this campaign. By 2003 Washington was not only supporting the use of poisonous chemicals over peasant lands but also the spraying of Agent Green, a genetically engineered pathogenic fungus developed in the US Department of Agriculture's research station in Beltsville, Maryland. The United States was then funding the production of the fungus by Ag/Bio Company, a private laboratory in Bozeman, Montana, while the organism was also being produced at a former Soviet bioweapons factory in Tashkent, Uzbekistan.[93]

It was known that the fungi being produced posed a threat both to human beings and to non-target species, so putting both Washington and the Colombian regime in violation of the UN Convention on the Prohibition of Military or Any Other Hostile Use of Environmental Modification Techniques (ENMOD), a legal instrument sparked by American use of Agent Orange and other toxic chemicals during the Vietnam war. Such Colombian neighbours as Ecuador and Peru were protesting at the US-Colombian biowar campaign. There was a grim irony in the fact that *while the United States was denouncing Iraq's alleged chemical and biological weapons, Washington was supporting the use of toxic chemical and biological weapons against Colombian agricultural land in violation of international law.*

By 2003, according to congressman Robert Barr, at least 22 US helicopters had been shot down by rebel forces, a figure that the Pentagon refused to confirm or deny; but in November 2002 the State Department reported that three US aircraft over Colombia were struck by groundfire on the same day. In December Powell said that the permanent fleet of US attack helicopters in Colombia would be increased to 24; and the State Department, often a cover for CIA activities, revealed that new pilots were being trained at 'a classified location' in New Mexico.

In early 2003 almost one hundred Green Berets were training Colombian troops, an escalating development that was enmeshing the United States further in the Colombian conflict and giving leftwing guerrillas an added incentive to target American assets in the country.[94] About 450 Colombians were being trained in basic infantry skills, intelligence and rapid response to rebel threats. Major Julio Burgos of the Colombian 18th Brigade commented: 'The United States is interested in oil the same way it interests any other country in the world. There is a US company that has its interests in this country. The US is defending its interests.'

ELEVEN

War Without End? (November 1999 to ...)

The Escalating Conflict

One of the principal targets of the paramilitaries and the Colombian army was trade unionists, often associated with community groups and political reform organisations. Through the 1990s around 2500 trade unionists were murdered in Colombia, according to the International Confederation of Free Trade Unions: 'Many more have been kidnapped, tortured, threatened with their lives and persecuted in numerous ways, while thousands have been forced to flee.' It was now obvious that the sporadic peace talks, seemingly irrelevant to many of Colombia's deep-seated problems, were doing nothing to discourage further outbreaks of violence and protest. On 11 November 1999 a car bomb in Bogota killed at least eight people and injured 45, in what the mayor said was probably a reaction to the resumption of the extradition of drug dealers to the United States. The 154lb bomb, packed with shrapnel, destroyed a two-storey house and a restaurant.

In the southern demilitarised zone the FARC guerrillas were

consolidating their grip on the territory and the people. Details are given in one report of how the rebels were seeking to impose their own system of justice. A coca farmer, accused of paying too little child support to his estranged girlfriend, was sitting before a guerrilla called Rayo ('Thunderbolt'), who served as judge and jury at the rebels' Office of Complaints. Rayo ran through a list of the man's assets whereupon, after a clipped discussion, the farmer agreed to increase his child support payment from $40 to $52 a month.[1] This was the sort of scene that was worrying the international human-rights organisations and critics of President Pastrana thought to have abandoned an area twice the size of Wales to the FARC guerrillas. The rebels, along with many other groups in Colombia, were known to be practising murder, kidnapping and the forced eviction of whole villages. It seemed that nothing could be done to impose a national system of justice that would win the approval of international observers. Carlos Salinas, Latin American advocacy director for Amnesty International, said: 'There is a vacuum in the administration of justice. We do not believe that the FARC has the capacity or the legal standing to supply such a service.'[2]

The FARC rebels, monitored by Amnesty, admitted to six recent killings, but it was acknowledged that since the guerrillas had taken control of the region the number of violent deaths had declined substantially. In 1998 the hospital at San Vicente del Caguan registered 95 violent deaths; by November 1999 there had been about two dozen. Critics were charging that the FARC guerrillas were taking advantage of the demilitarised (*despeje*) zone to stockpile arms, to train more soldiers and to recruit minors. Such matters seemed a greater priority than the halting peace talks – and it was not only the FARC rebels that were ordering their priorities in such a fashion. President Pastrana was insisting that the war should be conducted as effectively as possible, even while preparations were being made for peace negotiations, and US arms were continuing to pour into the country. Even sources within the American Drug Enforcement Administration (DEA) were privately admitting that their priorities in Colombia had 'been sidelined by the geopolitical concerns of cold war cronies in the CIA and the Pentagon – that while aggressive rhetoric and military hardware is aimed at the guerrillas, the US will tolerate drug-running by effective rightwing counter-insurgency forces, even if they happen to be illegal'.[3] There was nothing in this for a secure peace achieved through negotiation, only for a protracted and escalating war. On 17 November the Colombian authorities reported a new guerrilla offensive in five rural states.

A number of police officers surrendered to guerrillas during an attack on the town of Dolores, Tolima state, Four policemen had been wounded and the local police station destroyed, before the rebels claimed a local victory and released the captured police officers. Elsewhere in the country, around 80 people had been killed, including policemen and Colombian army troops. There was sustained fighting in Puerto Inirida, capital of the southeastern department of Guainia, with Admiral Sergio Garcia claiming that Colombian marines had killed at least 30 of the rebels. It was also being claimed that a bombing raid by the Colombian air force had killed between 30 and 40 rebels travelling in a convoy of lorries. The reports noted that the attack on Puerto Inirida was against 100 police and 500 marines who had been trained by the US Special Forces – the first time that any of the five US-trained river warfare units had been involved in the war.[4] The Colombian authorities continued to notch up successes in the war on drugs, and on occasions were aided by other Latin American states (for example, in November Pablo Escobar's widow and son were arrested in Buenos Aires[5]), but such successes were failing to impede the production and distribution of cocaine or to affect the course of the escalating civil war.

The official campaign against the traditional cocaine cartels (Medellin and Cali) had created a host of 'mini-cartels' and shifted the centres of the drug trade to fresh Colombian sites and elsewhere. According to the DEA's Thomas Constantine, a cartel based in the Mexican border town of Tijuana was 'one of the most powerful organised crime syndicates in the world today' (November 1999). In this case, members of the cartel, using bribery and intimidation to secure the co-operation of local officials, were acting as 'gatekeepers' for 1000 miles of frontier and for the busy border crossing at San Ysidro.[6] It was known that the Tijuana cartel was using encrypted cellphones, satellite communications and the Internet to avoid detection. Mexico had promised a $400 million 'total war' on drug smugglers, but no major traffickers were being indicted in Mexico, and drug hauls, arrests and seizures of drug vehicles had all declined.[7] US-sponsored anti-drug successes in Colombia had merely dissipated the problem. On 21 November the alleged drug baron Jaime Orlando Lara was put on a plane in Bogota for extradition to the United States, the first Colombian set to stand trial in the US in nine years – another minor US victory that would change nothing.

The escalating civil war, enmeshed with the drugs trade, was rooted also in all the privations of abject poverty. Tens of thousands of peasants, teachers and tribespeople had blocked Colombia's main road link with the rest of South America. In the southwest of Cauca, where more than 1.2 million people were living in poverty, the demonstrators had erected barricades along almost 60 miles of highway to demand development money from the Bogota government. Fernando Varas, president of the Asoinca teachers' union, declared: 'We need things as basic as piped water, drainage, roads and schools.' The protest pushed the Colombian government into signing a deal worth around $50 million, a fraction of what had been demanded. Victor Collazos, one of the negotiators, commented that the agreement was a start: 'The government say they will comply with all they promised – we're giving them the chance to show they mean it.'

The Colombian government was again looking to the possibility of a negotiated peace with the rebel factions, while prosecuting a growing war with mounting US support. In Sweden, Colombia's foreign minister Guillermo Fernandez declared that Colombia was nearer to peace than ever before, 'but you have to take into account it will be complex and will take time'. The government and the FARC rebels were again negotiating and had agreed a common agenda, but Fernandez was keen to emphasise that the United States and Europe were duty bound to provide aid to Colombia because they were partly to blame for the country's drug problems:

> The international community is responsible for some of the problems in Colombia. The drugs are consumed in the US and Europe, the chemical precursors for the drugs come from the US and Europe, and money is laundered in the US and Europe. The drug problem is not just the problem of the producer country. It is a problem for the whole international community and, since it also affects the conflict in Colombia, we must see co-responsibility.[8]

President Pastrana was now confirming that the FARC guerrillas would continue to control the agreed demilitarised zone, beyond the time originally specified for the possible re-militarisation of the region. (At the same time the Colombian government was alarmed that Iran had offered to invest around $3 million in a cold storage plant in San Vicente, deep in FARC-controlled territory, with the implication that Iran might be willing to supply arms to the rebels.[9]) The violence was continuing unabated at a time when some hope was being breathed into the peace talks. On 7 December leftwing rebels bombed Colombia's second-largest oil export pipeline, for the 70th time in 1999, forcing a halt to the oil pumping operations. Two days later, a gun battle between rival gangs in Bogota's notoriously violent La Modelo prison resulted in the deaths of about a dozen inmates with four wounded. On 13 December some 40 Colombian marines were killed when rebels overran the naval base near Jurado, Choco province, close to the sensitive border with Panama. The storming of the base came just hours before the formal ceremony in Panama to mark the US handover of the Panama Canal to the Panamanian government. About 600 FARC guerrillas had attacked a 147-strong marine detachment, at the same time skirmishing with police near the Capurgana tourist resort. Colombian Captain Carlos Humberto Pineda said: 'We have reports from the parish priest of Jurado of 40 marines dead and 40 others wounded. The situation is very serious.'

A rebel attack was also launched by a combined force of FARC and ELN guerrillas on the town of San Luis, Antioquia, killing at least eight policemen and two town hall officials. The provincial governor, Alberto Builes, commented: 'The attack was really ferocious ... The police are not shock troops. It's impossible for them to fight 200 guerrillas.' Three days later, the Colombian security forces launched a major offensive against rebel positions in southern and central regions of the country, with the military claiming that 147 guerrillas had been killed. Soon television broadcasts were showing that the entire central area of Hobo, southwest Huila, had been reduced to piles of ruins, while the police operations chief General Alfonso Arellano was reporting that 66 guerrillas had died when the Colombian air force bombed a retreating FARC column. In another clash in the mountains northwest of Bogota, Colombian troops killed eight FARC insurgents and proudly paraded the bodies of six rebels on television. On 17 December a car bomb exploded in southwest Putumayo province, racked by fighting between leftwing guerrillas and rightwing paramilitaries. Acting governor Alvaro Salas reported four dead and 27 wounded.

On 20 December the FARC rebels announced a unilateral Christmas ceasefire that would last until 10 January – 'so that the Colombians can celebrate the new year and the start of a new millennium with their friends and family, without the turmoil and death caused by the armed conflict'. President Pastrana welcomed the ceasefire and called on the country's other armed factions to follow suit. (In 1998 the paramilitaries had declared a Christmas ceasefire, and then massacred more than 120 civilians in January.) The Colombian army then issued Christmas cards for each of the country's 20,000 rebels, wishing them a happy yuletide – and urging them to desert: 'Guerrilla: Make your family happy, share the festive season with them. Abandon your squad, and enjoy freedom:' On 29 December the Colombian military claimed to have killed at least 30 leftwing rebels in three days of fighting. General Eduardo Herrera, commander of the Fourth Army

Brigade, declared that hundreds of troops – backed by helicopter gunships, air force planes and the recently inaugurated élite army counter-insurgency unit – had destroyed 11 ELN camps in a mountainous region of northwest Antioquia province. Christmas had changed nothing: it was military business as usual.

On 31 December 1999 President Pastrana vetoed a Bill that would have established mandatory jail sentences for violent crimes – because the legislation might have led to the prosecution of Colombian soldiers fighting leftwing rebels. The Bill, approved by Congress on 30 November, would have allowed for cases involving the trial of troops to be heard before civilian rather than military courts. The Bill's first Article, criticised by Pastrana, called for a maximum 60-year jail term for anyone convicted of killings aimed at the destruction of a political group. Pastrana noted in this context that the Colombian government had been required by law to grant political status to the FARC group before opening peace talks.

The arrival of the new millennium was marked by continued war, continued murders and continued peasant protest. On 5 January about 100 displaced people, forced off their land by the paramilitaries, stormed the offices of the International Committee of the Red Cross (ICRC) in Bogota and took a number of staff hostage. The protesters waved Colombian tricolour flags, forced their way past riot police and occupied the building. They then released 33 ICRC officials, but continued to hold Robin Wave, mission head in Colombia. For the previous three weeks a group of displaced peasants, including women and children, had been camping in makeshift tents outside the Red Cross offices, demanding help from the government and ICRC staff. Josefina Jaimes, one of the protesters, said: 'Paramilitaries forced me off my plot of land and I had to come to the city with my husband and five children to beg, live in poverty and rely on other people's goodwill.' Another protester, Gustavo Cepeda, declared that the people would not leave until their demands had been met. Nothing was settled, but the world was reminded yet again of the long struggle of the Colombian people.

Aid, War and the UN

In early January 2000 President Bill Clinton was continuing to press for a massive increase in US aid to Colombia. Again, the plan was for a two-year $1.2 billion aid package – nominally to help Colombia with a slumping economy, the drugs war, and the battle against the guerrilla insurgency. Coca production was at record levels, and – opined some observers – Colombian democracy was under massive threat. Already Colombia was third on the list of countries receiving US aid, after Israel and Egypt, but unless the United States did more it was clear that Colombia was, from Washington's perspective, facing disaster. There was still some frustration in the Clinton administration that President Pastrana seemed to be overwhelmed by Colombia's problems, but at least one thing was clear to Washington – following McCaffrey's agitations: no useful distinction could be drawn between the drug traffickers and the leftwing insurgents, with the useful corollary that a war on the one was a war on the other.

The peace talks were due to reconvene, Gabriel Garcia Marquez had agreed to dine with US Secretary of State Madeleine Albright after the US aid offer, and leftwing rebels were bombing 22 high-voltage power pylons after the International Monetary Fund (IMF) ordered the Colombian government to privatise the power company ISAGEN and the national power grid ISA. The bombing of the pylons caused power blackouts, cuts in water supplies and interruptions in telephone services across the northwest provinces of Antioquia, Choco and Cordoba. The bulk of the energy supplies were quickly restored, but 'drastic' rationing was demanded later in the day. It was judged that the rural areas of much of the northwest would be without power for several weeks. The guerrillas, rarely so successful in targeting the national power facilities, were objecting to IMF insistence that without an ISAGEN-ISA privatisation, likely to yield more than $1 billion, financial loans would not be granted. Carlos Caballero, mines and energy minister, admitted that the bombings would hamper the planned privatisation.

On 18 January rightwing death squads murdered at least 26 peasants in two raids. In the village of La Loma, northwest Antioquia, 50 heavily-armed paramilitaries dressed in combat fatigues dragged 19 peasants from their homes, bound their hands behind their backs, and then shot them dead in front of other villagers. In the hamlet of Estados Unidos, northern Cesar, the paramilitaries killed at least seven peasants. In 1999 the rightwing death squads carried out 402 politically-motivated massacres in which 1860 civilians died. Now, a year later, the ACCU paramilitaries were routinely carrying out the same campaign of slaughter: 'For each pylon or electrical facility that is attacked, we will execute 10 base elements or rural guerrillas.'

At the end of January Manuel Marulanda condemned the surge in US military aid to the Colombian government, insisting that it would only intensify the civil war: 'What we have here is hunger, misery and exploitation and that's not going to end with rifles, machine guns or bombs.' Marulanda then rejected the familiar charges that FARC was deriving vast profits from the drug trade, denouncing this 'invention' of the press and the crude pretext to deepen US involvement in Colombia: 'The FARC disagrees with this aid from the United States because assistance should be for social spending and peace, not for increasing the conflict with the blessing of the few who directly benefit from the war.' President Pastrana had recently said to the *Boston Globe* that the FARC guerrillas had been branded a 'narco-guerrilla' group unfairly: 'They're not a narco-guerrilla group. They're a guerrilla insurgency who really want to fight drugs.'[10] This Pastrana comment can hardly have improved his reputation in Washington.

The peace talks between the Colombian government and the FARC rebels, this time being conducted in Sweden, were said to be moving towards a lasting agreement – though no details were being reported. In Colombia, hundreds of hostages held by ELN rebels were freed following an army siege of a guerrilla-held stretch of road linking Bogota with Medellin. Elsewhere, in northern Sucre province, 200 members of a paramilitary death squad shot and hacked to death at least 27 peasants in a three-day rampage. It seemed likely that such atrocities would continue under the terms of the Clinton aid package designed to supply arms to army and other units with an appalling human-rights record. On 22 February 2000, Klaus Nyholm, a UN Drug Control Programme official criticised the aid plan as containing 'too much stick and not enough carrot'; and he pointed out also that the United States was the 'world's biggest marijuana grower'. As the US Congress was debating the massive aid plan, Human Rights Watch published details of the links between the Colombian army and both the drug traffickers and the death-squad paramilitaries. Here there was further evidence, were it needed, that US military aid would be used to fund corruption and atrocity.

On 17 February the UN-linked International Labour Organisation (ILO), representing trade unions in 200 countries, denounced the Colombian government for failing to protect trade unionists from the threat of violence or assassination from the rightwing death squads. It was thought that the ILO might propose punitive sanctions against the Colombian regime for doing nothing to prevent the murder of nearly 3000 union members over the last decade by death squads linked to the Colombian military. The government had also taken steps to repress the traditional union rights by restricting the freedom to strike and to negotiate collective wage agreements. Wilson Borja, a public-sector union spokesman, commented: 'We have succeeded in showing that the government violates the constitution and the labour code, and that there is persecution of the union movement.' Job redundancies had soared because of Colombia's worst recession on record, and in early 2000 the unemployment rate was standing at nearly 20 per cent, one of the worst rates in Latin America. The paramilitaries were continuing to target union campaigners as one of the many groups working for better worker conditions and an acknowledgement of international standards of social justice. In northern Bolivar province, a rightwing death squad dragged three civilians from their cars at an illegal road block and shot them to death before escaping in a helicopter. In a separate incident in the same province, paramilitaries murdered three civilians in the town of Salado.

On 21 February the United Nations office in Bogota reiterated its recognition of the political status of the FARC and ELN rebel groups, bolstering Pastrana's negotiation position but outraging US opinion intent on representing all the leftwing guerrillas as no more than terrorists to be exterminated. Pastrana was now pledged to expanding the peace talks to include the ELN, but there seemed to be no prospect of an early peace agreement with any of the rebel groups. Now the paramilitaries, leading their own peasant groups, were protesting at the agreed demilitarisation of the FARC-controlled territories. The scene was set for a further escalation in the conflict. In central Bogota hundreds of beggars fought with riot police to prevent evictions from their only home, a shanty-town near to the presidential palace. More than 500 riot police, armed with plastic shields, fired tear gas and high-pressure water jets as they fought running battles for more than two hours. At least 15 police officers and many of the homeless were injured in the conflict.

Against the inevitable backdrop of continuing violence, the Colombian government and the FARC rebels announced the formal opening of the peace talks on 29 February 2000. Some observers regarded this as a decisive phase of dialogue, designed to deal with a range of socioeconomic topics. Victor Ricardo, Colombia's high commissioner for peace, regarded the negotiations as historic, expressing the common desire for reconciliation and an end to the bloody fratricidal war. Raul Reyes, FARC commander and negotiator, urged widespread participation in the public hearings to facilitate discussion of the main problems that were facing the majority of Colombians. Topics to be discussed included unemployment, agrarian reform, education, housing and medical services. In March Raul Reyes issued a communiqué, summarising the principal FARC considerations (see Appendix 4). Already it was clear that there was no prospect of an early peace.

On 6 March the Colombian authorities confirmed that the rightwing death squads had been committing further massacres throughout the country in recent days. In one incident, 100 paramilitaries raided the village of San Miguel del Tigre, northwest Antioquia, shooting dead six peasants, including three brothers, and kidnapping others who were probably later murdered. The US involvement continued to escalate, with little distinction drawn by Washington between the drug traffickers and the leftwing insurgents. US aid to Colombia had grown 10-fold since 1995 while the number of American troops in the field was also rapidly increasing. In 1999 Colombia received $366 million in equipment and training, including four river-combat courses for the Colombian marines in Puerto Leguizamo. A Colombian Lieutenant, German Arenas, commented: 'US training is useful here because they gained so much experience on the rivers in Vietnam. They lost a lot of men, but they learnt plenty.' (Arenas, trained by the US Green Berets, might have been more circumspect in his reference to the site of an earlier US defeat and humiliation. Already many commentators were warning of the US being sucked into 'another Vietnam'.) Lucas Caquimbo, a local peasant leader, hoped that Plan Colombia would 'bring help for ordinary Colombians, not just helicopters and bullets'; if it did not, 'the conflict will just get worse'.[11]

Again the FARC rebels were protesting that the Colombian government was doing nothing to stem the wave of paramilitary massacres throughout the country. More than 60 peasants had been murdered in northern Colombia over the past month. Thus Raul Reyes declared: 'The genocide, unleashed by the Colombian state using its paramilitary army, makes it difficult for us to trust the government's good faith in peace talks with the FARC. If the paramilitary policy continues growing, it could lead to an end in the talks that we have undertaken with President Andres Pastrana.' Again the ELN was dynamiting power facilities, this time 11 pylons and two substations in separate attacks; and rebel attacks on personnel – 24 police officers and six civilians recently killed in northern Colombia – were continuing despite the peace talks.

The US Colonel James Hiatt, formerly in charge of the US military's anti-drugs campaign in Colombia, was admitting that he had covered up his wife's illegal heroin smuggling and money laundering;[12] President Pastrana was contemplating dissolving the Congress as the only way of rooting out widespread corruption (government investigators were focusing on 550 shady contracts worth millions of dollars that had been signed by the lower house of congress);[13] and Pastrana was pressing for European, Canadian and Japanese aid to supplement US efforts. Mary Robinson, UN human-rights representative, revealed on 14 April that the murders in Colombia had escalated to more than 2000 over the previous year. She declared in a speech to the UN Commission on Human Rights that executions, torture and death threats had been attributed to government-backed death squads, as well as to the police and the Colombian army. In the annual UN report on Colombia Mary Robinson urged the government to dismantle paramilitarism and to prosecute its leaders, 'including public servants' involved in it: 'This deterioration has seen a rise in the number of allegations of extrajudicial executions – many of these having taken the form of massacres – the persistence of torture and enforced disappearances and an increase in the number of death threats.' She urged the state to protect prosecutors, judges, victims and witnesses, as well as other potential targets, such as human rights advocates, trade unionists and journalists: 'In some cases, victims recognised members of the military forces who formed part of the paramilitary groups that committed the massacres.'

Some 1836 men and women were murdered in 1999, many of whom were university professors, students, trade union leaders, human-rights advocates, representatives of indigenous peoples, members of religious orders, journalists and peasants. The number of the murdered had risen some 36 per cent on the previous year. Camilo Reyes Rodrigues, the Colombian UN ambassador, claimed that his government was fighting the death squads, which he described as 'self-defence' groups, and would not tolerate complicity with them.[14] In fact the death-squads were meeting little government opposition, and there was ample evidence that government bodies were aiding the activities of the rightwing paramilitary groups.[15]

Victims, Protest and Politics

The human-rights abuses in Colombia were continuing through 2000, despite the on-off peace talks and spasms of international agitation. As one index, the likelihood of being kidnapped for ransom had doubled over the previous five years, with Colombia and Mexico topping the world league. (By March 2001 Colombia had become the world's kidnap capital, with someone abducted every three hours to impose a $150 million a year drain on the state.) In April 2000 the FARC rebels threatened to kidnap any millionaires who refused to pay a 'war tax' to help to fund the insurgency (in 1999 there were 2945 kidnappings).

At the end of April the FARC group, together with worker and peasant supporters, launched the clandestine 'Bolivarian Movement for a New Colombia' in the hamlet of Villa Nora on the outskirts of San Vicente del Caguan. The assembled guerrillas greeted the formation of the new political movement, waved weapons and revolutionary banners, and urged the audience to join the broad-based organisation that aims to represent the poor of the region and the rest of Colombia. Manuel Marulanda, appearing with six of the seven-man FARC ruling council, declared: 'It is necessary to make changes in the structure of the state using the impetus of the Bolivarian Movement in the cities and countryside. The FARC, the army of the people, will be its guarantee against extermination' (3500 members of the Patriotic Unity party, representing the poor, had been wiped out by the rightwing paramilitaries). It seemed likely that the Bolivarian Movement would be targeted also by the Colombian army. In mid-May government troops claimed that 10 suspected FARC rebels had been killed while transporting a kidnap victim near Bogota. One soldier had been killed and another injured. At the same time there were unconfirmed reports that four armed guerrillas had used a 'necklace bomb' to decapitate a woman who had refused to pay 'war taxes'. The bomb, packed in a 3in tube had been glued to the neck of 53-year-old Elvitt Cortez, a dairy farmer, but she had managed to call the police. A bomb squad, trying to remove the device, accidentally triggered a built-in pressure-release mechanism and detonated the bomb, killing the woman and an army technician, and injuring three soldiers. President Pastrana responded by suspending the peace talks, due to resume later in May: 'The men of violence have placed a necklace of dynamite ... around the hope of all Colombians.'[16]

The Colombian army called the incident an 'atrocious experiment' in psychological torture, with General Fabio Bedoya noting that it was the first time that such 'a macabre act' had been witnessed. Ivan Rios, a FARC commander, told Radionet Radio, that the guerrillas 'had nothing to do with this condemnable act'; and Camilo Gomez, Colombia's peace commissioner, was prepared to declare that it was 'increasingly clear that it wasn't the FARC' which had committed the atrocity. The United States immediately supported the suspension of the peace talks, describing Pastrana's decision as 'courageous'.[17] It has not been established who was responsible for the 'necklace' device.

On 1 June Luis Fernanda, Colombian defence minister, again rejected the FARC demand that captured policemen be exchanged for leftwing guerrillas. The Colombian government was still not prepared to regard the rebels as prisoners of war: 'The guerrillas were sentenced. Colombian justice requires that anyone who has been condemned should serve his sentence in prison.' But the FARC leadership continued to press for the imprisoned rebels to be granted prisoner-of-war status, not least because such recognition would legally transform the FARC group into a 'belligerent party' to the conflict. FARC was suggesting that prisoners from both sides could be handed over, if not to their own sides then to the International Committee of the Red Cross or to a neutral country until the armed conflict was resolved.

The FARC guerrillas were continuing the armed struggle while consolidating their hold on the demilitarised zone. On 7 June the Colombian military reported that leftwing rebels had blown up three jeeps in an ambush near the town of Cordoba, Bolivar province, and that 17 rightwing paramilitaries had been killed in the encounter. In what some journalists were now calling 'FARClandia', the rebels were bringing a measure of order under the terms of guerrilla law. Thus Omar Moreno, a teacher in San Vicente, commented: 'There used to be 12 or 13 killings a week here. Now there are none. Everyone in Colombia would like to live like this.'[18] Not everyone was in agreement. Miguel Angel Serna, a parish priest in the town, was an outspoken critic of the FARC movement, declaring that arms were a sign of weakness 'because it means that you don't have the authority without them'.[19] It remained to be seen what would happen. FARClandia, the demilitarised *despeje* zone, a 'laboratory of peace', had been given an extension by the Colombian government until the end of the year. By then there would be mounting pressure on the Pastrana administration, not least from the United States, to roll the troops – supported by the rightwing death squads – back into the region.

On 19 June it was reported that the peace talks between Colombian officials and the leftwing guerrillas (now controlling 16,000 square miles of Colombia) would move to Venezuela for mediation by President Hugo Chavez. Critics were claiming that Chavez himself, a leftwing populist attracting US hostility, was supplying arms to the Colombian rebels – a charge that he denied: 'We have been in close contact with the Colombian government, and not so close contact with the Colombian guerrillas, and this is working successfully.' On 29 June Western diplomats from Europe, Japan and Canada began talks with Colombia's leftwing rebels to consider ways of tackling the drug trade, with the United States refusing to attend as it prepared to implement the massive military aid package recently approved by US lawmakers. The European Union was due to meet in Madrid on 7 July to discuss contributing to President Pastrana's Plan Colombia.

In the event the Madrid conference brought together 23 countries, including some that were not in the European Union. Spain itself pledged $100 million in support of the Plan Colombia project and as an incentive to other countries to support the Pastrana scheme. Javier Solana, EU foreign policy tsar, had already given his support for Plan Colombia on his official visit to Bogota: 'The Commission backs the plan – it is a question of an opportunity for dialogue that has to be seized.' With a slight shift of emphasis Enrique Iglesias, Inter-American Development Bank chief, commented that the purpose of the Madrid conference was not to discuss the merits of Plan Colombia but to discuss the future funding of 'social projects' to rebuild Colombian society.

On 10 July rightwing death squads massacred six peasants in a village square in San José de Apartado, the self-styled 'peace community' intent on avoiding paramilitary attacks. A Colombian army helicopter hovered overhead and soldiers were on patrol in the vicinity, indicating yet again how atrocities could be conducted under the eyes of the Colombian armed forces. Gustavo Bell, Amnesty International vice-president, expressed his 'energetic condemnation' of the incident: 'How many times do killings committed by the security forces or their paramilitary allies have to be denounced before the Colombian government brings the perpetrators to justice?' On 16 July Colombian troops claimed to have killed at least 20 leftwing rebels after a column of about 200 FARC guerrillas fired propane gas tanks packed with explosives at a police station in Roncesvalles, Tolima province, southwest of Bogota. Colonel Paulino Coronado, army spokesman, said that 13 of the 17 police had been shot at point-blank range, and that the police station and 25 civilian homes had been destroyed: 'We know that there are considerable casualties among the rebels and the troops have reported at least 20 bodies.' Two days before, FARC guerrillas had launched simultaneous attacks on four towns near to the demilitarised zone.

The ex-commander of the now defunct M-19 rebel group, Alonso Lucio, who became one of the country's most controversial senators, had reportedly been assassinated by the Carlos Castano death squads – as a reprisal for his efforts in trying to broker a peace deal between the Colombian government and the ELN guerrillas. The death squads were also fighting ELN guerrillas for control of a region in northern Bolivar province

(Castano: 'The idea is to force them out of the only sanctuary that they have left'). Jaime Martinez, a colonel in charge of the regional national police, reported that 60 rebels and 15 paramilitaries (members of Castano's AUC death squads) had been killed. On 24 July peace talks between the ELN on the one hand and Colombian government, civil and religious leaders on the other began in Switzerland, with the intention of creating a troop-free enclave for the ELN guerrillas analogous to 'FARClandia'. The United States remained opposed to any conciliatory treatment of the leftwing rebels but there was some acknowledgement that the Colombian government was complicit in the atrocities. Thus US senator Paul Wellstone called on the Clinton administration to investigate recent civilian massacres by death squads linked to the Colombian military: 'This is no longer Colombia's business. It is our business because we provided the money for a military that is complicit in human-rights violations and the murder of innocent people, including small children.' In a surprise move at the end of July, the Colombian government formally charged four army generals and a colonel with ignoring a wave of death-squad attacks that resulted in the massacre of 18 civilians in May 1998.

On 31 July 2000 a contingent of FARC rebels overran security-force positions in Arboleda, an Andean town in Caldas province, killing 25 policemen. General Ernesto Gilibert, Colombia's national police chief, admitted that bad weather had prevented helicopter-borne reinforcements from flying into the area, and that an army unit trying to reach the town on foot had been ambushed. In early August the United States cancelled a meeting with human-rights groups concerned about US military involvement in Colombia, and Colombian oil workers began a strike against the US-backed Plan Colombia and the austerity measures being introduced by the Colombian government. (A spokesman for a solidarity picket outside the Colombian embassy in London emphasised that the Blair administration, working closely with the US government, had 'great responsibility for escalating the war situation' in Colombia.) On 4 August a bomb attack on the Cano Limon-Covenas pipeline, following a wave of similar attacks and coinciding with the oil workers' strike, meant that the Cano Limon oilfield, Arauca province, had been paralysed for 12 days, the longest delay of the year.

On 7 August FARC guerrillas were again clashing with security forces, this time near the town of Carmen de Atrato, Choco province, and at an ELN roadblock in the Norte de Santander province. More than a dozen people were killed, and much of eastern Colombia was left without electricity after ELN rebels blew up two power pylons. Now a growing number of US Special Forces trainers were beginning to arrive, as US C-17 transport planes brought 83 military personnel to the southern military base of Larandia, close to rebel-held territory. On 9 August an AUC death squad dragged 11 peasants from their homes and killed them, while death-squad leader Carlos Castano claimed to have received a message from the US Drug Enforcement Administration (DEA) requesting his help in wiping out the drug trade: 'I received a call saying that the DEA was opening the doors so that Colombian drug-traffickers could surrender to US justice and ... it needed a significant force in Colombia that would induce these people to take that decision.'

The massacres were continuing, despite mounting adverse publicity and the declared resolve of the Pastrana administration to stamp out such atrocities. On 27 August the rightwing death squads killed 22 peasants in Cienega and in three towns near the Pacific port of Buenaventura, after the paramilitaries announced that they would target 'collaborators' of the leftwing rebels. At the same time the FARC guerrillas announced that one of their senior commanders, Adan Izquierdo, head of one of FARC's seven main fighting divisions, had died in an 'unfortunate accident', but no details were reported. In London, a protest organised by the Latin American Solidarity Collective outside the US embassy warned the United States to stop interfering in Colombia's internal affairs. Spokesman Alberto Garcia declared: 'The same ugly power that backed Pinochet's coup and caused so many problems for the Chilean people back in the 1970s is today intervening in our country. That power is the United States of America. Clinton is using the drugs issue as a smokescreen for direct military intervention in Colombia. Quite simply, Plan Colombia is a plan for war.'

Now there were signs of unrest about Plan Colombia in Ecuador, Panama, Peru, Venezuela and Brazil. Thomas Pickering, US under secretary of state for political affairs, was continuing to deny that the scheme would convert Colombia into another Vietnam or that US combat troops would become involved in the civil war, but he acknowledged that US trainers were being assigned to two more Colombian army battalions. The conflict was continuing to escalate, with hundreds of people fleeing across the Colombian borders to escape the death-squad paramilitaries, and with the leftwing rebels remorselessly harrying the Colombian armed forces. In early September more than a dozen Colombian soldiers were killed when FARC rebels attacked a communications centre in western Colombia and when an AC-47 support aircraft crashed into Mount Montezuma, the site of a communications relay installation. Already US pride, the same vainglorious condition that had led to the catastrophe of Vietnam, was at stake. How could Washington allow the leftwing guerrillas to tighten their grip on half of Colombia, and to expand their influence to the rest of the country and beyond?

Prisoners of Conflict

On 12 September 2000 the Colombian authorities reported that Carlos José Restrepo, editor and publisher of two regional publications in Tolima province, had been shot dead and his body dumped on a remote roadside. He was the fourth journalist to be murdered by death squads during the year. Witnesses said that Restrepo had been led away in handcuffs before being killed after accusations that he had collected money on behalf of the FARC guerrillas. Alexander Lopez Maya, a trade union leader prepared to criticise Plan Colombia, was also under threat and needed bodyguards to protect him from the rightwing death squads. Lopez, head of the workers union Sintra Emcali, said that Plan Colombia was about forcing through industrial privatisation – an aim that was facilitated by killing trade union activists. (In 1999 some 160 union members were murdered, 30 had suffered assassination attempts, 40 had disappeared and 200 had been forcibly displaced.) Death threats to union activists were common (676 in 1999), a device used by the death squads to discourage industrial and political campaigning. In mid-September Dr Mo Mowlam, British Labour parliamentarian, declared after a fact-finding mission that before Europe could feel confident about contributing to Plan Colombia the country would have to give more evidence of progress in the human-rights field. In late-September the AUC's Colima Front death squad, linked to the Colombian army, dragged nine peasants out of their homes at dawn and summarily executed them. It was estimated that the Colima Front had been responsible for 200 killings and the displacement of more than 10,000 people since it was formed around Cali in July 1999 with the support of Colombian army officers.

The issue of prisoner exchanges was now again being considered. In early October, following a visit of two women to see their imprisoned relatives, a film broadcast on television showed the plight of Colombian soldiers held in FARC camps deep in the jungle. Monsignor Pedro Rubiano, archbishop of Bogota, described the muddy compounds as 'worse than a

Nazi concentration camp'; while Juan Manuel Ospina, a government negotiator, said that the film underlined the need for a prisoner exchange: 'We have to make some decisions. The government can't continue ignoring this situation.'[20]

Over the previous two years the FARC rebels had captured 468 Colombian servicemen in combat, and was hoping to exchange them for around 500 guerrillas convicted of crimes ranging from rebellion to kidnapping and murder. Marlene Orjuela, one of the visitors to the remote jungle camps, told the Bogota daily *El Tiempo* newspaper that the captives were tied together with nylon nooses around their necks, to stop them fleeing if the army arrived. Orjuela had talked with FARC representatives for two years in order to secure permission for a visit: 'I'm very demanding, but above all, I'm discreet and respectful. This is not about attacking people, but looking for solutions.' President Pastrana, rejecting an exchange deal, had argued that the captured Colombian soldiers were kidnap victims, not prisoners-of-war. And human-rights observers had warned that an unconditional release of rebel prisoners could open the doors to a blanket amnesty for human-rights violators.

On 12 October FARC guerrillas ambushed a group of AUC paramilitaries, killing about 20 of the death-squad members. Teddy Tornbaum, a Red Cross spokesman, said that the killed paramilitaries all wore combat fatigues and the trademark AUC armbands, adding that their weapons had been carried off after the ambush. Now the Colombian army, in a bid to improve its appalling human-rights image, was planning to discharge more than 300 officers who were under investigation for rights abuses and corruption. An army officer, asking not to be identified, said: 'The measure is part of a restructuring and modernisation programme of the armed forces. There are some officers who do not meet the requirements of service, their performance is not the best and that's why they are leaving.' The US Congress had already rubber-stamped the financial allocations for Plan Colombia, ignoring all the abuse allegations against the Colombian armed forces.

On 20 October the FARC rebels shot down a helicopter gunship, killing the 22 troops on board, with dozens of Colombian soldiers killed elsewhere in a week of heavy fighting. The sophisticated helicopter, valued at around $15 million, was hit by FARC ground fire just before it crashed in the town of Dabeiba. It was not lost on observers that this was only one of Colombia's US-supplied Black Hawks and that Plan Colombia provided for the supply of 60 more attack helicopters, including 18 Black Hawks. Now

Washington was finding it easy to blame the rebels for the lack of progress in the peace talks. Philip Chicola, a senior US diplomat, commented: 'You've got to have the political will to do things you would not otherwise do. Thus far, FARC has not done this. Plan Colombia is not the ailment. Plan Colombia is the prescribed medicine.'

The peace talks, already faltering, were now coming under attack by the death squads. On 2 November Carlos Castano, AUC leader, claimed responsibility for kidnapping eight Colombian senators and other political candidates, in the run-up to the nationwide elections for state and local offices, as a way of disrupting the government peace talks with the leftwing guerrillas. Castano said: 'This should be interpreted to mean that the AUC has rebelled against the government. It's a way of telling the president that we're not going to tolerate or put up with his mistaken policy on negotiations any more.' The political hostages would be held, said Castano, until a senior government official was sent to see him, whereupon Castano would voice the complaints of 'hundreds of thousands of Colombians who don't believe in the negotiating process'. International human-rights groups continued to insist that Castano's AUC death squad was working alongside the Colombian security forces. In early November the AUC paramilitaries killed another seven people in Barrancabermeja, just one day after the death squads had executed 15 people in the town of Granada in western Colombian. The local police chief in Granada said that his men were fighting off gunmen who had attacked the police station: 'While we were defending ourselves, other assailants were killing civilians in different parts of the town.'

On 15 November the FARC negotiators broke off peace talks, again in protest at the failure of the Colombian government to take any effective action against the death-squad paramilitaries, and at the government's willingness to tolerate the escalating Vietnam-style US military intervention. FARC was maintaining that Plan Colombia was part of a conspiracy by the Colombian government and the ruling élites to pave the way for 'open military participation by the United States in our country' – 'the first step toward an invasion'. Again FARC was comparing the US military build-up in Colombia with the US aggression against Vietnam:

> It would seem that President Pastrana and his team are leaning towards the militaristic option, given the hopes raised by Plan Colombia and promises from gringos who think that they're invincible. They quickly erased the defeat that they suffered at the

hands of the heroic people of Vietnam from their history books. But reality remains the same and people subjected to the will of the empire remember it as a banner for struggle.[21]

On the following day the death squads murdered Gustavo Ruiz Castillo, another journalist (the sixth killed in 2000), shot down in Tivijay, Magdalena province. A few days later a massacre began in the village of Nueva Venecia, northern Colombia, after death-squad members in combat fatigues and brandishing automatic weapons stormed into the area and began calling out the names of people on a 'hit list' of alleged collaborators with leftwing guerrillas. The number of dead in this massacre has remained uncertain: at least 36 and perhaps as many as 86 peasants summarily executed in the worst Colombian massacre for three years. For some days after the death squad had left the village, bullet-riddled bodies were still being found around Nueva Venecia.

On 5 December 2000 Mary Robinson, the UN high commissioner for human rights, accused the Colombian government of standing by while the AUC carried out massacres: 'The government, despite a commitment voiced to me very strongly today, has not tackled adequately the violence of paramilitary groups ... I'm aware of certain commitments made, but I'm looking at the practical implementation and I have grave concerns about the process of tackling this problem in an effective way.' It was necessary to bring the AUC warlords to justice, to 'break the impunity' with which the paramilitaries were operating. She also urged the FARC rebels to end their long-standing campaign of kidnapping.

The Colombian government was now signalling that it was nearing an agreement on the issue of prisoner exchanges, but there were still many sensitivities about the possible legal implications. A prisoner exchange would clearly have meant a significant breakthrough in the peace talks, but few observers were that optimistic. The talks were accomplishing little and now it seemed unlikely that the government would be willing to extend the life of the demilitarised zone through 2001. One consequence would be that the FARC guerrillas would come under mounting pressure from both the Colombian army and their paramilitary allies, both enjoying growing support from the United States under the terms of Washington's interpretation of Plan Colombia. There were suggestions that the Colombian public was becoming increasingly disenchanted with the slow pace of the peace talks, giving President Pastrana more scope for developing a robust anti-FARC policy.

At the end of 2000, peace seemed no nearer than it had done through all the bitter years of the civil war. The FARC rebels and their allies had created a secure base of support throughout much of Colombia; the rightwing death-squad paramilitaries, with the likelihood of covert military aid through the US version of Plan Colombia, were keen to expand their bloody activities; the Colombian army, with its appalling human-rights record, knew that its abuses would not limit its access to US-supplied military hardware and training; there was no prospect of rolling back the thriving drugs business, the epitome of capitalist free enterprise; and the American White House had a new president-elect – who, having secured his post by comprehensive ballot-rigging and having only a risibly dim comprehension of foreign affairs, was nonetheless smilingly happy to sign any military appropriations when invited to do so. The prospects for Colombia through 2001 and beyond were less than benign.

Over to Bush

In December 2000 the Colombian military was declaring its willingness to retake the vast swathe of territory that had been ceded to the FARC rebels. Thus General Jorge Enrique Mora, army commander, said: 'The Colombian army is ready and it is prepared for anything.' In response to the time limit specified by President Pastrana for the rebels to reach a land-for-peace deal, General Mora commented: 'I think that this bit about 55 days sends a message to these bandits that the country is tired. Also that territory must belong to the Colombian people and that the army of Colombia has a constitutional mission.' It was obvious that the Colombian army could rely on the support of the paramilitaries. On 15 December a three-man assassination squad brandishing automatic assault rifles opened fire on Wilson Borja, head of the public-sector workers union Fenaltrase and a member of the central committee of Colombia's Communist Party. Borja's bodyguard, shot in the face, managed to return the gunmen's fire. Borja, shot in the leg and with one bullet grazing his head, was rushed to hospital where he was said to be in a stable condition. Four days later, a rightwing death squad shot dead Alberto Elias Torres, the mayor of the central Colombian town of Quipile, in the 19th murder of a local leader in the year.

On 23 December the ELN guerrillas announced Christmas plans to free 45 military and police officers: 'The National Liberation Army has considered the importance of the process that is advancing talks with the government and we want to take advantage of the opportunity presented by the Christmas holidays to send a clear message.' While releasing the captives the ELN rebels urged them to 'be happy' in a gesture that Colombian officials said would aid the prospect of peace talks.

The incoming US administration of George W. Bush was now indicating its views on the Colombian issue. Already Robert Zoellick, set to be appointed to an international policy post in the new government, had indicated the shape of what would become Bush policy: 'If the Colombian people are willing to fight for their own country, then the US should offer serious, sustained and timely financial, material and intelligence support.' Zoellick had always regarded the Clinton posture – of offering substantial aid but staying largely out of active combat embroilment – as essentially soft on the leftwing guerrillas: 'We cannot continue to make a false distinction between counter-insurgency and counter-narcotics efforts. The narco-traffickers and guerrillas compose one dangerous network.' It was of no concern, in this perspective, that the rightwing death squads were carrying out the bulk of the 4000 annual political murders; or that the Colombian army was implicated in massive human-rights abuses. In fact there was no distinction here between the policies of the outgoing Clinton administration and what would be the attitude of the Bush regime. Clinton had been criticised for ignoring human-rights abuses – and this posture was not about to change.[22] On 29 December 47-year-old Diego Turbay, president of Colombia's congressional peace commission, his mother and five other people were shot dead in an ambush staged by rightwing paramilitaries. In 2000, 38,820 Colombians, 10 per cent more than in 1999, died in violent circumstances.

It was now being predicted that the Colombian issue would present the soon-to-be President George W. Bush with a 'baptism of fire'. Plan Colombia, initially proposed by President Pastrana under US pressure, would soon be rolling into effect. At a conservative estimate, some 500 US troops were already supporting a Colombian army known to deal in drugs, to perpetrate gross human-rights violations, and to collaborate in operations staged by the death-squad paramilitaries. It seemed that an escalation in the US involvement was inevitable, but Plan Colombia was itself running into significant American criticism – to the point that some commentators were declaring that the scheme was in crisis. Thus William Ratliff, from the conservative Hoover Institution at Stanford (formerly run by Bush's National Security Advisor, Condoleezza Rice), declared that Secretary of State Colin Powell 'must have noticed the large and war-oriented US aid package to Colombia flies in the face of his own famed doctrine: clarity of objective, use of massive force, certainty of victory and exit strategy, and public support'.[23] When the body bags began coming home, opined Ratliff, there would be public protest.

The Clinton administration had recently signed contracts for 30 Black Hawk helicopters, scheduled for early delivery to Colombia. The manufacturers were keen to promote the virtues of their products: each helicopter could carry 'up to 11 fully outfitted troops or four stretchers'. FARC, in its New Year message, was promising to 'defeat the evil war plans of the governments of the United States and Colombia'; and President Hugo Chavez in neighbouring Venezuela, an erstwhile paratroop colonel, was refusing US warplanes permission to fly over Venezuelan territory from their new bases in the Dutch Antilles. Chavez was bitterly critical of Plan Colombia, as was President Mireya Moscoso of Panama, who had denied the Pentagon permission to reoccupy the former Canal Zone bases that the US had been obliged to relinquish a year before. José Vicente Rangel, Venezuela's foreign minister, had publicly challenged Washington to explain why – in view of the much-hyped US anti-drugs campaign – $4 billion-worth of marijuana was being grown in the United States. It seemed unlikely that George W. Bush, despite his famed mental agility, would find an early solution to the many problems surrounding the Colombia issue.

In the first Colombian massacre of 2001, rightwing death squads shot dead 11 people in the town of Yolombo, Antioquia, an event which had reportedly caused 'anxiety, panic and commotion'. Perhaps president-elect Bush was aware of such events when he ordered the Central Intelligence Agency (CIA) to recommend how US resources might be deployed most effectively in Colombia. Some senior Republicans were urging a more aggressive US stand in Colombia, while others appeared to have learned something from the American defeat and humiliation in Vietnam. Thus Roger Fontaine, a Colombian specialist in the Reagan administration, commented: 'Bush will spend at least three months re-evaluating the whole thing. There is growing scepticism about US involvement in Colombia – it's a death trap.'[24] Hundreds of US troops were already deployed in Colombia, and 'Agent Green', reminiscent of the catastrophic US use of 'Agent Orange' in Vietnam, was already being sprayed on Colombian jungles and plantations.

On 7 January the two-year anniversary of the peace talks passed in a general atmosphere of pessimism: nothing substantial had been accomplished and the negotiations had been frozen since mid-November.

There were reports that the FARC rebels were intending to release more than 100 soldiers and police officers by the middle of February, but it was clear that such a conciliatory move would do nothing to address the fundamental differences between the two sides. A bomb was detonated in a shopping mall in Medellin, with no faction claiming responsibility; while the Cano Limon oil pipeline was again inoperative after being bombed for the first time in 2001.

On 11 January the Colombian government announced new measures, in line with various previous commitments, to crack down on the rightwing death squads. Two days later, a rightwing death squad – 20 men in camouflage gear and brandishing assault rifles – drove into the northern town of Valledupar, killed three men, including a 17-year-old, threw a grenade into a nearby house, and then drove to another neighbourhood where they executed four men and a woman. At the same time Colombian guerrillas and rightwing paramilitaries were clashing outside a small town in Ecuador's Amazon jungle, the first time that the two factions had fought each other on Ecuadorian territory. Now there were growing worries – in Ecuador, Venezuela, Peru and Panama – that the US implementation of Plan Colombia would cause the Colombian conflict to spill over into the adjoining states. But some commentators were regarding such a development as inevitable. Patricio Falconi, political analyst, commented: 'Plan Colombia is not the cause of this problem. Plan Colombia is more like a medicine, applied to a problem that has existed for a long time. The medicine could be good, regular, bad or worse than the sickness, but the problem existed before.' On 16 January a number of Colombian governors from the coca-cultivation regions condemned the US-backed policy of spraying the plantations, one aspect of Plan Colombia, saying that this would imperil the livelihoods of thousands of poor peasants. Alfonso Jaramillo, governor of Huila, said: 'The real problem is the terrible situation in which thousands of peasants live in Colombia. We can't trample on their livelihoods without giving them opportunity to grow other crops.'

The United States was now saying – presumably to sanctify increased US action – that the Colombian government and armed forces had improved their human-rights record over the previous six months; while the United Nations was charging that rightwing death squads, linked to the Colombian military, had killed 170 civilians in the first 18 days in murders and massacres. Thus the Colombian office of the UN Commissioner for Human Rights declared: 'The alarming degradation of the Colombian conflict prompts the office to strongly appeal to the authorities so that they protect the civilian population from threats and actions carried out by armed groups.' On 23 January the FARC rebels, told by the Colombian government to end kidnappings and the use of homemade bombs, decided not to resume the peace talks, whereupon President Pastrana declared: 'If Manuel Marulanda wants an extension of the safe haven, he has to sit at the negotiating table.' Already some 600 Colombian troops had been airlifted to sites near the demilitarised zone.

On 31 January President Pastrana announced that he would extend the safe haven for four more days to allow peace talks to begin, whereupon Manuel Marulanda agreed to meet with the government on 8 February. Pastrana duly travelled to the FARC demilitarised zone and stayed overnight in the region to extend the demilitarised (*despeje*) zone, the so-called 'FARClandia', for eight more months, and to negotiate arrangements for a prisoner exchange programme and a ceasefire. At the same time Luis Alberto Moreno, the Colombian ambassador in Washington, was saying that despite the complexity of the security situation in Colombia the government would not accept counter-insurgency aid from the United States: such aid 'would open a huge debate in our country – and the US – that would not be sustainable … From the standpoint of the Colombian government the insurgencies are to be dealt with internally'. The Moreno contribution seemed difficult to comprehend, since Washington was already supplying massive counterinsurgency aid to the Colombian armed forces. Perhaps, as Plan Colombia rolled into effect, the Colombian government was keen to signal a placatory mood to the FARC leadership. The peace talks, for the moment, were again on track but few observers were optimistic. The US Congress had agreed the massive military appropriations for Colombia, Washington had its own agenda, and a new American president was not about to 'wimp out' where US interests were at stake.

The Elusive Peace

On 5 February the Colombian government admitted that attacks by the rightwing death squads, often linked to the military, had soared. According to the Defence Ministry, the number of killings of civilians by paramilitary groups had risen to 1560 in 2000 from a mere 18 in 1995. Nearly 700 paramilitaries had been imprisoned by 2000, but the paramilitary ranks had increased over eight years from 2000 to around 8000 members. In every category of outrage, the death-squad paramilitaries were having an increasing impact. There were more intimidations, kidnappings, murders and massacres; and a rapid increase in the number of forced displacements, with hundreds of Colombian civilians being compelled to seek safety elsewhere in the country or across the Colombian borders. Over a period of a few days, 400 Colombians had crossed the River Rio de Oro into the western Venezuelan state of Zulia. The peasants, from four Colombian villages, were now forced to live in makeshift shelters on the Venezuelan side of the river, after paramilitaries stole their livestock and burned their homes.

The rightwing death squads were also continuing to threaten any groups considered sympathetic to political reform and social justice. Thus members of Peace Brigades International (PBI), an international human-rights group, was informed by paramilitary gunmen that they were now considered to be a 'military objective' because of their work with community groups in Barrancabermeja. The various PBI teams – which include British, Canadian and Australian volunteers – provide unarmed escorts for community activists, trade unionists and human-rights workers who are often the target of the rightwing death squads.

In early February two gunmen broke into the offices of the Popular Women's Organisation (OFP), a local women's group, during a peace demonstration – and then, having declared their AUC membership, confiscated the mobile phones, a passport and other items: 'From this moment onwards, you are targets.' One of the main OFP activities was to run soup kitchens for war refugees and other homeless people in Barrancabermeja. Yolanda Becerra, an OFP organiser, commented of the paramilitaries: 'We know that when they make a threat they're not playing around.' It was suspected that the Organisation was being targeted because of OFP criticisms of paramilitary abuses. Said Becerra: 'They are recruiting boys as young as 12 … they seduce them with £150, a cellphone and a gun. As women and mothers, we cannot allow this. The paramilitaries don't understand that a women's group can have an independent political position. They say that we're a front organisation for the insurgents.'[25] Denise Cauchi, a British PBI volunteer, noted that threats were being made on a daily basis: 'I wouldn't say you ever get used to [the danger], but there's no time to get carried away by your emotions. There's only time to focus on what you have to do.'[26]

There seemed no prospect that the Pastrana-Marulanda peace talks would remove the paramilitary threat to the PBI, the OFP and the many other organisations working to improve the situation of the Colombian people. On 12 February, with the bulk of the news services focusing on the peace talks, the 'US Out of Colombia Committee' of the New York-based International Action Centre issued a statement demanding that President Bush immediately repeal Plan Colombia. Teresa Gutierrez, Committee chairwoman, commented: 'The reality is that the US government is the chief obstacle to genuine peace in Colombia. Its interventionist scheme called Plan Colombia is designed to accelerate US support for the Colombian military and its paramilitary adjuncts. The US's Plan Colombia is the real problem in Colombia today. As long as the paramilitaries of Colombia are allowed to continue to operate in the manner they have been operating, an end to the conflict cannot be expected. As long as the Colombian and US governments utilize the death squads, the people of Colombia will find no real peace.' Gutierrez noted that all the demands to resolve the conflict were being made to the FARC and the ELN rebels: *'Why don't the US and the Colombia governments impose a plan in Colombia that will put an end to the rightwing death squads?'*

On 13 February a death-squad paramilitary group killed Ivan Villamizar, a former regional ombudsman (1996-99) in the Norte de Santander province. On the next day, the bodies of six men and three women, executed by a shot to the head, were reported as having been pulled from a ravine near Purace, southwest of Bogota. On 15 February two people were killed and a trade union leader, Wilson Borja (head of the Federation of State Workers), wounded. On 23 February the Ecuadorean government warned that the Colombian conflict was again spilling over the border – an issue that was complicated by the US deployment of warplanes to the Manta military base in Ecuador. Now President Bush seemed wary about the escalating American commitment to the region: 'I am worried about ever committing the United States military to an engagement in that part of the world. I know we're training – and that's fine. But the mission ought to be limited to just that.'

The United States remained concerned that President Pastrana was not committed to a full military victory over the leftwing rebels. A US diplomat, speaking inside the heavily-fortified embassy in Bogota, said: 'The problem is, we don't know whether Pastrana truly wants to fight this war. You have to be sceptical when you see him in action lately.' President Pastrana had recently gone alone into the Colombian jungles to meet the FARC guerrillas on their territory; he had trustingly placed himself in the hands of those who were committed to his defeat, and who habitually used kidnapping as a political and economic weapon; he had extended the period of the demilitarised zone; and he had looked favourably on the possibility of a deal covering prisoner exchanges and a ceasefire. Pastrana was convinced that Manuel Marulanda was sincere: 'I have looked in his eyes and I see it. He wants peace, not decades more of war.'[27] Pastrana was trying to make peace before the United States managed to escalate the seemingly endless Colombian conflict.

The US-sponsored campaign of spraying the Colombian jungles and plantations with herbicidal poisons was already having a disastrous impact on peasant life. On one occasion the toxic clouds engulfed a school, a Roman Catholic church and other village buildings. Miriam Rodriguez, a teacher at the school in La Concordia, said: 'The effects have been catastrophic. They sprayed the coca, but they also killed all our food crops.' The children were complaining of rashes, headaches and vomiting after the chemicals were dumped on the land, killing fruit trees and maize plants as well as the coca plants.[28] Spy planes and US satellites were used to guide the crop-dusters as they criss-crossed the skies of the southern Caqueta state and the Middle Magdalena region in the north. The pilots, some US contract workers, were flying up to five missions a day, spraying on average 3.8 litres of glyphosate herbicide on every hectare – destroying, in addition to coca, thousands of hectares of pasture and food crops, wrecking local economies, and sowing deep resentment among the local poor.[29]

The spraying of poison on Colombia, a principal element of Plan Colombia, was an effective way of destroying sectors of coca cultivation – and it destroyed, and continues to destroy, much else. There were reports that the herbicides had destroyed plots of banana and yucca, and contaminated fish stocks. Subsistence crops were devastated, and the poisoned land would take time to recover.[30] There were no reports yet on the effects of the poison on human health, on the sick and the old and on pregnant women. How many of the gung-ho pilots, the hawkish politicians and the rightwing US strategists had glanced at the literature on Agent Orange? How many had visited – or even knew of – the museums of deformed foetuses in Vietnam? How many would be surprised when the same thing started to happen in Colombia, among the poor farmers of La Mormiga and elsewhere?

The United States had no interest in a negotiated peace with leftwing rebels. The toxic spraying would continue, as would the supply of arms to the Colombian military and their death-squad allies. Washington would continue to pour arms into the maelstrom, while preparing to inject US combat troops into an unwinnable foreign war. The United States, declared

President Bush, would not take part in peace talks: 'We'll be glad to help Colombia in any way to make the peace (sic). We'll be glad to help the Colombian economy through trade. But I won't be present for any discussions.'[31] Instead the military aspects of Plan Colombia would be prosecuted with vigour, even if this meant more Colombian suffering, more displaced people, more massacres, long-term poisoning of the land, and an ever more disenchanted and angry people.

President Bush was resolved not to attend any peace talks; nor would he even send an envoy to observe the proceedings – a posture that was being criticised in Colombia and elsewhere. President Pastrana, visiting Washington in early March 2001, urged the US to participate in the imminent meeting between the Colombian government, the rebels, the United Nations and diplomats from dozens of countries. But President Bush was not about to agree to that sort of involvement in Colombian affairs: the talks were 'an issue that the Colombian people and the Colombian president can deal with'.[32] Later President Pastrana pulled back, suggesting that the United States had never been invited to the talks: 'There was a lot of misinformation.' Was this revised posture preferable to an outright rejection by one of the principal parties to the war? Then Ciro Ramirez, president of Pastrana's ruling Conservative Party, urged Bush to reconsider his decision not to attend the talks.

On 8 March envoys from 26 countries met FARC rebels at Los Pozos, a guerrilla stronghold 430 miles south of Bogota. Officials from the UN, Europe and Latin America – but not the United States – attended in an effort to end the 37-year conflict that had claimed 130,000 lives. This was the first time that members of the international community had been invited by President Pastrana and Manuel Marulanda to join in a dialogue to end the hemisphere's longest and bloodiest battle.

As the diplomats left their buses a group of about 100 mothers, waving pictures of men being held by the FARC, broke into chants of 'Freedom for our sons!'. Then Marulanda walked over and shook hands with the women: 'Have faith and hope. We hope to reach a humanitarian solution soon.' Later Marulanda said, of the American absence: 'If they don't want to come, that's their business. We've invited them several times. It may be that they come in the future.' Three days later, on 11 March the FARC temporarily suspended the peace talks in protest against a new army offensive against rebel groups.

A Curfew on Men

On 11 March 2001 the men of Bogota were under a curfew from 7.30pm, a 'Night Without Men' imposed by Antanas Mockus, the city's philosopher-turned-mayor. The measure, designed to highlight the alarming incidence of street crimes and to improve the safety of women for a few hours, did not have the force of law but the few men who left their homes during the six-hour period were asked to carry an explanatory police pass. Mockus, variously described in the media as 'zany' and 'wacky', won notoriety in 1993 as a professor of logic prepared to flash his naked bottom at students in the National University to gain their attention. He married in 1996 in a circus tent, seated with his bride on an elephant in a cage full of Bengal tigers to show his disdain for the Roman Catholic Church.

The brief curfew was an extraordinary episode in Bogota's recent violent history. Thousands of women attended female-only concerts, strolled down barricaded streets and danced in the central park. A strip club that normally employed women hired men for the evening instead. Women staffed the city's fire engines and most male police officers were given the night off, leaving their 1500 female colleagues to patrol the streets. At the same time statistics were being compiled on bar room brawls and armed arrests to illustrate that most violent crime was caused by men. Roberto Pombo, a columnist for *El Tiempo*, was dismissive: 'Showing there is violence and that it is mostly male is like discovering warm water.'

The episode provided entertaining newspaper copy and some serious commentary. It did nothing to curb the escalating levels of violence in Colombian society.

The Spreading Conflict

There was now a growing international concern that the ongoing conflict would spill over Colombia's borders. On 20 March the Organisation of American States (OAS) warned that Ecuador could be affected by a planned US-backed offensive against the guerrilla rebels. Ecuador had already complained that Plan Colombia could encourage the spread of violence into various countries. Luigi Einaudi, OAS general secretary commented that 'the United States didn't evaluate from a regional and strategic perspective' what Plan Colombia's impact would be on neighbouring countries Ecuador, Venezuela, Peru, Brazil and Panama.

On 22 March the Colombian government moved to dismiss 20 military officers and 50 other soldiers linked with the rightwing death squads, at the same time criticising a UN Commissioner on Human Rights report accusing the regime of not doing enough to fight the paramilitaries. At the end of March, as a conciliatory gesture to the 5000-member ELN, the government began to withdraw troops from the northern province of Bolivar, a leftwing stronghold. General Carreno, commenting on what would become a demilitarised enclave similar to FARClandia, said that the move was intended to stimulate an initial dialogue between the government and the guerrillas. Washington remained opposed to all such conciliatory policies and urged a more vigorous campaign against the various rebel factions.

On Easter Sunday leftwing guerrillas stormed the paramilitary-held village of La Caucana, killing nine people and burning houses and cars in north-western Antioquia province. Two days later, ELN rebels freed all but 17 of 92 employees of Occidental Petroleum taken hostage at the Cano Limon oilfield. The conflict was continuing to escalate with increased US military aid and a small but growing British involvement. In April 2001 the British government admitted sending two generals and the former head of security at the Northern Ireland Office to help train Colombian government forces. Britain had also made £100,000 available to the UN Drug Control Program to monitor the effects of chemical defoliant spraying on coca plants. It was known that fields of plantain, cassava and maize had been inadvertently destroyed by herbicides.

The last of more than 3000 Colombian troops had been withdrawn from the designated ELN enclave, but Washington remained determined to advance the military aspects of Plan Colombia. The Andean states – Venezuela, Colombia, Ecuador, Peru and Bolivia, coming together in the Andean Community organisation – were arranging talks with President Bush in Quebec to discuss a counter-proposal to the US-run Plan Colombia, but few observers doubted that the American priority would remain the protection of the US corporate interests throughout the region. On 20 April the ELN again suspended the peace talks with the government, charging that nothing was being done to curb paramilitary excesses, and that in fact the army and the rightwing death squads were still collaborating to wipe out the ELN and other rebel groups.

Nuclear Ambitions?

In April six Colombian secret policemen, along with members of the prosecutor general's office and geologists, arrived at the home of Alfonso Sandoval in a western suburb of Bogota. On entry they discovered a computer, a spectrometer for measuring the purity of radioactive elements, and two lead canisters with 600 grams of highly concentrated uranium. The geologists' Geiger counters immediately showed heavy signs of radiation, and Sandoval's computer files revealed detailed information on uranium enrichment processes. It seemed that Sandoval 'was engaged, however implausibly, in a high-risk, home grown uranium enrichment exercise'.[33] Initial enquiries revealed no links with other illicit networks and it was not obvious how the uranium had arrived in Colombia. The police, and an American FBI team hurriedly drafted in, were then speculating about the prospect of a black market in atomic bombs. Said Ismael Malaver, head of the Colombian investigating team: 'What is certain is that he was planning to sell it.' There were thoughts that since the collapse of the Soviet Union an unregulated and lawless Colombia might serve as a secret bazaar where pariah states might try to acquire uranium smuggled out of Russia.

Sandoval, an animal feed salesman, claimed that he had merely found some radioactive ore on his farm, but natural uranium has to be treated to reach the levels of enrichment found in his bathroom. Sandoval had visited Russia for unknown reasons in February 2000. Had he really only stumbled across the radioactive material on his land? In any event this was not the first case of its kind. In 1991 a Colombian passing through Frankfurt on his way from Moscow was arrested with a quantity of plutonium in his suitcase, though this turned out to be a 'sting' operation by German intelligence. The Bogota find was the first such discovery in Latin America but experts were not surprised that Colombia – where smugglers of drugs, arms and emeralds operate with virtual impunity – should have emerged as a player in the uranium trade. David Kyd, a spokesman for the Vienna-based International Atomic Energy Agency (IAEA), commented that the Bogota haul might indicate that 'the Colombian mafia is diversifying to the extent that it is introducing uranium into its sales brochure'.[34] We may speculate on the extent to which Plan Colombia, in encouraging paramilitary excesses, encouraged a lawless social order in which enterprising criminals might make uranium available to pariah states.

War on the People

The suffering of the Colombian civilian population continued through 2001, with no relief from kidnappings, torture, assassinations and civil conflict. In May the police assaulted Carlos Gonzalez, president of the University of Valle de Cauca trade union, and Jesus Antonio Gonzalez, a trade union human-rights representative, during a demonstration in Cali. Seven other trade unionists were also arrested, held incommunicado and beaten in custody. On 18 May a car bomb exploded in Medellin, killing seven people and injuring 138. General Tobias Duran, National Police director, blamed rightwing paramilitaries and criminal elements: 'All indications are that this is a retaliation stemming from a war between the AUC and criminal bands, specifically The Terrace band.' The blast followed the AUC killing of the leader of The Terrace, a notorious criminal gang.

In three days of fighting the Colombian army killed 41 rebels in various parts of the country, and military operations were continuing against various guerrilla factions. On 16 May teachers and public-health workers across Colombia launched a strike against IMF-imposed spending cuts designed to slash federal expenditure on social services. At the same time more than 12,000 Indians in Cauca state began a five-day march in protest against the massacre of Indians by rightwing death squads. One massacre, in Naya province, one such incident among many, left more than 100 people dead in furtherance of the AUC policy of weakening the FARC presence in the region by killing off the peasants at will. As always, trade union members were being targeted by AUC death squads, leading to a shortage of teachers in some 300 schools leaving around 20,000 children with no school places. Miguel Antonio Caro, a union leader, said that 31 trade unionists, including 13 teachers, had been murdered in the first three months of the year.

It seemed plain that the United States, under the terms of Plan Colombia, was providing funds to support such paramilitary atrocities. Amnesty International had already recorded: 'Colombian army personnel, trained by US special forces, have been implicated ... in serious human rights violations, including the massacre of civilians.' And an official human rights ombudsman in Colombia had noted, in the same vein: '*The paramilitary phenomenon ... is the spearhead of Plan Colombia; to create territorial control and to control the civilian population. This is a terror tactic.*'[35] The United States, with the help of the Colombian government, 'is waging yet another dirty war in Latin America'.[36]

In this context Plan Colombia, involving the destruction of peasant agriculture and widespread murder, has been rightly viewed as an attack on both leftwing guerrillas and grassroots democratic movements, in order to facilitate the seizure of the country's most valuable land:

> The US envisages a new inter-oceanic canal through the north of the country, to bypass the congested Panama canal. Its companies have identified billions of dollars' worth of oil and mineral deposits. So ... soldiers and paramilitaries have been murdering community leaders and expelling local people. *The places identified for economic development by Plan Colombia are the places now being savaged by the paramilitaries* (my italics).[37]

Such information, all in the public domain, can be obtained relatively easily but the United States is understandably reluctant to encourage discussion in this area. It is far preferable in propaganda to portray the Colombian conflict as a mindless battle between extremist factions, which a virtuous Washington is trying to address by waging war on drugs and terrorism. But it is obvious that the aims of Plan Colombia cannot be comprehended without due consideration of the American corporate interest and the wider US strategic goals.

On 25 May two more bombs exploded in Bogota, killing at least four people and wounding many others, following the bigger blast a week before. Some progress was being made on the issue of prisoner exchange, while other aspects of the war continued unabated. In early June fake bank notes, worth $1 million, were found near Cali under a small hill with coffee and bananas growing on top – an unsurprising discovery in a disordered society. Violence, taking its usual toll of innocent life, remained endemic in rural and urban areas. The toxic spraying of agricultural land continued, despite mounting Colombian opposition, with the consequences of this practice – banned in international law – then becoming increasingly obvious.

The fate of the tiny indigenous Kofan community of Santa Rosa de Guamez was typical of great swathes of agricultural Colombia. Here the peasant land had been sprayed with 'Roundup Ultra' containing cosmoflux 411F, a weedkiller being sprayed on Colombia in a concentration 100 times more powerful than was legally permitted in the United States. The produce of the villagers had been destroyed; the pineapples were stunted and shrivelled; the banana plants had been reduced to blackened sticks; and other food crops had been devastated. The villagers were hungry – and suffering also in other ways. Babies and children were falling ill, and families were fleeing the poisoned land. The indigenous peasant tribes, already miserably poor, were being torn apart and whole communities forced into exile.[38]

Villagers were reluctant to describe their plight for fear of reprisals by the US-funded government forces and their death-squad allies. Children were showing serious skin conditions which abated but continually recurred. At one school in El Placer about 230 of the 450 pupils were suffering from diarrhoea, respiratory diseases and severe skin infections. Dogs, pigs and other livestock were dying. Elsa Nivia, a Colombian agronomist working with the Pesticide Action Network, had ridiculed US government assertions that Roundup Ultra was safe, writing that in the first two months of 2001 the Colombian local authorities had reported 4289 people suffering skin or gastric disorders linked to the chemicals, while 178,377 creatures – including cattle, horses, pigs, dogs, ducks, hens and fish – had been killed by the spraying.[39]

The Vietnamisation of the region – stimulated by the post-September 11 sensitivities of the Bush administration and the perennial greed of corporate America – was well under way. In August 2003 Donald Rumsfeld, US defence secretary, visited President Uribe in Bogota to signal Washington's escalating involvement in Colombian affairs. On 19 August, interviewed by TV Caracol in Bogota, Rumsfeld declared that the situation in Colombia may 'end up having both a military solution as well as a political solution'.

It seemed that the grim toll of human life could only grow in the years to come. After the US-led invasion of Iraq in 2003 there were few constraints on American ambition or American power.

TWELVE

War on Terrorism? (September 2001 to ...)

Exploiting 11 September

The events of 11 September 2001, horrific in themselves, were of immense help to a Bush administration determined to drag the United States and the world to the ideological Right. The resulting US-led 'war on terrorism' helped Washington to increase its military spending, to launch devastating wars against Afghanistan and Iraq, to expand American military penetration around the globe, and to strike massive blows against human rights in the United States and elsewhere (Figure 1). Without the attacks on Washington and the Twin Towers many of the subsequent events would still have occurred – the political trends were plain – but after 11 September the Bush administration was emboldened to display a brash arrogance and a contempt for international law that was remarkable even by US standards.

The American use of atomic-scale thermobaric bombs in Afghanistan, the horrific missile onslaught on Iraq at the start of the 2003 war, the abrogation of many human rights in the United States, the abuse of caged prisoners at Guantanamo Bay, the routine American torture of suspects at

Canada – new law facilitates the freezing or seizure of assets, and requires individuals to supply all relevant information to a judge

United States – Patriot Act allows indefinite detention on security grounds of non-US citizens who cannot be deported; non-US nationals can be tried by military commissions

Cuba – expanded anti-terrorism law reaffirms the death penalty in the most extreme cases

United Kingdom – new law allows the internment of foreigners without trial; suspension of British obligations under the European human rights Convention; increased surveillance powers; provisions for the retrospective use of the law

France – expanded security in airports, stations and other public buildings; a dozen new anti-terrorism measures significantly expand police surveillance and search powers

European Union – anti-terrorism legislation, already in the pipeline, was speeded through; EU-wide arrest powers with automatic extradition between member states

Netherlands – lower house voted for investigation of country's 800,000 Muslims

South Africa – proposed anti-terrorism law could criminalise strikes, allow detention without trial and give police wider search powers

Italy – new laws allow police to detain and question alleged Islamists with the same powers they have used against the leftwing Red Brigades

Egypt – reinforces existing harsh measures – formerly criticised by Europe and the United States

Jordan – new law to allow closure of newspapers for publishing false information that could 'undermine national unity or the country's reputation'

Israel – considers hard-line policies vindicated; Sharon calls Yasser Arafat 'our Bin Laden'

Australia – police given increased surveillance powers; proposed law would allow detention of suspects as young as 10 for indefinite time

Russia – claims vindication of harsh policies on Chechnya

India – new law allows suspects to be held for three months without charge

New Zealand – new laws allow tightening of immigration policy and seizure of assets

China – thousands of arrests reported by human rights groups

Philippines – arrest and torture of alleged Abu Sayyaf members

Figure 1. Worldwide impact of 11 September 2001 on human rights

Bagram in Afghanistan, the 'green light' to Sharon's atrocities in Palestine – all this and much more, highly congenial to George W. Bush and his corporate coterie, was directly facilitated by the successful terrorist attacks on the prime symbols of American power: global capitalism and vast military might.

The Bush administration also felt encouraged to expand a number of proxy wars around the world, not least in Colombia – all in the name of an alleged 'war on terrorism'. The Colombian civil war, four decades long, was in essence a struggle between the people (workers, peasants, professionals) and successive US-friendly repressive regimes. In 2003 the leftwing guerrillas controlled almost half the country, a wholly intolerable situation for a Bush administration determined to donate Colombian natural resources – including oil – to American corporations. The result was a growing US military intervention, a progressive 'Vietnamisation' of the region. Here the toll of civilian casualties – tortured, injured, killed, displaced, bereaved, traumatised – was already numbered in the millions. With the escalating American involvement the dreadful toll was set to swell through 2003 and beyond.

Enter the IRA

On 3 August 2001 it emerged that Colombian police had arrested three alleged IRA members who were travelling on false passports. At first it was assumed in Northern Ireland that the three men – James Monaghan (travelling as Edward Joseph Campbell), Martin McCawley (John Joseph Kelly) and Niall Connolly (David Bracken) must have been on a weapons-buying mission, but then the Colombian army made a specific charge – the trio had spent two weeks in a remote rebel-held part of the country where they were teaching bomb-making techniques to guerrillas of the Revolutionary Armed Forces of Colombia (FARC). The men were arrested at the El Dorado airport and were still being held in Bogota. It was further reported that Monaghan, a convicted member of the Provisional IRA, had already served two prison sentences in Britain and the Irish Republic, spending ten years in the republic's high-security Port Laoish jail. The men, if convicted of training the FARC rebels, faced prison terms of up to 20 years.

The Colombian army had been tipped off by 'an international security organisation', enabling the trio to be placed under surveillance upon their arrival on 30 June. Gustavo Bell, the Colombian defence minister, commented: 'Given their route plan [variously arriving in Bogota via Paris, Madrid and Caracas] and their backgrounds, they weren't likely to be involved in legal activities ... The FARC didn't learn how to build mortar bombs from gas cylinders from the internet.' The Royal Ulster Constabulary (RUC), happy to see the incarceration of Irish citizens in Colombia, was soon exchanging photographs and fingerprint information with the Colombian authorities. The case, set to last months, was already raising questions of extradition and human rights.

In August 2001 the Colombian political situation was rapidly deteriorating. The Colombian Foreign Ministry estimated that at least four million Colombians had fled the country, while customs authorities were suggesting that half of those travelling abroad had no plans to return. Colombians were leaving the country in droves, desperate to escape kidnapping, record levels of violence and crime, an escalating US-fuelled civil war and a worsening economic situation. In 2000 there were more than 3700 abductions, more than one every three hours, and the FARC rebels, heartened by their territorial gains, were demanding a nationwide tax. Unemployment was more than 20 per cent, $2 billion had left the country over the previous two years, and murders were running at the rate of 26,000 a year. The rightwing death squads, funded indirectly by the United States and often aided by the Colombian army, were carrying out massacres throughout the country.

Impoverished peasants, protesting at their plight, set up road blocks, whereupon the police moved in with teargas and armoured vehicles; two protesters were killed. The Movement for Farm Salvation was urging the government to ban farm imports and to write off farmers' debts in circumstances where the farming sector had been drastically affected by the removal of trade barriers and subsidies in the interest of US multinational corporations. The death-squad paramilitaries were killing protesting peasants and trade unionists, in part to clear land coveted by the corporations. On 8 August the Spanish authorities revealed that more than 60 international peace activists, including 37 Spaniards, had been captured in the Bolivar region – at a time when peace activists from 11 nations were setting out on a 'life caravan' to deliver food and medical supplies to impoverished families in an area controlled by the paramilitaries. Shortly after the kidnappings President Pastrana broke off peace talks with the ELN, then judged to be weakened by the rise of the paramilitary forces. Thus Arturo Valenzuela, a former US government advisor, said: 'The ELN is sort of caught between a rock and a hard place, because their bargaining position has gotten weaker and weaker as the paramilitaries have gotten more effective.'

The peasants, constantly terrorised by the paramilitaries, were facing various other threats to their livelihood and survival. The United States, as part of its Plan Colombia, was supporting the campaign to spray toxic chemical and biological agents on agricultural land – in violation of international law. The nominal aim was to destroy the coca crops and so combat the drugs industry, but in fact human beings, animals and non-target agricultural species were also being devastated. At the same time coffee prices, another index of peasant enterprise, were falling drastically, forcing farmers to switch to coca and poppy, the raw materials for cocaine and heroine. Octavio Asavedo, a farmer with a typical seven-acre plantation in Antioquia, northern Colombian, commented: 'We are beset on all sides. The gringos [Americans] are spraying chemicals on us anywhere they see a coca leaf, killing all plant life. The guerrillas and paramilitaries are killing us. Now the international coffee market is killing our livelihood. We have no choice, it is drugs or joining the fighting.'[1]

In 2001 (up to August) the United States sprayed toxic defoliants on more than 125,000 acres of drug crops – and watched an increase in the cultivated area, estimated by the UN Drugs Control Program at 500,000 acres. Over the previous two years the number of paramilitaries doubled to more than 8000, and the strength of the leftwing guerrillas, then numbering 22,000, was continuing to grow. Hence the peasant farmers were being poisoned, terrorised and exploited in equal measure. Ian Breminar, managing director of Complete Coffee, a medium-sized roasting company in London, commented on the plight of the Colombian farmers:

> For the first time in my working life I am ashamed to be working in this industry. I find it unacceptable to be in one of the consuming countries responsible and to allow this situation to increase beyond all proportion. I know these people. I have made friends with many of their growers ... and they are making no money at all. We have all known that this was coming.[2]

The London-based Economist Intelligence Unit reported that whereas farmers had received 20 per cent of the price paid in supermarkets, that share was reckoned to have fallen to below 10 per cent, with retail prices not falling in proportion. Colombian coffee-growing was being decimated by the policy of the supermarkets and high-street chains.

On 10 August Colombian troops killed at least six ELN members, following the collapse of peace talks, and clashes were continuing near the northern town of La Bodega. Witnesses at the bottling plant in the town of Carepa, northern Colombia, said that rightwing paramilitaries had shot union leader Isidro Segundo Gil on 5 December 1996 and set the trade union's headquarters on fire. The paramilitaries then assembled the workers outside and told them to resign from the union or be killed. A number of workers had gone into hiding to escape the death squads. A week later Sinaltrainal, the food industry union, received 43 typed resignations, all with the same wording, from its members at Carepa. Javier Correa, Sinaltrainal national president, said: 'I am always getting threats over the phone at my house. The last time, they left a message saying "We're going to cut you up" and then they turned on a chainsaw.'

There were still few developments in the case of the three IRA suspects. On 16 August Sinn Fein was being asked to clarify the republican position, whereupon it issued a statement accusing British intelligence of exploiting the arrests in order to stall moves towards demilitarisation in northern Ireland. The three men – Monaghan, McCauley and Connolly – had made their first court appearance to be accused of using false passports and travelling illegally. It was alleged that initial tests showed traces of explosives on the men's skin, but there were doubts that convictions on terrorist-related charges could be achieved. The men claimed that they had visited the FARC area merely to check on the peace process between the Colombian government and the rebel army, while military officials suggested that the training offered to FARC personnel was a prelude to a guerrilla campaign in the cities. The suspects allegedly told prosecutors that they had visited the rebel enclave only because 'it is a very pretty area'.

It was then emerging that Niall Connolly had worked in Cuba for the previous five years as Sinn Fein's Latin American representative, a revelation set to embarrass the Irish republicans who had strenuously denied any association with the suspects. Colombian police were claiming that Connolly had contacted the FARC using a codename provided by Cuban intelligence, and that he was the link between the IRA and various revolutionary movements in Latin America. One Colombian security officer claimed that the men's mission was to supply FARC with expertise in electrical and remote detonation for car bombs and in mixing highpowered synthetic explosives. The Irish suspects were supposedly met by a FARC escort, and driven north towards the village of La Macarena, where the rebels maintained a number of large training camps. It was known that the

FARC was then using mortars fashioned from gas cylinders filled with explosives and shrapnel, with unnamed diplomatic sources suggesting that the IRA men might have been working to improve their accuracy.[3] It was then being suggested that the fate of the three suspects would be made clear over the coming days.

On 18 August the British security forces claimed that the IRA suspects were testing a 'super-bomb' or 'vapour-bomb' capable of killing hundreds of people. Such a device, relying on a mixture of gas and explosives that vaporises oxygen and creates a huge fireball, would have the power of a 'small nuclear device'.[4] In the early 1990s the IRA had allegedly tried but failed to develop such a 'fuel air bomb', though the relevant technology was widely known throughout the world. A swab taken from the clothing of one suspect was said to have yielded traces of vapour-bomb ingredients, and two other tests showed up drugs and explosives. In one account the vapour-bomb was likened to napalm. Said one senior intelligence source: 'It is terrifying used against economic targets such as oil depots, or as an anti-personnel bomb that sets people alight.' A lawyer for Monaghan and McCauley appointed by the Colombian government claimed that subsequent forensic tests had revealed no traces of explosives.

It now seemed clear that the IRA's alleged links to FARC would cost it support on both sides of the Atlantic. FARC was known to have been implicated in the kidnap and often murder of scores of Americans, Britons and other Westerners. In the United States opposition was growing to Sinn Fein's traditional practice of fundraising, and the republican leadership in Northern Ireland was thrown into confusion. Few independent observers doubted that the venture of the three suspects was sanctioned by the IRA Army Council and that the issue had cost Sinn Fein dear.

On 20 August the Bogota magazine *Cambio* published what it claimed were radio intercepts implicating the IRA men with the FARC's urban bombing campaign. In the messages, intercepted by army intelligence staff, FARC commander Jorge Briceno appeared to be referring to IRA advice on Semtex:

> We have to rattle the cities. There are a lot of ways to make a big noise, to make it thunder. The thing about Semtex was very interesting. It's very important and they have it and they know how to use it ... We have to prepare how the material they're going to send us will arrive. We can use Venezuela – there are people there who can help us, and the routes are working and they're safe.[5]

Later Briceno supposedly commented on the lessons learnt from the three Irishmen:

> We have to take advantage of this instruction for everyone. It's very technical, it's not easy, but the three blondies gave us very thorough lessons here.[6]

There was no way to validate the *Cambio* story, but the Colombian army confirmed that the military had collaborated with the magazine on the details. After hints that the three suspects might be deported, the men were charged on 21 August with 'training for illegal activities' and travelling on bogus passports. Now the IRA trio could be held for eight months in a high-security jail while the Colombian government prepared its case. On 26 August a fourth Irishman, Kevin Noell Crennan, arrested at a roadblock two weeks before, was released without charge.

Once in jail, Bogota's notoriously violent Modelo prison, the three men faced further hazards as news emerged of an assassination plot by rightwing inmates. In response the prison authorities banned the trio from taking exercise or eating in the prison canteen, and a 24-hour guard was posted outside their cell. Their state-appointed lawyer commented: 'If they step out of their cell, they'll be killed. If they stick a finger out, it would be cut off.'

The Culture of War

In the latest of a series of offensives, thousands of Colombian troops were being flown to the eastern jungles to locate and destroy guerrilla forces. This action coincided with reports suggesting that the United States was growing increasingly impatient with President Pastrana's attempts to seek accommodations with the leftwing rebels. Washington, as with Iraq, believed that military force should be used effectively in Colombia as a realistic alternative to negotiation.

The new offensive, relying on US-supplied helicopters and other military aid, involved 6000 troops dropped along a river dividing Guaviare and Meta states in an effort to stop FARC forces reaching the demilitarised zone that Pastrana had agreed. General Carlos Fracica declared: 'This will end in a massive guerrilla surrender, if we don't bring them back in body-bags first. Only when the rebels are annihilated will we leave the region.'

The FARC column had marched out of the demilitarised zone in late July, aiming to attack towns and military bases towards the Venezuelan border. On 10 August a rebel attack was launched on the village of La Co-operativa, resulting in the destruction of dozens of houses with homemade gas cylinder mortars. Then the army responded with a massive operation, which forced the guerrillas to scatter into the jungle. More than 1000 further rebels emerged from the demilitarised zone but were intercepted by helicopter gunships equipped with night-vision sights. Before long, television news broadcasts showed FARC guerrillas being cut down by cluster bombs and machine-gun fire.

The United States, angered by the FARC's military use of the agreed haven, was urging a more robust government response, at the same time increasing the flow of munitions to the Colombian armed forced and their paramilitary allies. The arrest of the IRA suspects had further incensed Washington, and there was mounting pressure from the Bush administration for President Pastrana to abandon all thought of talks with the guerrilla factions. On 24 August 2001 the *New York Times* quoted a senior White House official as saying that there was 'no reason to believe' that there could be a substantive deal with either of the main guerrilla groups, the FARC and the ELN, in the future. There was still an element of policy confusion in the US government. Thus Peter Rodman, assistant secretary of defence, said: 'I think we as a country are not quite sure where we are heading. Is it just narcotics, or is there some wider stake we may have in the survival of a friendly democratic government?'

The United Nations had a somewhat different focus. At a time when a high-level US delegation was arriving in Bogota to press President Pastrana to adopt a more aggressive approach, Jan Egeland, Kofi Annan's special advisor on Colombia, said that the UN Secretary-General was 'deeply concerned by the deteriorating situation in Colombia'. With Pastrana having until 7 October to decide on allowing the FARC rebels continued use of the demilitarised zone, Egeland was declaring that only talks would avoid greater bloodshed: 'Seeking a negotiated end to the conflict should become a state policy in Colombia, no matter who is president.' But the possibility of talks seemed increasingly remote. On 31 August 2001 the rightwing death squads offered their leadership job to Salvatore Mancuso, a hardline paramilitary set to replace Carlos Castano who had resigned saying he could no longer control the death-squad extremists.

There was little doubt that Mancuso would continue the horrific policies of the ultra-right United Self Defence Forces of Colombia (AUC) whose members, sometimes using chainsaws and sledge hammers, had tortured and murdered thousands of peasants thought to be sympathetic to the leftwing rebels. Castano, anticipating even more horrific death-squad policies, declared himself 'not responsible' for Mancuso's actions.

In early September four Colombian police officers died after being attacked with a mortar bomb filled with poison gas, which suggested an IRA link. General Fernando Tapias commented:

> The guerrillas have started using poisonous gas bombs which we believe they learnt how to make from IRA terrorists. The rebels, who have long kept to jungle battles, are trying to show us that they have been trained in lethal urban terror tactics.

It now seemed obvious that the conflict would escalate and that the demilitarized zone, ceded to the FARC rebels two and a half years before, would not survive. On 6 September President Pastrana was forecasting the possibility of all-out war, particularly if he was forced to annul the Switzerland-sized guerrilla sanctuary and instruct the army to take over the territory. Pastrana and Armando Estrada, interior minister, seemed prepared to tolerate the enclave but there was mounting pressure from Washington for the Colombian military to attack the leftwing rebels wherever they were. Now the AUC faction, responsible for many of the 40,000 civilians killed in the previous decade, was forming its own political party, the so-called Democratic and National Movement, to be headed by Carlos Castano.

The three IRA suspects were claiming that international intelligence agencies had falsely incriminated them in order to derail the Irish peace process: 'We are not terrorists' (Connolly). The men had already been held in their cell for several weeks, 24 hours a day, with no opportunity to go outside: 'We can't see the light of day, and we haven't had enough access to our lawyer.' On 10 September the Colombian authorities announced that they had moved the men from the top-security prison to prevent their being murdered by rightwing paramilitary prisoners. The lawyer representing Connolly said that an explosive had already been tossed into their cell and that there was a plot to kill them. A week later, General Jorge Enrique Mora declared: 'Military intelligence has done valuable work that did not end with the capture of the three Irish. We have detected a bigger presence of IRA members in the demilitarised zone.' Moreover, it was revealed that Padraic Wilson, the former IRA commander in the Maze prison in

Northern Ireland, had visited Colombia some months before, with the Colombian police claiming that no fewer than 14 Irish republicans had already visited the demilitarised zone.

It had always been plain that the relatively successful FARC struggle against the Colombian authorities had attracted revolutionary interest from around the world, and that the civil war had provided a congenial environment for criminal activity. The leading drug trafficker Fabio Ochoa, said to have bathed his 1500 thoroughbred horses in whisky and kept them in carpeted stables, was being arraigned before a Miami court after extradition from Bogota. Having resisted extradition for years, he was reported as saying: 'Better a grave in Colombia than a cell in the United States.'

The extradition, like earlier US successes of the same kind, had fuelled tensions throughout Colombia, and the police announced that they had foiled an assassination attempt against the popular rightwing presidential candidate, Alvaro Uribe Velez. The plot reportedly involved a suitcase-bomb packed with explosives in hollowed-out Bibles, to be detonated at one of Uribe's campaign offices in Bogota. The trial of Ochoa, the biggest since the 1991-2 prosecution of Panama's General Manuel Noriega, was unlikely to end with a lenient sentence. Earlier cases had involved the strategy of negotiated sentences but it seemed probable that Ochoa would spend the rest of his life in prison.

On 21 September 2001, with the world still preoccupied with the terrorist attacks on the Twin Towers and Washington, the Colombian army claimed to have killed dozens of FARC rebels during a six-week offensive. The guerrillas had separated into small groups and were retreating to their demilitarised enclave. In retreat, a FARC group kidnapped 56-year-old Consuelo Araujo, the wife of the Colombian attorney-general and a former minister. When she was exhausted by the chase and could not continue, the guerrillas promptly executed her with two shots to the head, so seemingly ending any real chance of effective peace talks with the government. But on 5 October Camilo Gomez, President Pastrana's chief negotiator, met guerrilla leaders in the demilitarised region of Caqueta, the safe haven that FARC stood to lose unless Pastrana extended its life. Three days later, it was announced that the guerrillas could continue to occupy the enclave until January 2002 – the ninth time that the life span of the enclave had been extended since 1998.

This did little to arrest the deteriorating situation. Government forces around the enclave were growing, threatening the fragile peace process.

'Under these conditions', said Manuel Marulanda, 'we are not inclined to mobilise ourselves to attend the meetings at the negotiating table.' But the military buildup and the patrols by security forces were set to continue, with Marulanda charging that government agents were being sent into the demilitarised zone 'disguised as salesmen and coca pickers'. At the same time Pastrana warned that the Colombian congress would move to create a 'fiscal dictatorship' if senators failed to agree the 2002 budget. This meant that the budget, shaped by US-approved IMF proposals, would be implemented by the Pastrana regime even if the elected parliament failed to approve it. Dissident congressmen knew what to expect: earlier in October two had been shot dead by rightwing paramilitaries. And the killings of trade unionists continued.

Some 69 unionists had been murdered by the death squads in 1999, 112 in 2000 and 100 in the first nine months of 2001. One of the killings was that of Dario Soto, shot while walking home with his youngest daughter. As a union representative in negotiations between Colombian workers and a local bottling plant, he was a typical target. Manual Pajao Peinado, treasurer of the Public Service Workers Union in Barranquilla, had been refused government protection when he and other members of his union reported being followed by a group of heavily armed men. Soon afterwards, he was shot dead, probably by AUC paramilitaries who frequently killed peasants and trade unionists.

On 21 October British trade unionists reported on their visit to Colombia to talk with Alexander Lopez, the Colombian mineworkers' president and a guest of UNISON in Britain the previous year: 'We were due to meet the mineworkers' president last Wednesday, but he was shot dead the previous night.' Tony Staunton, Plymouth TUC secretary and a delegation member, commented on the situation in Colombia:

> Seven million people have been thrown into poverty in the last three years because of privatisation. That is more than a thousand a day as public services are closed down, schools and hospitals shut and utilities demolished. The state was the largest employer in 1991, now over 60 per cent of state industries have gone with a fourfold increase in unemployment and no state support. Hospitals have been privatised and can no longer afford the medicines now controlled by drug companies demanding outrageous prices.

Such trends threw into graphic relief the underlying reasons for the war, where US-sponsored economic policies designed to protect American transnational companies were being forced on Colombia and many other countries; and where, in Colombia and elsewhere, private militias were used to silence dissident opinion.

At this time a British backpacker, Jeremy Parks, was reported killed by Colombian troops in clashes with ELN rebels. His face had been mutilated and one report said he had been decapitated. It seemed unclear why the 28-year-old man had become involved. Was he a tourist in the wrong place at the wrong time? Was he a kidnap victim (the ELN were known to kidnap hundreds of people a year for ransom)? Local reports suggested he had come from Northern Ireland, suggesting an IRA link. The British embassy in Bogota began investigations.

In early November Colombian and US forces captured Juan Pablo Rubio, the alleged FARC financial chief and money-launderer, according to *El Tiempo*. Documents linking him to the cocaine trade were reportedly found in his possession, though no details were given. At the same time gunmen on motorcycles murdered Carlos Arturo Pinto, a special prosecutor who had been investigating a paramilitary group and rival guerrillas. Pinto was a successor to the prosecutor Maria del Rosario, who was killed in July. Now, in the context of this mounting carnage, there were signs that the ELN and the Colombian government were about to resume talks; while the FARC Marulanda denounced the government for calling the guerrillas drug traffickers and 'terrorists', thereby providing 'a pretext for intervention by the United States in the internal affairs of Colombia'.

On 28 November 2001 Anders Kempass, UN High Commissioner for Human Rights in Colombia, condemned the prisons in the country as an overcrowded 'hell' where most inmates had yet to receive a final sentence and were crammed into filthy cells: 'You don't have to look for a hell anywhere else, because hell is here.' More than 54,000 prisoners, many of them untried and without legal representation, were crammed into 167 prisons throughout the country, with a further 5000 being held in police stations, where conditions were even worse. A joint study by the United Nations and Colombia's official human rights agency, the People's Defence Office, emphasised many shortcomings of the prison system; for example, sewage facilities inadequate and food sometimes contaminated by faeces. The jails were crowded with petty offenders who had received no definitive sentences, while the perpetrators of serious crime often bribed officials to keep them out of prison. Wealthy and powerful prisoners obtained the best cells, and the poorest lived in cardboard shacks in the open air. With a

Colombian poverty rate of more than 50 per cent, much petty crime was being committed out of desperation and basic need.

In early December Aury Sara Marrugo, president of the Cartagena branch of the oil workers' union, United Workers Union (USO-CUT), was kidnapped by paramilitaries. A few days later his body was found: a highly popular Cartagena community leader, he was the fourth USO member to be killed in 2001. The AUC had already admitted to the abduction and declared that Marrugo would face a paramilitary 'trial', inevitably a prelude to his murder.

Such events served Washington's aim of weakening the power of organised Labour throughout Colombian industry, and the European Union (EU) was prepared to adopt the same attitude. In mid-December the EU banned members of FARC and the ELN, from entering the bloc, signalling implicitly that whereas Colombians with links to the rightwing death squads would not be excluded guerrilla leaders struggling against corporate corruption and government repression would not be allowed into Europe. In 2000 a group of FARC commanders had gone on a 'Euro tour' that included Sweden, Norway, Italy, the Vatican, Switzerland, Spain and France, but now the EU policy on the matter was being shaped in Washington. The FARC then issued a statement accusing Brussels of trying to 'win over the United States' and condemned the EU decision as a 'violation of the people's sovereignty'. It was plain that Brussels had resolved to act as the junior partner of Washington, at least as far as corporate interests in Colombia were concerned, in the US business-friendly world order.

Fresh peace talks between the Colombian government and the ELN were scheduled to begin early in 2002, though few observers were optimistic about the likely outcome. On 17 December the ELN called a Christmas truce but it seemed unlikely that there would be no violent incidents through the holiday period. The war was continuing to expand, affecting all sectors of Colombian society and even drawing children into the conflict. An estimated 6000 children were fighting alongside the rebels and the paramilitaries, the majority of them volunteers but around a quarter press-ganged. Rocio Mojica, Save the Children, estimated that about 3m of the country's 14m children had no access to education: 'There are very few opportunities for work or education, and joining an armed group gives young people a sense of importance and belonging that they can't find elsewhere.' But in such circumstances the children, assigned no rights, are abused and brutalised. The 15-year-old Miguel testified that he was ordered to torture and kill a suspected rebel: 'The "paras" said that if I didn't kill him, they'd shoot me because I knew too much. Once you've done that three or four times you don't respect anything. You just kill for the sake of killing.' After the murder of one victim Miguel's commander forced him to drink the man's blood.[7]

American funds and military assistance were indirectly (and perhaps directly) aiding the rightwing paramilitaries – at first in the alleged 'war against drugs' and then in the war against the Marxist rebels. The war against drugs, if such were ever a serious project, had manifestly failed; and it could even be argued that US policies were *stimulating* such production and trafficking. The Colombian cartels, like all successful entrepreneurs, were constantly searching for new markets and new opportunities. Experts judged that, despite all supposed official efforts, the flow of drugs into the United States was continuing unabated – indeed the American market was saturated, a circumstance that inevitably shifted a part of the trafficking to Europe and particularly Britain. Colombian exporters were paying around $2000 for a kilo of cocaine, worth $20,000 in the United States and $30,000 in Britain. One estimate suggested that consumption in the UK had increased from about one ton a year 20 years ago to anything between 25 and 40 tons in 2001.[8] There is some irony in the fact that American and British consumers were providing some part of the funds used by Colombian rebels and paramilitaries to wage their endless internecine war.

The military conflict was continuing, as was the paramilitary assassination of anyone thought to be unsympathetic to corporate greed and exploitation. Through 2001 nearly 200 trade unionists were assassinated by the rightwing death squads, known to have strong links with the US-funded Colombian army. Over the past decade more than 30,000 people – workers, peasants, human rights activists, leftwing political leaders, teachers and health workers – had been killed by the armed forces and their allies. To combat the endless stream of official propaganda urging a 'war against terrorism' some leftwing activists have stressed the simple facts of the Colombian case:

> The Pastrana government and the death squads support the same reactionary landlords and bankers, which explains their close military relations, while the close FARC ties to peasant and worker unions is based on the similarity of their programmes. Almost all death squad killings are directed at peasants not landlords, trade unionists not bosses, human rights lawyers not government officials, resistance sympathisers not US military advisors.[9]

In this context Colombia has been described as a 'death-squad democracy'[10] in which an electoral facade provides political cover for a murderous regime to which there is little public commitment. It is significant that the greatest repression – for example, the murder of trade unionists – has occurred in areas where government troops predominate and the paramilitaries can operate without constraint. Where the FARC was strong, trade unionists had been able to function normally; in the demilitarised zone, where the FARC ruled, not a single trade unionist had been attacked.

The Colombian regime has been sustained by foreign loans and military power, much of the latter supplied by Washington. The country's economic programme has been shaped by American and European bankers, and by the US-dominated IMF. The nation's military and strategic policies are run by the Pentagon and implemented by local officers and mercenary US helicopter pilots. Unemployment, murder and the displacement of entire communities are increasing while US corporate strategists eye the next piece of attractive Colombian real estate to be targeted for early acquisition.

On 1 January 2002 around 800 Colombian trade unionists entered the second week of their occupation of their employer Emcali's central administrative building, an action caused by the appointment of Oscar Halim Reveiz as general manager. The union suspicion was that the move was intended to pave the way for the privatisation of the company. Already Halim had been a manager of a corporation implicated in a range of corruption investigations concerning a bribery scandal. The Colombian government was restarting its peace talks with FARC, at the same time claiming that up to 25 IRA members may have entered the country to train local 'terrorists' over the previous decade.[11] Then the possibility of a useful outcome to the peace negotiations quickly evaporated, under US pressure, and a deepening of the conflict seemed imminent.

Thus Camilo Gomez, the government peace commissioner, commented on the collapse of talks: 'The government brought proposals and alternatives to give hope to the peace processes. The FARC has cast them aside.' The government was now giving the rebels 48 hours to leave the main municipalities of the demilitarised zone, after which the security forces would re-establish their presence in those areas. Raul Reyes, FARC spokesman, denied that FARC had walked away from the negotiating table: 'The government lied to the nation and the international community.' An escalation of the fighting between FARC, ELN and other rebel groups on one hand and government forces and their death-squad allies on the other was anticipated, a conflict that was already costing 3500 lives every year.

On 11 January Colombian troops were preparing to make a massive incursion into the former safe haven of the FARC rebels. James LeMoyne, Kofi Annan's special representative, said that he was in contact with FARC and the Colombian government: 'The objective of peace is worth so much and the cost of war so terrible that I urge the parties to do everything possible to find a solution.' When the FARC-government talks began in 1998 the troops were withdrawn from the designated region and San Vicente was suddenly deep within rebel territory, the capital of the new demilitarised fiefdom. Then guerrillas manned checkpoints on all major roads and rebel commanders resolved all disputes, from bar-room brawls to family feuds. San Vicente, protected from the war's violence, enjoyed an economic boom: bars and bordellos were open at breakfast time, and stores were crammed with goods. Outside the zone many Colombians resented the haven's relative tranquillity and the extent to which the FARC used its new opportunities to train guerrilla fighters and to launch raids from its secure territory.

The inhabitants of the haven were now fearful that the dreaded death-squads would arrive in the wake of the Colombian army. All the civilians in the region had been obliged to co-operate with the guerrillas; all therefore would be regarded by the paramilitaries as legitimate targets for elimination. Said Maria Prudencia, a restaurant owner in the zone: 'The government tells us not to worry about our security, but who will guarantee that we'll be safe? What happens if the "paras" arrive before the army?' Dimas Vargas, a seller of sugar cane juice, was philosophical: 'We were scared before the troops left, scared of the guerrillas while they were here, and scared of what will come next. We're kind of used to being scared.'[12] On 13 January President Pastrana, addressing the nation, declared that the United Nations had failed to find a way out of the crisis. The FARC proposals were inadequate and the peace process was in tatters.

On 14 January the FARC rebels began to move out of some areas of the haven, but then fresh peace talks were agreed in order to avert a bloodbath. Paul Reyes, FARC negotiator, said that he was satisfied that the military controls placed around the safe haven would not endanger the new negotiations. In a televised address Pastrana commented: 'The peace process continues. There's less than a week left to decide whether to extend the life of the enclave. We haven't reached that goal yet.' Annan and James LeMoyne, speaking for the United Nations, were happy to welcome the fresh prospect of talks. Some 12,000 Colombian troops, backed by US-supplied helicopter gunships, had moved to the edge of the zone, as FARC rebels dismantled their checkpoints and began to vacate the zone's five main towns.

Opposing Privatisation

Any attempt to understand the Colombian situation must take into account the dynamics of world politics; in particular, the persistent US pressure for privatisation, the crushing of workers' power and the erosion of public services – a raft of mutually supportive objectives that rely on transnational propaganda and military suppression of dissident opinion. The Colombian people, like courageous and politically aware people everywhere, have struggled to resist the worldwide trends that serve the ambitions of corporate greed.

On 18 January 2002 the British trade union movement showed its solidarity with the Colombian workers occupying the public-utilities headquarters in Cali. Thus in a live video link from the TUC headquarters in London John Edmonds (GMB general secretary), Mick Rix (ASLEF general secretary), Andy Gilchrist (FBU general secretary) and Alison Shepherd (UNISON executive member) sent messages of support from their unions. John Edmonds declared:

> We stand with you in your campaign against privatisation and corruption. Like you, we face privatisation. Already we have seen privatisation of our trains and transport systems, parts of our municipal utilities and, now, privatisation of the NHS ... Your fight to keep public services for the working people does you proud and is an inspiration to us in our struggle here.

In Cali eyewitnesses described the occupation of the central administration tower of Emcali, which runs the city's public services, as solid. The mayor and the government were entering into negotiations, forced to address the demands of the union activists. Community council leaders in the rural areas around Cali issued a joint statement in support of the occupation and the struggle to defend public services, and community leaders in poor areas stood ready to launch civic strike action.

At the same time the FARC negotiators and the Colombian government reached an agreement on talks sufficient to halt the imminent invasion by 12,000 troops and tanks into the rebel enclave. The newspaper *El*

Colombiano voiced a widespread opinion: 'Just when there was talk of open war, suddenly there's a chance of peace ... an imperfect peace process was preferable to a perfect war.' *El Pais*, more sceptical, urged support for Pastrana's 'tough stance.' And the US involvement in the course of events was widely assumed. The *San Francisco Chronicle* suggested an enlarged American intervention: 'President Bush and Congress have a solemn responsibility to prevent the formerly demilitarised zone from turning into a new killing field.'

There was speculation also about the manifest impunity of Carlos Castano, former AUC head and self-confessed assassin. He remained free to carry out his business deals from his farms in Colombia, and there appeared to be no US pressure for Pastrana to follow up any of the arrest warrants for the known death-squad organiser:

> Could it be that, when Washington put $25 million on bin Laden's head, it had no money left over to have Colombia's number one hitman arrested? Or is it that the terrorists of the world will only have problems with Washington and London if they hit the wrong targets.[13]

In reality Castano, in running a campaign of assassination against trade union members, had served American interests – as AUC continued to do under Salvatore Mancuso, Castano's hard-line successor.

The occupation of the Emcali tower was continuing, sustained by immense local solidarity. When union leaders left the building for talks with community activists, workers blocked off the surrounding roads to prevent attacks on the union men. The Internationale was blaring from loudspeakers while the workers were donning bulletproof vests and brandishing machine-guns. The Colombian army and its death-squad allies had failed to intimidate the workers and it seemed that events were moving to a new and more dangerous level. President Pastrana had been forced to extend the FARC safe haven until 10 April to allow peace talks to continue but there was mounting US pressure for decisive action against the Marxist rebels. Now James LeMoyne, UN envoy, was appealing directly to the death-squad paramilitaries: 'Please, stop assassinating, killing, displacing, kidnapping and committing massacres against the Colombian people.'

The Cali occupation was heightening the political consciousness of the people. Inside the tower a newly formed women's group was formulating proposals to address male attitudes, asking why no woman had ever been a member of the executive board of Sintraemcali, the public-sector union. Aydee, a spokeswoman, commented: 'We are in the front line of the struggle to defend Emcali, and male attitudes inside the tower are changing towards us. When we leave, we want to change the attitudes of those outside as well.' She also described the practical and cultural activities being organised:

> Tomorrow, we have computer classes and English classes, and we are organising a cleaning party, jointly with the men, to keep the tower clear. We are also circulating the words of the Internationale and the anthem of Sintraemcali to every floor, so that everyone can learn the songs by heart. Tomorrow, we will have a competition with a prize for the floor that sings them the best.

Outside the tower there was a festival atmosphere. A dance group from Agua Blanca, the poorest district in Cali, was performing and a crowd was swaying in time with the music. A rap band from the same part of the city was chanting a tribute to social protest. On the roof of an adjoining building workers wearing balaclavas danced together in this people's celebration.

The occupation of the Emcali tower was now stimulating an international solidarity movement. Messages of support were being received from the British TUC, the Central Workers Federation of Indonesia, the Norwegian Socialist Party and an anti-imperialist organisation in the Philippines. In Cali a youth march was held, with hundreds of children, a folk band and 13-foot-high puppets parading in support of public services. The Cali mayor had refused to use force to end the five-week occupation, despite growing government frustration at the workers' solidarity and the support for them shown by the local community. The government had made some concessions but refused to put them in writing, prompting Alexander Lopez, Union head, to comment: 'How can we accept a verbal agreement with the government, when the government is notorious for reneging on agreements, even when they are written on paper in the presence of lawyers?' At one stage the union was facing financial collapse – and then the workers starting donating their salaries to keep the occupation going. Each day, Sintraemcali journalists were producing press releases along with the posters, documents and leaflets being generated by the union and the municipal strike command.

On 24 January 2002 the photographer Marcos Ayala, who worked for the newspaper *El Caleno* specialising in Cali crime, was killed by unidentified gunmen while he was carrying film to be developed at a nearby laboratory. This was the first killing of a journalist in the year; 10 had been murdered in Colombia the previous year, about 100 since 1980. At this time the main trade union federation, the CUT, was revealing the scale of atrocities being perpetrated against trade unionists by the rightwing paramilitaries (figures for 2001): 160 assassinations, 79 disappearances (presumed killings), 30 attempted assassinations and scores of displacements and death threats. In the first 15 days of 2002 three trade unionists had been killed, two had disappeared, three had suffered assassination attempts and three had been threatened with death. The National Hauliers association was considering an indefinite cross-country strike starting on 18 February to protest against the increasingly lawless roads.

The public-sector workers in Cali were condemning the country's press for launching a smear campaign against the unionists occupying the Cali tower. Thus the *El Pais* newspaper had claimed that the occupation was part of a terrorist plan to destabilise the city through 'road blocks, the occupation of churches, public buildings and other buildings' as part of the workers' action. On the 28 January there was a widespread strike in Cali in support of the Emcali occupation.

On the same day one hundred members of the Sintraemcali union declared a permanent occupation of the offices of the superintendent of public services, with workers still entrenched in the Cali tower. The new occupation, in Bogota, was quickly surrounded by riot police and the situation was tense. Lopez declared:

> We urge all those affected by the rises in prices of public services, increases in school enrolment fees and the deterioration of health services that, together, we can build the forces necessary to defend our national heritage.

The IMF had recommended 'rapid progress' on slashing pensions, a move that would need to be approved by the Colombian congress and which was a key part of the government's austerity plan. It was to this sort of retrograde social legislation that the workers were responding with such determination and commitment. Then the army introduced martial law and banned all public assemblies in Cali.

On 30 January the mayor of Cali and the government suddenly and unexpectedly agreed to meet all the union's demands. The Emcali tower had been occupied since 25 December with the Sintraemcali union developing a range of strategies to ensure that Emcali remained a public company. The agreement included guarantees that the company would not be privatised, that there would be no price increases in 2002, and that a high-level anti-corruption enquiry would begin to bring to justice all those people who had siphoned off public resources from the company.

When the news arrived of the government's capitulation many of the workers in the tower joked and laughed with relief, while others cried tears of tension and joy. This was a significant victory in the battle against privatisation, showing how the 'neoliberal model' could be confronted and defeated. The workers had formed new friendships and achieved a deeper political understanding. When it came to the moment of 'salida' (leaving the building) thousands of people were filling the streets, the Internationale was playing and the workers filed out of the building in military parade, faces covered with balaclavas and flags held high. The streets filled with the roar of the crowd as the huge flag of Sintraemcali was lowered by ropes from the 17th floor.[14]

The workers of Cali had demonstrated what could be accomplished with solidarity and courage. The occupation of the tower was over but no-one doubted that the government and the paramilitaries would want revenge: 'One battle has been won, but the dirty war continues.'[15]

Plunging into Turmoil

On 1 February 2002 the Colombian government and the ELN agreed to extend the peace talks being held in Cuba, with a joint declaration at the end of the preliminary session calling for the protection of children, the elimination of antipersonnel mines and an ending of attacks on the Colombian infrastructure. The talks were also attended by representatives from various non-governmental organisations (NGOs) and representatives of the 'Group of Friendly Countries' – Cuba, Switzerland, France, Spain and Norway. Jaime Bernal, a member of Colombia's peace commission, commented: 'There was progress. Society is demanding we move to concrete agreements.' But the killings continued. One casualty was the 41-year-old Orlando Sierra, deputy editor of *La Patria* and one of Colombia's most influential newspapermen. Two hours before he was shot dead by two unknown gunmen, Sierra was on television denouncing 'acts of terror'.

Amnesty International and Human Rights Watch were highlighting the deteriorating human rights situation in Colombia. Political violence had increased through 2001 and massacres of civilians had doubled – against the background of ever increasing US military aid. Alexandra Arriaga, Amnesty director of government relations, said: 'The facts are clear. Colombia has not met the conditions for human rights set by Congress and instead there is evidence of backsliding.' José Miguel Vivanco, Human Rights Watch, pointed out that military officers implicated in human rights abuses had remained on active duty and in some cases had been promoted. Ken Cameron, chairman of Justice for Colombia (London), commented that the American posture was another example of the increasing lawlessness of the Bush administration.

It was obvious that US aid was no longer linked to Colombian progress on human rights. On 11 February Anne Patterson, American ambassador in Bogota, declared that decisions of future US aid would depend on the success of a new initiative to train and equip the Colombian army. She emphasised that there were more than 300 sites in Colombia with infrastructure of strategic importance to the United States and that securing oil supplies in Latin America was particularly important with growing tension in the Middle East. Patterson also admitted the real reason for US intervention:

> It is true that this is not an anti-narcotics issue, but it is something that we have to do. It is important for the future of the country [the US], for our petroleum supplies and for the confidence of our investors.

The events of September 11, 2001, were already impacting on Colombia. Colombian officials, asking to remain anonymous, commented that the United States was more willing to take military action in Colombia as part of Washington's global 'war on terrorism'. The 'war on drugs', despite its lingering propaganda value as a slogan, was history. As Senator Patrick J. Leahy, Democrat chairman of the US foreign operations subcommittee, observed: 'This is no longer about stopping drugs. It's about fighting the guerrillas.'

The paramilitaries, with US support, were already taking revenge for the Emcali occupation. On 12 February 2002 Julio Galeano, involved in the Sintraemcali action, was shot dead, and the Colombian Communist Party, having already seen thousands of its members assassinated, was reporting raids on the homes of its members. A party statement noted the deteriorating situation:

> Such acts of intimidation and repression are all too familiar in
> Colombia, but the fact that state security forces … appear now to be
> openly carrying out persecution campaigns takes us back to a period
> of all too recent Latin American history which no-one ever wanted to
> see repeated.

The human rights situation throughout the country was worsening with
fewer than ever constraints on the excesses of the death-squad
paramilitaries and the US-trained Colombian army. The Colombian
prosecutors were announcing plans to try the three IRA suspects, while
peace talks between the government and the FARC rebels were thrown into
jeopardy when rebels forced an airliner to land on a remote highway and
kidnapped a senator and at least one other passenger.

On 21 February the government ended the three years of peace talks and
ordered military action against the FARC enclave. Rebel positions were
bombed and 13,000 troops invaded the former safe haven. The final straw
was the hijacking of the domestic passenger plane and the kidnapping of
Senator Jorge Gechem Turbay, chairman of the peace talks committee, after
which the guerrillas retreated into the jungle, blowing up a bridge behind
them to prevent pursuit. President Pastrana declared in a televised
broadcast:

> Today the guerrillas have unmasked and shown their true face, the
> face of violence without reason. The FARC have opted for terrorism.
> I have decided not to continue the peace process with the guerrillas
> … and from midnight tonight I have given orders to the armed forces
> to retake the guerrilla safe haven.

A few hours later, the bombing began against more than 85 strategic FARC
positions, including camps, warehouses and clandestine airfields. The
troops, backed by tanks, then launched their incursion into the FARC
territories. There had been 117 rebel attacks over the previous month and
now there was widespread fear in the population about what an all-out war
would bring. The US Southern Command was reporting that there were
currently about 250 American military personnel, 50 civilian employees and
100 civilian military contractors in Colombia. It remained to be seen how
the United States would respond to this new escalation of the civil war. In
any event President Pastrana, pending increased US military aid, was
invoking ethereal help. He ended his televised address to the nation with a

prayer for the Archangel Michael 'to protect us'. It seems that Michael was well experienced in such matters, having driven Satan and his demons out of heaven.

The Colombian army launched more than 200 bombing missions using US-supplied Black Hawk helicopters and A-37 and AC-47 jets to attack 'strategic targets' in the zone. Paul Reyes, FARC chief spokesman, denied knowledge of the kidnapping of Turbay, one of the ruling 'oligarchs' who owned most of the country's wealth, and declared that the military invasion showed the government's commitment to war and that the Colombian army was 'one of the main perpetrators of state terrorism in this country'. Mario Novelli, Colombia Solidarity Campaign, emphasised that the US-backed regime was determined to destroy all the forces that opposed the neoliberal economic programme which has thrown 60 per cent of the population into poverty.

The small Colombian élite had grown increasingly wealthy on the back of a privatisation programme that had forced up prices and cost thousands of workers' jobs:

> For the trade union movement, the end of the talks is likely to lead to further assassinations of their leaders, 3500 of whom have been assassinated by state and parastate forces since 1986. For the peasants it will lead to more massacres in rural areas as the military and paramilitaries clear the land for the transnationals.[16]

Now the Colombian army was entering FARC territory, encountering little resistance as the rebels retreated into the jungle. The invasion, 'Operation Death', seemed likely to exacerbate tensions throughout the country. Some 200 rapid deployment troops were the first to arrive at an abandoned FARC base, ferried to the site in US-supplied Black Hawk helicopters. Jets packed with 500lb bombs attacked targets around San Vicente in what was what some observers described as a 'carpet-bombing' assault. The people of the region, not consulted when the safe haven was declared in 1998, were now fearing paramilitary reprisals against civilians assumed to have collaborated with the rebels. One resident, Maria Magdalena Mayorga, cradling her five-month-old baby, said: 'We are scared over what could happen now and that evil armed men could come. We lived quietly here with the FARC, who made their own laws.'

The six countries that make up South America's Mercosur trade bloc – Argentina, Brazil, Uruguay, Paraguay and associate members Chile and

Bolivia – issued 'a passionate call for the total respect of human rights and the principles of international human rights'. Richard Boucher, US State Department spokesman, expressed American support for Pastrana's invasion of the FARC enclave.

The conflict was now deepening, with fears that the displaced FARC rebels would take their campaign into the Colombian urban centres. On 23 February FARC forces kidnapped Senator Ingrid Betancourt as she was driving to San Vicente. The government had advised her against entering the conflict zone and had refused her request for transport in a military helicopter. Others kidnapped with Betancourt were later released but the rebels continued to hold the senator and Clara Rojas, her campaign manager. At the same time Gilberto Torres Martinez, leader of a pipeline subdivision of the oil workers union (USO), was kidnapped by paramilitaries and taken to an area strongly guarded by army personnel. A few weeks before, Aury Sara Marrugo, USO regional president, and his bodyguard Enrique Arellano had been kidnapped and assassinated by the paramilitaries.

In early March the Colombian army, without explanation, arrested Hugo Alberto Pena Camargo, president of the Arauca Campesino Association (ACA) and detained him without a legal warrant. The ACA had been oranising a regional workshop for campesinos and displaced people, an initiative resented by the Colombian authorities. Following the collapse of peace talks the army had been given the power to impose a curfew and to demand that civilians show identification on demand, developments that were increasing the fear of death threats, assassinations and forced displacements. On 17 March Archbishop Isaias Duarte, known for his criticism of leftwing rebels and drug traffickers, was shot dead in Cali after conducting a group wedding service for 100 couples. The assassins, after shooting the Archbishop at point blank range in the head and chest, escaped on a motorcycle. A week later, the oil-workers union issued a statement protesting against the 'genocide' being committed against Colombian trade unionists.

Questions were now being raised about the background of the leading presidential candidate Alvaro Uribe Velez. US Drug Enforcement Administration (DEA) documents revealed that the DEA had seized 50,000 kilos of potassium permanganate – a necessary chemical in the production of cocaine – in 1997-98 destined for a company owned by Uribe's campaign manager Pedro Juan Moreno Villa. These unreported shipments were sufficient to produce half-a-million kilos of cocaine hydrochloride, with a street value of $15 billion. Donnie Marshall, DEA chief, noted in one of the documents (3 August 2001) that Moreno's company, GMP Chemical Products, was the single largest importer of the chemical from 1994 to 1998. This was roughly the same period that Uribe was governor of the state of Antioquia and Moreno was his chief of staff.

In March 2002 Uribe was interviewed by Joseph Contreras, a *Newsweek* correspondent. At this time Uribe was presidential frontrunner and popular in Washington.[17] It is useful to note the tone of Uribe's response to *Newsweek*:

> *Newsweek*: In 1997 and 1998, agents of the DEA seized 50,000 kilos of a chemical precursor used in the processing of cocaine … allegedly purchased by a company belonging to Pedro Juan Moreno, who served as your cabinet chief when you were governor of Antioquia.
>
> *Uribe*: I became aware of that only after my term as governor ended … I believe that an error was made in his case.
>
> *Newsweek*: According to a best-selling book about the drug trade … you spoke out on behalf of a low-income housing program in Medellin that was funded by drug lord Pablo Escobar when you were mayor …
>
> *Uribe*: I asked the attorney general's office to investigate, and I was completely cleared of those charges … I had nothing to do with that.
>
> *Newsweek*: Well-informed sources say that a record number of pilot's licences and airstrip construction permits were issued by the civil-aviation authority when you headed that agency … when drug trafficking was on the rise …
>
> *Uribe*: Let's not talk further …
>
> *Newsweek*: Your deputy at the aviation authority was a man named Cesar Villegas, later sentenced to five years in prison for his links to the Cali cartel and murdered earlier this month …
>
> *Uribe*: I refuse to accept that you foreign correspondents come here to ask me these kinds of questions and repeat slanders made against me … I have been honorable and accountable. We have nothing else to discuss.

Despite such revelations it seemed likely that Alvaro Uribe would do well in the forthcoming presidential elections. President Pastrana's policy of engagement with the rebels had come to nothing, the war was intensifying, and he was widely seen as having been too lenient with the Emcali demonstrators. There was no sign of any slackening in the incidence of atrocities, and it was clear that the rebel tactics were now expanding to the cities. On 7 April a car bomb exploded in Villavicendio, a regional capital, killing at least 12 and injuring more than 70. No group claimed responsibility but Pastrana commented: 'The first indications point towards the FARC. Terrorists will have no refuge anywhere in the world.' Ivan Dario Solano, a local journalist described what he saw:

> The scene was Dantesque: mutilated bodies, the wounded, people collapsing. It was terrible, terrible. The people closest to the car died instantly. The bodies were unrecognisable.

On 9 April a car with a body inside blew up near Bogota, killing two police explosives experts; and later in the day two homemade mortar bombs were fired at the presidential palace but neither exploded. Two small bombs exploded in a commercial area of Bogota, injuring four people including a six-year-old girl who was reported to be in a critical condition. Two days later, Marxist rebels disguised as an army bomb squad burst into a regional parliament building in Cali and kidnapped 12 politicians, while in the street outside the rebels herded 17 people into a minibus and headed into the nearby mountains. Four assembly staff and a state deputy were later freed by the kidnappers. During the same week more leading trade unionists were kidnapped and assassinated.

Diofanol Sierra Vargas, a Sinaltrainal activist and a member of the OFP women's organisation, was taken by force from her family home and murdered by a paramilitary group that operated in the oil city of Barrancabermeja. At the same time Oscar Alfonso Jurado, a leading member of the Sintraquim union, was murdered; and Arturo Vasquez Galeano, of the CUT union federation, was kidnapped near Medellin. Jesus Antonio Gonzalez, CUT human rights head, commented:

> These barbarous acts form the dramatic situation in which we in the CUT are suffering as a result of all the assassinations, disappearances, kidnappings, death threats, detentions, forced displacement and temporary or permanent exile.

On 14 April presidential candidate frontrunner Uribe survived an apparent assassination attempt. An explosive-packed bus was detonated just as Uribe's campaign caravan passed en route to the airport. Two policemen and many civilians were injured.

On 23 April Gerry Adams, Sinn Fein president, refused to attend a congressional hearing in Washington on the IRA's alleged links with Colombian terrorists. Henry Hyde, chairman of the House of Representatives international relations committee, accused Adams of ducking an opportunity 'to offer some explanation about why two IRA explosive experts and a Sinn Fein political officer were arrested last August following a visit to a safe haven' controlled by the FARC. Adams claimed that his appearance would only damage the Northern Ireland peace process, and that he had been advised not to testify by lawyers representing the IRA trio. At a subsequent press conference he declared: 'Irish Republicans pose no threat to US national security interests in Colombia.'[18]

There was no break in the continuing carnage. On 3 May 2002 Colombian officials reported that around 100 people seeking refuge in a church in north-western Colombia had been injured and at least 60 killed. Peasants trying to protest against BP encroachments on their land were forcibly moved by the Colombian army. The men were beaten and a woman was raped by the army troops, crimes for which the soldiers have impunity. On 18 May it was reported that aid workers employed by the US government would be evacuated from their offices after a sophisticated car bomb was defused outside their offices in Bogota.

Electing an Extremist

Throughout May Alvaro Uribe was the undisputed frontrunner for the forthcoming presidential elections but since the bomb attack on his motorcade he was seldom seen in public: 'The other candidates are walking around the country. Here I am in Bogota in this van and I cannot go to any place because of the violence.' Uribe was in the lead but Colombians were deeply divided over the country's political future. Many feared that Uribe's campaign slogan, 'A firm hand and a big heart', would take the country deeper into war. With alleged past links to drug traffickers and rightwing paramilitaries, Uribe was planning to drastically increase military spending and to create a controversial million-man civilian defence network to be known as the 'Convivir' system. When governor of Antioquia in the 1990s he created the rudiments of such a body – and it quickly became a network of murderous vigilantes. Now Uribe wanted to revive the concept on a national scale. No aspect of his campaign had caused more alarm.

On 26 May the Colombian people voted in the presidential election as guerrillas tried to sabotage the likely victory of Alvaro Uribe, the hardline Oxford- and Harvard-educated candidate. More than 210,000 police and troops were deployed but the Marxist rebels were still able to blow up power lines and a bridge in one northern province. The mayor of a southern town was kidnapped and later found dead. The 49-year-old Uribe, whose father was killed by guerrillas and who was keen to encourage increased US military aid, was elected with just over half of the popular vote – enough to clinch victory without a June runoff. Horacio Serpa, of the centre-left opposition Liberal Party, was second with 36.6 per cent of the vote. One woman was killed during the election when guerrillas dynamited the election headquarters in the northern town of San Luis, and car bombs were placed on at least four roads connecting provincial capitals. Two guerrillas were killed and two soldiers wounded in clashes between rebels and government troops.

Mary Robinson, UN human rights commissioner, had criticised Uribe for supporting the paramilitaries and for policies that would tip the country into an all-out civil war. He planned to enlist 150,000 extra troops and police officers, to begin the mobilisation of 30,000 reservists and to encourage a greater US involvement in the Colombian civil war. Human rights monitors feared that his enthusiasm for the Convivir idea would simply draw more civilians into the civil war and breed a new generation of paramilitary extremists. In a *New Yorker* interview Uribe praised the paramilitary death-squads for bringing 'relative peace' to some regions. In some areas Colombians were instructed by the paramilitaries to vote for Uribe on pain of death.

Washington, like the paramilitaries, favoured a Uribe victory and were not disappointed. Already the US ambassador in Bogota had predicted that the US would have a close relationship with their preferred candidate – a man close to the paramilitaries and with self-admitted family links to the drug-trafficking Ochoa cartel of Medellin. The Bush administration was confident that Uribe would implement policies in line with Washington thinking, and that generous US military aid to defeat the Marxist rebels was likely.

In a leader headed 'Despair in Colombia' *The Guardian* (London) recorded that victory had been handed to 'the hard man' and noted that the thrust of his approach was 'clearly military'. Uribe, who described himself as 'the first soldier of the nation', was promising to defeat the rebels by purely military means, an approach that included the granting of judicial powers to the armed forces. Gustavo Chirolla, a philosophy professor, commented: 'I'm scared – not just by Uribe, but by the huge number of people who supported him. It's as if the people want repression.' Soon after his election victory Uribe called on the rebels to lay down their arms. Said a taxi driver in Bogota: 'Uribe may not defeat the guerrillas right away, but he's the only one who will stand up to them. This is the start of the real war.'

Washington was heartened by Uribe's tough approach and it was obvious that he had been the favoured candidate of the Bush administration. Even before the final results were announced Anne Patterson, the US ambassador, arrived at the Uribe headquarters to congratulate him on his victory: 'Colombians are fed up with terrorism', she said, promising that the United States would have a 'very close' relationship with Mr Uribe. In the event Uribe had won 53 per cent of the votes cast, with a 47 per cent turnout – which meant that less than a quarter of those eligible had voted for him. The 'overwhelming victory' claimed by rightwing pundits was a myth. The main paramilitary group, the AUC, deeply implicated in thousands of death-squad assassinations, issued a communiqué congratulating Uribe on his victory.

Uribe began peacefully enough, announcing that he was asking the United Nations for a talks mission and the international community for debt relief to help him overcome the poverty that fuelled rebellion. But his underlying message remained clear. In his acceptance speech he had said: 'The international community should know that Colombia has expressed its desire to recover civility and order. The world should be told of our determination to defeat violence.' He had already asked for an interview with Kofi Annan, inviting the UN to lead a mission to establish contacts with the insurgent movement 'to seek a peace process which will start with a cessation of hostilities and an end to terrorism'. He added that the paramilitaries could be included in the peace process. Doubtless Uribe was happy to know that the European Union (EU) was adding FARC rebels to its blacklist of terrorist organisations.

On 8 July the Colombia Solidarity Campaign (London) called for a mass picket of Downing Street in protest at the visit of president-elect Uribe the following week. The Blair administration was set to increase its levels of aid to the Colombian regime.[19]

It was noted that Uribe's policies included slashing public spending, doubling the size of the armed forces and draconian restrictions on the Colombian opposition parties. Carlos Castano, death-squad leader, had described Uribe as 'the man closest to our philosophy'. In summary, Uribe's policies included:

- Opening negotiations with the paramilitaries as a first step to their legalisation;
- Restriction on democratic opposition and the possible abolition of congress;
- The creation of a one-million-strong armed vigilante group;
- The doubling of the size of the army;
- Refusal to negotiate for a peaceful solution with the guerrilla movements;
- Cutting the already decimated health and education spending in favour of diverting funds to war and internal repression.

Such policies, highly congenial to Washington, and seemingly to London also, seemed guaranteed to attract increased American and British military support.

The war was now bringing growing numbers of women and children into the conflict. One estimate suggested that at least one third of FARC's 18,000 soldiers were women, with the guerrilla organisation forced to rely increasingly on its female warriors as the intensifying war put the rebels under greater pressure. One battle, according to the Colombian army's General Mora, had been intense and bloody, but when his soldiers collected the bodies of the rebels killed in the conflict near the town of La Plata they were surprised to find that most were young women. The FARC was now training girls as young as 13 to be soldiers, and women had been used to hijack airliners. One former FARC fighter told *The Observer* (London) that women were braver fighters than men.[20]

The guerrillas seven-strong leadership was all male, but some women have risen through the ranks to win the *commandante* titles. Olga Lucia Marin was a FARC ambassador to the long peace talks that ended the previous February. Typically, the women were joining up during their teens, keen to escape the boredom of the villages and the drudgery of marriage. Some had been seduced by FARC's revolutionary ideals. The 6000 children in the ranks of the rebels and the paramilitaries had similarly often joined up to find the excitement of a violent life. At least one, referred to as José, became disillusioned when he was ordered to kill innocent people.[21] Some, once they had escaped, found their way to safe houses in Bogota and elsewhere.

On 24 July a video was released by FARC in which appeared Senator Ingrid Betancourt, the Franco-Colombian politician, and Clara Rojas, her campaign manager. Betancourt denounced the government for abandoning Colombia and leaving her 'rotting' in the jungle: 'I have spent 82 days in terrible solitude', she said, indicating that the film was made on 15 May. She asked: 'How can you explain that for five years we have 50 officers from both the police and armed forces rotting in the jungle like us?' FARC had said it was prepared to exchange Betancourt and other prisoners for rebel commanders held in state prisons, but to no effect. By August 2003 the French government was being criticised for supposedly bungling its own attempts to arrange her release.[22] On 30 July FARC guerrillas invaded Puerto Alvira, 160 miles south of Bogota, and kidnapped all but eight of its 700 inhabitants. More than two million Colombians had been displaced from their homes during the four decades of civil war.

Now, with the Uribe presidential victory, the United States was set to increase its military involvement in Colombia. Otto Reich, Bush's advisor on Latin America, had visited Uribe soon after Anne Patterson had rushed to congratulate him, and had written in the *Washington Times*: 'Our values, our security and the future of our hemisphere are tied to Colombia's victory in its war against terror.' In one commentary, a widespread perception, 'America has taken off the gloves and is preparing for a bloody escalation in the 38-year civil conflict'.[23] Fernando, a rebel militiaman, had fought the Medellin drug cartel, rightwing paramilitary death squads and the state. Now he was preparing to take on the Americans: 'The gringos just do not seem to learn their lessons. Any reasonable person after Vietnam, Nicaragua and September 11 would realise that if you stick your nose in other people's business you will get it punched.' And he was happy to give his prophecy on the Uribe administration: 'Blood, blood and more blood. Maybe even some gringo blood.'[24]

A bomb exploded in Bogota as Alvaro Uribe was being sworn in as president, killing 13 people and injuring two dozen more. Bodies were lying in the street and in a house five blocks from the presidential palace. Three smaller devices exploded around the palace, injuring three people. Fragments hit the facade of the palace, while other devices were detonated on a helipad. Uribe, fearing further attacks, opted out of the open-air inauguration and was sworn in inside the parliament building. Thousands of troops supported by tanks were patrolling Bogota, if only to prevent yet another assassination attempt against Uribe. During his first day in office he launched his civilian militia programme designed to help the security forces fight the insurgents. Sceptical observers considered that he was merely adding to the population of death-squad paramilitaries.

On 20 August, in conditions of rising violence, Fernando Londono, Colombia's interior and justice minister, read out a catalogue of war crimes that included massacres, kidnappings, forced displacements and the destruction of villages by illegal armed groups; and then he declared that Colombia's democracy was under threat: 'The nation is subject to a regime of terror in which democratic authority is sinking and where the economic activity is increasingly more difficult, multiplying unemployment and poverty for millions of Colombians.' Since President Uribe took office a few days before, more than 100 people had been killed in civil conflict, after which Uribe responded by declaring a state of emergency. Now the government could raise an emergency tax to raise more than $700 million in defence funds to finance the creation of two élite battalions, totalling 3000 soldiers, as well as 10,000 new police officers.

The United States was well pleased with the Uribe posture that only force could solve Colombia's problems. *The Wall Street Journal*, lauding Uribe, called him 'Colombia's George W. Bush', which was presumably intended as a compliment. Now Amnesty International was expressing fears that America's increased involvement in Colombia's internal affairs would increase the violations of human rights in the country, not least because Washington was already supporting Uribe's emergency measures.

The new policies were plainly intended to limit basic freedoms and civil rights in general. The state security forces were allowed to detain people on suspicion of supporting the rebels – in the absence of evidence. And the army and police were permitted to break into homes without a warrant. Freedom of movement was restricted, as was freedom of the press, and the state could ban meetings, protests and similar activities deemed to be against state policy. One union leader in Bogota commented:

> What I fear is that these new regulations will be used against people such as trade unionists, human rights workers, land reform activists, student leaders and independent journalists, all of whom Uribe hates, as he says they are guerrilla sympathisers.

When Fernando Londono, interior and justice minister, was asked which laws and rights could be restricted by Uribe's actions, he answered: 'All of them.'

The Impact of Uribe

One of the first moves of President Uribe was to encourage people to report on their neighbours. The first people to do so, wearing balaclavas and baggy clothes to hide their identities, were televised receiving bundles of cash for their efforts. Marta Lucia Ramirez, defence minister, declared on 2 September 2002: 'Starting today, the state security forces in each and every province will enact the programme, making Monday reward day.' Uribe was also setting up his 'million-man militia', a vast spy organisation that would be authorised to take vigilante action against suspects.

Uribe had declared the 'state of national emergency', had begun fusing ministries – such as the interior and justice ministries – and was contemplating the concentration of power in one house of congress instead of two. His principal aim was to prevent any constitutional challenge to his presidential decrees. Soon after the army and police had been given extra powers, the family home of the Director of the Human Rights Department of the Central Trade Union Federation was raided – and nothing was found. The new powers, apart from arbitrary arrest and detention, also extended to the interception of private communications and the banning of mobile phones, these latter the only means in rural areas of warning against impending massacres. Such repressive measures had long been practised by the army and the paramilitaries but Uribe's contribution was to legalise them and to encourage their universal application.

His moves to establish a nationwide 'Convivir', the countrywide militia, were based on his experience as governor of Antioquia between 1995 and 1997. There, what emerged were private armies, funded and armed by the state, and associated with a dramatic increase in the number of massacres, assassinations, forced disappearances, forced displacements and 'social cleansing' operations. One early consequence of the Convivir scheme was that the ranks of the death-squad paramilitaries expanded rapidly – a development that Uribe seemed intent on introducing throughout Colombia. More military prisons were to be built, penalties for a wide range of crimes would be harsher, and under-16s would be criminally accountable. Top military posts were being filled with ultra-right generals accustomed to scorched-earth practices and indiscriminate bombing.

It was plain also that Uribe's economic policies would be highly congenial to Washington, the IMF and the World Bank. More than 65 per cent of Colombians were living in conditions of extreme poverty, while 25 per cent existed in absolute poverty. A quarter of the working population was unemployed or underemployed, while in these circumstances Uribe was proposing a 16-hour working day, reduced overtime pay, an end to holiday pay and 'reforms' that would enable employers to discharge people without notice or compensation. The United States was applauding the 'democratic' election of Uribe where less than a quarter of eligible people had voted for him and where thousands of potential voters had been effectively disenfranchised through paramilitary terror. Britain was giving unspecified aid to the Colombian security forces and American military involvement was set to increase.

On 5 September 2002 a leading human rights group, Consultant for Human Rights and the Displaced (CODHES), said that the Colombian government-supported paramilitaries were the main cause of the country's refugee crisis, in which 2.7 million people had been forced to flee their homes. In 2001 some 300,000 people were forced to leave their home, 204,000 in the first six months of 2002. Rebel groups were judged to be responsible for 43 per cent of all refugees. War refugees, sometimes entire families, were a common sight in Colombia's major cities where they are typically forced to beg for a living. At the same time the number of registered informants was growing, as part of the network launched a day after Uribe took office.

The Uribe administration was also blocking the possibility of Colombians being arraigned before the International Criminal Court for war crimes. The Court would not be allowed to prosecute indicted war criminals for a period of seven years – a move similar to Washington's decision to protect American war criminals from justice. One consequence was that Colombian rightwing death squads which had carried out gruesome massacres with sledgehammers and chainsaws would stand no chance of prosecution either domestically or before an international court. This contempt for natural justice was not unique to Colombia but characterised the repressive postures of many governments following September 11 (Figure 1).

On 16 September Colombian state employees held a one-day strike to challenge government cost cuts designed to increase the war spending. The new Uribe plans included wage cuts, reductions in benefits and a raising of the retirement age. The Confederation of Democratic Colombian Workers reported: 'Things are going really well. We have the health sector paralysed and the oil sector stopped, as well as the courts and the state auditing offices.' But the police responded with repressive measures. A large number of demonstrators were mistreated by the army and the police as thousands of people protested throughout the country against government policies designed both to intensify the conflict and to follow IMF recommendations for cuts in public spending.

In Bogota Mauricio Rubiano, a CUT youth worker, was arrested, moved to various locations, and eventually released after being beaten. Other young demonstrators in Bogota were detained with several injured and a number missing. A peasant meeting in Tolima was raided by the army, arresting some people and stealing food from the building. In Sumarez further arbitrary arrests were carried out while unidentified men in civilian dress tried to detain farmers' leaders. Paramilitary groups in the region of Cauca stopped a peaceful demonstration with the open complicity of the army and the police. Elsewhere the paramilitaries set up roadblocks, stole food and made death threats to marchers. In Caldas some 90 families were detained by troops for taking part in the demonstration, while the paramilitaries were announcing that they would assassinate protesters.

On 27 September about 80 Colombian police officers, including a former top anti-drug official, were arrested after being accused of stealing more than $2 million of American aid. The arrests took place just 48 hours after President Uribe met President Bush in the White House to discuss increases in aid. At the same time the three IRA suspects were due to attend their arraignment but were protesting that a fair trial was impossible. On 4 October, when the men refused to leave the jail, the trial was postponed. A spokeswoman for the prison service could not confirm reports that the three men had been beaten when they refused to leave La Picota jail.

Seven people were killed in Medellin when far-right paramilitaries clashed with local leftwing activists, bringing to well over 300 the number of civilians killed in the year. A few days later, on 18 October, troops encircled the Comuna 13 district after further deaths and orders from Uribe for the army to retake the lawless slums that had become virtually inaccessible to police. Some 3000 police and troops, accompanied by hooded informers, assaulted the poor neighbourhoods and then began searching homes, shops and bars. The guerrillas had retreated and were hiding in the surrounding hills. The police and army had succeeded in this major operation but the rebels were now bringing the war to the streets of the main Colombian cities.[25] An army major commented on the urban fighting:

They [the rebels] remove a brick or punch a hole in the wall and shoot at us through them. They dig tunnels from the basement into other houses so they can escape quickly. The fighting here has been very hard.

A car packed with 90lb of explosives had blown up in central Medellin, shattering windows in offices and shops. According to Leonardo Gallego, the Medellin police chief, more than 100 rebels were still hiding in the shantytown of Comuna 13 but it was being emphasised that the security operation would continue until all the guerrillas were captured, killed or driven out. This was all part of the harsh Uribe approach. The president's first military decree on 10 September had allowed for the creation of 'Zones of Rehabilitation and Consolidation', where direct military rule would replace existing local government.

In the reoccupied demilitarised zone, the former FARC safe haven, the soldiers and the paramilitaries were taking their revenge on the helpless inhabitants of the region. Amnesty International was reporting an increasing number of corpses being found in the San Vicente municipality. There was no official attempt to establish the identities of the bodies or the circumstances of the deaths. Some reports were claiming that bodies were being buried in mass graves, and that the former DMZ, no longer under FARC control, was being run by a killer network of paramilitaries and security forces. Arbitrary intelligence, some from children, was being gathered before assassinations and massacres were carried out as the usual 'cleansing' operations. Women were being harassed, houses arbitrarily searched and property stolen or destroyed. In Ciudad Bolivar, on the outskirts of San Vicente, the troops were burning houses, beating civilians and taking men and women away to unknown destinations. Amnesty International had also collected testimonies of torture by troops in San Vicente and La Macarena. One man was forced to witness the torture of his brother.

One victim, arrested along with ethers by Mobile Brigade No. 6, a counter-insurgency unit, was at first handcuffed and then punched and kicked. He was then nearly suffocated with a wet towel, burned with cigarettes, and had his arms, feet and stomach cut with a machete. Finally the soldiers threatened to amputate his testicles before knocking him out with a blow to the head. Then he was offered money to work as an informer and forced to sign a document without reading it. When the man eventually returned home he found everything ransacked and his livestock gone. With the arrival of the army, the paramilitaries were allowed to operate freely in the former safe haven and in the south of Caqueta, Mesetas, La Macarena, Uribe and Vista Hermosa.[26]

There seemed to be no prospect of any relief from the continuing conflict and the suffering of the Colombian people. In November 2002 Monsignor Jorge Enrique Jimenez, a senior Roman Catholic bishop, was kidnapped by rebels and later rescued by Colombian troops; guerrillas again blew up the Cano Limon pipeline, used by the US firm Occidental Petroleum, forcing 280 people living nearby to escape the oil spill; and Gilberto Rodriguez Orejuela, a leading drug trafficker who had headed the Cali cartel, was released after serving seven years of a 15-year sentence. In late-November the Colombian government was negotiating with the paramilitaries, but to what purpose was unclear. What was plain was that such talks would not be allowed 'to stand in the way of the all-important tasks of killing unionists, displacing peasants, and preventing peace with the guerrilla movement' – the customary activities of the Colombian army aided by the death squads: 'Those tasks are ordered from the US, and it is unlikely that they will stop until the US changes its orders.'[27]

Fighting Capitalism

It has long been apparent that the violent struggle in Colombia, like violent struggles elsewhere, is largely about the acquisition of natural resources, the control of commercial enterprise and the exploitation of national peoples. Put simply, the conflict in Colombia is largely about the capitalist penetration of a country. Here the problem is compounded by a rightwing regime eager to hand over national assets to foreign, primarily US, corporations and to perpetrate any repression that aids the process.

On 29 November 2002 Ecopetrol, Colombia's state oil company, announced that it wanted to cut benefits for the roughly 50 per cent of its workforce who belonged to a trade union. Rodolfo Gutierrez, the Workers Union president, commented on the possibility of industrial action: 'We have declared ourselves on a state of alert and, at any moment, we will be calling a national meeting of leaders to take decisions. We have total authority from our members to fix the hour the strike starts.' The union had already been striking for a 12 per cent rise in 2003, and Ecopetrol was claiming that it would have to cut its workforce by a sixth and sell assets. Already the company had started court action to alter the working conditions agreed with the union – to hive off oil-well maintenance, to cut pension benefits for new workers, to cut health care costs and to be able to sack union members more easily. The company also wanted to cut spending on food and schooling for refinery workers' families: 'The objective of the court action is to recover our capacity to manage the company.'

The trial of the IRA suspects was about to begin, though it seemed that the government case was collapsing through lack of reliable evidence. Observers assumed that the men had been involved with the FARC rebels but there was no evidence to establish the nature of their activities. The men were still refusing to leave their cell, forcing the trial to continue in their absence. As a significant corollary to the developing proceedings, President Uribe had been supplied with a British military jamming device for his car to prevent attack from IRA-style bombs. This suggested that, absence of evidence notwithstanding, the British government assumed that the IRA trio had been training the FARC in bomb-making.

On 2 December the IRA suspects, though absent from court, went on trial. Now their defence lawyers were claiming that a fair trial was impossible since top government and judicial figures had already made statements convicting the men. In court, Major Carlos Eduardo Matiz Ramirez produced a manual, allegedly taken from FARC rebels, that explained how to build IRA-style weapons. He suggested that the manual must have been written by someone with expert knowledge, which the FARC did not possess: 'The gas cylinder system was first used in Northern Ireland, not in Colombia.' Such evidence was merely circumstantial and inconclusive; and, in any case, on the following day the trial descended into chaos. Two key witnesses, both FARC deserters, failed to arrive in court and the trial was suspended. Perhaps, suggested Judge Jairo Acosta, a special commission could be set up to visit the witnesses in hiding outside Bogota, and written questions could be put to them by the court.

At the same time the courts were powerless to protect Marta Hinestroza, a lawyer who had been acting for farmers claiming that their livelihoods had been ruined by a pipeline part-owned by BP. She graduated in Médellin at a time when BP was discovering oil in the region. Here the oil was first pumped through the Oleoducto de Colombia (ODC) pipeline, the construction of which had wreaked havoc with the local ecosystems and ruined local farms. Then BP took a 15 per cent stake in a new company, Ocensa, created to construct and operate an 800km pipeline passing from the Cusiana-Cupiagua fields through four states, 40 municipalities and 192 villages to the port of Covenas in northwest Colombia. The new pipeline passed through the municipality of Zaragosa, not far from Hinestroza's hometown of El Bagre.

The construction of the new pipeline destroyed hundreds of water sources and caused landslides that ruined local farmers. To protect the pipeline an exclusion zone was created around it – denying the farmers more of their land. Hinestroza began to hear the complaints of many farmers, but it proved impossible to represent them effectively in the courts. Four of her colleagues – ombudsmen in neighbouring municipalities – were assassinated by the paramilitaries. Then Hinestroza began to receive death threats. A short time later, the paramilitaries arrived at the home of her aunt, dragged her out, tied her hands behind her back, made her kneel down, and then in front of the villagers shot her through the back of the head. Hinestroza resigned but continued to represent her clients. BP has since paid out £180,000 to 17 families affected by the ODC pipeline, but offers of less than £100 per person to other claimants have been rejected: some 1600 people are holding out for claims worth a total of around £20 million. Hinestroza, having fled to London, commented:

> When your work might make all the difference for more than 200 helpless and impoverished families, it is difficult to walk away. But in the end you have to ask, 'What use am I to anyone dead?' I'd already had to move my office in the city because the people I shared with were frightened by the vile phone calls I was receiving. I'd only been in the new place a few days when they began again, and then a couple of very dodgy characters turned up on the doorstep.

The pattern was familiar. The peasants would be evicted and abused, often in the plain interests of the corporations, and anyone who tried to protect them would be threatened or worse. The intimidation and assassination of trade union leaders was part of the same framework of terror. Thus on 18 December 2002 Nicodemus Luna, a leader of the oilworkers union (USO) was beaten by five men in civilian dress carrying rifles and hand weapons. A watchman who witnessed the assault called the police who quickly arrived and took Luna away. For several hours his whereabouts was not known, until it was admitted that he was being held by Gaula, the anti-extortion unit of the army's Third Brigade. This was alarming since the men who had beaten and kicked Luna claimed that they were Gaula members.

It was clear that under the Uribe administration social protest and trade union activism were being criminalised. Nicodemus Luna had already suffered systematic threats by paramilitary groups and continuous judicial persecution by the state, forcing him to move several times from 29 October 1992 to March 1995, and during a second period from 21 December 1997 to 18 December 1999. In December 2002 trade unions and human rights activists began a campaign of protest at the unexplained detention of Luna.

The government had declared a 'State of Internal Commotion' and passed the highly repressive Decree 2002. By 2003 the whole of Colombia was termed a 'zone of rehabilitation and consolidation', with zones containing the richest natural resources specifically designated for special measures. Such areas were effectively under martial law and the people were living in terror. In Arauca more than 500 people were taken into a stadium and marked with ink, demonstrating the power of the army and police, acting on their own suspicion, to capture, process and imprison anyone for supposed terrorism. Dozens of trade unionists had been rounded up and, without charge or trial, thrown into jail in Bogota.

Some 300 state bodies were scheduled for privatisation or closure, affecting 150,000 workers – with the government aim of raising funds to support an expansion of the army and mounting state repression. A Public Order Law, law 418, had been passed, granting to the president the legal power to negotiate with armed groups – for example, the paramilitary death squads – to grant pardons or amnesties. The law meant that the assassins would not be brought to justice but incorporated into the state system of terror and repression. Hence the role of the private armies would be reinforced while new laws were being devised to criminalise trade unions. Decree 2002 was already criminalising all forms of protest as terrorism.

Alexander Lopez, the Colombian opposition deputy, has described some aspects of the Uribe 'reforms':

> The proposed labour reform will reduce work contracts down to just one hour and it will remove all protection from the workers. The proposed pension law puts two conditions for receiving a state pension – that you are 62 years old and that you have completed 1300 weeks of paid-up work. Very few people will be able to get a pension. On average, the Colombian worker has just 16 weeks of work in a year. At that rate, it would take over 80 years of work to qualify[28]

Lopez emphasised that the United States saw Colombia as essential to its interests: 'If they get away with introducing another wave of neoliberalism in Colombia, then it will open up that possibility across the whole of Latin

America.' The conflict in Colombia was not just a civil war but a 'direct confrontation with neoliberalism and with the US empire'.[29]

In November 2002 Nestlé was found to have imported 200 tons of powdered milk into Colombia in sacks stamped with false production dates – presumably designed to give the product a longer shelf life. Senator Jorge Enrique Robledo charged the company with using sub-standard contaminated milk, 'a serious attack on the health of our people, especially the children'. This scandal followed persistent complaints that Nestlé was indifferent to human rights. Since 1982 eight trade unionists, members of the Food and Drink Workers Union, Sinaltrainal, and employees of Nestlé, have been assassinated by the paramilitaries. When the AUC death squad organisation declared local union leaders as military targets, Nestlé workers were on the list.

There was no evidence that Nestlé was collaborating with the AUC paramilitaries but the company was known to be hostile to the trade union. In late 2001 the management of Comestibles La Rosa, a Nestlé subsidiary, told the workers that they must either renounce union membership or lose their jobs. In February 2002 the company took steps to abandon a collective agreement covering 400 employees, to sack 96 workers and to break the contracts of another 58 workers so that jobs could be contracted out through labour agencies.

The corporate ambitions are clear and run to a common pattern. In 2000 the massive mining corporation BHP-Billiton and the Swiss-based multinational Glencore bought 50 per cent of the El Cerrejon organisation from the Colombian state – a deal that caused a scandal because the $384 million paid was only a third of the state's accumulated investment in the company. The other 50 per cent of Cerrejon was owned by Intercor, a subsidiary of ExxonMobil bought out by Billiton-Anglo-Glencore in early 2002.

These mining corporations then accelerated their exploitation of Colombian natural resources. Settlements of the Wayuu people and Afro-Colombians were cleared to give the companies easy access to the land. On 9-10 August 2001 the village of Tabaco was destroyed, displacing 350 families from their homes. Two hundred police and soldiers fought the helpless villagers as Intercor bulldozers smashed down their houses. And forcible ejection was being backed up by the usual panoply of terror. The nickel mine Cerro Matosa, another Billiton operation, was in an area where the paramilitaries held the people in a grip of fear. On 4 November 2002 shareholders at the first annual general meeting of BHP-Billiton approved chief executive Brian Gilbertson's remuneration package – worth $5.06 million per annum.

One significant case was that of Alfredo Porras Rueda, a former president of Sinaltrainal forced to leave his job due to persecution, death threats, assassination attempts and illegal searches. On 31 December 2002 Porras was detained by the security forces, while General Jairo Duvan Pineda, commander of the Fifth Division of the Colombian army accused him publicly of being a member of ELN.

Another Coca-Cola worker and former Sinaltrainal leader, Adolfo de Jesus Munera, was also forced to leave his job because of death threats. On 31 August 2002 he was assassinated in the city of Barranquila.

On 10 January 2003 the Colombian security forces raided the offices of the United Workers Federation (CUT) in Cali. Carlos Lozano, director of *Voz*, the weekly newspaper of the Colombian Communist Party, commented: 'This is a serious incident; the CUT is the country's principal trade union centre, a very respectable organisation to which thousands of workers are affiliated. The raid is an open attack on the popular, social and trade union movement in Colombia.' Agents of the attorney general and the Department of Administrative Security (DAS) were reportedly inspecting the files and other documents belonging to the union.[30]

Rodolfo Gutierrez Nino, national president of the oilworkers union (USO) was also receiving death threats – during discussions with the government and the Ecopetrol administration about the deteriorating state of the corporation: falls in reserves and production, low refining yields, and the leasing out of pipelines and the fuel supply system. Ecopetrol was then demanding the elimination of trade union rights, sackings, new disciplinary procedures and the criminalisation of certain union activities. Management efforts to restructure Ecopetrol, allied to official oil policy, were designed to assist the acquisition by the US multinationals of the Colombian oil industry. At the same time leading union individuals were being targeted: death threats against Gutierrez and measures taken against Hernando Hernandez, USO's secretary for foreign affairs.

In the first ten days of 2003 the paramilitaries carried out massacres in the poor districts of Camilo Daza and Antonia Santos and elsewhere, resulting in the deaths of about 60 people. On 9 January the paramilitaries, carrying long-range and automatic weapons, descended on the poor districts, immobilised two security guards and then shot them dead. Then they moved off to search for more victims. In Los Olivos they shot a 17-year-old boy and then murdered his 22-year-old brother-in-law. Later the paramilitaries shot the 18-year-old Rafael Ricardo Vanegas Mejia in the head and murdered the 39-year-old Maria Rubiela Poveda Sanchez, a community worker and pregnant. Her 18-year-old son Raul was shot three times. Then the paramilitaries arrived at the home of the 23-year-old Olider Miguel Zafra Serpa, dragged him out of the house in front of his partner and children, and then shot him dead in the street.

At 3 am on 10 January a group of paramilitaries entered the suburbs of Dona Nidia in the west of Cucuta. When they arrived at the house of labourer Reinalso Camacho Gil they banged on his door and demanded that he open it, identifying themselves as members of the security forces. Then they dragged him out of his home onto the street and shot him dead. On the same day President Uribe confirmed that he would be talking to the paramilitaries. A week later, a car bomb exploded in Medellin, killing five people, including a four-year-old boy, with 32 wounded.

On 16 January workers at Ecopetrol began a 24-hour strike in protest at an arrest warrant issued for Hernando Hernandez, a senior USO official. It was assumed that the government intended to put Hernandez under house arrest. The paramilitaries had already tried to assassinate him in a hospital bed when he was recovering from cancer, and now the government was taking retaliation for the union's defence of Ecopetrol and its workers. In 2001 alone more than 200 trade unionists were killed or disappeared, and the murders were continuing.

The Constitutional Court was considering Uribe proposals for a national referendum to approve the government's new austerity measures, necessarily involving IMF requirements for severe cuts in public spending. The rebels responded with yet another attack on the Cano Limon pipeline and 'retained' (kidnapped) a British reporter, Ruth Morris, and an American photographer, Scott Dalton, for a period that would depend on undefined 'political and military conditions'. The ELN said that the two had become victims because they had strayed into rebel territory on a freelance assignment for the *Los Angeles Times* without proper permits:

> You must take into account that Arauca state has been declared a war zone by the American government and the Colombian state. For that reason the National Liberation Army is on a war footing and is acting in defence of the dignity of all the people of eastern Colombia.

The 'lives and security of these journalists' would be guaranteed.

On 23 January 2003 Eve Maria Uribe, superintendent of public services, issued Resolution 141 designed to 'modify the administration of Emcali ... and take possession of it in order to liquidate it and, in consequence, from the time of this resolution on to carry out the necessary actions to initiate the liquidation process'. The intended privatisation followed the policy of the Uribe administration, as laid out in the proposal for a 'communitarian state' with the intention of handing over state assets to US corporations. Following the issuing of the resolution, groups of protesting workers were surrounded by state security forces, and in some cases death threats were being made.

On 9 August 2002, just two days after taking power, President Uribe had travelled to Cali to show his intention of privatising the state organisation through a proposed 'shareholder company'. In January 2003 the union was again rallying the workers to resist the donation of state assets to foreign multinationals.

On 1 January the two kidnapped journalists were freed by the ELN, a seeming act of clemency in a worsening human rights situation. Colombia remained in the midst of a humanitarian crisis of massive scale, with civilian casualties being 80 per cent of the total. It had been estimated that the rebel movements were responsible for about five per cent of the deaths, the army ten per cent, and the paramilitary forces about 85 per cent. In summary the statistics described the character of Colombian society:

> A union leader was assassinated every three days, accounting for the vast majority of all trade unionists killed worldwide. More than 2.5 million campesinos had been forced from their land by economic conditions, toxic crop-spraying and death-squad intimidation. 1.5 million displaced people were living in Bogota alone, surviving in appalling conditions in shanty-towns. One person was murdered every 15 to 20 minutes. With the encouragement of Uribe the paramilitaries had grown more than 80 per cent over the past year, extending their terror over 40 per cent of the country.

In this context about 42 per cent of Colombia's budget was being used to service foreign debt, with nearly a third of the budget being used to fund the police, security services and armed forces. Even then, the IMF and the World Bank were pressing for further reductions in state spending on health and education. State assets were being donated to foreign corporations, and draconian laws were hitting at trade unions, civil protest and human rights. The United States, pleased with this course of events, was pouring billions of dollars into the Colombian armed forces and the corporations, while supporting the poisoning of peasant land and the escalating war against the Colombian people.

Intensifying the Conflict

On 28 November 2002 a delegation of Irish parliamentarians, human rights activists and international legal observers went to Colombia where they visited the three IRA suspects in La Modelo jail. The delegation also met a number of legal and political figures in Bogota and attended the first stage of the trial. On 5 February 2003 the trial resumed before a single judge and without a jury. The judge had formerly ruled that the prosecution witnesses should attend the February hearing but then gave permission for one witness to be interviewed in Medellin, while the Colombian authorities claimed that they could not afford the $200 airfare to transfer the witness to Bogota. The delegation concluded that:

> The men could not obtain a fair trial.
>
> The men had not obtained a fair legal process to date.
>
> The men had been transferred from jail to jail on several occasions which has prejudiced the preparations for their trial.
>
> Threats had been made against the defence lawyers which had made it more difficult to prepare for trial hearings.
>
> The men had been held in dangerous and unsuitable conditions, in breach of internationally accepted human rights conventions, since their arrest in August 2001.
>
> Pre-trial publicity in Colombia and internationally had undermined the principle of presumption of innocence.
>
> Statements by the former and present presidents of Colombia and senior Colombian and US officials and elected representatives had further undermined the possibility of a fair trial.
>
> The Irish government should send an official legal observer to attend the trial at all stages.
>
> The men should be held in Bogota in a safe location for the duration of the trial.

There was no sign that the Colombian authorities or the Irish government were responding to these observations.

On 3 February the Uribe administration rejected a UN plan to hold regional peace talks in Arauca state where rebels had recently bombed two electrical towers and left the region without power. Martha Lucia Ramirez rejected the UN suggestion, saying that peace talks had to be handled on a national level. On the following day, Carlos Castano gave a 47-minute radio interview on the main breakfast show. Here, with reference to Uribe's referendum project, he declared that the leaders of the abstention campaign should be targeted for elimination and that he had no problems with the armed forces. The Uribe administration had no problem with the death squads: Castano had been granted immunity from prosecution.

When the trial of the three IRA suspects resumed on 5 February, little progress was made. One witness, Edwin Giovanni Rodriguez was brought into the chamber wearing a bullet-proof vest, whereupon Judge Acosta asked for him to be put into the witness protection program saying that his evidence would soon be heard. The suspicion remained that the trial would not be fair. Caitriona Ruane, Bring Them Home Campaign, expressed the defence complaint that a witness was to give evidence in Medellin: 'We have complained about that. We have put in an appeal. We expect that we will be back and forth like yo-yos and we think it is a tactic of the Colombian state.' Then the trial was adjourned until the following Friday. In Bogota the political situation was worsening as confrontation between the Emcali workers and the security forces seemed increasingly likely.

The workers were gathering in their workplaces and being threatened by armed police surrounding the plants. The police had already broken up one Sintraemcali rally with arrests, beatings, tear gas and explosive grenades. Uribe, determined to confront all forms of dissent, had recently spoken at the launch of the 13,000-strong Sixth Division, charged with the task of hunting down the main leaders of the FARC organisation: 'The decisive moment has arrived for the military forces to deliver results.' It seemed that the rebels did not have the option of surrender, that if they relinquished their arms they would be executed. Thus the newspaper *El Espectador* reported that many demobilised members of the Maoist EPL group had met a gruesome fate: some 250 ex-combatants and 350 sympathisers had already been assassinated. As part of the alleged 'war on terrorism', all radical and leftwing movements were being treated as enemies to be eliminated. One leftwing activist commented: 'In this country, we don't have a bourgeoisie. We have mafias.' As always, the trade unionists were a primary target. Thus a leader of the union at Bavaria beer company reported that the membership of Sinaltrabavaria had plunged from 3000 to 580 workers – the consequence of death threats, beatings and assassinations. One union leader, forced into exile in Chile several years ago, returned recently to his home city of Barranquilla for a family visit. He arrived at the airport and was assassinated on the way home.

On 6 February the three IRA suspects were ordered back to the notorious Bogota jail where they had received death threats. The judge would decide their fate following a court procedure that seemed largely indifferent to the judicial rights of the accused. At the same time FARC rebels, allegedly trained by the Irishmen, were again blowing up the Cano Limon pipeline, producing a gush of crude oil near the village of La Ceiba that was expected to cause lasting environmental damage. Specialists from Ecopetrol were reportedly rushing to the area. Already the many guerrilla attacks on the pipeline had cost Occidental Petroleum hundreds of millions of dollars: $445 million in 2001, more in 2002.

President Uribe was now recruiting as many people as possible to expand the Colombian armed forces. Supposedly sympathetic peasants were being given compulsory military training and retired troops were being brought back into the armed forces. The government was even working to enlist the private sector to adopt a military role in the national conflict, with companies in the telecommunications and private security sectors heading Uribe's list of draftees. A recent decree had placed obligations on the country's 160,000 security guards – a force bigger than the police or the army – to pass potential intelligence to the authorities. A 27-member platoon of top business leaders had pledged support for the defence industry, creating a series of support committees to aid the government in such fields as logistics, administration and information technology. The government had already imposed a one-off tax on companies and wealthy individuals to raise $800 million for military spending, in turn creating business confidence that the rebels would be defeated and foreign investment would be boosted. But some of the companies were nervous about their growing involvement in the conflict. Thus Jaime Higuera, National Association of Private Security (Andevip), representing about 150 security companies employing around 150,000 people, commented: 'People have always been willing to co-operate. What we don't want is anyone saying that an arrest or operation was due to information from a specific company. We don't want to become targets.'[31]

In the same vein another business leader declared: 'People do not want publicly to assume positions of collaboration. We have 30,000 deaths a year in this country and people get killed for publicly appearing in these ways.' But the corporations were trying to support Uribe's militarisation policy, with one consequence being a vastly increased flow of intelligence information to the Colombian authorities. It remained to be seen whether the government would be able to sift through the stream of information in any useful way.

In February 2003 more than 1000 young farmers were being trained to handle weapons, to patrol and to engage in urban warfare. Forced to attend three-month boot camps the farmers were being issued weapons and military uniforms, and being taught such skills as how to cross a street under fire and how to enter a house where the enemy was hiding. The scheme required the soldier-farmers to remain attached to the army for two years and to receive a monthly salary of about $17. The government was aiming to train 12,000 farmers in this fashion by the end of the year. Human rights activists were suggesting that this plan would accomplish nothing more than to expand the ranks of the death-squad paramilitaries, an outcome that might not have been unwelcome to Uribe.

On 22 January President Uribe had already begun talks with the AUC paramilitaries of Carlos Castano and Salvatore Mancuso. Shortly before the talks began, Uribe issued a decree designed to give immunity to the 14,000-strong band of murderers, extortionists, torturers and drug traffickers. The paramilitaries had tortured and assassinated many thousands of campesinos, social workers, community activists, students and indigenous leaders – in collusion with the armed forces and with state backing. It says something about the Uribe administration that it saw the paramilitaries as its natural allies, having no interest in curbing their crimes and working instead to swell their ranks. It was significant also that the United States regarded this as a highly congenial arrangement.

The US had long been involved in efforts to support successive Colombian regimes working to protect the corporations and the financial élites and to repress any hint of social protest. It was as early as 1962 that the Colombian authorities, the Pentagon and the US State Department began to develop Plan Laso, a counterinsurgency programme aimed at crushing any signs of leftwing opposition to the US-friendly regime. Washington claimed to be combating 'communist proponents', but the term was rapidly expanded to include suspected communists, social protesters, human rights activists and trade unionists. Thus General Luis Carlos Camacho Leyva, Colombian defence minister (1978-82), commented that social protest was 'the unarmed branch of subversion'. Over the subsequent decades the Colombian people have been forced to live under the conditions imposed by such repressive measures, all the legal paraphernalia of a police state where broad judicial and political powers have been progressively transferred to the military with no effective overseeing civilian authorities to keep their activities in check.

These trends have come to define the condition of Colombia in the 21st century. Through 2003 the paramilitary murders continued, generally with the tacit approval of the Uribe administration and his US backers; and the guerrillas continued to prosecute what they saw as a 'people's struggle'. On 8 February a massive car bomb ripped through an exclusive club in Bogota, killing 32 people and wounding more than 160. An estimated 400lb of explosive detonated in the car park of El Nogal Club, a gathering place for the capital's corporate and cultural élite. One witness said he though a plane had crashed.

On 10 February Martha Lucia Ramirez, Colombia's defence minister, flew to Miami with a US military commander to seek more military aid to combat the leftwing rebels. On the following day leaders from Central American countries – Panama, Costa Rica, Guatemala, El Salvador, Honduras and Nicaragua – signed a joint declaration of solidarity with Colombia in its fight against the rebels. At the same time the European Union (EU) strongly condemned the attack on the El Nogal Club, applauding President Uribe's efforts to combat terrorism and to establish the rule of law throughout the country.

A few days later a US spy plane crashed in southern Colombia, leading to the rebel execution of two Americans and the kidnapping of three more. US-supplied Black Hawk helicopters quickly located the crashed Cessna with two bodies nearby. At the same time rebels exploded a house full of mortars in southern Colombia, killing at least 15 people and injuring 30. And on the 18 February further doubts were aired about the Colombian government's case against the IRA suspects. Caitriona Ruane, Bring Them Home Campaign, protested that the Irish government should intervene in the case: 'There is a miscarriage of justice occurring. The Colombian state is going to great lengths to fabricate a case against these three Irish citizens, and we are calling for the Irish government to call for their release and get them sent home to their families.'

The Uribe administration, contemptuous of human rights, was developing its policies of repression and militarisation. The ranks of the death-squad paramilitaries were expanding, partly as a result of deliberate government policy. In March 2003 Gloria Ramirez, a prominent Colombian trade unionist, told a TUC conference in London: 'We're supposedly democratic because we hold elections, but we have seen 30,000 killed, the same level as Pinochet's Chile'.[32]

The Bush administration, enjoying the pretext of its alleged 'war on terrorism', was knowingly aiding the repression of the Colombian people in the interest of corporate profit. There seemed no end in sight.

Agreed Agenda for Peace Talks between Colombian Government and FARC Rebels (6 May 1999)

1. A Negotiated Political Solution
A political solution to the serious social and armed conflict is being sought, one which will bring a new Colombia through political, economic and social change, creating consensus to build a new state, founded on social justice and conserving national unity.

Acts of peace will occur as negotiations advance. This means that all Colombians must commit to the construction of peace without regard to economic, social or religious interests, or political parties.

2. Protection of Human Rights as a responsibility of the State
    2.1   Fundamental rights
    2.2   Economic, social, cultural and environmental rights
    2.3   International human rights treaties

3   *An Integrated Agrarian Policy*
   3.1   The democratization of credit, technical assistance and market access
   3.2   Redistribution of unproductive land
   3.3   Recuperation and distribution of land acquired through drug-trafficking and illegal enrichment
   3.4   Stimulating production
   3.5   Integral ordering of territory
   3.6   Illicit crop substitution and alternative development

4.   *Exploitation and Conservation of Natural Resources*
   4.1   Natural resources and their distribution
   4.2   International treaties
   4.3   Protection of the environment based on sustainable development

5.   *Economic and Social Structure*
   5.1   Revision of the economic development model
   5.2   Income redistribution policies
   5.3   Expansion of internal and external markets
   5.4   Stimulating production through small, medium and large-scale private enterprise
   5.5   Cooperative support for the economy
   5.6   Stimulation of foreign investment that benefits the nation
   5.7   Social participation in economic planning
   5.8   Investment in social welfare, education and scientific research

6.   *Justice reform, fighting corruption and drug trafficking*
   6.1   Judicial system
   6.2   Control institutions
   6.3   Mechanisms to fight corruption
   6.4   Drug trafficking

7.   *Political reform to broaden democracy*
   7.1   Reform of political parties and movements
   7.2   Electoral reforms
   7.3   Equal opportunity for the opposition
   7.4   Equal opportunity for minorities
   7.5   Mechanisms for citizen participation

8.   *State reform*
   8.1   Congressional reform

8.2 Administrative reform to improve the efficiency of public administration
8.3 Decentralization and strengthening of local power
8.4 Public services
8.5 Strategic sectors

9. *Agreements about International Humanitarian Law*
    9.1 No child involvement in the conflict
    9.2 Land mines
    9.3 Respect for the civil population
    9.4 Respect for international agreements

10. *Armed forces*
    10.1 Defense of sovereignty
    10.2 Protection of human rights
    10.3 Combating self-defense groups
    10.4 International treaties

11. *International relations*
    11.1 Respect for non-intervention and free self determination
    11.2 Latin American regional integration
    11.3 Foreign debt
    11.4 Treaties and international state agreements

12. *Formalizing the agreements*
    12.1 Democratic instruments to legitimize the agreements

(Signed)

For the government
Victor G. Ricardo
Fabio Valencia Cossio
Maria Emma Mejía Vélez
Nicanor Restrepo Santamaria
Rodolfo Espinsosa Meola

For the FARC
Raúl Reyes
Joaquin Gómez
Fabián Ramirez

APPENDIX 2

Plan Colombia

(a) Content and Scope of Plan Colombia (10 December 1999) as Promoted by Colombia Government to International Community – Extract

Plan Colombia has been designed by the government of President Andres Pastrana as a set of strategies to support the most pressing needs of the Colombian people in relation to peace, economic and social growth and the strengthening of the State.

Plan Colombia has been conceived as an integrated plan which seeks to create a climate favourable to peace through economic recovery, the strengthening of national defense and security, the justice system, the defence of human rights and democratization and social development.

Plan Colombia is a set of strategies designed to materialize the government's commitment to recover the central responsibilities of the State in relation to:

- the promotion of democracy
- a monopoly in the application of justice
- territorial integrity

– the general of conditions for increased employment
– respect for human rights and human dignity
– the preservation of public order
– the strengthening of the rule of law

If the state is to recover this capacity, there must be a process of reconstruction of society and communication, and of concertation. Here, peace is not simply a matter of political will. Rather, we need to build peace gradually, and for this, there must be progress in the institutionalization and strengthening of the State in order to guarantee security and the respect for human rights and freedom of all citizens in all parts of the country.

The presence of drug trafficking has affected Colombia more than any other country in the world. No other country has suffered the human cost of the problem on the same scale as we.

Drug trafficking has weakened our institutions, democracy, principles, values, and indeed the economy.

Drug-trafficking has also had a great influence on the escalation of the conflict and violations of human rights, to the extent that it has become an important source of finance mainly for the guerrillas and the paramilitaries. Drug trafficking has also had a devastating effect on the environment.

Therefore, Plan Colombia is a plan which seeks the cooperation of the entire international community to solve the problems derived from drug trafficking, on the principle of shared responsibility in the struggle against the world problem of drugs.

Plan Colombia has five central strategies:

1. The Peace Process
2. Stabilisation of the Economy
3. The Anti-drugs Strategy
4. Reforms to the Justice System and the Promotion of Human Rights
5. Democratization and Social Development

1. The Peace Process

The strategy of the peace process is designed to start a process of negotiation for peace agreements with the guerrillas, on the principle of territorial integrity, democracy and human rights, which should also strengthen the rule of law and the struggle against drugs everywhere. The main difference between this

strategy for negotiated peace and efforts made in the past is that it is not limited
to the idea of demobilization and reinsertion of former combatants into society.
It also recognizes the need for political, judicial, social and economic change in
order to prevent confrontation and build a lasting peace.

Its objectives are:

–   To achieve a peace agreement which seeks not only demobilization and
    reinsertion of combatants but also recognizes the need for political,
    judicial, social and economic change in order to prevent confrontation
    and build a lasting peace.
–   Peace, as the result of a broad social consensus which involves society as
    a whole: economic, political and armed agents.

2. Stabilization of the Economy

The goal of stabilization of the economy is to recover confidence in it through
a series of fiscal adjustments. These measures will be the basis for sustained
growth in investment and production; and stronger private investment will
enable jobs and opportunities to be created for all.

The expansion of international trade, along with better access to foreign
markets and free trade agreements, which attract domestic and foreign
investment, are key factors in the modernization of our economic base and in
the generation of employment. This strategy is essential at a time when
Colombia faces its worst economic crisis in 70 years. With unemployment at
almost 20%, the government's capacity to combat drug trafficking and the
violence which it creates will be a severe strain on our resources.

Colombia expects the support of the international community to
consolidate economic reform, increase the flow of resources to satisfy the social
needs of the Colombian people and so, to generate conditions favourable to the
construction of peace and to support the armed forces in the maintenance of
public order.

3. Anti-drugs Strategy and National Security

The principal aim of this strategy is to strengthen the presence of the State in
all parts of the country and reduce the growing, processing and distribution of
drugs by 50% in the next six years.

In association with other countries involved in one or more of the links in
the drug-chain – production, distribution, sale, consumption, asset-laundering,

precursors and other materials, arms dealing – Colombia aims to combat all components of the cycle of unlawful drugs and prevent the flow of the proceeds of that traffic – which fuels violence – to the guerrillas and other outlawed groups.

If we are to achieve these objectives, we must restructure and modernize the armed forces and police so that they may restore the rule of law and guarantee security throughout the country against the actions of organized crime and armed groups; and to protect and promote human rights and international humanitarian law.

We must also neutralize the financial system of the drug traffickers and make the mechanism of confiscation of assets for the State more effective.

An essential part of this effort is the strategy for Alternative Development. The aim of this strategy is to encourage forms of agriculture and other profitable activities among peasant farms and their families who are currently engaged in the growing of unlawful crops. Alternative development also contemplates economically-viable activities in environmental protection in order to conserve jungle areas and stop the dangerous spread of unlawful crops across the Amazon Basin and the vast natural parks which are also areas of immense biodiversity, of environmental importance to the international community. In this context, the strategy includes sustainable, integrated and participatory productive projects, combined with the infrastructure required, and pays special attention to regions which combine high levels of conflict with low levels of State presence, fragile social capital and serious degradation of the environment, such as the Middle Magdalena, the High Andes and the south-western Colombia.

4. *Reforms to the Justice System*

The reforms to the judiciary are designed to produce an impartial and effective system of justice who objectives are:

- To secure the rule of law
- To expropriate the proceeds of crime by efforts to combat asset-laundering
- To improve the credibility of the judicial system
- To combat contraband and strengthen interdiction of drug trafficking
- To eliminate corruption

5. Democratization and Social Development

Democratization and Social Development is designed to achieve a gradual and systematic reduction in the causes and manifestations of violence by strengthening civil participation and creating collective awareness.

The objectives are:

– *To promote respect for and to protect human rights and provide care for the victims of violence*

One of the goals of the peace strategy is to provide appropriate humanitarian aid to the victims of armed conflict in accordance with the principle of international humanitarian law and internal legislation. This includes insurance, compensation, physical and psychological rehabilitation, mechanisms to quantify and identify victims and special programs for those most affected (children, women heads of household, the elderly and ethnic groups). The government will define standards for minimum quality levels and regular institutional responsibilities based on indicators and supervision.

Based on the United Nations Convention of the Rights of the Child, humanitarian assistance will mainly concentrate on the physical and psychological needs of the children and promote their development, keeping them away from the armed groups. In addition, there will be rehabilitation, psychosocial treatment, training, and special education for the handicapped, depending on their individual and collective needs. Finally, the strategy includes action to identify and eliminate anti-personnel mines and to reduce the risks of settlement in high-risk areas and zones of conflict, through economic and social integration.

– *Assistance for the displaced*

Here, activities are designed to return the displaced to their homes and secure their stability there through social and productive investment programs in the zones of conflict. The government's strategy in providing assistance to the displaced is closely linked to the peace process and the efforts to increase the capabilities of local government. Assistance to the displaced will be the responsibility of municipal government and local NGOs under the leadership of the Social Solidarity Network. The government will also invite international organizations to play a part at municipal level in the mobilization of resources and in setting up mechanisms for verification of the local situation.

As laid down in the Guiding Principles for Assistance for the Internally Displaced, the government's actions seek to neutralize the causes of displacement by improving security in high-risk areas. In zones of conflict the government structures an early-warning system to detect the imminent threat of violence so that it will be able to act promptly. If displacement cannot be avoided, the government will provide whatever is necessary to meet local needs.

Measures will be taken to secure the protection of the rights of all the displaced and mechanisms will be set up to offer emergency humanitarian assistance such as water, nutrition, health and protection. Special attention will be paid to the needs of the different age groups, with special services for children, women and ethnic minorities. Where possible, the government will support and promote the Peace Communities to which the displaced may return and receive social services and physical protection.

– *To strengthen sustainable development in environmentally fragile areas*

Armed conflict affects the natural habitat in the same way as the expansion of the agricultural frontier (lawful and otherwise, this has destroyed close to a million hectares of woodland since 1974). These zones include a high proportion of conservation areas and natural parks, and there is plenty of evidence to suggest that the process of expansion is a serious threat to the rest of the Amazon Basin.

In order to combat this problem, actions taken include the restoration of some areas as natural parks, the recovery of woodland in accordance with world objectives for the preservation of the Amazon Basin (as observed in the Convention on Climatic Change). Further, the government will facilitate the transition from unsustainable agriculture to crops better suited to local and regional conditions. Finally, among the activities planned there will be support for small-scale replanting of woodland and the consolidation of green markets to generate local potential for trade.

– *To strengthen the credibility and effectiveness of State agencies at national and local level*

People look for security, order, employment, basic services and a better future for their children. National programs, such as those for alternative development, environmental protection, the displaced and assistance for the zones of conflict, aim to materialize these expectations and thus reduce the incentive to migrate or to grow unlawful crops. Local communities and municipal councils play a basic role in ensuring that these programs reach their destination.

Greater capabilities in local government in the execution and evolution of national investment plans, the work of the NGOs in problem-solving and the efforts of all agents are essential to the strategy for social investment and alternative development in Colombia.

The government will act through the Social Solidarity Network, the Ministries and the NGOs to support municipal administration in the management of technical resources and skills, the management of the displaced, alternative development and the struggle against poverty. About 150 communities which live in areas where conflict and unlawful crops have interrupted the supply of basic services, where the environment has been degraded and where there are high levels of poverty will be selected over years to take part in programs to strengthen institutions. Community leaders will be trained in techniques of government. Local government will be trained to promote community participation in decision-making processes and in the solving of social and economic problems. The training of local leaders will make it possible to establish priorities in local needs and initiatives to design the basic services required, so that available resources will be employed as effectively as possible.

In order to maximize efficiency, local government will work with central government, local business and NGOs. Municipal government will seek to invest local revenues, transfer from the central budget and donations to support local organizations in satisfying local basic needs.

Estimated cost of Plan Colombia

Plan Colombia is estimated to cost $7,500 million over three years. Colombia will provide $4,000 million, and it is hoped that $3,500 million will be provided by the international community.

(b) Summary of Plan Colombia According to US Institute of Peace Library – Extract

Plan Colombia: Plan for Peace, Prosperity and the Strengthening of the State

Table of Contents

Preface

Plan Colombia: Plan for Peace, Prosperity and the Strengthening of the State
    Elements of the Plan

The Peace Process
    The Armed Conflict and Civil Society
    The Current Situation
    The Role of the International Community

Approach to the Colombian Economy
 Stabilization Measures

Counter-Drug Strategy
 Strategy Based on Human Values
 Strategic Objectives
 Basic Elements of the Strategy Against Narcotrafficking

The Reform of the Justice System and the Protection of Human Rights
 Securing the Rule of Law
 The Accountability of the Judicial System
 The Promotion, Respect and Protection of Human Rights
 Eliminate Corruption
 Deprive Criminals of Illegal Profits
 Combat Contraband and Strengthen Narcotics Interdiction
 Reduction of Demand

Plan for Democratization and Social Development
 Assistance for the Victims of Violence
 Assisting the Internally Displaced
 Alternative Development Strategy
 Sustainable Development in Environmentally Fragile Areas
 The Role of Local Communities and Municipalities

Elements of the Plan

1. An **economic strategy** that generates employment, supports the ability of the State to collect tax revenues and allows the country to have a viable counterbalancing economic force to narco-trafficking. The expansion of international trade, accompanied by enhanced access to foreign markets and free trade agreements to attract foreign and domestic investment are key to the modernization of our economic base and to job creation. Such a strategy is crucial at a time when Colombia is confronting its worst economic crisis in seventy years, with unemployment reaching 20%, which in turn greatly limits the government's ability to confront drug trafficking and the violence it generates.

2. A **fiscal and financial strategy** that includes tough austerity and adjustment measures, in order to boost economic activity and recover the historically excellent prestige of Colombia in international financial markets.

3. A **peace strategy** that aims at a negotiated peace agreement with the guerillas on the basis of territorial integrity, democracy and human rights, which should further strengthen the rule of law and the fight against drugs.

4. A **national defense strategy** to restructure and modernize the armed forces and the police, so that they will be able to restore the rule of law and provide security throughout the country, to combat organized crime and armed groups and to protect and promote human rights and international humanitarian law.

5. A **judicial and human rights strategy** to reaffirm the rule of law and assure equal and impartial justice to all, while pressing ahead with the reforms already initiated in the forces of law and order to ensure that they play their proper role in defending and respecting the rights and dignity of all.

6. A **counter-narcotics strategy**, in partnership with other countries involved in some or all of the links of the drug-chain: production, distribution, sale, consumption, asset laundering, precursor chemicals and arms dealing. And, at the national level, to stop the flow of drug-money the fuel of violence – to the insurgent and other armed organizations.

7. An **alternative development strategy** that will promote agricultural schemes and other profitable economic activities for peasant-farmers and their families. Alternative development will also consider economically-feasible environmental protection activities, designed to conserve the forest areas and end the dangerous expansion of illegal crops across the Amazon Basin and Colombia's vast natural park-areas of immense bio-diversity, of vital environmental importance to the international community. Within this framework the strategy includes sustainable, integrated and participatory productive projects combined with the required infrastructure. Particular attention is paid to regions which combine high levels of conflict with low levels of State presence, fragile social capital and serious environmental degradation, such as the Middle Magdalena valley, the Macizo Colombiano and the south-west.

8. A **social participation strategy** aimed at collective awareness. This strategy seeks to develop more accountability in local government, community involvement in anti-corruption efforts, and continued pressure on the guerrillas and other armed groups to end kidnapping, violence and the internal displacement of individuals and communities. This strategy will also include co-operation with local business and labour groups, in order to promote innovative and productive models in the face of a more globalized economy and thus strengthen our agricultural communities and reduce the risks of rural violence. In addition, this strategy seeks to strengthen institutions, both formal and informal, to foster changes in the cultural patterns through which violence develops and reinforces itself. It includes the promotion of mechanisms and educational programs to increase

tolerance, the essential values for peaceful co-existence, and participation in public affairs.

9. A **human development strategy** to promote efforts to guarantee, within the next few years, adequate education and health, to provide opportunities to every young Colombian and to help vulnerable groups in our society, including not just those affected and displaced by violence by also those in conditions of extreme poverty.

10. An **international-oriented strategy** to confirm the principles of shared responsibility, integrated action and balanced treatment of the drug issue. The role and support of the international community is also vital to the success of the peace process provided that it conforms to the terms of international law and is requested by the Colombian government.

Clinton Proposal (11 January 2000) and Senate Proposal (20 October 1999) in Response to Plan Colombia

Clinton Administration Proposal

On January 11, 2000, the Clinton Administration unveiled a large package of anti-drug assistance to Colombia for 2000 and 2001, with an unprecedented emphasis on the military. The administration's aid package follows along the lines of at least the military and police aspects of the 'Plan Colombia', a September 1999 Colombian government document outlining Bogota's economic and military needs over the next few years. During 2000 and 2001, the proposed package would add about $1,005 billion in new military and police assistance; the vast majority is destined for Colombia, though an undetermined amount would go to Colombia's Andean neighbours. The package is to be submitted for congressional approval in two segments: as a supplement appropriation for 2000; and as part of the regular 2001 budget request.

The aid proposal falls into five categories:

1. **Push into southern Colombia growing areas.** $600 million over two years, for the following efforts:

   - Training and equipping two additional counternarcotics battalions within the Colombian Army.

   - 30 UH-60 Blackhawk helicopters and 33 UH-1H Huey helicopters for the counternarcotics battalions.

   - Intelligence for the counter narcotics battalions.

   - USAID assistance that will, according to a White House document, 'provide shelter and employment to the Colombian people who will be displaced during this push into southern Colombia'.

2. **More aggressive Andean region interdiction.** $341 million over two years, for the following efforts:

   - Radar upgrades.

   - Airplane and airfield upgrades.

   - Provision of intelligence.

   - Support for the US Forward Operating Location (FOL) at Manta, Ecuador ($38.6 million).

   - Assistance for interdiction efforts in Peru, Bolivia and Equador.

3. **Colombian National Police support.** $96 million over two years, for the following efforts:

   - Upgrades to existing aircraft.

   - Purchases of additional spray aircraft.

   - Secure bases for increased operations in coca-growing areas.

   - Provision of intelligence.

4. **Alternative economic development.** $145 million over two years, for the following efforts:

   - USAID assistance to provide economic alternatives for former coca-growers.

   - USAID assistance to increase local government's ability to provide for citizens' basic needs.

5. **Boosting governing capacity.** $93 million over two years, for the following efforts:

   - USAID and Justice Department assistance to increase protection of human rights, reform the judicial system, increase the rule of law, and crack down on money laundering and other high-tech crimes.

- Training of Colombian government representatives to prepare them for peace negotiations.

Most of the military and police assistance in the package will be managed by the State Department's International Narcotics Control (INC) program. A sizeable portion of the first two categories (the push into southern Colombia and Andean interdiction), $144 million, will be funded through the Defense Department's 'Section 1004' counter narcotics budget authorization. The defense budget portion will fund equipment and training for the counter narcotics battalions, a headquarters for a three-battalion counter-narcotics brigade, helicopter maintenance, military reform assistance, intelligence, aircraft upgrades, a new ground-based radar facility, support for the Manta FOL, and a broad-based drug interdiction program.

Senate Proposal

On October 20, 1999 Sen. Paul Coverdell (R-GA) introduced a separate proposal, the 'Alliance with Colombia and the Andean Region (Alianza) Act' (S.1758). If approved, this legislation would authorise – but not appropriate – $945 million in new assistance for Colombia's security forces during 2000, 2001 and 2002. This would include support for the creation of at least three counter narcotics battalions in the Colombian Army. Additional Army support would include fifteen UH-60 'Blackhawk' helicopters, intelligence, surveillance and refueling aircraft, airfield construction, and other equipment and training. Colombia's navy would receive patrol aircraft, helicopters, patrol boats and forward-looking infrared radar systems. The country's National Police would get additional spare parts, upgrades, transport aircraft, base construction assistance, and training.

The legislation also includes some human rights provisions. Among them, the bill would require the Secretary of State to notify Congress about, and to cut off funding for, Colombian military units that provide material support to paramilitary or narcotrafficking groups, even if gross human rights violations are not a direct result. The bill would also authorize $100 million to assist Colombia's judicial system, government human rights institutions, non-governmental human rights organizations, and internally displaced populations, and $50 million for alternative-development programs in drug cultivation areas.

While any new aid package for 2001 is likely to multiply US assistance for Colombia's armed forces, several other military co-operation initiatives – many begun in 1998 and 1999 – are already underway.

Text of FARC Communiqué (March 2000)

1. Despite the fact that we are currently immersed in a process that should lead to democratic peace in Colombia the State continues to strengthen its legal and illegal armed forces with the national budget in order to plant a seed of terror among the people.

2. As if that were not enough, the Government of the United States of America continues to pursue its interventionist policies in our country by sponsoring and participating in our internal war. Most recently this has been done under the pretext of the fight against drugs and is supported under Plan Colombia. This will bring traffic consequences to our country.

3. International corporations continue to exploit our riches and the work of our people.

4. The efforts to face this aggression of which our country is a victim demand enough money so that to guarantee the objectives of the new Colombia.

5. The resources acquired from donations of our fellow countrymen and those of our own investment are not enough to cover the necessities of the FARC-EP.

6. International corporations and the wealthy continue to tax the State in order to increase their aggressions toward the people and finance the paramilitaries.

7. We have not yet been able to reach substantial agreements with the Government at the negotiating table because it is obvious that Colombia has two powers that are fighting head-on for the political direction of the country.

We resolve:

First Article – those people whose net worth exceed one million dollars will be charged the tax for peace.

Second Article – as of today, all those who fulfill these criteria should come forward and make their payment. A second call will mean an increase in the tax amount.

Third Article – those who do not pay will be retained. Their liberation will depend on the prompt payment of an amount that will be determined on a case-by-case basis.

Consent for the implementation of this law has been granted and should be made public
FARC-EP
With Bolivar for peace and national sovereignty
The Mountains of Colombia, March 2000

Notes

Introduction
1. Jenny Pearce, *Colombia: Inside the Labyrinth*, Latin America Bureau, London, 1990.
2. Joe Gill, 'Veil across class war', *Morning Star*, London, 24 November 2000.
3. Karl Penhaul, 'In the line of fire', *Morning Star*, London, 5 September 2000.
4. R. T. Naylor, *Hot Money and the Politics of Debt*, Unwin, London, 1987, pp. 293–4.
5. Jeffrey Robinson, *The Laundrymen*, Simon and Schuster, New York, 1994, pp. 252–3.
6. Simon Strong, *Pablo Escobar and the Cocaine Wars*, Macmillan, London, 1995, pp. 192–7.
7. *Ibid.*, p. 193.
8. Alfred W. McCoy, *The Politics of Heroin: CIA Complicity in the Drug Trade*, Lawrence Hill Books, New York, Chapter 9, pp. 436–492; Gerald L. Posner, *Warlords of Crime: Chinese Secret Societies – the New Mafia*, McGraw-Hill, New York, 1988, pp. 66–77, Christopher Robbins, *Air America*, Corgi, London, Chapter 9, pp. 235-56.
9. Hugh O'Shaughnessey, *Pinochet: The Politics of Torture*, Latin American Bureau, London, 1999; Hugh O'Shaughnessey, 'Revealed: Pinochet Drug Link', *The Observer*, London, 10 December 2000.

10. Michael C. Ruppert, 'The Bush-Cheney Drug Empire', *Nexus*, Australia, Volume 8, Number 2, February–March 2001, pp. 11–16.
11. David Adams, 'US fooled into destroying drug cartel's enemies', *The Times*, London, 26 January 2004.
12. William Raynor, 'A lethal brew of oil and blood', *The Independent on Sunday*, London, 31 August 1997.
13. Judy Mann, 'Waging Chemical Warfare in Colombia', *Washington Post*, 16 March 2001.
14. Hugh O'Shaughnessy, 'Revealed: how America's war on cocaine is poisoning Ecuador', *The Independent on Sunday*, London, 31 August 2003.
15. Antony Barnett, 'UK in secret biological war on drugs', *The Observer*, London, 17 September 2000.
16. *Ibid.*

Chapter 1
1. Quoted in J. H. Parry, *The Discovery of South America*, Paul Elek, London, 1979, p. 117.
2. *Ibid.*, p. 119.
3. Quoted in Peter Bakewell, *A History of Latin America*, Blackwell, Oxford, England, 1997, p. 32.
4. Quoted in J. B. Trend, *Bolivar and the Independence of Spanish America*, Bolivarian Society of Venezuela/Macmillan, New York, 1951, p. 41.
5. Quoted in David Bushnell (ed.), *The Liberator, Simon Bolivar: Man and Image*, Alfred A. Knopf, New York, 1970, p. 86.
6. David McCullough, *The Path Between the Seas: The Creation of the Panama Canal, 1870–1914*, Simon and Schuster, New York, 1977, p. 32.
7. *Ibid.*, p. 66.
8. Quoted in *Ibid.*, p. 135.
9. *Ibid.*, p. 136.
10. *Ibid.*, p. 379.

Chapter 2
1. F. A. Kirkpatrick, *Latin America, A Brief History*, Cambridge University Press, Cambridge, England, 1938, p. 262.
2. *The Memoirs of Cordell Hull*, Hodder and Stoughton, London, 1948, p. 170.
3. George Scott, *The Rise and Fall of the League of Nations*, Hutchinson, London, 1973, p. 249.
4. *Ibid.*, pp. 249–52; *The Memoirs ... op. cit.* pp. 310–311.
5. Quoted in Jenny Pearce, *Colombia: Inside the Labyrinth*, Latin America Bureau, London, 1990, p. 22.
6. *Ibid.*, p. 51.
7. *Ibid.*
8. Alfredo Molano, *Sela adentro: una historia oral de la colonizacion del Guaviare*, El Ancora Bogota, 1987, p. 46.
9. Americas Watch, *The Killings in Colombia*, Human Rights Watch, New York, April 1989, pp. 50–51.

10. *Fuerzas Militares de Colombia, Instrucciones de Contra-guerillas*, (no date), translated by Human Rights Watch, New York.
11. Carlo Reyes Posada, *El Espectador*, Bogota, 10 December 1961; cited in Hugh Thomas, *The Cuban Revolution*, Weidenfeld and Nicolson, London, 1986, p. 28.
12. *Morning Star*, London, 3 May 2003.
13. Quoted in Thomas, *op. cit.*, who opines: This report must surely have owed much to imagination', p. 30.
14. Quoted in Thomas, *op. cit.*: another imaginative report?
15. Norman Smith, Scotland Yard, reported in *El Tiempo*, Bogota, 12 April 1961.
16. Pearce, *op. cit.*, p. 79.
17. Penny Lernoux, *Cry of the People*, Penguin Harmondsworth, England, 1982, p. 209.
18. Roger Burbach and Patricia Flynn, *Agribusiness in the Americas*, Monthly Review Press, North American Congress on Latin America, 1980, pp. 64–65, 67.
19. Hubert Humphrey, Policies and Operations of PL 480, Senate Committee on Agriculture and Forestry, Hearings, 84th Congress, 1st Session, US Congress, 1957, p. 129.
20. Michael McClintock, *Instruments of Statecraft; US Guerilla Warfare, Counterinsurgency and Counterterrorism, 1940–1990*, Pantheon Books, New York, 1992, p. 187.
21. Headquarters, US Army Special Warfare School, 'Subject: Visit to Colombia, South America, by a team from Special Warfare Centre, Fort Bragg. North Carolina, 26 February 1962', Kennedy Library, Box 319, National Security Files, Special Group, Fort Bragg Team, Visit to Colombia, 3/62; quoted in McClintock, *op. cit.*, p. 222.
22. *Ibid.*
23. Richard Goodwin, 'Our Stake in a Big Awakening', *Life*, 14 April 1967.
24. Lernoux, *op. cit.*, pp. 214–217.
25. *Ibid.*, p. 216.
26. *Ibid.*, p. 289.
27. Noam Chomsky, *Deterring Democracy*, Verso, London, 1991, p. 127.
28. E. G. Valliantos, *Fear in the Countryside*, Ballinger, 1976; quoted in Chomsky *op. cit.*, p. 227.
29. See Pearce, *op. cit.*, pp. 119–135.
30. Cited in Pearce, *op. cit.*, p. 136.
31. Pearce, *op. cit.*, p. 154.
32. Lernoux, *op. cit.*, p. 24.
33. Lernoux, *op. cit.*, p. 37.

Chapter 3
1. Testimony of Diego Viafara Salinas to the Procuraduria, 22 February 1989; translation by Human Rights Watch.
2. Information in this section derives from material accumulated by Human Rights Watch.
3. Rafael Pardo, speech in Latin American Program, 'Colombia: Human Rights

and the Peace Process.' No. 212, Working Paper Series published by the Woodrow Wilson International Centre for Scholars, Washington D. C., 4 April 1995, p. 14.

4. Simon Strong, *Whitewash: Pablo Escobar and the Cocaine Wars*, Macmillan, London 1995, p. 38.

5. *El Espectador*, 4 October 1988.

6. Richard B Craig, 'Illicit drug traffic: implications for South American source countries', *Journal of Interamerican studies and World Affairs*, vol. 29, No.2, Miami, Summer 1987.

7. Fabio Castillo, *Los Jinetes de la cocaina*, Documentes Periodisticos, Bogota, 1988, p. 224; cited in Jenny Pearce, *Colombia: Inside the Labyrinth*, Latin America Bureau, London, 1990, p. 192.

8. Pearce, *op. cit.*, p. 193.

9. *Ibid.*

10. *Ibid.*

11. Quoted in *Ibid.*, p. 194.

12. Alfonzo Gomez Mendez, quoted in *La Prensa*, 20 September 1989.

13. Pearce, *op. cit.*, p. 269.

14. *Impunity*, Pax Christi Netherlands and the Dutch Commission Justitia et Pax, October-November 1988.

15. Brook Larmer, 'US, Mexico try to halt chemical flow to cartels', *Christian Science Monitor*, 23 October 1989 (reporting on the lack of any serious attempts and the blaming of Mexico); cited by Noam Chomsky, *Deterring Democracy*, Verso, London, 1991, p. 117,136.

16. Thomas E Skidmore, *Modern Latin America*, 5th edition, Oxford University Press, Oxford, England, 2001, pp. 391–92.

17. Strong, *op. cit.*, p. 38.

18. US Congress, Senate, Committee on Foreign Relations, Subcommittee on Terrorism, Narcotics, and International Operations, *Drugs, Law Enforcement, and Foreign Policy*, 100th Congress, 2nd Session, US Government Printing Office, Washington D. C., December 1988, report, pp. 26–29.

19. *Forbes*, 25 July 1988, p. 64.

20. Strong, *op. cit.*, p. 168.

21. Ian Brodie, 'Cocking a snook at Uncle Sam', *The Daily Telegraph*, London, 23 August 1989.

22. Simon Fisher, 'Barco moves too late to break the drug barons', *The Independent*, London, 12 October 1989.

23. Philip Wearne, '50 murders a day as cocaine war explodes', *The Sunday Telegraph*, London, 6 May 1990.

24. Tim Ross, David Adams and Colin Harding, 'Israeli general in drug cartel arms link', *The Independent*, London, 4 October 1990.

25. 'Export and Die', *The Economist*, London, 2 March 1991.

26. Malcolm Coad, 'High in the Andes', *The Guardian*, London, 26 July 1991.

27. Hugh O'Shaugnessy, 'Drugs terror tightens grip on Colombia', *The Observer*, London, 24 November 1991.

28. Timothy Ross, 'Escobar escape humiliates Colombian leaders', *The Guardian*, London, 24 July 1992.
29. Adrian Croft, 'US sends military help to Colombia for Escobar hunt', *The Independent*, London, 31 July 1992.

Chapter 4
 1. Phil Reeves, 'Anti-drug agents crack pet ruse of the drugs cartel', *The Independent*, London, 29 October 1992.
 2. 'Writers scold Colombia's rebel front', Associated Press (AP), *The Guardian*, London, 23 November 1992.
 3. Timothy Ross, 'Mystery group unleashes terror wave on Colombian drug baron', *The Sunday Times*, London, 21 February 1993.
 4. Douglas Farah, 'Cali drugs cartel quietly takes over Medellin's share of $30 billion business', *Washington Post*, reprinted in *The Guardian*, London, 10 March 1993; Phil Davison, 'Rivals muscle in on Escobar drug empire', *The Independent*, London, 23 March 1993.
 5. Quoted by Jenny Pearce, *Colombia: into the Labyrinth*, Latin America Bureau, 1990, pp. 101–102.
 6. Mike Reid, 'The black hole', *The Guardian*, London, 21 November 1992.
 7. *Ibid.*
 8. Isabel Hilton, 'The illicit miners', *The Independent*, London, 29 November 1992.
 9. *Ibid.*
10. Hugh O'Shaughnessy, 'Child miners slave in City of Angels', *The Observer*, London, 2 December 1992.
11. Timothy Ross, 'End of the line for the king of cocaine', *The Sunday Times*, London, 5 December 1993.
12. Simon Strong, *Whitewash: Pablo Escobar and the Cocaine Wars*, Macmillan, London, 1995, pp. 291–293.
13. 'Escobar's death "was suicide",' Reuter, *The Guardian*, London, 6 December 1993.
14. Ross (5 December 1993) *op. cit.*
15. *Ibid.*
16. Isabel Hilton, 'The king is dead ... long live cocaine', *The Independent*, London, 11 December 1993.
17. *Ibid.*
18. *Ibid.*
19. *Ibid.*
20. Harry Clegg, 'Escobar's shoes filled by the men in suits', *The Observer*, London, 5 December 1993.
21. Howard Foster and Richard Palmer, *The Sunday Times*, London, 16 January 1994; 'MP calls for inquiry into bungled £1bn Colombia Cocaine "sting",' *The Guardian*, London, 17 January 1994.
22. Gustavo de Greiff, *Washington Post*, quoted in Patrick Cockburn, 'Drug barons promote heroin in the hunt for fatter profits', *The Independent*, London, 9 April 1994.

23. Timothy Ross, 'Colombia at odds with itself again over narcotics', *The Guardian*, London, 21 May 1994.

Chapter 5
1. Timothy Ross, 'Little to choose in neck and neck presidential race', *The Guardian*, London, 27 May 1994.
2. *Ibid.*
3. Adrian Levy and Ian Burrell, 'Named: Britain's top drug barons', *The Sunday Times*, London, 15 January 1995.
4. Ulises Estrada Lescalle, 'Toward a lasting peace', Granma International, Havana, 7 June 1995.
5. *Ibid.*
6. Michael S. Serrill, 'A drug deal?', *Time*, 7 November 1994.
7. *Ibid.*
8. 'Drug baron seized in cupboard', *The Observer*, London, 11 June 1995.
9. Phil Davison, 'Bomb kills 30 after cocaine baron's arrest', *The Observer*, London, 12 June 1996.
10. Phil Davison, 'The "Chess Player" offers a gambit', *The Independent*, London, 14 June 1995.
11. Michael S. Serril, 'Narco-democracy now?' *Time*, 4 July 1994.
12. *Ibid.*
13. *Ibid.*
14. Gabriel Escobar, 'Tape links new leader to old vice', *Washington Post*, *The Guardian*, London, 13 July 1994.
15. Michael S. Serrill, 'Drug diplomacy', *Time*, 25 July 1994.
16. Noll Scott, 'Minister resigns over "drug money"', *The Guardian*, London, 3 August 1995; Noll Scott, 'Colombian President "took campaign gift from cartel"', *The Guardian*, London, 5 August 1995.
17. President-elect Ernesto Samper Pizano, interview with Tom Quinn, 'We're going to win this war', *Time*, 8 August 1994.
18. Christopher Bellamy, 'SAS help to free UK soldier in Colombia', *The Independent on Sunday*, London, 10 December 1995.
19. Tom Brown, 'Scot of the Andes backs president', *The Guardian*, London, 8 June 1996.
20. Arnold Kemp, 'Farmers riot in Cocaine battle', *The Observer*, London, 4 August 1996.
21. 'Colombian "coup" thwarted,' Reuter, *The Guardian*, London, 20 August 1996.
22. 'Blackmail diplomacy', *Granma International*, Havana, 28 August 1996.

Chapter 6
1. Mary Matheson, 'Colombia's drug cartel city counts cost of arresting the kingpins', *The Guardian*, London, 2 November 1996.
2. *Ibid.*
3. *Ibid.*
4. Mary Matheson, 'Cartel leaders are in jail but there is no stopping the cocaine train', *The Guardian*, London, 19 November 1996.

5. Elizabeth Nash, 'Cocaine fleets bring wealth and death to the end of the earth', *The Independent on Sunday*, London, 24 November 1996.
6. 'Toward constitutional reform', *Granma International*, Havana, 6 November 1996.
7. Gerhard Dilger, 'Mauss trap slams shut', *Die Tageszeitung*, *The Guardian*, London, 27 November 1996.
8. Jeremy Lennard, 'A hundred ways to make an honest peso', *The Guardian*, London, 13 December 1996.
9. Jeremy Lennard, 'Urban disciples revive fortunes of Colombian shaman', *The Guardian*, London, 28 December 1996.
10. Jeremy Lennard, 'Colombian strike leaves Samper out in the cold', *The Guardian*, London, 11 February 1997.
11. Bob Graham, 'Behind the white lines', *The Sunday Times*, London, 23 February 1997.
12. *Ibid.*
13. *Ibid.*
14. Colin Harding, 'Concern at Colombian killings', *The Daily Telegraph*, London, 15 March 1997.
15. Phil Davison, 'British aid for Colombian refugee crisis', *The Independent*, London, 5 April 1997.
16. *Ibid.*
17. Phil Gunson, 'Colombia's war of terror against revels drags Panama into the fire', *The Guardian*, London, 24 July 1997.
18. Ian Burrell, 'Crisis as Colombian refugees flood into Britain', *The Independent*, London, 21 August 1997.
19. *Ibid.*
20. *Ibid.*
21. Jeremy Lennard, 'Rebels hold Colombian democracy to ransom', *The Guardian*, London, 4 September 1997.

Chapter 7
1. *The New York Times*, 16, 17 and 18 September 1989; Ursula Marquez, *The Guardian* (New York), 11 October 1989; Colombian Human Rights Committee, POB 3730, Washington D. C. 20010; cited by Noam Chomsky, *Deterring Democracy*, Verso, London, 1991, pp. 129–30.
2. Colombia Update, 1, 4 December 1989l; cited by Chomsky, *op. cit.*, pp. 130–131.
3. *Ibid.*
4. Chomsky, *op. cit.*, p. 131.
5. *Ibid.*
6. Phil Davison, 'Figurehead rumbas while Colombian military rules,' *The Independent*, London, 26 July 1993.
7. *Ibid.*
8. Michael Meacher, letter, 'Political killings in Colombia', *The Guardian*, London, 29 July 1993.
9. Gavin O'Toole, 'Living in the shadow of Colombia's death squads', *The Guardian*, London, 18 August 1993.

10. *Ibid.*
11. See, for example, *The Observer*, London, 15 May 1994, p. 17.
12. *Women in Colombia: Breaking the Silence*, Amnesty International, J-AMR 23/41/95.
13. Amnesty International, London; International Federation of Human Rights (FIDH), Paris; International Service for Human Rights, Geneva; World Organisation for the Protection of Human Rights Defenders, Paris.
14. Listed in *War Without Quarter, Colombia and International Law, IV. Paramilitary Violations of International Humanitarian Law*, Human Rights Watch, New York, October 1998, 15pp.
15. These and other examples in this section are taken from *ibid.* (sources in *ibid.*).
16. Examples given in *ibid., V. Guerrilla Violations of International Law*, 19 pp.
17. *Ibid.*
18. Source in *Ibid.*
19. Timothy Ross, 'Death warning terrifies Bogota street children', *The Guardian*, London, 13 August 1993.
20. *War Without Quarter, VI, Little Bells and Little Bees, op. cit.*, 5 pp.
21. Sources in *ibid.*
22. Sources in *ibid.*
23. *War Without Quarter, VII, Forced Displacement, op. cit.*, 5 pp.
24. Sources in *ibid.*
25. Sources in *ibid.*
26. Sources in *ibid.*
27. Ruth Morris, 'Refugees, guns and cocaine spill over the border', *The Independent*, London, 2 December 2000.
28. *Ibid.*
29. *Colombia: Human Rights Defenders Under Increasing Attack*, Amnesty International, AMR 23/017/1998, 20 March 1998.
30. *Ibid.*
31. *Ibid.*
32. *Ibid.* Detailed examples are provided in each of these categories (pp. 6–16).
33. *Ibid.*, p. 16.
34. *Colombia: Barrancabermeja: A City Under Siege*, Amnesty International, AMR 23/36/99, May 1999, 16 pp.
35. Sources in *ibid.*
36. *Ibid.*, pp. 5–6 (sources in *ibid*).
37. *Ibid.*, p. 14.
38. In November 1997 the Colombian Constitutional Court ruled that the creation of civilian vigilante associations (CONVIVIR) was constitutional, but that they should not be allowed to act as 'death squads' nor to violate human rights.
39. Ramon Osario had been arrested in January and then released because of irregularities in the arrest procedure.
40. *AI Report 1998: Colombia*, Amnesty International, report for period January to December 1997: plus *Update* for period from January to June 1998.
41. See, for example, *Colombia: Paramilitaries, 'Disappearance' and Impunity*,

Amnesty International, AMR 23/039/1998, 1 June 1998; *Colombia, Human Rights Developments*, World Report 1999, Human Rights Watch, New York; *AI Report 1999: Colombia*, Amnesty International.

42. *AI Report 1999: Colombia*, Amnesty International.
43. *Colombia: Human Rights Developments*, World Report 2001, Human Rights Watch.
44. *Ibid.*
45. *Ibid.*
46. *Ibid.*
47. Appendix to *War Without Quarter, op. cit.*
48. *War Without Quarter, op. cit.*
49. The International Court is itself not relevant, though the spirit of its provisions may be regarded as universally binding, since the Court only addresses disputes between states. (The Court may become relevant if, as one hypothesis, a Colombian government wanted to take legal action against unilateral violations of Colombian sovereignty – see Chapter 9 of present book).
50. *War Without Quarter, op. cit.*
51. Listed for all parties in *ibid.*
52. See *ibid., Summary and Recommendations*, 7 pp.
53. José Migel Vivanco, executive director, Americas Division, Human Rights Watch, 'Colombia: Human Rights Watch testifies before Senate', Foreign Operations Subcommittee, Senate Appropriations Committee, 11 July 2001.
54. *Ibid.*
55. In his book *My Confession* (Black Sheep Press, 2001) Carlos Castano, AUC Leader, admitted to having personally killed more than 50 people, some of them high-profile individuals, including a presidential candidate.
56. *Washington Post*, 28 January 2001.
57. Nick Dearden, 'Colombian crusade', *Morning Star*, London, 1 August 2002.
58. David Rhys Jones, 'Law of the Assassin', *Morning Star*, London, 6 December 2002.
59. Meg Williams, 'Coca-Cola – blood on its hands', *Morning Star*, London, 6 December 2002; 'Bottling Coke and spilling blood', *New York Daily News*, 11 November 2003; 'Students call for Coke boycott', *Atlanta Business Chronicle*, 24 November 2003; 'Soft drink, hard times: Colombians boycott Coca-Cola, *Time Europe*, 4 August 2003; 'Coca-Cola sued over death squad killings', *The Times*, London, 27 July 2001.
60. Jose Otero, 'Fear and pain in Paya, attack leaves four dead, *La Prensa*, 23 January 2003.
61. George Monbiot, 'First it was the Reds, then drugs, then terror. So who have the US really been fighting in Colombia?', *The Guardian*, London, 3 February 2003.

Chapter 8
1. Jon Mitchell, 'Panama's jungle villages fall victim to a foreign war', *The Guardian*, London, 18 October 1997.
2. Jeremy Lennard and Steven Ambrus, 'Elusive supremos redraw drugs map', *The*

Guardian, London, 28 November 1997.

3. *Ibid.*

4. Jeremy Lennard and David Harrison, 'Headcutters dodge the state's axe', *The Observer*, London, 7 December 1997.

5. The RCN radio network received telephone calls for the 'Extraditables', a group originally formed by Pablo Escobar, saying that they had seized Parra.

6. Again the Maripiran massacre was being cited as evidence of collaboration between the Colombian army and the paramilitaries.

7. Lennard and Harrison, *op. cit.*

8. Castano's brother, Fidel, known as 'Rambo', was once a close ally of Pablo Escobar. It was Fidel who helped to establish the paramilitaries' reputation for extreme violence.

9. Jeremy McDermott, 'Colombian army seeks US help to fight rebels', *The Daily Telegraph*, London, 27 March 1998.

10. Jeremy McDermott, 'Kidnap victim freed in jungle', *The Daily Telegraph*, London, 3 April 1998.

11. Caroline Davies, 'Inquiry into drugs film accused of sham', 'Heroin packages "just crushed mint",' *The Daily Telegraph*, London, 7 May 1998.

12. Jeremy Lennard, 'Colombian death squads' bloodshed by appointment', *The Guardian*, London, 18 May 1998.

13. *Ibid.*

Chapter 9

1. Carey Scott, 'Colombia votes in a war zone', *The Sunday Times*, London, 31 May 1998.

2. *Ibid.*

3. Jeremy Lennard, 'Colombia votes for new order', *The Guardian*, London, 2 June 1998.

4. Jeremy McDermott, 'Colombian president may seek sanctuary in Britain', *The Daily Telegraph*, London, 4 June 1998.

5. On 8 June 1998 the United Nations held a drug-trade summit in New York to discuss the plan. Colombia's Colonel Leonardo Gallego attended, in part to signal Bogota's good faith.

6. John Simpson, 'On board Bogota's mission impossible', *The Sunday Telegraph*, London, 7 June 1998.

7. *Ibid.*

8. John Simpson, 'Gunfire sounds on the road to everyone's ruin', *The Sunday Telegraph*, London, 14 June 1998.

9. Peter Beaumont and Jeremy Lennard, 'Land where "headcutters" rule', *The Sunday Telegraph*, London, 21 June 1998.

10. *Ibid.*

11. John Simpson, 'The quiet suburban life of cocaine cartels', *The Sunday Telegraph*, London, 21 June 1998.

12. *Ibid.*

13. Jeremy Lennard, 'Colombia puts faith in change', *The Guardian*, London, 23 June 1998.

14. Jeremy Lennard and Anne McIlroy, 'Mine owner volunteers to be a hostage', *The Guardian*, London, 12 November 1998.
15. Jeremy McDermott, 'Sex offender held for 29 Colombian child murders', *The Daily Telegraph*, London, 1 January 1999.
16. Talks between the government and the National Liberation Army (ELN) were scheduled to begin in February 1999.
17. '250 killed in Colombian earthquake', *The Daily Telegraph*, London, 26 January 1999; Jeremy McDermott, 'Quake city survivors cry out for water', *The Daily Telegraph*, London, 27 January 1999; Jeremy Lennard, 'Rubble slowly gives up the dead', *The Guardian*, London, 28 January 1999.
18. Jeremy Lennard, 'Colombian victims take law into their own hands', *The Guardian*, London, 29 January 1999.
19. *Ibid.*
20. Jeremy McDermott, 'British rescuers quit as looters open fire', *The Daily Telegraph*, London, 31 January 1999.
21. Isabel Hilton, 'Death squads exploit quake', *The Independent on Sunday*, London, 31 January 1999.
22. Jeremy Lennard, 'Quake masks death squad attacks', *The Guardian*, London, 3 February 1999.
23. *Ibid.*
24. Isabel Hilton, 'The silent murders', *The Guardian*, London, 5 February 1999.
25. 'Colombian rebels killed Americans', *International Herald Tribune*, 13 March 1999.
26. Jeremy Lennard, 'Colombian death squads threaten the new Atlantis', *The Guardian*, London, 1 April 1999.
27. *Cambia*, Colombian News Weekly, edited by Gabriel Garcia Marquez, 19 April 1999.
28. *Ibid.*
29. Jeremy Lennard, 'Colombian rebels free five from hideout', *The Guardian*, London, 7 June 1999.
30. To boost the economic figures, the government decided to include illegal drug revenues as a component of national income.
31. 'UN condemns Colombia on death-squad links', *Morning Star*, 27 August 1999.

Chapter 10
1. As, for example, in Eric Williams, *From Columbus to Castro: The History of the Caribbean, 1492–1969*, Andre Deutsch, London, 1978, ch.24.
2. A. H. Allen, *Great Britain and the United States, A History of Anglo-American Relations (1783–1952)*, Odhams, London, 1954, p. 199.
3. *Ibid.*, p. 369.
4. Anna Rochester, *Rulers of America: A Study of Finance Capital*, Lawrence and Wishart, London, 1936, p. 260.
5. The 20th Century saw dozens of US interventions in Latin America and the Caribbean states. Some 5000 marines were sent to Nicaragua in 1926 to quell a revolution, and a US occupying force was maintained there for seven years. In

1917 the US invaded the Dominican Republic for the fourth time, maintaining troops for eight years. The US intervened for the second time in Haiti in 1915, and kept troops there for 19 years. Between 1900 and 1933, the United States invaded Cuba four times, Nicaragua twice, Panama six times, Guatemala once, and Honduras seven times. (See Howard Zinn, *A People's History of the United States*, Longman, London, 1980, p. 399.) Thereafter, the United States variously invaded Brazil, Panama, Haiti, El Salvador, Nicaragua and Grenada; and intervened diplomatically and economically in all the states of the area.

6. Noam Chomsky, *Profit Over People: Neoliberalism and Global Order*, Seven Stories Press, New York, 1999, p. 50.

7. Quoted in *ibid.*

8. Simon Strong, *Whitewash: Pablo Escobar and the Cocaine Wars*, Macmillan, London, 1995, p. 58.

9. Alfred W. McCoy, *The Politics of Heroin: CIA Complicity in the Global Drug Trade*, Lawrence Hill Books, New York, 1991; Gerald L. Posner, *Warlords of Crime, Chinese Secret Societies – the New Mafia*, McGraw-Hill, New York, 1988, pp. 68–77.

10. Strong, *op. cit.*, pp. 58–60.

11. McCoy, *op. cit.*, p. 479.

12. US Congress, Senate, Committee on Foreign Relations, Subcommittee on Terrorism, Narcotics, and International Operations, *Drugs, Law Enforcement and Foreign Policy*, 100th Con., 2nd session, US Government Printing Office, Washington D. C., December 1988, report, p. 37.

13. *Ibid.* p. 39.

14. *Ibid.* p. 38.

15. Drug running was commonplace in CIA operations. See, for example, Christopher Robbins, *Air America*, Corgi, London, 1988, Chapter 9, pp. 235–6.

16. US Senate Committee on Foreign Relations, *Drugs, Law Enforcement and Foreign Policy*, report, *op. cit.*, p. 36.

17. *Ibid.*, pp. 53–8.

18. Christie Institute, *Inside the Shadow Government*, Christie Institute, Washington DC, June 1988, pp. 100–14.

19. McCoy, *op. cit.*, pp. 481–4.

20. Strong, *op. cit.*, pp. 84–5.

21. Paul Eddy, Hugo Sabogal and Sara Walden, *The Cocaine Wars*, Century, London, 1988, pp. 307–8; Strong, *op. cit.*, pp. 104–5.

22. Noam Chomsky, *Deterring Democracy*, Verso, London, 1991, p. 132.

23. *Ibid.*, pp. 132–3.

24. 'Organisation of Hired Assassins and Drug Traffickers in the Magdalena Medio', Department of Security Administration (DAS), Colombia, 20 July 1988.

25. Eugene Robinson, *Washington Post*, 9 August 1989; Chomsky, 1991, *op. cit.*, pp. 133–5.

26. Ron Ben-Yishai, *Yediot Ahronot*, 30 August 1989; Uriel Ben-Ami, *Al Hamishmar*, 31 August 1989; Danny Sadeh, *Yediot Ahronot*, 29 August 1989; quoted by Chomsky, 1991, *op. cit.*, p. 134.

27. Quoted in Chomsky, 1991, *op. cit.*, p. 134.
28. Strong, *op. cit.*, pp. 180–182.
29. Ian Brodie, 'Cocking a snook at Uncle Sam', *The Daily Telegraph*, London, 23 August 1989.
30. Chuck Call, *Clear and Present Danger: the US Military and the War on Drugs in the Andes*, Washington Office on Latin America (WOLA), Washington D. C., October 1991, p. 1.
31. Examples in this section appear in Human Rights Watch, *Colombia's Killer Networks, The Military-Paramilitary Partnership and the United States*, New York, November 1996.
32. *Ibid.*
33. *Ibid.*
34. Quoted in Michael S. Serrill, 'Glove-off approach', *Time*, 13 March 1995.
35. Jonathan Freedland, 'Former US officials linked to drug cartel', *The Guardian*, London, 7 June 1995.
36. *Ibid.*
37. Phil Davison, 'US lawyers linked with Cali Cartel', *The Independent*, London, 7 June 1985.
38. Statistics provided by the Colombian Drug Prevention Division of the National Police Force revealed that 2356 Colombian drug dealers and 98 foreigners had been apprehended, and confiscations made of 25,771kg of cocaine, 21,395kg of coca paste, 339,490kg of coca leaves, 177,937kg of marijuana bricks, 128,844 grams of heroin, 289,604 grams of morphine and 171,718 grams of opium paste. A total of 24,304 hectares of coca leaves were destroyed, along with 39 hectares of marijuana and 3959 hectares of poppies. In addition, 518 drug processing laboratories were dismantled. Six out of the seven most important members of the Cali cartel were imprisoned. (All figures published in 1995.)
39. Jeremy Lennard, 'Jungles face US "toxic rain"', *The Guardian*, London, 20 April 1998.
40. *Ibid.*
41. *Ibid.*
42. *Colombia's killer networks ... VI*, The US Role, *op. cit.*
43. Includes aid from Fiscal Year 1989 to FY 1995. The aid was provided on a grant basis, except for a $20 million loan in FY 1991. The aid was provided through the Foreign Ministry Financing, MAP Merger, and IMET programs, as well as through special presidential emergency drawdown authority under Section 506 of the Foreign Assistance Act of 1961. US Department of Defence Security Assistance Agency, Foreign Military Sales, *Foreign Military Construction Sales and Military Assistance Facts. As of 30 September 1995* (1996) cited in *ibid.*
44. Warren D. Hall III, Memorandum for Commander-in-Chief, US Southern Command, Department of Defence, 8 April 1994.
45. Human Rights Watch (*Colombia's Killer Networks, op. cit.*) has indicated an inquiry initiated by US ambassador Myles Frechette that named the specific units of the Colombian army, 'all implicated in serious human rights violations', that were receiving substantial US military aid. Cosmetic US efforts to combat human-rights abuses have been hugely ineffectual.

46. *Colombia's Killer Networks, op. cit.*

47. 'Colombia report on human rights practices for 1997', US State Department, Washington DC, 454.

48. Charles Wilhelm, testimony before the House International Relations Committee, 31 March 1998.

49. Quoted by Colonel Vicente Ogilvy, US Southern Command spokesman, to Human Rights Watch, 28 May 1998; 'Colombia no es alarma: Wilhelm', *El Espectador*, Colombia, 9 May 1998.

50. David Smith, 'US war machine sucked into Colombia's fire', *The Observer*, London, 26 April 1998.

51. Brian Denny, 'Colombian rebels defy US aggression', *Morning Star*, London, 7 July 1999.

52. David Adams, 'Embassy in Bogota "is base for drug smuggling",' *The Times*, London, 17 August 1999.

53. Ed Vulliamy, 'US hawks fuel war in Colombia', *The Observer*, London, 22 August 1999.

54. 'Castro warns of "colossal disaster"', *Morning Star*, London, 21 August 1999; 'The gringos make a war', *Morning Star*, London, 7 September 1999; Martin Hodgson, 'Colombian drugs force raises fear of US role', *The Guardian*, London, 15 September 1999.

55. 'FARC stresses the US force in Colombia', *Morning Star*, London, 29 September 1999.

56. Gabriella Gamini, 'Colombia militia join war against civilians', *The Times*, London, 6 October 1999.

57. *Ibid.*

58. John Pilger, 'Phoney war', *The Guardian*, London, 19 October 1999.

59. David Smith, 'US pours in combat experts to train drug-busting squads of Colombia', *The Independent*, London, 22 October 1999.

60. *Ibid.*

61. David Smith, 'SAS secretly helps Bogota fight rebels', *The Independent*, London, 22 October 1999.

62. Andy Buchanan and Martin Koppel, 'US military escalation in Colombia targets working people, guerrillas', *The Militant*, New York, 1 November 1999.

63. 'US plans military boost for Colombia', *Morning Star*, London, 17 January 2000.

64. Isabel Hilton, 'Colombians do not need help like this', *The Guardian*, London, 21 June 2000.

65. Julian Borger, 'US Senate clears way for Bogota drugs-war aid', *The Guardian*, London, 23 June 2000.

66. Ed Vulliamy, 'US sprays poison in drugs war', *The Observer*, London, 2 July 2000; Tom Rhodes, 'Agent Green casts shade of Vietnam over Colombia', *The Sunday Times*, London, 27 August 2000; Kristian Carter, 'Still throwing toxins around the globe', *Morning Star*, London, 16 August 2000.

67. Ted Szulc, 'The Ghost of Vietnam now haunts "Plan Colombia"', *Los Angeles Times*, 20 August 2000.

68. Duncan Campbell, 'Drugs under fire', *The Guardian*, London, 20 July 2000.
69. Richard Boucher (spokesman for US State Department), 'Plan Colombia certification requirements', press statement, Washington D. C., 23 August 2000.
70. Deb Riechmann, 'Clinton visits Colombia to support anti-drug plan', The Associated Press (AP), 30 August 2000.
71. Andy McInerney, 'First victims of Plan Colombia', *Workers World*, 31 August 2000.
72. Simon Jenkins, 'Clinton's billions keep a drugs war alive', *The Independent*, London, 1 September 2000.
73. Mark Honigsbaum, 'US reaps a bleak harvest', *The Observer*, London, 3 September 2000.
74. 'Vietnam south of the border', *Atlanta Constitution*, 23 February 1981; 'El Salvador – will it turn into another Vietnam?', *US News and World Report*, 90, 16 March 1981; 'The Vietnam shadow over policy for El Salvador', *Business Week*, 18 March 1981.
75. See Geoff Simons, *Vietnam Syndrome: Impact on US Foreign Policy* (London: MacMillan, 1998).
76. In some commentary, Dow's reluctance was caused by how the US government left the company to pick up the legal fallout from the use of Agent Orange in Vietnam.
77. 'Clinton's drug war pledge raised "Vietnamisation" fears', *Jane's Defence Weekly*, 18 September 2000.
78. Quoted in *ibid*.
79. It was considered too dangerous for Clinton to visit Bogota. In Cartagena he was protected by 350 US agents and 5000 Colombian soldiers.
80. 'The US plan for Colombia', *Socialism Today*, 51, October 2000.
81. *International Herald Tribune*, 4 September 2000.
82. Quoted in *ibid*.
83. Matthew Engel, 'This drugs war is just like Vietnam', *The Guardian*, London, 13 March 2001.
84. David Bacon, 'Blood for coal', *Morning Star*, London, 22 September 2001.
85. Quoted in *ibid*.
86. Liz Atherton, 'Continuing US fumigations in Colombia, United States terrorism by proxy', *Colombia Peace Association*, October 2001.
87. Liz Atherton, 'The peace process ends – and now the US war begins', *Morning Star*, London, 23 February 2002.
88. Martin Hodgson, 'US takes role in Colombia to new level', *The Guardian*, London, 21 March 2002; Tony Allen-Mills, 'Bush ponders new front in Colombia', *The Sunday Times*, London, 24 February 2002.
89. Doug Stokes, 'Perception management and the US terror war in Colombia', *ZNet Colombia Watch*, 7 June 2002.
90. Quoted in *ibid*.
91. David Adams, 'US military aid turned against Colombia rebels', *The Times*, London, 22 August 2002.
92. Did Colin Powell know then that the United States intended to intercept the

important Iraqi declaration and, in flagrant violation of SCR 1441, make only selected parts of the document available to other Security Council members? It was Colombia that agreed to hand over the 12,000 page document to the United States, which was returned a week later minus 8000 pages.

93. Two kinds of killer fungus were being produced: fusarium oxysporum (for use against marijuana and coca plants), and pleospora papveracea (for use against opium poppies).

94. Rachel Van Dongen, 'US focus in Colombia expands from drugs to oil', *The Christian Science Monitor*, 5 February 2003; Scott Wilson, 'US moves closer to Colombia's war', *Washington Post*, 7 February 2003.

Chapter 11

1. Ruth Morris, 'Colombia rebel army metes out rough justice', *The Independent*, London, 12 November 1999.
2. *Ibid.*
3. Jeremy Lennard, 'A war run on drugs', *The Guardian*, London, 13 November 1999.
4. 'Colombian rebels target US navy', *Morning Star*, 19 November 1999; 'Scores die in rebel offensive', *The Times*, London, 19 November 1999.
5. Jan McGirk, 'Escobar's widow arrested and may face trafficking charges', *The Independent*, London, 18 November 1999.
6. Tony Thompson, 'Cocaine cartels return to war', *The Observer*, London, 21 November 1999.
7. *Ibid.*
8. 'Colombian civil war edges towards peace', *Morning Star*, London, 4 December 1999.
9. Jeremy McDermott, 'Terrorism fear over Iran aid to Colombia', *The Daily Telegraph*, London, 4 December 1999.
10. 'FARC leader attacks US interference', *Morning Star*, London, 10 April 2000.
11. Martin Hodgson, 'Colombians braced for fight on all fronts', *The Guardian*, London, 10 March 2000.
12. Martin Kettle, 'Anti-drugs colonel had role in wife's smuggling', *The Guardian*, London, 5 April 2000.
13. 'Pastrana plans dissolution of congress,' *Morning Star*, London, 6 April 2000.
14. 'UN reveals growth in Colombian death toll', *Morning Star*, London, 15 April 2000.
15. Martin Hodgson, 'Innocent catch flak in dirty war', *The Guardian*, London, 19 April 2000.
16. David Adams, 'Necklace bomb is terrorists' new tactic', *The Times*, London, 17 May 2000.
17. 'FARC rebel group absolved of blame', *Morning Star*, London, 23 May 2000.
18. Duncan Campbell, 'Heart of Darkness', *The Guardian*, London, 19 June 2000; 'Awaiting the world's dawn chorus', *The Guardian*, London, 21 June 2000.
19. 'Bogota squad leader claims US mandate', *Morning Star*, London, 11 August 2000.
20. Martin Hodgson, 'Plight of soldiers shocks Colombia', *The Guardian*, London,

11 October 2000; 'Colombians back swap of prisoners', *Morning Star*, London, 12 October 2000.

21. 'Colombian rebels end peace talks', *Morning Star*, London, 16 November 2000.
22. Martin Kettle, 'Bush advisor talks tough on Colombia', *The Guardian*, London, 28 December 2000.
23. Hugh O'Shaughnessy, 'US's drug war will put Bush in the firing line', *The Observer*, London, 31 December 2000.
24. Tom Rhodes, 'Bush feels the heat as critics lie in wait for his first big decision', *The Sunday Times*, London, 7 January 2001.
25. Martin Hodgson, 'Colombian death squads target British volunteers', *The Guardian*, London, 10 February 2001.
26. *Ibid.*
27. David Smith, 'Colombia appeases its drug lords to stop US-backed war', *The Independent on Sunday*, London, 25 February 2001.
28. Martin Hodgson, 'Colombian farmers count cost of airborne assault on drug fields', *The Guardian*, London, 27 February 2001.
29. *Ibid.*
30. James Wilson, 'Plan Colombia fails to find its mark', *The Financial Times*, London, 6 March 2001.
31. Alfredo Corchado, 'US rejects taking part in Colombia peace talks', *The Dallas Morning News*, 28 February 2001.
32. Jared Kotler, 'US criticized for shunning peace talks in Colombia', *Chicago Tribune*, 2 March 2001.
33. Ian Traynor and Stephen Dudley, 'Hot house', *The Guardian*, London, 25 April 2001.
34. Matthew Campbell, 'Bogota police foil "atom bomb" sale', *The Sunday Times*, London, 29 April 2001.
35. George Monbiot, 'Bush's dirty war', *The Guardian*, London, 22 May 2001.
36. *Ibid.*
37. *Ibid.*
38. Hugh O'Shaughnessy, 'Revealed: The innocent victims of war on drugs', *The Observer*, London, 17 June 2001; Liam Craig-Best and Rowan Shingler, 'Campesino crush', *Morning Star*, London, 20 June 2001.
39. Quoted in O'Shaughnessy, *op. cit.*

Chapter 12
1. Jeremy McDermott, 'Poverty and strife boost drug harvest in Colombia', *The Daily Telegraph*, London, 11 August 2003.
2. Catalina Stogden, 'Industry fears for fate of the farmers', *The Daily Telegraph*, London, 11 August 2001.
3. Jamie Wilson, Richard Norton-Taylor, Martin Hodgson and Julian Borger, 'Trio's trip to jungle costs IRA dear', *The Guardian*, London, 18 August 2001; Tony Allen-Mills, 'Rumbled in the jungle', *The Sunday Times*, London, 19 August 2001.
4. David Bamber and Alan Murray, 'IRA suspects "were testing super-bomb"', *The Sunday Telegraph*, London, 19 August 2001.

5. Martin Hodgson, 'Claim that IRA suspect promised Semtex to Colombian terrorists', *The Guardian*, London, 21 August 2001.

6. *Ibid.*

7. Martin Hodgson, 'Children swap murder for maths', *The Guardian*, London, 17 December 2001.

8. Martin Hodgson, 'White mischief', *The Independent*, London, 22 December 2001.

9. James Petras, 'Death squad democrat', *Morning Star*, London, 22 December 2001.

10. *Ibid.*

11. David Lister, 'Colombia says IRA sent 25 to train rebels', *The Times*, London, 8 January 2002.

12. Martin Hodgson, 'Troops close in on Colombia's rebel haven', *The Guardian*, London, 12 January 2002.

13. Heinz Dieterich Steffan, 'Death's dealer', *Morning Star*, London, 19 January 2002.

14. Mario Novelli, 'Colombian Victory', *Morning Star*, London, 1 February 2002.

15. *Ibid.*

16. 'Bogota bombs rebel territory', *Morning Star*, London, 22 February 2002.

17. Alvaro Uribe, interview with Joseph Contreras, 'I have been honourable', *Newsweek*, 25 March 2002.

18. 'Sinn Fein's big blunder', *The Observer*, London, 28 April 2002; David Bamber and Francis Elliott, 'Terror International', *The Sunday Telegraph*, London, 28 April 2002.

19. *The Guardian*, London, 9 July 2003.

20. Sandra Jordan, 'Girls go to war as Colombia's frontline killers', *The Observer*, London, 14 July 2002.

21. Sibylla Brodzinsky, 'Colombia's child soldiers swap guns for home', *The Times*, London, 1 August 2002.

22. *The Sunday Telegraph*, London, 3 August 2003; 'Kidnapped', *The Guardian*, London, 20 February 2004.

23. Jeremy McDermott, 'Colombia's gunmen aim for gringo blood', *The Daily Telegraph*, London, 3 August 2002.

24. *Ibid.*

25. David Sharrock, 'Colombian cities on the front line as rebels close in', *The Times*, London, 19 October 2002.

26. Liz Atherton, 'Silent abuses', *Morning Star*, London, 29 October 2002.

27. Justin Podur, 'The Uribe administration's negotiations with itself', *ZNet Colombia Watch*, 27 November 2002.

28. Alexander Lopez, talking to Andy Higginbottom, 'Solidarity now', *Morning Star*, London, 21 December 2002.

29. *Ibid.*

30. *El Tiempo*, 11 January 2003.

31. James Wilson, 'Colombia's private sector receives its call-up papers', *Financial Times*, London, 6 February 2003.

32. *Morning Star*, London, 24 March 2003.

Bibliography

Bagley, B. *et al*, *State and Society in Contemporary Colombia*, 1988.

Bakewell, Peter, *A History of Latin America*, Blackwell, Oxford, 1997.

Burbach, Roger and Patricia Flynn, *Agribusiness in the Americas*, Monthly Review Press, New York, 1980.

Bushnell, David (ed.), *The Liberator – Simon Bolivar: Man and Image*, Alfred A. Knopf, New York, 1970.

Cameron, Ian, *The Impossible Dream: The Building of the Panama Canal*, Hodder and Stoughton, London, 1971.

Chomsky, Noam, *Deterring Democracy*, Verso, London, 1991.

Chomsky, Noam, *Profit Over People: Neoliberalism and Global Order*, Seven Stories Press, New York, 1999.

Dix, R. H., *The Politics of Colombia*, 1986.

Eddy, Paul, Hugo Sabogal and Sara Walden, *The Cocaine Wars*, Century, London, 1988.

Galvis, Constanza, *The Heart of the War in Colombia*, Latin America Bureau, London, 2000.

Hartlyn, I. *The Politics of Coalition Rule in Colombia*, 1988.

Harvey, Robert, *Liberators: Latin America's Struggle for Independence, 1810-1830*, John Murray, London, 2000.

Hull, Cordell, *Memoirs*, Hodder and Stoughton, London, 1948.

Kirkpatrick, F. A., *Latin America: A Brief History*, Cambridge University Press, Cambridge 1938.

Kline, H. F., *Colombia: Portrait of Unity and Diversity*, 1983.

Lernoux, Penny, *Cry of the People*, Penguin Books, Harmondsworth, England, 1982.

McCoy, Alfred W., *The Politics of Heroin: CIA Complicity in the Global Drug Trade*, Lawrence Hill Books, New York, 1991.

McCullough, David, *The Path Between the Seas: The Creation of the Panama Canal, 1870-1914*, Simon and Schuster, New York, 1991.

Naylor, R. T., *Hot Money and the Politics of Debt*, Unwin, London, 1987.

Oquist, P., *Violence, Conflict and Politics in Colombia*, 1980

Parry, J. H., *The Discovery of South America*, Paul Elek, London, 1979.

Pearce, Jenny, *Colombia: Inside the Labyrinth*, Latin America Bureau, London, 1990.

Posner, Gerald L., *Warlords of Crime: Chinese Secret Societies – the New Mafia*, McGraw Hill, New York 1988.

Robbins, Christopher, *Air America*, Corgi, London 1988.

Robinson, Jeffrey, *The Laundrymen*, Simon and Schuster, New York, 1994.

Skidmore, Thomas E, *Modern Latin America*, 5th Edition, Oxford University Press, Oxford, 2001.

Sterling, Claire, *Crime Without Frontiers*, Little, Brown and Company, London, 1994.

Strong, Simon, *Whitewash: Escobar and the Cocaine Wars*, Macmillan, London, 1995.

Thomas, Hugh, *The Cuban Revolution*, Weidenfeld and Nicolson, London 1986.

Trend, J B, *Bolivar and the Independence of Spanish America*, Bolivarian Society/Macmillan, New York, 1951.

Weeks, John and Phil Gunson, *Panama*, Latin America Bureau, London, 1991.

Williams, Eric, *From Columbus to Castro: The History of the Caribbean, 1492–1969*, Andre Deutsch, London, 1978.

Zinn, Howard, *A People's History of the United States*, Longman, London, 1980.

Index

273, 274-5, 282, 284, 290, 311, 312, 315, 318, 333

Caballero, Carlos 253
Cadogan, Pat 87
Caicedo, Luis 167
Calderon, Elsa 127
Calderon, Enrique 104
Calderon, Mario 127
Cali, Municipal Workers Union (Sintraemcali) 10, 299-303
Calixto, Mario Humberto 153
Camargo, Alberto Lleras 38, 48
Camargo, Hugo 307
Camargo, Jimmy 186
Camejo, Rosario 168
Cameron, Ken 304
Camargo, Rodrigo Polonia Gonzales 73
Campaign, Against US Intervention in Colombia 232
Cancino, Antonio José 106, 108
Candela, Vito 179
Cano, Guillermo 63
Cantalapiedra, Ricardo Lorenzo 201
Caquimbo, Lucas 256
Caraballo, Francisco 145-6
Cardenas, Stella 145
Cardona, Londono 81
Caro, Miguel Antonio 279
Carranza, Victor 57, 176-7
Carrizosa, Alfredo Vasquez 133
Cartagena manifesto 22
Carter, Jimmy 12
Casadiego, Carlos Arturo 78
Castano, Carlos 128, 140, 148, 156, 161, 173, 174, 191, 193, 200, 205, 231, 260-1, 262, 265, 290-1, 300, 313, 329, 331
Castano, José 137
Castano, Mario 79
Castano, Oscar 137
Castano Gil, Fidel 156
Castellanos, Henry 203
Castillo-Agudelo, Arnulfo 174
Castillo, Gustavo Ruiz 266
Castro, Fidel 44-6, 95, 210, 228
Castro, Jorge Eliecer 141
Castro, José Fernando 180
Castro-Maza, Heriberto 77
Catton, Trevor 110
Cauchi, Denise 272
Celeyta, Berenice 15
Central Intelligence Agency (CIA) 12, 45, 49, 66, 209, 210-11, 223, 248, 269
Central Workers Federation (Indonesia) 301

Centre for Investigation and Popular Education (*Centro de Investigacion y Educacion Popular,* CINEP) 57
Cenu people 18
Cepeda, Gustavo 252
Cepeda, Manuel 94-5
Cerro, President (Peru) 37
'certification' (drugs) 123, 126, 219, 220, 224
Chacon, José Miller 95
Charles V (Spain) 20
Charrua, Luis Angel 163
Chase Manhattan 82
Chavez, Errol 211-12
Chavez, Hugo 205, 259, 269
chemical warfare 245-6
    see also cosmoflux 411F
        crop spraying
        glyphosate
        tebuthiuron
Cheney, Richard 12
Chia, Alfredo Colmanares 163
Chibcha people 18, 20
Chicola, Philip 264-5
children, 144-7, 190-1, 202, 295-6, 313-4
Chirolla, Gustavo 312
Chomsky, Noam 134, 209
Christie Institute (New York) 211
CIA
    see Central Intelligence Agency
Cifuentes, Ricardo Emilio 108
CINEP
    see Centre for Investigation and Popular Education
Clayton, John 28
Clayton-Bulwer Treaty (1850) 28-9
clearance (*despeje*) zone
    see demilitarized zone
Clinton, Bill (Clinton administration) 11, 162, 163, 171, 176, 188, 203, 219, 221, 223, 225, 229, 230, 232-3, 235, 237, 239, 252, 253, 268, 269
coal 81-3
Coca-Cola company 325
CODHES
    see Consultancy for Human Rights and the Displaced
Coffey, Kendall 218
Cohen, William 225
Cole, Thomas 209
Colima Front death squad 263
Collazos, Victor 250
Colombian Institute of Agrarian Reform (*Instituto Colobiano de Reforma Agraria,* INCORA) 62